THE RENAISSANCE OF EMPIRE
IN EARLY MODERN EUROPE

This book brings together a bold revision of the traditional view of the Renaissance with a new comparative synthesis of global empires in early modern Europe. It examines the rise of a virulent form of Renaissance scholarship, art, and architecture that had as its aim the revival of the cultural and political grandeur of the Roman Empire in Western Europe. Imperial humanism, a distinct form of humanism, emerged in the earliest stages of the Italian Renaissance as figures such as Petrarch, Guarino, and Biondo sought to revive and advance the example of the Caesars and their empire. Originating in the courts of Ferrara, Mantua, and Rome, this movement also revived ancient imperial iconography in painting and sculpture, as well as Vitruvian architecture. While the Italian princes never realized their dream of political power equal to the ancient emperors, the Imperial Renaissance they set in motion reached its full realization in the global empires of sixteenth- and seventeenth-century Spain, France, and Great Britain.

Thomas James Dandelet is Associate Professor of History at the University of California, Berkeley. He previously taught at Bard College and Princeton University. Dandelet was awarded the Rome Prize from the American Academy in Rome in 1999 and a Guggenheim fellowship in 2007. His first book, *Spanish Rome, 1500–1700* (2001), won the Sixteenth Century Studies Conference Roland Bainton Prize for best book in history and theology in 2002.

D1547747

THE RENAISSANCE OF EMPIRE IN EARLY MODERN EUROPE

THOMAS JAMES DANDELET

University of California, Berkeley

CAMBRIDGE
UNIVERSITY PRESS

32 Avenue of the Americas, New York, NY 10013-2473, USA

Cambridge University Press is part of the University of Cambridge.

It furthers the University's mission by disseminating knowledge in the pursuit of
education, learning, and research at the highest international levels of excellence.

www.cambridge.org
Information on this title: www.cambridge.org/9780521747325

First published 2014

Printed in the United States of America

A catalog record for this publication is available from the British Library.

Library of Congress Cataloging in Publication data
Dandelet, Thomas James, 1960–
The renaissance of empire in early modern Europe / Thomas James Dandelet,
University of California, Berkeley.
pages   cm
Includes bibliographical references and index.
ISBN 978-0-521-76993-8 (hardback) –
ISBN 978-0-521-74732-5 (pbk.)
1. Europe – History – 1492–1648.   2. Imperialism – Economic aspects – Europe –
Colonies – History.   3. Europe – Civilization – Roman influences.
4. Europe – Colonies – History.   I. Title.
D228.D36   2014
940.2′3–dc23   2013048939

ISBN 978-0-521-76993-8 Hardback
ISBN 978-0-521-74732-5 Paperback

CONTENTS

ILLUSTRATIONS AND MAPS

Illustrations

Maps

vii

ACKNOWLEDGMENTS

Many people and institutions helped in the creation of this book, and I wish to thank them here. I first had the chance to explore the broad themes of this project in the context of a chapter I was asked to contribute to *The Renaissance World*, edited by John Martin. Encouragement to develop the theme further came from my editor, Beatrice Rehl, whose generosity with both time and comments over the years has been very valuable. A term as a Fellow of the Townsend Center at the University of California at Berkeley also provided a helpful context to present an early chapter of the book and get helpful comments from other Fellows. Similarly, students in both undergraduate and graduate seminars dedicated to the topic of Renaissance Empire provided insightful observations on the topic. Two years in the city of Bologna, Italy, as the director of the University of California education abroad program gave me critical access and time to work in the rich collections of that great city and other Italian and European libraries. The staff of the University library and the city library of the Archiginnasio in Bologna were most gracious. So, too, were the librarians of the Ambrosiano library in Milan, the Laurenziana library in Florence, the National libraries of Madrid and Paris, the British Library, the Vatican Library, and the Bancroft Library. The rare book collections in these great libraries provided the tools without which this book could not have been written. My colleague and mentor at Berkeley, Randolph Starn, provided valuable criticism of a first draft of the text, and my old colleague at Princeton, Tony Grafton, offered characteristically generous comments and encouragement at a critical juncture in the project. Molly Everett provided much help with gathering images and publication rights. Finally, I dedicate the book to Gloria for her good humor and support, to Sophie for the same, and to Luca, young fan of the Caesars, whose excitement, wonder, and music did much to sustain me through the years of research and writing.

INTRODUCTION

ROME WAS

> Consider Rome, our common fatherland, our mother: she lies there – O shameful spectacle! – trampled by all whom she, the conqueror of all lands and seas, once trampled.
>
> Francesco Petrarch, *Letters on Familiar Matters*, trans.
> Aldo S. Bernardo (New York: Italica Press, 2005)[1]

In 1341, Francesco Petrarca, the most important early intellectual protagonist of the Renaissance in Europe, traveled to Rome at the invitation of the city's Senator to accept the honor of the poet's laurel wreath. This imagined revival of the ancient Roman ritual honoring the best poets was both an acknowledgment of Petrarch's early literary fame and an act of faith in his future for the poet and his powerful patron. At the age of thirty-seven he had written many celebrated sonnets in Italian, a number of Latin poems that demonstrated a rare Ciceronian Latinity, and he was at work on *Africa*, his great epic in the manner of the Latin poets. His studies of ancient authors and his Latin letters imitating their style were all the more intense and provocative because he and his patrons increasingly acknowledged that the grandeur of ancient Rome was a distant memory.

The Capitoline Hill where the prize was given made this abundantly clear as it looked out over the ruins of the ancient Roman forum. Once the monumental center of the Roman Republic and Empire, graced by temples, basilicas, triumphal arches, the Senate house, and many statues honoring the gods and emperors, the forum in Petrarch's time had been reduced to a place of smoking lime pits, grazing cows, and the ruins of Rome's former glory.

---

[1] Francesco Petrarch, *Letters on Familiar Matters*, trans. Aldo S. Bernardo (New York: Italica Press, 2005), vol. 2, XV, 7, p. 267. Petrarch's lamentations on the sad and decrepit state of Rome in his own day were expressed often in his vast correspondence. This example is found in a letter to Stefano Colonna, the senator of Rome, from circa 1350.

The ancient center of Rome, still the location of a modest twelfth-century palace that housed the office of the Senator, stood isolated from the main population center of the city surrounding the forum. The largest metropolis of the ancient world when it boasted an estimated population of 1 million, Rome had been reduced to a large town of roughly 30,000 people by the time of Petrarch's visit. In an earlier letter to Pope Benedict XII from late 1334 or early 1335, Petrarch expressed the melancholy sentiment evoked by the decline of the ancient capital with the poignant lament: "Meanwhile in murmur sad the words rang forth: Rome was."[2]

Three hundred years later, the intellectual successors and disciples of Petrarch had a decidedly different view. Visitors to Rome in 1650 saw a city dominated by Michelangelo's colossal dome. It crowned new St. Peter's Basilica, a monumental classicizing temple for a new age that dwarfed the ancient Pantheon. At least a hundred new palaces and dozens of churches, many designed with the classical orders of architecture and decorated with statues and paintings proudly recalling Roman imperial grandeur, lined broad new streets and piazzas where processions modeled on ancient triumphs were reenacted. The Capitoline Hill, too, was renewed with the ancient bronze statue of the emperor Marcus Aurelius at its center flanked on both sides by new classicizing palaces designed by Michelangelo. It had become "a monumental symbol in which the haunting dream of ancient grandeur became concrete."[3] Following the dreams and words of the fifteenth-century Roman humanist, Flavio Biondo, Rome had been restored and reborn as Europe's most dramatic urban stage and a central example of the Renaissance of Empire in early modern Europe.

Rome was not alone. By 1650, colossal palaces, majestic domed churches, villas that imitated those of ancient Rome, and equestrian statues dotted both urban and rural landscapes throughout Western Europe. In Madrid, Paris, and London, European monarchs, together with their viceroys, governors, navies, and armies, sought to emulate and move beyond the ancient Romans who had once ruled over their lands. A political Renaissance of Empire had witnessed the rise of numerous new empires or imperial states. The Spanish Empire had acquired global territories that made it larger than the ancient Roman Empire. By 1800, moreover, the major European maritime empires

---

[2] Ernest Hatch Wilkins, *The Life of Petrarch* (Chicago: University of Chicago Press, 1956), p. 11. The quote is part of a long metric epistle, or letter in Latin verse, also sometimes described as a poem. It urged the pope to return to Rome and also reflected the early conviction of Petrarch that Rome should be the seat of the Empire. It is found in Maud Jerrold, *Francesco Petrarca Poet and Humanist* (New York: Kennikat, 1906), p. 97.

[3] James S. Ackerman, *The Architecture of Michelangelo* (London: A. Zwemmer, 1966), p. 65.

of Spain, Portugal, Britain, and France had to varying degrees left a lasting and deep imprint on a substantial part of the world. Imperial power and pretension in the West had risen to a degree that Petrarch could not have imagined. Rome was again. More accurately, there were numerous new Romes all vying for the imperial mantle and all claiming to be the rightful successor to ancient Roman glory.

This revival of imperial ambition, this dream of a Renaissance of empire as an intellectual, cultural, and political project, was nothing less than the dominant master narrative that drove European political life for the entire early modern period – that is, for at least four centuries. Empires that matched or surpassed ancient Rome in territorial domination, military strength, large revenues extracted from their subject peoples, and the power to impose new laws, cultural aesthetics, and religious beliefs were the driving ambitions of rulers of the great age of early modern empire – Charles I of Spain (1500–1557), Philip II of Spain (1527–1598), and Louis XIV of France (1638–1715), to name the most formidable among them. Global empires were the ultimate prize of early modern political contest.

At the heart of this imperial revival lies a historical question that has occupied contemporary historians for some decades: Why the West? Why was it that Western Europe, a politically fragmented and economically unprepossessing part of the world with one-sixth of the population of China in the fifteenth century, rose to dominate the world in the period from roughly 1500 to 1900? China, a politically united power of 300 million people in the fifteenth century, certainly looked more likely to assume that role.

Although many other explanations have been offered, one largely neglected answer is the Renaissance of Empire. The revival and imitation of the memory, texts, cultural forms, intellectual accomplishments, and political aspirations of the Roman Empire animated imperial pursuit and distinguished Western Europe from any other part of the early modern world. What I argue here is that the widespread dissemination of imperial literary, political, and aesthetic ideals deriving from ancient Roman precedents created a common political culture and ambition throughout Western Europe that provided the broad foundations for the first global empires of Spain, Portugal, France, and Britain.

"Political culture" is a term used here to describe a broad collective political mentality and set of practices that developed among the European ruling class between the fifteenth and eighteenth centuries. It is not to be confused with a uniform political theory or a consistent set of formal policies or juridical definitions. Early modern empires, unlike their modern successors, were guided less by formal political theory than by a set of examples and

historical models derived from Roman antiquity and embodied in a growing body of humanist texts. This literature was characterized by an evolving
set of ideas and reflections on empire that were inspired by the revival, study,
and imitation of the texts, rulers, and example of ancient Rome above all
others. Numerous empires rose and fell in the early modern period, and
there was certainly a wide range of political forms and models, but all of
these empires shared the common reference of ancient Roman imperial
memories and models. Empire was increasingly seen as Europe's birthright
as the successor to ancient Rome both pagan and Christian.

As a scholar of later European imperialism noted, "the enterprise of
empire depends upon the *idea of having an empire*." A related axiom is that
"Empire follows Art," with art being broadly defined to include the literary
and plastic arts.[4] In the case of early modern Europe, it was the *longue durée*
of the Imperial Renaissance, of political ideas and artistic forms taken from
the ancient Roman empire, that were repeatedly used as both inspiration and
justification for European political ambition over the course of four centuries. It may be "Guns, Germs, and Steel" that answer the question of *how* the
West dominated much of the early modern Atlantic world – of the most
obvious material tools and causes that explain Western domination. But it
was the political mentalities and culture nurtured by the ideas and art of the
Imperial Renaissance that largely answer the question of *why* European rulers and peoples thought they should.[5] They were as central to the building
of empires as the more formulaic explanations of sails, credit, gold, guns, and
steel even if they do not lend themselves as easily to a deterministic-oriented
analysis concerned with causation.

Renaissances and Empires

The Renaissance has most often been treated as an intellectual, political,
and cultural movement focused on the revival of ancient Roman and Greek
civilization, which emerged in Italy in the middle of the fourteenth century
and spread to other parts of Europe to varying degrees over the next three
centuries. On the intellectual level, this was a movement characterized by the
revival, translation, imitation, and dissemination of ancient Roman and Greek
texts on an unprecedented level. Culturally, in the time-honored accounts,

---

[4] Edward Said, *Culture and Imperialism* (New York: Vintage Books, 1993), pp. 10–13. The close
relationship between Renaissance ideas and cultural forms has seldom been adequately
acknowledged or fully incorporated into studies of early European empire, a gap in the
literature that this study aims to fill.
[5] Jared Diamond, *Guns, Germs, and Steel* (New York: W.W. Norton, 1997).

it sought to imitate or revive the Vitruvian orders of classical architecture, to rediscover the ability to represent the natural world and human form in art, and to recreate the styles and insights of ancient authors. Politically, it was defined by the revival of two primary political systems from the ancient Roman world: the Republican and Imperial forms of government.

All of these themes, and many others, have been studied and debated, but not all have been treated equally or applied with the same analytical depth to varying European polities. In the realm of political interpretation, most especially, the emphasis on the revival of the ancient Roman Republican political tradition dominated Renaissance scholarship in the wake of World War II and the Cold War. So, for example, the most important single explanation for the interest in Italian Renaissance history in the United States in the twentieth century was the perception that the republicanism of the Florentine and Venetian city-states prefigured the rise of the "republican ideal" in Western Europe and the United States.[6] This was a Renaissance to celebrate like a heroic and virtuous ancestor. The threats to republicanism by the corruptions of power, internal division, and external enemies became an object lesson in the need for republican vigilance.

In regions of Italy with little or no Renaissance republican tradition, the political dimension of the Renaissance has been treated generally as the regional struggle between competing princely dynasties or despots like the Sforza in Milan, the d'Este in Ferrara, the Gonzaga in Mantua, the kings of Aragon in Naples, the Montefeltro in Urbino, and the various popes. In the rhetoric of earlier Renaissance history, these territories and their rulers could be characterized in terms of tyranny or despotism in contrast to the republican ideals of Florence and Venice. But a new political ideal of imperial revival was beyond their grasp, if not their dreams, and they had little impact on the great empires that rose later.

The popes, above all others, have represented the despotic Renaissance. In the prevailing view, the Imperial Renaissance in Rome was politically compromised by the military failures and limits of Alexander VI and Julius II, bankrupted by the extravagance of Leo X, and ultimately overshadowed by the Reformation. The Imperial Renaissance, in this scholarly tradition, was largely over by 1527 and the sack of Rome, although papal imperial ambitions continued, especially in the realms of artistic or architectural production in the Baroque period.[7]

---

[6] For a succinct summary of Renaissance history in the United States, see especially Edward Muir, "The Italian Renaissance in America," in *The American Historical Review*, Vol. 100, No. 4 (Oct. 1995), pp. 1095–1118.

[7] Charles Stinger, *The Renaissance in Rome* (Bloomington: Indiana University Press), 1998.

It follows that many scholars in the Anglo–American tradition would make little connection between the Italian Renaissance and political developments in other major European territories where republicanism was at best marginal and monarchs had greater aspirations than did makeshift Italian despots. Beyond the Alps, the Renaissance, and Italy more generally, was displaced in the conventional accounts by the Reformation or treated primarily as a cultural and intellectual movement void of a serious unified political program. The narrative teleology was not about Renaissance Empire but about national identity and national monarchies culminating in nation-states.

Adding further to the weakening of the Renaissance as a central aspect of early modern European political developments, even the traditional republican narrative has been called into question in recent decades. The strength and purity of the republican political program in Florence and Venice has been strongly qualified. Leonardo Bruni has been found, literarily, in bed with the Medici. His republican public writings, the foundations of the famous civic humanism thesis of Hans Baron, often contradict his private letters that are more pragmatic and accommodating to oligarchs. Florentine and Venetian oligarchies alike also engaged in imperial expansions such as the conquest of Pisa and the Veneto, respectively, without bothering to spread political liberty to the new colonies. In short, there was a good deal of imperial pursuit in the Renaissance republics, a fact that contemporary historians versed in democratic imperialism are quick to recognize.[8] After all, the ancient model most admired by Venice and Florence, Republican Rome, was itself a republican empire. Democratic Athens in the Golden Age also had its colonies.

This deconstruction of the republican narrative of the Renaissance has coincided with a broader questioning of the Renaissance and its place in the Grand Narrative tradition of Western history over the past generation. The Renaissance as a field has been a contested and fragmented territory in recent decades with varying revisions appearing in the thematic, chronological, and geographical emphases of the scholarship.[9] Although the volume

[8] Peter Burke, *The European Renaissance* (Oxford: Blackwell Publishers, 1998). The author opens his book asking the basic question: Why another book on the Renaissance? Part of his answer is that authors and groups that had been previously marginalized needed to be incorporated into the picture. See also James Hankins, "The 'Baron Thesis' after Forty Years and Some Recent Studies of Leonardo Bruni," in *The Journal of the History of Ideas*, Vol. 56, No. 2 (Apr. 1995), pp. 309–338.

[9] The chronology of the Renaissance has lengthened considerably over the past generation. While the postwar generation followed a much shorter chronology that usually had the Renaissance end where the Reformation began, around 1520, the contemporary boundaries

of Renaissance scholarship remains high, what is noticeably lacking in any major recent work is a unifying political theory or interpretation that ties the cultural and intellectual revival together with the political developments of European global empires.

This study proposes to offer just that. It argues on a broad level that it was the Renaissance of Empire on two primary levels that had the longest and most profound impact on both Western Europe and the parts of the world colonized by the new empires in the early modern period. On the level of intellectual and cultural life, the revival of ancient texts and cultural forms associated with the Roman Empire reshaped the political mentalities, architecture, and arts of the capital cities and courts of Europe like no other movement did. On the related political level, the ambition to revive real territorial empires equal to or greater than the Roman Empire contributed to the establishment of numerous new global empires that constituted the concrete manifestation of the intellectual and cultural Renaissance.

Far more influential in shaping the political mentalities and programs of European monarchs than the civic humanism and Renaissance republicanism of Northern Italy were imperial humanism and Renaissance imperialism.[10] The imperial humanists applied their rhetorical and grammatical skills to the tasks of recovering, editing, commenting on, imitating, and creating new versions of ancient Roman texts that were used to propagate an imperial political program and set of ideals. Working for princes, popes, monarchs, and emperors as tutors, secretaries, historians, and poets, they truly created a "cultural program and political outlook that reshaped European (and world) history."[11] Together with scholastic political philosophers and theologians, these scholars provided much of the intellectual framework for early modern

---

now stretch well into the seventeenth century. The Renaissance Society of America, for example, defines the period as roughly between 1300 and 1650.

[10] Certain imperial characteristics notwithstanding, the Renaissance Republics also had a larger degree of political representation, complete with institutions and laws, than their despotic, princely, or imperial neighbors. The Renaissance in Florence and Venice were distinct because of their republican politics, even if rhetoric did not always reflect reality. The simple fact that the *ideal* of civic humanism was created and held up as a possibility significantly transformed the political landscape in early modern Italy and beyond. Regardless of their imperial characteristics, the Florentine and Venetian Republics, as well as the Dutch Republic in the sixteenth century, did experience a political Renaissance and a form of civic humanism that was distinct from the centers of the imperial Renaissance that are the focus of this book. The subject of the lion's share of Renaissance scholarship over the last century, Florence and Venice are left to the side here, as is the Dutch empire.

[11] Quoted in Hankins, "The Baron Thesis." This is a paraphrase of Najemy's claim for civic humanism cited by Hankins.

empires that eventually swallowed up their smaller Republican counterparts like great predatory sharks.[12]

Seen from this perspective, the Renaissance in Florence does not end when the Republic falls. Rather, when Charles V, the first early modern emperor, conquered Republican Florence and installed the Medici as his de facto governors, the Republican Renaissance was overtaken by the Imperial Renaissance. Similarly, the Renaissance in Rome does not end with the ascendancy of the empire of Charles V. It is simply merged with the larger empire that more often than not takes up the role of protector and patron.

This should come as no surprise. As Petrarch's biography of Julius Caesar so clearly demonstrates, the Renaissance and Renaissance humanists, from their very beginning, also held a fascination with the imperial tradition that was always the other political option for Europeans committed to a revival of Roman antiquity. The imperial theme, with its great political lure and temptation of reviving large-scale empires, subsequently came to dominate the political imaginations of European Renaissance princes just as it had dominated ancient Rome throughout the centuries after Caesar.

Clearly, this Renaissance of Empire largely supplanted the republican tradition and the Renaissance republics by the middle of the sixteenth century. It was the revival of empires, not republics, both imagined and real, that came to dominate the literary, artistic, and political agendas of Europe's most powerful states, political writers, and monarchs. This Imperial Renaissance, moreover, continued to shape the political ambitions and agendas of both Catholic and Protestant monarchs and empires throughout the seventeenth and eighteenth centuries. Thus, taking the Renaissance of Empire seriously requires us to substantially revise and expand our traditional understanding of the impact and longevity of the Renaissance itself. From this political vantage point, the Renaissance as a cultural, intellectual, and political movement spans the better part of four centuries from roughly 1340 to roughly 1715, with powerful echoes beyond. It is thus the most influential political drama of the early modern period.[13]

---

[12] Paul Oskar Kristeller, *Renaissance Thought and Its Sources* (New York: Columbia University Press, 1978). Kristeller emphasized the importance of scholasticism as one of the major schools of Renaissance thought, along with humanism and neo-Platonism.

[13] Empire studies are clearly a hot field at the moment. See, for example, the special volume of the journal *History and Theory* entitled *The History and Theory of Empires*, ed. Philip Pomper, Vol. 44, No. 4 (December 2005). Interest in the theme of Empire across time and place has been spurred in part by the strong perception among many political scientists and historians that contemporary America continues to be motivated by imperial ambition as the direct heir of the European imperial tradition. This is perhaps most overtly stated, albeit from opposite sides of the political spectrum, by Niall Ferguson in his recent work *Empire*

This Renaissance may not have the same political appeal or inspire the same admiration as the Republican Renaissance, but it constitutes a critical part of the political and cultural legacy of the early modern period. The analysis and narrative of the Imperial Renaissance that follows here does not aim to celebrate Western triumphalism, but it does aim to reconstruct and resurrect a central early modern narrative that has been largely buried or minimized in the prevailing scholarship. This Renaissance was and remains central to understanding early modern European and global history – to understanding the intellectual and cultural patterns that constituted a substantial part of the genetic code of early modern empires and their ruling class. As such, it is a cautionary tale about the deep and expansive roots of imperial ambition in the West.

This theme, by the very nature of its broad chronological and geographical sweep, is history on the "grand scale" reminiscent of Fernand Braudel in spirit, if not in form.[14] It is a topic that demands a panoramic and macro-historical perspective. The chapters that follow subsequently employ a multilayered methodological approach that draws on various analytical tools from cultural, intellectual, and political historians. As a historical essay on the long Renaissance, it privileges those themes, texts, and locations that were central to the revival of Roman imperial antiquity.

Because the project covers a large topic over a long span of time, it is not the purpose here to offer thick historical detail for all of the empires covered. Rather, I aim to first establish the major intellectual themes, aesthetics, and

(New York: Basic Books, 2004) that primarily focuses on the modern British Empire, and by Antonio Negri and Michael Hardt in their work *Empire* (Cambridge, MA: Harvard University Press, 2000) that sees modern global capitalism as the contemporary embodiment of imperialism. Other works such as that by Harold James, *The Roman Predicament* (Princeton, NJ: Princeton University Press, 2008), point to the lingering reference to the old models of empire for builders of modern Europe. Still others, like Nigel Hamilton's recent *American Caesars* (New Haven, CT: Yale University Press, 2010), indulge in a Roman conceit with deep roots in the Renaissance by overtly modeling the study of the most recent twelve American presidents after the *Lives of the Twelve Caesars* by the ancient Roman writer Suetonius. Like these books, most recent work on empire in the nineteenth and twentieth centuries focuses on the British and American capitalist model of empire. What this literature often lacks, however, is a firm grounding in the expansive Renaissance intellectual and cultural roots of the imperial tradition in the West and more specifically in Renaissance Italy. It is one of the aims of this book to add this early modern perspective to modern debates and perceptions of the lingering lure of imperial ambition in the West.

[14] Fernand Braudel's *The Mediterranean and the Mediterranean World in the Age of Philip II* (New York: Harper and Row, 1972). The last paragraph of the introduction reads, in part: "I hope that I shall not be reproached for my excessive ambitions, for my desire and need to see on a grand scale. It will perhaps prove that history can do more than study walled gardens. If it were otherwise, it would surely be failing in one of its most immediate tasks which must be to relate to the powerful problems of our times."

locations of the Imperial Renaissance in Italy and then to examine how this cultural movement took root in, shaped, and was shaped by the major emerging empires of Spain, France, and Britain.

Two basic interrelated assertions or assumptions guide this work: first, that the long Imperial Renaissance has not been adequately studied, articulated, or acknowledged in the historical literature on the Renaissance to date; and second, that this Renaissance has subsequently not been fully incorporated into the history of early modern empires as the unifying intellectual and cultural movement that it constituted for Spain, France, and Britain.

Much work already exists on individual empires, but there is no work that seeks to analyze and understand the various empires as part of a single movement inspired and driven by a central intellectual, cultural, and political program with roots in the Italian Renaissance. The study that comes closest to this agenda and that provides both important points of comparison and contrast is Anthony Pagden's *Lords of All the World*.

Like this study, that work focuses its attention on Spain, Britain, and France as the three dominant global European empires of the early modern period. Like Pagden, I exclude the Holy Roman Empire, Russia, Venice, and the Ottoman Empire as empires that did not share the basic characteristics of the global empires: to varying degrees they were not major players in imperial competition for New World colonies and trade with the accompanying navies to advance this agenda; they did not witness the proliferation of art and architecture inspired by the ancient Roman Empire; and they did not share to the same extent the circulation of imperial humanist texts and ideas shared by the major empires.[15]

Importantly, the major political observers and actors of the period from Machiavelli to Louis XIV also understood the widening gulf between the new empires and the others. Machiavelli, for example, commenting on the German lands, called the Holy Roman emperor a "shadow of an emperor" who exercised "no direct power" there.[16] Almost two centuries later, Louis XIV ridiculed the German emperor as having no real empire to back up the

---

[15] Anthony Pagden, *Lords of All the World* (New Haven, CT, and London: Yale University Press, 1995), p. 4. Pagden notes that competition for American colonies, above all else, caused the Spanish, French, and British to measure themselves against one another and to borrow from one another "in their continuing attempts to understand the evolving shapes of the empires which they had created." Russian, German, and Scandinavian incursions into America, by comparison, were "too transitory to arouse much interest." In addition to Pagden's work, see *Theories of Empire, 1450–1800*, ed. David Armitage (Aldershot, UK: Ashgate, 1998) – a collection of essays that, like, Pagden's work, privileges the political theory of empires in the period.

[16] N. Machiavelli, *The Discourses*, vol. 1, p. 379.

title, in contrast to himself. Similarly, contemporaries understood clearly that one old Mediterranean commercial empire, Venice, was contracting, while another, that of Genoa, had joined itself to the Spanish empire as a de facto client state. Second- or third-tier powers, they simply did not have the same power or exercise the same influence as the emerging big three.

This also holds true for the Dutch empire. Although the quick rise of the republican commercial empire had the distinction of briefly competing for colonies in the Atlantic world in the seventeenth century, it could not compete with the major powers and failed to establish any permanent political presence. In Asia, where it had more success as a commercial power, its colonial influence and power still remained far weaker than that of the major powers. In short, the limited global imprint of the Dutch and other European powers in the early modern period in the realms of political, economic, and cultural influence compared to Spain, France, and Britain underlines the fundamental difference that distinguished the major empires from all of the others.

This is also the case with the Portuguese Empire, to a lesser extent. It represents a special case particularly because it was merged with the Spanish Empire in the critical period between 1580 and 1640. Portugal will be dealt with here in that context in Chapter 3, where a number of its distinctive characteristics will be analyzed. Among these was its weaker connection to the Italian Renaissance and subsequently to the ancient model of the Roman Empire.

A major factor that distinguished Spain, France, and Britain from Portugal and other early modern empires was the greater affinity that the dominant empires had with ancient Rome. As Pagden notes, for them, all roads led to the ancient Roman Empire. As a work of intellectual history that focuses first and foremost on the political theory and language of empire derived in part from ancient Roman law, Pagden's *Lords of All the World* provides an excellent examination of the terminology and definitions of ancient empire and its early modern adaptations and variations. Readers interested in the thick linguistic maze of empire will find much there, as will those in search of the juridical roads from early modern empire to the Roman Empire.[17]

This work, however, follows different paths that lead out of ancient Rome, which only occasionally cross the jurist's road of Pagden's study. The roads followed here, wider and with considerably more traffic, cover very different

---

[17] Ibid., p. 11. Pagden states that, "It was above all, Rome which provided the ideologues of the colonial systems of Spain, Britain, and France with the language and political models they required."

territory using different intellectual guides and lingering over the physical monuments on those roads. Most noticeably, this study spends far more time – the entire first chapter – in Renaissance Italy, something that neither Pagden nor any other work on any of the empires studied here offers. For it was in Italy that the ancient Roman conduits essential for the spread of the Imperial Renaissance were first being repaired to make possible the flow of ancient imperial ideas and models.

More specifically, it was in Renaissance Italy that the ancient historians of empire and the memory of the central emperors were being revived, rehabilitated, and imitated on an unprecedented level. The histories of Julius Caesar, Seutonius, Tacitus, and Plutarch took center stage in this movement. Numerous new editions and translations of their works appeared, and they became the new political primers for Renaissance rulers. Humanist editors of these texts often provided elaborate commentaries, and humanist historians like Petrarch, Biondo, and Giovio, among many others, wrote new histories of the ancient empire and emperors, as well as histories of the new empires, that were modeled on the ancient texts.

This study gives these texts pride of place in its analysis because they were the single most important location for the instruction and modeling of Renaissance empires and rulers. History was the primary *magister vitae* for the rulers of early modern empires. As the French humanist and councilor Jaques Amyot noted in the dedication to King Henry II of his translation of Plutarch's *Lives of Illustrious Greeks and Romans*: "Thus one can truly conclude that History is the teacher of Princes, from whom they are able to learn, without trouble, and passing their time with singular pleasure, the major part of that which their office requires."[18]

Above all else, history provided the ideas, examples, and agendas that inspired the imperial monarchs in the art of war and in the patronage of the arts. The importance and popularity of the ancient historians, as well as new histories of the ancient empire, were demonstrated by their extremely successful publication records as they went to print over and over again in many languages and editions. More often than not, these texts were dedicated to the monarchs and published with their blessing and support. They

---

[18] Plutarque, *Les Vies des Hommes Illustres Grecs et Romains*, translation by Jaques Amyot (Gent: Jacob Stoer, 1642). Not paginated, but the quote is found on the fourteenth page of dedicatory materials that open the text.

"Ainsi peut-on veritablement conclurre, que l'Histoire est la maistresse des Princes, de laquelle ils peuvent apprendre sans peine, en passant leur temps, et avec singulier plaisir, la meilleure partie de ce qui est requis a` leur office." The first French translation was published by Amyot in 1559.

subsequently played the central role in shaping and reflecting the political mentalities of their day that went well beyond those of any other genre of literature. Historians, not jurists, were the true intellectual guides to the revival of imperial rule.

Accompanying these texts as instruments of empire were the imperial arts. An essential lesson of the imperial historians and histories emphasized over and over again was that the glory and honor of the ruler were demonstrated in two major realms: war and patronage of arts and letters. Just as the history of Julius Caesar provided valuable advice and the most exalted example of military victory and conquest, so too did the history of his adopted son and heir, Augustus, provide the principal model of a ruler who knew how to use art and architecture to celebrate and give material substance to imperial power.[19]

The Renaissance monarchs were deeply influenced by this message and example, and the rebirth of the imperial arts is subsequently another major focus of this work. More specifically, the revival of the equestrian monument as a symbol of sovereignty, painting and sculptural cycles celebrating the Caesars, and opulent palaces and public buildings inspired by the revival of the architect of Caesar and Augustus, Vitruvius, take pride of place in this study because they were the most visible and important material manifestations of the Imperial Renaissance. As such, they constitute some of the strongest threads that tie the Imperial Renaissance in Italy, Iberia, France, and Great Britain together.

As the only surviving treatise from ancient Rome, the "Ten Books of Architecture" by Vitruvius played a singular role in the revival of imperial architecture in all of these locations.[20] Dedicating his work to the emperor Augustus, Vitruvius had made the explicit connection between empire building and architecture in the introduction to his book:

> When, however, I perceived that you were solicitous not only for the establishment of community life and of the body politic, but also for the construction of suitable public buildings, so that by your agency not only had the state been rendered more august by the annexation of entire provinces, but indeed *the majesty of the Empire had found conspicuous proof in its public*

---

[19] Indra Kagis McEwen, *Vitruvius* (Cambridge, MA: MIT Press, 2003), p. 38. McEwen argues that architecture in the age of Augustus and beyond gave "material substance to the abstract imperium."

[20] Ibid. McEwen argues that the difference between the rulers of Republican Rome, who certainly understood the role of architecture in projecting political power, and Vitruvius is that he thought and wrote carefully about "*why* architecture would 'increase' the commonwealth and *how* it would record Roman greatness."

works – then I thought that I should not miss the opportunity to publish on these matters for you as soon as possible, given that I was first recognized in this field by your Father [Julius Caesar].[21]

This was a message that had strong appeal to monarchs as they sought to provide "conspicuous proof" of their own greatness in their building programs. Following the example of the ancient emperors, and above all others Augustus, they embraced the belief that monumental architecture was both a reflection and a constitutive part of good government. The text of Vitruvius subsequently became "one of the most profoundly influential books to survive from antiquity."[22]

Italy was the first location to witness this revival as new editions of the ancient work were repeatedly published and translated. Moreover, important new texts inspired by Vitruvius, especially those of Alberti and Sebastiano Serlio, served as instruction manuals for builders of new monumental architecture. By the early sixteenth century there was a Vitruvian Academy in Rome dedicated to the revival of his architectural style. In Italy and Spain new colossal imperial palaces following Vitruvian orders appeared, marking the beginning of a revival that would dominate the capitals of the new empires for centuries to come. By the end of the seventeenth century, Paris and London had fully joined in the revival.

The five chapters of this work are subsequently arranged both geographically and chronologically beginning with fourteenth- and fifteenth-century Italy, where the book excavates the literary and artistic foundations of the Imperial Renaissance. It then moves to examine the first global empire built on those foundations, that of Charles V, in Chapter 2. A study of the Spanish Empire of his son and grandson, Philip II and Philip III, follows in Chapter 3, and Chapter 4 focuses on the rise of the French Empire. The final chapter charts the rise of the empire of Great Britain in the sixteenth and seventeenth centuries.

---

[21] Vitruvius, *Ten Books of Architecture*, translated by Ingrid Rowland (Cambridge: Cambridge University Press, 1999), p. 21.

[22] Vitruvius, *Ten Books on Architecture: The Corsini Incunabulum*, ed. Ingrid D. Rowland (Rome: Edizioni Dell'Elefante, 2003), p. 4. Rowland, presently one of our leading authorities on Vitruvius in the Renaissance, argues that "*De Architectura* must be regarded as one of the most profoundly influential books to survive from antiquity, not for its technical information, but for the way in which it links good architecture with good government."

Map 1.1. Italy.

ITALIAE NOVISSIMA
DESCRIPTIO AVCTORE
IACOBO CASTALDO
PEDEMONTANO

I

THE REBIRTH OF THE CAESARS

I gave him as a gift some gold and silver coins bearing the portraits of our ancient rulers and inscriptions in tiny and ancient lettering, coins that I treasured, and among them was the head of Caesar Augustus, who almost appeared to be breathing. "Here, O Caesar," I said, are the men whom you have succeeded, here are those whom you must try to imitate and admire, whose ways and character you should emulate.

Petrarch to the Emperor Charles IV in Mantua.[1]

Late in the 1330s, Francesco Petrarch began work on *De viri illustribus, or On Famous Men*. It was originally conceived of as a collection of biographies of twenty-three ancient Romans beginning with Romulus and ending with Julius Caesar, the de facto founder of the Roman Empire.[2]

As a work dedicated largely to important military and political figures, Petrarch's text served as an early literary guide to the two primary political streams that flowed out of ancient Rome: the Republican tradition and the Imperial tradition. For some of Petrarch's later disciples and admirers such as the Florentine humanist Leonardo Bruni, it was the Republican tradition that they most celebrated and sought to revive and emulate in their own city states. The great majority of Petrarch's famous men came from the Republican period, for example, whereas only Julius Caesar could be tied to the Imperial tradition.

---

[1] *Letters on Familiar Matters*, 19:3, trans. Bernardo, vol. 3, p. 79. Quoted in Leonard Barkan, *Unearthing the Past: Archeology and Aesthetics in the Making of Renaissance Culture* (New Haven, CT: Yale University Press, 1999), p. 28.
[2] Francesco Petrarca, *De Viris Illustribus*, ed. Guido Martellotti (Florence: Sansoni, 1964). This remains the most cited critical edition of the text where the writing chronology is reconstructed from references in other sources and from Petrarch's own writings. He argues that the earliest lives were begun sometime around 1338–1339, while the life of Caesar was his last work, completed in the few years before his death in 1374.

Yet Petrarch's elaborate treatment of the life of Julius Caesar, compared with his much shorter biographies of the other men, already suggested that the Republican phase of the Renaissance was a long prelude to the revival of empire. In a modern version of the text, for example, the lives of the first twenty-two Romans from Romulus through Scipione Africanus are covered in 268 pages. But Petrarch's life of Julius Caesar alone requires 238 pages.[3] In part, this may have been because Petrarch had more expansive historical sources for Caesar, including the works of Suetonius, Cicero, and the *Commentaries* of Caesar himself. But it also points to Petrarch's increased concentration on Caesar as he grew older. It was a strong and tangible sign that the founder of the Roman Empire was being presented as ancient Rome's most compelling and greatest political figure.

A younger Petrarch had given a great deal of attention to one of Republican Rome's central heroes, Scipione Africanus, whose biography was his second longest at 114 pages. Similarly, Petrarch's great early work, "Africa," celebrated the Republican victory over Carthage. In the political world of his own day he was supportive, initially at least, of Cola Di Rienzo's attempt to restore a Roman Republic in 1347, and he regularly criticized tyrants in his letters.[4]

But Petrarch obviously had a foot on both sides of the political fence from an early point in his life. His repeated appeals to Charles IV to restore imperial glory and rule to Italy in the 1340s and 1350s and his praise of King Robert of Naples as a new Augustus in the same period were more than just rhetorical.[5] Particularly after the failed Republican revival of Cola di Rienzo, Petrarch exhibited increasingly monarchist leanings and associations, and the long biography of Julius Caesar underlines the fact that

---

[3] Francesco Petrarca, *Gli Uomini Illustri Vita di Giulio Cesare*, ed. Ugo Dotti (Torino: Einaudi, 2007), p. 7. There is presently no English translation and/or study of this work, a telling omission in the historical literature that reflects the general lack of scholarly interest in English that this text has received when compared with Petrarch's other writings. Dotti also draws on a recent critical edition of *De Gestis Cesaris* by Giuliana Crevatin (Pisa: Scuola Normale, 2003). Included in Dotti's edition are eleven additional lives of biblical and ancient men, beginning with Adam and going through Hercules, that Petrarch decided to add to his text sometime between 1351 and 1353. For a concise account of the presumed writing chronology see Dotti, pp. 7–8.

[4] For a relatively recent synthesis of views on Petrarch as a historical figure, see Craig Kallendorf, "The Historical Petrarch," *The American Historical Review*, Vol. 101, No. 1, 1996, pp. 130–141. For a still-useful traditional biography, see Ernest Hatch Wilkins, *The Life of Petrarch* (Chicago: University of Chicago Press, 1956). His chronology of Petrarch's writings has been qualified somewhat by subsequent research.

[5] Petrarch, *Letters on Familiar Matters*. See, for example, the letters to Charles IV in 1351, vol. 2, Fam. X, 1.

in his writings, as in his own political life, he yearned for the revival of a strong imperial monarchy by the 1350s. Observing the communal strife of his own times and the constant battle for control of various parts of Italy that left the fourteenth-century peninsula politically weak and fragmented, Petrarch seems to have concluded that a full-scale revival of imperial power was the best hope for uniting Italy and ending all of the divisions and bloodshed. Repeatedly he urged the Holy Roman Emperor, Charles IV, to live up to his title. But he was repeatedly disappointed in the weakness of the emperor and empire of his own day. He regularly chided Charles IV in his correspondence and complained of how poorly both he and his empire compared to the ancient emperors and the Roman Empire.[6]

In Julius Caesar, however, Petrarch found a military and political model that embodied many of the virtues that he wished to see reborn in his own rulers. Although he did not shy away from criticizing some of Caesar's actions, particularly in the civil war, his overriding admiration for the founder of the empire was clear.[7]

The reasons for this emerge in the portrait that Petrarch paints of Caesar in his biography. As a piece of humanist historiography, the text sticks close to the sources and has an overarching didactic purpose. The early life of Caesar, where the records are sparse, is subsequently covered in just a few pages. After that, Petrarch largely contents himself with constructing a straightforward political narrative that charts Caesar's rise, his victories in Africa and Europe, and his victory in the civil war. The *Lives of the Caesars* by Suetonius and Caesar's *Commentaries* are the sources quoted most often, and Petrarch states that one of his own purposes was to more broadly develop their themes in the form of a chronicle.[8]

But the text is far more than a chronicle. It is full-blown humanist history with a clear agenda of using the lives of great men to promote certain

---

[6] C. C. Bayley, "Charles IV, and the 'Renovatio Imperii'", *Speculum*, Vol. 17, No. 3 (Jul., 1942), pp. 323–341. Based largely on a reading of his letters, Petrarch's views are described here as being marked by "the nostalgic yearning ... for a restoration of the secular despotism of the later Roman Empire." P. 338. Petrarch's biography of Caesar, which is not incorporated into the analysis here, changes this perspective insofar as it points to a desire for a restoration of the Empire from its earliest beginnings.

[7] Francesco Petrarca, *Gli Uomini Illustri Vita di Giulio Cesare*, ed. Ugo Dotti (Torino: Einaudi, 2007), p. 373. This is the perspective of Dotti, who argues that by the end of his life, Petrarch's political experience may have led him to abandon his earlier devotion to Scipione in favor of admiration for Caesar.

[8] Ibid., p. 539. After quoting Suetonius: "Tali le sue parole che qui noi, secondo il nostro proposito, abbiamo piu' ampiamente svolto in forma di cronaca."

values and provide examples to be imitated.[9] In the case of the life of Caesar, Petrarch uses his text to provide examples of how successful wars were waged and what particular virtues led Caesar to such a high level of success. It was a rhetorical performance meant to impress and move the audience with Caesar's example both as military strategist and ruler who knew how to maintain power once victories were won.[10] The text thus set a vital precedent for future positive humanist treatments of Caesar, and as such represents a central pillar of imperial humanism.[11] Because of its importance, and because no substantial commentary on the text exists in English, the following analysis outlines the major aspects of Petrarch's treatment of Caesar.

The majority of the text, or chapters 3 through 19, covers the period from 58 BC to 50 BC, the years of Caesar's great victories in Gaul, Germany, and Britain. The picture of Caesar that emerges throughout this section is overwhelmingly heroic and virtuous. After a great victory over the German, Ariovisto, for example, Caesar is depicted as deriving the greatest joy from having liberated his friend, Caio Valerio, from a cruel captivity.[12]

Later, in a hard battle against the Nervi, the Romans appeared to be in great danger of suffering a major defeat, and some were urging retreat. "But not Caesar, always great and exceptionally great when in great danger." Grabbing a shield, he went to the front lines, rallied some centurions around him, and turned the tide of the battle in the Romans' favor. The lesson was clear: "One saw then how the force of spirit of one single man knew how to inspire in everyone an ardent and extraordinary courage and how the voice and example of one captain was of such a quality as to reanimate the legions."[13]

---

[9] For a concise treatment of Petrarch's historical methods and views of history that is directly related to *De viris illustribus*, see Benjamin G. Kohl, "Petrarch's Prefaces to deViris Illustribus," *History and Theory*, Vol. 13, No. 2 (May, 1974), pp. 132–144.

[10] Anthony Grafton, "Historia and Istoria: Alberit's Terminology in Context," in *I Tatti Studies*, 1999, p. 49. Grafton provides one of the most succinct descriptions of the purposes of humanist history writing. Most germane to Petrarch's life of Caesar were the words Grafton quotes from the later humanist Lapo da Castiglionchio, who, in a letter to Flavio Biondo, emphasized that history was a rich source of wisdom for "the method of ruling the state, the reasons for undertaking wars, how they should be waged, and how far they should be prosecuted."

[11] Andrew Pettegree, *The Book in the Renaissance* (New Haven, CT: Yale University Press, 2011), p. 187. The author credits this work of Petrarch with nothing less than the revival of history: "The revival of history was initiated by Petrarch, whose sequence of biographies, *De viris illustribus* (Lives of Famous Men), became an extremely popular genre in the fifteenth and sixteenth centuries, and was widely imitated."

[12] Petrarca, *Vita di Giulio Cesare*, p. 423.

[13] Ibid., p. 433. "Si vide allora come la forza d'animo d'una sola persona avesse saputo infondere in tutti un ardente e straordinario coraggio e come la voce e l'esempio del solo comandante fossero stati in grado di rianimare le legion ..."

In yet another battle against the Gauls in the following year, similar inspirational qualities were demonstrated. A battle was won by the power of the Roman navy but also by the valor of the men, which was superior to that of their opponents "all the more so because the presence of Caesar increased their courage."[14]

The mere presence of Caesar inspired not only courage in the Roman legions but fear in his enemies. During the first British conquests in 55 BC, Caesar was approached by some British tribes, who offered him their obedience and tribute even before he reached the island, so fearsome was his reputation as a warrior. And when a group of 300 Roman soldiers was trapped by 6,000 British enemies, the arrival of Caesar with reinforcements sent the enemy into immediate retreat because his presence alone was enough to scatter a much larger army. For this victory, Caesar was rewarded with an unprecedented twenty-day feast proclaimed by the Roman Senate.[15]

For Petrarch, Caesar's strategic leadership and valor were all the greater because he was able to teach and inspire his officers to follow his example. In this way he was able to accomplish extraordinary victories, which increased both his own fame and that of Rome. At the same time, he was famous for the clemency that he was quick to grant former adversaries and the help that he was quick to give former enemies.

All of these virtues and victories in war were also joined with equal wisdom in times of peace. Having conquered all of Gaul by 51 BC, and having placed soldiers throughout the country, Caesar was free from the obligation to spend his winter planning the next summer's campaign. Instead, he focused on "extinguishing all reasons for conflict and on sweet discourses about peace, with conserving old friendships and making new ones, with doing harm to no one and good to all, and with imposing no new taxes but diminishing or eliminating the old ones." Through these means, the whole region remained pacified, and he was able to celebrate a proper triumph with his army. In Petrarch's judgment that summed up the long section on the Gallic Wars, "Things went even better than were hoped, and not for no reason, but because Caesar was the best both in war and in peace, in conquering and knowing how to reconcile the spirits of men."[16]

[14] Ibid., p. 440.

[15] Ibid., p. 458.

[16] Ibid., p. 539. The text reads: "E le cose andarano ancor meglio di quanto avesse sperato; non per nulla, del resto, Cesare era il migliore sia in guerra che in pace, sia nel vincere che nel sapersi conciliare gli anime."

Up to this point in his biography, Petrarch not only follows Caesar and Suetonius closely in recounting the details of the wars, but he also adds rhetorical flourish and instruction to the story. Petrarch's Caesar is more heroic and virtuous than Caesar as depicted by himself. By comparison, the *Commentaries* of Caesar read like an exercise in humility and literary restraint. Without question, Petrarch's long section on the Gallic wars presented Renaissance readers with a leader most worthy of imitation.

Petrarch's briefly changes tone when he reaches the Civil Wars in chapter 21. Although he acknowledges from the beginning of this section that Caesar did not lack notable justifications for his actions, he nonetheless concludes that "to make war against one's own country always remains unjustifiable."[17] Still, he seems to empathize with Caesar's plight because "glory never escapes jealousy." Moreover, when he describes the causes of the Civil War, he points out the duplicity and plotting of Caesar's enemies in Rome, above all those of Pompey.[18]

Moreover, after briefly recounting the opinions of those who blamed Caesar for the Civil War, summed up by Cicero, who claimed that Caesar was willing to violate the principles of justice for the sake of gaining power, Petrarch turns to Caesar's defense. He points out that all of the negative opinions of Caesar came from enemies who wanted to discredit him. But Petrarch claimed that he had in his own hands letters of Caesar and others that painted a decidedly different picture, namely of a Caesar who wanted peace.[19]

In this two-page-long digression from the historical narrative, Petrarch goes further to point out the inconsistencies in Cicero's own accounts of Pompey's motives, and he pointedly asks the reader, "And you, reader, what do you think? To what extent do you believe that the cause of Pompey was more just than that of Caesar?"[20] Certainly, Petrarch does not think that, and he concludes his inquiry with the judgment that the motives of Caesar and Pompey were not so different and that both aspired to power. The text thus placed equal responsibility for the war on Pompey and subsequently lifted the disproportionate blame that Cicero and other ancient authors had given to Caesar, in Petrarch's view.

Petrarch's ode to Caesar, like his admonition to the Holy Roman Emperor, Charles IV, to imitate Caesar Augustus and other Roman emperors, was an

---

[17] Ibid., p. 540.
[18] Ibid., p. 545. "La gloria non si scompagna mai dall'invidia."
[19] Ibid., p. 547. "Ho qui riferito intorno a una sola questione opinioni diverse, tutte per`o d'uomini che avevano un solo intento: screditare Cesare. Ame inve`ce, che sono molto interessato a questi problemi, sono venute in mano alcune lettere dello stesso Cesare e conosco altresi' certi suoi detti e moltissime sue risposte nelle qauli si mostra sempre desiseroso di pace."
[20] Ibid., p. 548. "E tu, lettore, che ne pensi? Di quanto credi che la causa di Pompeo fosse piu' giusta di quella di Cesare?"

act of early Renaissance political counsel and historical revision that explicitly urged a break with the medieval past. The true ancestors of Charles IV were the Christian Carolingian emperors starting with Charlemagne in the ninth century, a fact Petrarch certainly knew. But his obvious desire was to see the revival of *pagan* imperial political models and ancient Roman imperial power like that held by Julius Caesar.

As the first advocate for an expansive intellectual and cultural *renovatio* of antiquity that was also tied to the *imitatio*, or political imitation of Caesar and his empire, Petrarch was the principal early practitioner of an expansive form of imperial humanism.[21] This was a radical conception of history for the fourteenth century, and the biography of Caesar, in particular, distinguished Petrarch from his most important medieval predecessors in this regard.[22]

First among these was Dante, the most famous medieval advocate of the Ghibelline idea that the Holy Roman Empire was the heir to the ancient Roman Empire in an unbroken succession. In the *Divine Comedy*, the author of the founding imperial myth of Rome, Virgil, famously served as Dante's guide through hell. There, on the very fringes of hell, among the heroes of antiquity damned not for any ill deeds but only because they were born before the time of Christ, was Caesar with his hawklike eyes. Admired but still damned, Dante's Caesar represented the medieval view of the best pagan Caesars. Lacking Christian faith, their usefulness as role models was limited.

But the empire they ruled over was another matter for Dante. Rome was the power destined to be the political vehicle for the spread of Christianity. In book six of the *Paradiso*, most especially, he acknowledged the role of Julius Caesar in imposing the imperial eagle on much of the known world as part of the divine plan. But it was the sixth-century Christian Byzantine emperor, Justinian, who had pride of place in Dante's vision. As the virtual role model for emperors, Justinian was found in paradise speaking about his own

[21] Angelo Mazzocco, "Petrarch: Founder of Renaissance Humanism?" in *Interpretations of Renaissance Humanism*, ed. Angelo Mazzocco (Boston: Brill Academic Publishers, 2006), pp. 215–242. Mazzocco argues that many of the fourteenth- and fifteenth-century successors to Petrarch, especially Flavio Biondo, saw him as the founder of the humanist movement not only because he revived the studia humanitatis, but because he also urged the broad imitation of ancient Roman cultural and political accomplishments including the deeds of the emperors. See especially pp. 231–233.

[22] For a more lengthy treatment of Petrarch's view of the medieval period, see Theodore E. Mommsen, "Petrarch's Conception of the 'Dark Ages'" in *Medieval and Renaissance Studies*, ed. E. F. Rice, Jr. (Ithaca, NY: Cornell University Press, 1959), 106–129. While he placed hope in Charles IV for the revival of ancient Roman glory, Petrarch was under no illusion that the Holy Roman Emperors or Empire represented an unbroken line of descent from the ancient Roman Empire.

Christianity, and it was clearly the emperor's central vocation as the guardian of a Christianized Roman empire that Dante wanted to highlight.[23]

This caesaro-papist view served Dante's political agenda of supporting imperial power over that of the pope, a position most clearly articulated in his treatise "On Monarchy." As a piece of imperialist polemic, this treatise, like that of Marsilio of Padua of the same title, certainly provided important ideological parallels to Petrarch's imperial politics a century later. In that text, Dante elaborated on the theme that ancient Rome's rise was part of God's plan, a point best illustrated by the birth of Jesus during the first decades of the empire.[24]

But Dante did not call for a rebirth of the ancient Roman Empire, because his own historical perspective presumed that it had never ended. Nor did he advocate the imitation of the ancient pagan Caesars with any great specificity or detail. His literary production stopped far short of producing expansive historical texts like Petrarch's life of Caesar as tools for the promotion of that cultural and political project. Rather, Dante's political concerns and agenda were more local and limited, as was his choice of political models from antiquity. In short, he used the ancient example of Rome to advocate for the supremacy of the Holy Roman Empire and emperor over the pope in his own day, but not for the revival of the ancient Roman Empire. Justinian served this cause well, but Julius Caesar much less so, if at all.

This was obviously not the case with Petrarch and many later followers who held up the ancient Caesars as the political examples most worthy of imitation in their own day. This was illustrated in Petrarch's admonition to Charles IV that opened this chapter, but it was also reflected in other writings in which the poet's highest flattery of contemporary political figures came in the form of comparing them to the ancient Caesars.

The Roman nobleman Stephano Colonna, for example, in whose house Petrarch stayed during his 1343 soujourn in Rome, was described in the following way: "Good God! What a majestic personality.... I thought I was looking at Julius Caesar."[25] Although this may seem like rhetorical bluster,

[23] Frances A. Yates, *Astraea* (London: Routledge and Kegan Paul, 1975), pp. 14–16. Yates points out that the need Petrarch felt for the "re-Romanizing of the Empire" was the result of his new view of medieval history that took a dark view of the Holy Roman Empire, the major contrast between him and Dante.

[24] Ibid., pp. 2–11. Yates provides a good synthesis of various medieval views of the Roman Empire in the introduction to her work that includes a succinct rendering of the Ghibelline position on the continuity between the ancient and medieval empires most famously championed by Dante in his treatise "On Monarchy."

[25] From a letter written to one of Petrarch's most important patrons, Cardinal Giovanni Colonna, the son of Stephano. The more complete passage reads: "Tuttavia prima di riposarmi potei

Petrarch's classical flattery both nurtured and reflected the Italian nobility's desire to tie itself to the ancient Roman past. By the seventeenth century, the descendants of Stephano Colonna were having family histories written by their own court humanists that included genealogies relating the Colonna directly to Julius Caesar.[26]

This preference for the ancient Romans was not surprising given Petrarch's own intellectual agenda. The student of Caesar and Suetonius knew well that the best of the Roman emperors had been learned philosophers, historians, and great patrons of letters and the arts. No medieval pretenders to the title could claim the intellectual talents or the political skills and power of the ancients. Neither Charlemagne nor Frederick II, perhaps the most illustrious of the medieval western emperors, could really compare with Julius Caesar, Caesar Augustus, or Marcus Aurelius for Petrarch and many of his humanist successors. Moreover, the fact that the ancient Caesars were not Christian does not exclude them or limit their usefulness as central political models. As Petrarch's treatment of Caesar vividly demonstrates, religious identity is largely put to the side, and there is a decidedly more secular approach to his life that emphasizes his military, political, and literary accomplishments.

A new moment that elevated the examples and culture of the pagan empire was clearly at hand by the early fifteenth century, but it did not first take root in the court of the Holy Roman Emperor. Rather, the revival of ancient imperial texts and models as inspiration for new forms of political and material culture first found its richest soil near Petrarch's birthplace in the courts of northern Italy and in Rome.

The Imperial Renaissance in the Northern Italian Courts

Certainly, I often take great pleasure in looking at the heads of the Caesars on bronze coins – bronze having survived more commonly than gold or silver – and they impress me no less than the descriptions of their appearance in Suetonius and others. For the latter are apprehended by the mind alone.

Leonello d'Este, quoted in Angelo Decembrio's *De Politia Litteraria*[27]

---

vedere il tuo magnanimo Genitore.(Stefano). Dio buono! Quale maest`a della persona, qual voce, qual fronte, quale aspetto, quale portamento, quale vigore di animo in quella età, quale forza del corpo? Mi sembrò di vedere Giulio Cesare, o Scipione Africano." Quoted in A. Coppi, *Memorie Colonessi* (Rome: Salviucci, 1855), p. 125. From Petrarch's *Rer. Famil. Lib. V, epist. LXX.*

[26] Filadelfo Mugnos, *Historia della Augustissima Famiglia Colonna* (Venice: Turrini, 1658).

[27] Michael Baxandall, "A Dialogue on Art from the Court of Leonello d'Este: Angelo Decembrio's De Politia Litteraria Pars LXVIII," *Journal of the Warburg and Courtauld Institutes*, Vol. 26, No. 3/4, 1963, p. 324. (pp. 304–326).

As Petrarch's biography so vividly demonstrates, Caesar's reputation was rising in the early Renaissance, and this included his fame as a historian. A growing number of new editions and/or copies of Caesar's *Commentaries* served as the most tangible sign of this increased fascination with the founder of the Empire, owing in no small part to Petrarch himself. At least 10 new manuscript copies of the *Commentaries* appeared in the fourteenth century and more than 150 new manuscript copies appeared in the fifteenth century.[28] Among these was that of Guarino Guarini (da Verona), for instance, who dedicated an important new edition of the *Commentaries* to his pupil, Leonello d'Este (1407–1450), marquis of Ferrara, in 1433.[29]

Leonello d'Este as a New Caesar

One of the first Renaissance princes to have both an excellent humanist teacher and the natural abilities to benefit from him, Leonello was also among the earliest of European rulers to bring together the ideas and arts of the Imperial Renaissance in his court. Ferrara subsequently became a central location and laboratory in which humanist learning advanced side by side with the revival of artistic production.[30] The result was a court in which the material culture gave form to the ideas of the imperial revival found in the texts.[31]

Guarino, who had established a school in Ferrara under the patronage of Leonello's father, Niccolò, was a major protagonist of this development, together with other prominent humanists including Giovanni Lamola,

---

[28] Virginia Brown, "The Textual Transmission of Caesar's Civil War," *Mnemosyne*, Special Supplement Volume (Leiden: Brill, 1972). This study identified 160 manuscript versions of the *Commentaries* produced in the fourteenth and fifteenth centuries and also assumes that there are additional copies in private collections. These later copies were derived from eight earlier surviving Latin editions from the tenth, eleventh, and twelfth centuries now found in Rome, Naples, Paris, Florence, London, and Austria. See especially pp. 42–65. The author also points out that the *Commentaries on the Civil Wars* and the *Commentaries on the Gallic Wars* were virtually always presented together in these manuscript editions. Brown asserts that "the *Commentaries* first came into real prominence in the Trecento with the attention given to Caesar by such figures as Petrarch and Coluccio Salutati." P. 49.

[29] *Epistolario di Guarino Veronese*, ed. Remegio Sabbadini (Venice: C. Ferrari, 1919), vol. 3, p. 307. Guarino was followed by dozens of other authors who saw the usefulness of the text as a political instruction manual for Renaissance princes.

[30] *Gli este a Ferrara: Un corte nel Rinascimento*, ed. Jadranka Bentini (Milan: Silvano Editore, 2004). This collection of 23 essays by leading historians and art historians provides a good sampling of recent scholarship, especially on the arts in Renaissance Ferrara.

[31] For a useful collection of studies on classical learning and humanist culture in Ferrara, see *L'ideale classico a Ferrara e in Italia nel Rinascimento*, ed. Patrizia Castelli (Florence: Leo S. Olschke, 1998).

Giovanni Marasio, Angelo Decembrio, and Leon Battista Alberti. The founding of the university by Leonello in 1442 under Guarino's supervision elevated and institutionalized humanist learning while also making it clear that Guarino was the leader of that movement in Ferrara.[32]

It was also Guarino who advanced Caesar as the primary political role model for Leonello. In a number of letters to the prince, Gaurino praised Caesar's many virtues and triumphs while also drawing parallels between the magnificence of the d'Este princes and that of Julius and Augustus Caesar.[33] The lessons were embraced by Leonello, who made good use of the edition of the *Commentaries* that Guarino dedicated to him. He was reputed to prefer Caesar to all other ancient authors.[34]

Guarino's praise of Caesar, and Leonello's admiration of him, was far from being merely academic. Rather, it struck at the heart of one of the major humanist political debates of the time: the debate between the champions of the Republican Renaissance and the Imperial Renaissance. Guarino was himself at the center of the debate when he engaged with Poggio Bracciolini in an exchange of letters that specifically compared the respective virtues and faults of Scipione Africanus and Julius Caesar.[35]

Poggio had provoked the argument in 1435 when he wrote a letter to the Ferrara humanist Scipione Mainenti that compared the two Romans. In his analysis, Scipione was worthy of praise for retiring after his many military victories, a selfless act that preserved the Republic. Caesar, however, succumbed to the temptations of power, murdering his opponents and imposing a tyranny on Rome. The contrast between the two men was clear. Scipione was celebrated for "justice, temperance, dignity, moderation, continence, integrity," but Caesar was condemned for "plundering, deceit, internal opposition, civil struggle, immoderate lust for power" and numerous other personal faults.[36]

Guarino's response to Poggio was a thirty-three-page treatise that praised both Scipione and Caesar while making it quite clear that Caesar was the more successful and important of the two because of the combination of his military greatness, political virtues, and literary production.[37] In this sense,

---

[32] Rinaldi, pp. 31–35. Rinaldi provides a concise summary of the humanist circle in Renaissance Ferrara.

[33] Maria Grazia Pernis, "Fifteenth-Century Patrons and the Scipio-Caesar Controversy," *Text*, Vol. 6, 1994, p. 185. (pp. 181–195).

[34] See especially Remegio Sabbadini, *La Scuola di Guarino Guarini Veronese* (Catania: Francesco Galati, 1896), p. 146.

[35] Ibid., p. 146.

[36] Pernis, p. 182.

[37] *Epistolario di Guarino Veronese*, ed. Remegio Sabbadini (Venice: C. Ferrari, 1919), pp. 221–254, vol. 2, lett. 670, pp. 221–254. This is among Guarino's longest letters, which underlines

Guarino echoed Petrarch's view as he provided a condensed version of the comparison and contrast provided by the two Petrarchan biographies of Caesar and Scipione. Guarino had also written a letter to Leonello prior to responding to Poggio, in which he cited both contemporary and ancient authors who had judged Caesar favorably.[38]

These included the humanist friend of Petrarch, Coluccio Salutati, chancellor of Florence from 1375 to 1406, who had largely absolved Caesar of the charges of tyranny in much the same way Petrarch had. In his *Treatise on Tyranny* (1400), Salutati cited Seneca's account of all of the honors and titles heaped on Caesar by the Senate and people after his assassination and concludes that "Caesar was not a tyrant, having a good right to govern and not one that was illegally held."[39]

In earlier scholarship on the debate between Guarino and Poggio, the central political issue has been presented as a contest between liberty and tyranny. Poggio's perspective, in a view promoted by Hans Baron, was a central plank in the political platform of the civic humanists that won the day in fifteenth-century Florence. By implication and neglect, Guarino's position, a central plank of imperial humanism, has been largely left out of this picture, even though it clearly won the day in fifteenth-century Ferrara, Mantua, Milan, Rome, sixteenth-century Florence, and beyond.[40]

The debate between Gaurino and Poggio was, on one level, a scholarly argument between two humanist friends who disagreed on the interpretations and historical contrast between the two men, Caesar and Scipione. But on a larger scale, this debate was also about the competing political models of Roman Republic and Roman Empire. Guarino's student and patron,

---

the importance of the topic for him. This was part of a debate that stretched out over five years and also included lengthy letters against Poggio defending Caesar from Ciriaco d'Ancona and Pietro Del Monte. For the details, see Sabbadini, vol. 3, p. 325. It is also worth noting Sabbadini's opinion that both Leonello and Guarino saw in Caesar "everything beautiful, everything good, everything great." Vol. 3, p. 323: "tutto bello, tutto buono, tutto grande."

[38] Sabbadini, *La scuola*, p. 146.

[39] Coluccio Salutati, "De Tyranno," trans. and ed., Francesco Ercole (Bologna: Nicola Zanichelli, 1942), p. 174. "Per cui concludo con questo capitolo che Cesare non fu un tiranno, avendo a buon diritto e non illegalmente tenuto ed esercitato il governo."

[40] That Renaissance humanism included alternatives to Baron's civic humanism has long been recognized. Paul Oskar Kristeller, for example, noted that "the civic humanism of Florence was opposed by the despotic humanism of Milan, Ferrara, and other centers." While accurate insofar as it describes humanist production under the patronage of princes depicted by critics as despots, despotic humanism falls short of describing the expansive political program of imperial revival that was the larger agenda of imperial humanism. Paul Oskar Kristeller, "Studies in Renaissance Humanism in the Last Twenty Years," in *Studies in the Renaissance* Vol. 9, 1962, pp. 7–30. Quotation, p. 14.

Leonello, would obviously not have described himself or his ancestors as tyrants or despots. Nor would he have acknowledged following the example of a tyrant. Rather, he modeled himself after the ruler of the ancient world's greatest empire. It was Caesar as wise ruler, author, and compassionate leader of the Roman Empire that inspired imitation and admiration.[41]

For Guarino, Leonello, "the humanist prince, was none other than a new Caesar," and in various texts including his edition of Caesar and a letter written on the occasion of Leonello's wedding in 1435, this Caesar of Ferrara is praised for all of the virtues associated with Julius Caesar, most especially his clemency and love of peace.[42]

Other humanist clients of Leonello also dedicated treatises to the prince that carried strong imperial echoes. Alberti, for example, revealed himself to be a humanist who knew how to advocate for the politics of the *rule of one*, as political writers frequently described monarchical or imperial rule. In his work *Theogenius* (1441), dedicated to the d'Este family, he made it clear that republics were marked by disorder and corruption, but principalities brought peace. Similarly, in his parody, *Momus sive de principe*, produced a few years later when he was still living in Ferrara, he produced a humorous story of the struggles among the ancient pagan gods, with Jupiter playing the main role as king of heaven. Faced with the challenge of ruling over proud and often difficult deities, the clear message of the text was that the good monarch embraced the virtues of action, zeal, diligence, and constancy while avoiding ambition, envy, and laziness. The goal of this prince was glory and popularity.[43]

This "political" work of Alberti was far from that of contemporary or later political treatises in form and content as it safely stayed away from any specific historical or contemporary references or advice. In this sense it was not overtly imperial in its references to the ancient Roman Empire. But combined with other counsel, it provided a supporting ideological reference point that bolstered the growing political aspirations and image of

---

[41] For the most famous treatment of the debate over Caesar, see Hans Baron, *The Crisis of the Early Italian Renaissance* (Princeton, NJ: Princeton University Press, 1966), pp. 123–128. For later elaboration on the theme of Republican liberty that emerged in this debate, see Ronald Witt, "The Rebirth of the Concept of Republican Liberty in Italy," in *Renaissance Studies in Honor of Hans Baron*, ed. Anthony Mohlo and John Tedeschi (Florence: G. C. Sansoni, 1971) pp. 175–199.

[42] Marianne Pade, "Guarino and Caesar at the Court of the Este," in *The Court of Ferrara and its Patronage, 1441–1598*, ed. Marianne Pade, Lene Waage Peteersen, and Daniela Quarta (Ferrara: Edizione Panini, 1990), p. 87.

[43] Leon Battista Alberti, *Momo o Del Principe*, trans. and ed. Giuseppe Martini (Bologna: Nicola Zanichelli, 1942), pp.296–297.

the prince in the mold of Caesar. More specifically, Alberti also provided humanist advice for Leonello in his role as patron of the arts.

In an age when political power and reputation increasingly went hand in hand with artistic power and reputation, the d'Este faced stiff competition from wealthier cities that had expansionist agendas animated by their own literary, political, and artistic Renaissance. In the case of Florence, pretender to the title of the new Roman Republic thanks to the works of the humanist chancellor Leonardo Bruni, the city's political rhetoric and pretensions were backed up by new monumental architecture such as the great Duomo of Brunelleschi, the sculpture of Donatello, and the painting of Masaccio, just to name the most famous early-fifteenth-century Florentine masters. Venice, too, harnessed the artistic power of Veneto masters like Bellini, Carpaccio, Titian, Tintoretto, and Veronese to paint the narrative history and myth of their own Republican Empire over the course of the fifteenth and sixteenth centuries.

The d'Este, like the Gonzaga of Mantua, responded to the challenge not by claiming any Republican heritage but by claiming ties to empire both past and present and by creating a distinctive imperial iconography and aesthetic in many media, including sculpture, painting, and medals. They also recruited Florentine and Venetian artists to serve this cause, underlining the fact that the production of great art and architecture was not inspired by Republican polities alone, a view promoted by at least some fifteenth-century humanists like Poggio Bracciolini.

Moreover, because the surviving examples of ancient imperial art and architecture scattered around Italy and Europe were more plentiful and expansive than that of the Republic, the patrons and artists of the imperial Renaissance courts had a broader range of models and forms to draw from. In the realm of statuary, for example, there were the four main ancient types: the figure in a toga; the statue in military uniform, the nude heroic figure, and the equestrian statue.[44] Among these, the statue of a ruler in his military uniform and the equestrian statue were most frequently imitated in the courts of the Imperial Renaissance.

In this realm, the d'Este took the lead: in a dramatic early example of the dynasty striking an imperial pose, in 1441 Leonello commissioned the casting of a great bronze equestrian statue of his father, Niccolò III (1393–1441). A copy still graces the original position of the monument in the central public square between the d'Este castle and the cathedral in Ferrara (Figure 1.1).

[44] Donald Strong, *Roman Art* (Harmondsworth: Penguin Books, 1982), p. 84.

1.1. Antonio di Cristofaro and Niccolò Baroncelli, Replica of Bronze Equestrian Statue of Niccolò III, 1451. (Photograph by author.)

Among the first of their kind to be cast in Western Europe since the fall of the Roman Empire, the bronze horse and rider announced the true arrival of Ferrara as a competitor in the realm of Renaissance art patronage. Alberti acted as the judge of the competition for the works and composed a special commemorative treatise in 1444 to further celebrate the event. Titled *De equo animante*, the treatise subtly evoked comparisons between the d'Este and the ancient Caesars by referring to the ancient imperial precedent of the great funeral monuments of Augustus and Julius Caesar, both of which included sculptures of their horses.[45] His treatise, a literary companion and parallel to the sculpture, underlined the close relationship between imperial humanism and artistic production.

The commissions were awarded to Antonio di Cristoforo, who executed the figure of Niccolò d'Este, and Niccolò Baroncelli, who executed the fine bronze horse. Both were Florentines who had worked with Brunelleschi, and they were among the first artists in Ferrara who had the knowledge to cast

[45] Leon Battista Alberti, *De Equo Animante*, trans. and ed. Antonio Videtta (Napoli: Ce.S.M.E.T., 1991), pp. 90–91.

large bronze statues.[46] When the pair of sculptures was completed in 1451 under Borso d'Este (1450–1471), they bore a strong resemblance to a similar monument of the emperor Justinian (or Theodosius) in Constantinople. At the same time, they evoked a strong parallel with the famous ancient statue of the emperor Marcus Aurelius that stood in the piazza of St. John Lateran in Rome. This was the more obvious model given the proximity of Rome and likelihood that one of the artists had seen the statue, and it highlighted the imperial associations clearly cultivated by Leonello and the humanists in his court.[47]

This was also true of the more well-known equestrian monument by Donatello that honored the Venetian condotierre, Gattamelata, or Erasmo da Nardi in roughly the same period. Occupying a prominent place in the piazza in front of the Basilica of Sant'Antonio in Padua, where Gattamelata requested to be buried, the bronze monument was yet another magnificent equestrian statue that evoked ancient Roman glory. Often described as the first monumental bronze equestrian statue cast since antiquity, it carried heavy political meaning of its own because it was placed in a city conquered and ruled by the Venetian Republic.

In the case of the Ferrara statue that honored Leonello's father, Niccolò, the political and cultural implications of the work point more to the present and future rather than celebrating past imperial conquests. More specifically, the monument, placed on a column modeled after a triumphal Roman arch, was itself a public triumph. More modest, perhaps, than that of Marcus Aurelius, it nonetheless celebrated both the high cultural and political accomplishments of the d'Este under Niccolò and especially Leonello, the most intellectually capable and culturally refined of the d'Este princes up to his time.

Leonello's imitation of the arts of antiquity also extended to the realm of fine bronze medals cast by Pisanello in Ferrara in the 1430s and 1440s. Marked by both the technical precision of their casting and the artistic beauty of their relief portraits, these medals successfully imitated ancient Roman coins and medals in a way that was unequalled in preceding centuries. Leonello may not have been the Holy Roman emperor in either political power or aspirations, but he was following the advice of Petrarch quoted at the beginning of this chapter when he imitated the ancient emperors in their artistic and cultural tastes and habits. Among the subject matter of his

---

[46] Marcello Toffanello, *Le arti a Ferrara nel QuattroCento, gli artisit e la corte* (Ferrara: Edisai, 2010), p. 92 and pp. 391–419. See also C. M. Rosenberg, *The Este Monuments and Urban Development in Renaissance Ferrara* (Cambridge: Cambridge University Press, 1997), pp. 54–61.

[47] Ibid.

medals, moreover, may have been a relief portrait of Caesar. Leonello had already paid Pisanello for a portrait of Caesar in 1435, yet another sign of his fondness for the subject.[48]

Leonello's successors continued the imperial iconographic tradition over the course of the following century. Ercole I (1431–1505), for example, renovated the family castle by adding a three-level balcony to the family residence, also known as the Palazzo del Corte, which he adorned with medallions of the twelve Roman emperors of Suetonius. The tradition of placing images of the Roman emperors, frequently busts of the twelve emperors of Suetonius, on the facades of Renaissance palaces or in the interior was a tradition that appeared very early in Ferrara. It would be imitated in many other locations in the sixteenth century that will be noted in the pages that follow.[49] More generally, the practice points to the fact that sculptures of the ancient Roman emperors, as well as paintings, were becoming a common element of Renaissance iconography in the smaller courts that sought to accentuate their connections to empire.

Ercole I also began a process of the urbanization of Ferrara that broke with the medieval past as it carved out larger public space and wider streets that were more amenable to public spectacles and political pageantry that also increasingly took their inspiration from ancient Roman examples. The dramatic urban plan begun by Ercole I and realized especially in the northern half of the city over the next century led Jacob Burckhardt to describe Ferrara as the first modern city.[50]

One last concrete sign of this that was planned but never finished was a monument to Ercole I composed of two triumphal columns that supported an equestrian monument of the prince. The monument was unfinished at the time of the papal annexation of Ferrara under Pope Clement VIII (1596) with only a column completed. This column would later support the statue of one last ruler of Ferrara who claimed the title of Caesar, namely Napoleon.[51]

---

[48] See Toffanello, *Le arti a Ferrara*, p. 219, for information on Pisanello's portrait of Caesar. See pp. 21–28 for a sketch of the artist's work in Ferrara.

[49] For a detailed analysis of the architectural and urban patronage of Ferrara in the age of Ercole I, see especially Thomas Tuohy, *Herculean Ferrara* (Cambridge: Cambridge University Press, 1996). On the medallions of the twelve Caesars that decorated the balcony, see pp. 193–194.

[50] Jacob Burckhardt, *The Civilization of the Renaissance in Italy*, trans. S. G. C. Middlemore (London: Penguin Books, 2004), p. 48. The author famously wrote: "Ferrara is the first really modern city in Europe."

[51] For the proposed designs of the monument to Ercole I, see M. Toffanello, *Le Arte a Ferrara*, p. 466, and especially the more detailed treatment by C. M. Rosenberg, *The Este Monuments and Urban Development in Renaissance Ferrara*, pp. 153–181.

Equestrian monuments on triumphal arches, columns, medals, and relief sculptures of the ancient emperors created by artists who successfully revived and imitated the arts of the ancient Roman Empire effectively connected the d'Este to the iconography of the Roman imperial tradition. But the family also had concrete political aspirations and dynastic strategies to accompany their artistic and humanistic program. The imperial images were a clear declaration of political sympathies and alliances, and as the family's fortunes and reputation rose in the fifteenth century, they married up into the house of the kings of Aragon, the Borgias in the age of Pope Alexander VI Borgia, and King Louis XII of France.

The d'Este alliance with France in the sixteenth century did nothing to diminish their attraction to the imperial theme. On the contrary, it provides an important example of how Italian members of the French faction, imitating French Renaissance humanists, saw the kings of France as having their own claim to the imperial heritage, as we will see in Chapter 4. There was subsequently no contradiction in the imperial imagery with which they surrounded themselves.[52]

The rise of the d'Este court in the fifteenth century took place in the context of the almost perpetual contest for political, military, and cultural pre-eminence that consumed the Po Valley courts of Northern Italy. The leading men of the families owed their substantial estates and position to their military skills, first and foremost. As effective *condottiere*, or military captains, they and their armies frequently served as well-paid mercenaries for the Holy Roman Emperors. It is thus no surprise that they admired the Caesars and increasingly sought to imitate them not just as warriors but in the way they lived.[53]

Wealth was not the only prize they sought. Dynastic advancement was the other major goal. In this realm, they were particularly dependent on one of the primary overlords of Northern Italy, the Holy Roman Emperor, who had the right to grant titles to rulers of imperial cities over which

---

[52] Besides the court in Ferrara, imperial aesthetics also dominated the d'Este court in Modena, especially in the later sixteenth and seventeenth centuries. After the city of Ferrara had been claimed by the papacy in 1596, the d'Este dukes continued the imperial theme in their new court. The façade of the ducal palace was decorated with life-size statues of the d'Este duke in imperial dress and a statue of Hercules. The interior, in the meantime, was decorated with busts of the emperors, including Julius Caesar and a young Marcus Aurelius, that are preserved in the Modena museum that houses the palace collection today.

[53] *Alla corte degli Estensi*, ed. Marco Bertozzi (Ferrara: Università degil Stidi, 1992) provides a good sample of contemporary scholarship that seeks to analyze the relationship between the intellectual and cultural life of the court.

they claimed lordship. These included the cities of Ferrara, Milan, Mantua, Modena, and Reggio Emilia, among others.

In the course of the fifteenth and early sixteenth centuries, the Holy Roman Emperors Frederick III, Maximilian I, and Charles V, respectively, granted the titles of Duke of Modena and Reggio to Leonello's son, Borso d'Este, in 1452; Duke of Milan to Gian Galeazzo Sforza in 1493; and Duke of Mantua to Federico II Gonzaga in 1530. This bond to the emperors further explains the rise of a distinctly imperial aesthetics in these courts and above all others in that of the Gonzaga.[54]

The Gonzaga and Imperial Palace Culture

Although Ferrara arguably took the lead as the center of the ideas and arts of the Imperial Renaissance in the age of Leonello and Guarino, Mantua increasingly became the northern Italian center of this revival in the latter half of the fifteenth century. The dynasty rose to prominence under the condottiere and first marquis, Gianfrancesco Gonzaga (1395–1444), who received that title from the Holy Roman Emperor Sigismondo IV in 1433 for faithful military service. His son, Ludovico II (1412–1478), was married to the emperor's granddaughter Barbara of Brandenburg to strengthen the political bonds with those of blood. It was an effective strategy, and the Gonzaga remained among the strongest Italian allies of the Holy Roman Emperors and the Spanish monarchy through the sixteenth century.[55]

Tutored by the humanist friend of Guarino, Vittorino Rambaldoni (da Feltre), Ludovico and his siblings were the beneficiaries of an education comparable to that of Leonello d'Este with classical Greek and Latin texts forming the core of their curriculum. After his father's death in 1445, Ludovico II took his place as head of the family, continuing the martial tradition of his father. But he also increased his role as a cultivated patron of the arts in much the same way as Leonello d'Este. The two princes and their courts were much like Northern Italian twins, often commissioning works from the same artists including Pisanello, Mantegna, and Alberti.[56]

[54] For an insightful and comparative treatment of the courts at Milan, Ferrara, and Mantua, see especially Rinaldo Rinaldi, "Princes and Culture in the Fifteenth-Century Italian Po Valley Courts," in *Princes and Princely Culture 1450–1650*, ed. Martin Grosman, Alasdair MacDonald, and Arjo Vanderjagt (Leiden: Brill, 2005), vol. 2, pp. 23–42.

[55] For a comprehensive genealogy of the Gonzaga, see Giancarlo Malacarne, *I Gonzaga di Mantova* (Modena: Il Bulino, 2010), six volumes. Vol. 6, *Gonzaga Genealogie di una dinastia*.

[56] For a concise account of Mantuan political history in this period, see M. J. Rodríguez-Salgado, "Terracotta and Iron: Mantua Politics" (ca. 1450–ca. 1550), in *La Corte di Mantova nell'età di Andrea Mantegna*, ed. Cesare Mozzarelli, Robert Oresko, and Leandro Ventura

The reign of Ludovico II, however, had the distinct advantage of lasting much longer than that of Leonello d'Este, spanning more than three decades versus only nine years for the unfortunately short-lived prince of Ferrara. Mantua subsequently witnessed the rise of both its political stature in Italy and a deepening of its role as a center of the Imperial Renaissance on the critical and interwoven levels of politics and art.

Serving as both a sign of Mantua's rise and a catalyst for this development was the decision of the humanist pope, Pius II, to call a council of the church in 1459 in the city to address the crisis caused by the fall of Constantinople in 1453 and the very real military threat that the Ottomans posed to Italy and Europe more generally. If it was the internal strife of Italy that caused Petrarch to yearn for the revival of ancient Roman power and to offer his biography of Caesar as a source of inspiration for the emperors of his own day, the Ottoman threat was an even greater spur that led the popes after 1450 to revive the memories of ancient Roman grandeur and the hope for a new Caesar to lead Europe. The papal decision to hold the council in Mantua was a clear sign of the military strength of Ludovico II, and the pope counted him among those who could lead the fight.

Pius II was himself fond of Caesar's *Commentaries*, and his court was the location of important new historical reflections on the glory of the Roman Empire that went hand in hand with his concrete political agenda. More specifically, Flavio Biondo, papal secretary in the Roman Curia and leading court humanist, was busy at work on a series of scholarly works aimed at restoring the historical memory of ancient Rome. Indeed, in 1459, the same year the council was held, he had just finished his *Roma trionfante*, a celebratory description of the ancient Roman triumphs. He presented the text, no less, to the pope in Mantua. A more detailed analysis of this text will soon follow in the section on Rome. But it is important to note it here in the context of the Gonzaga court because it almost certainly served as the initial textual inspiration for one of the most important series of Renaissance paintings celebrating the imperial theme created in the entire period, namely Andrea Mantegna's *The Triumphs of Caesar*.[57]

(Rome: Bulzoni, 1997), pp. 15–59. Also see Giancarlo Malacarne, *I Gonzaga di Mantova* (Modena: Il Bulino, 2010), vol. 2, *Il sogno del potere da Gianfrancesco a Francesco II (1432–1519);* and vol. 3, *I Gonzaga Duchi da Federico II a Guglielmo (1519–1587).*

57 Maria Agata Pincelli, "La *Roma triumphans* e la nascita dell'antiquaria: Biondo Flavio e Andrea Mantegna," in *Mantegna e Roma*, ed. Teresa Calvano, Claudia Cieri Via, and Leandro Ventura (Rome: Bulzoni, 2010), pp. 79–98. She notes that Ludovico requested a copy of the text from Biondo already in a letter from 1460 and that the first printed edition of Biondo's work was done in Mantua, another sign of the popularity of the text for the Gonzaga. Pp. 79, 88.

Recent scholarship has made a convincing argument that conversations in Mantua in 1459 among Mantegna, Flavio Biondo, and the Gonzaga prince led to the commissioning of the series of nine large paintings by Ludovico II soon thereafter. It is generally agreed that the series was not completed until the early 1490s, but the origins of the project most likely date to the 1460s, and it is possible that the first two pieces of the series painted, canvases 8 and 9 that include the portrait of Caesar in the triumphal carriage, were painted much earlier than the rest (Figure 1.2).[58]

The portrait of Caesar, in particular, serves as an illustrated version of the biographical portrait created by Petrarch insofar as it presents him in a flattering light as the clement prince with the outstretched and open hand. Mantegna almost certainly knew of and drew from Petrarch's text because it had been translated into Italian by Donato degli Albanzani and brought to press in Mantua in 1476 with the help of Mantegna's friend, the humanist Felice Feliciano.[59]

Mantegna's masterful series of paintings were the first in the Renaissance to so overtly celebrate Julius Caesar and the ancient Roman Empire. As a historical narrative cycle, they constituted a painted celebration of the new editions of Caesar's *Commentaries* like that of Guarino, as well as both classical literary portraits of Caesar, such as the one created by Suetonius, and new versions like Petrarch's. When finished, they became favorite possessions of the marquis Francesco II (governed 1484–1519), who hung them in his new palace of San Sebastiano.[60] From the time of their completion, they strongly influenced the historical perception of the ancient triumph.[61] Moreover, they became the most highly praised work of Mantegna that elevated both his historical reputation as well as that of the Gonzaga.[62]

[58] Paola Tosetti Grandi, *I Trionfi di Cesare di Andrea Mantegna* (Mantua: Sometti, 2008), p. 5. Her view that Biondo's text served as a major inspiration for Mantegna, bolstered by the research of Agata Pincelli, is also supported by Clifford Malcom Brown and Rodolfo Signorini in their introductory remarks to the volume.

[59] For details on the translation and more specific associations with Petrarch's biography of Caesar, see P. Tosetti Grandi, pp. 131–133.

[60] For a careful study of "The Triumphs of Caesar," see Andrew Martindale, *The Triumphs of Caesar by Andrea Mantegna* (London: Harvey Miller, 1979). For a lucid description of the relationship between early textual revivals of the ancient triumph, images of the triumph, and actual triumphal processions, see Starn and Partridge, *Arts of Power*, pp. 158–159.

[61] For an evocative description of Mantegna's work placed in the historical context of the ancient triumph, see Mary Beard, *The Roman Triumph* (Cambridge, MA: Harvard University Press, 2007), pp. 153–159. This study of the ancient triumph describes Mantegna's cycle as "probably the most influential visualization of the Roman victory parade ever." P. 154.

[62] The learned study of Mantegna by Paul Kristellar, *Andrea Mantegna* (London: Longman Green, and Co., 1901), went so far as to say that just as Augustus had gained luster from

1.2. Andrea Mantegna, The Triumphs of Caesar, after 1486. (Hampton Court, Royal Collection.)

Far from being mere palace decoration, Mantegna's *Triumphs of Caesar* were just one part of an expanding imperial decorative scheme in the various residences of the Gonzaga that served to underline the political connections between the dynasty and the hereditary Roman Empire founded by Julius Caesar. Described as "the fount and justification of Gonzaga authority in Mantua" by one contemporary scholar, the idea of sharing in a hereditary Roman imperial power was a central dimension of Gonzaga dynastic ideology.[63] It followed that their artistic and architectural tastes and commissions increasingly reflected and bolstered that self-perception.[64]

Vitruvius, so too did the house of Gonzaga attain "undying renown by the works of Mantegna." P. 278.

[63] A. S. Halliday, "The Literary Sources of Mantegna's Triumphs of Caesar," p. 193. His political interpretation follows that of R. Lightbown, *Mantegna*.

[64] For another elaboration on the relationship between art and power in the Gonzaga court that emphasizes the close relationship between family political ideology and the "precise

Mantegna, the most-favored artist of fifteenth-century Mantua who worked in the Gonzaga court from roughly 1460 until his death in 1505, was also responsible for another series of paintings that furthered this agenda and made more explicit the relationship between the Gonzaga family and the ancient emperors. It was in the renowned Camera degli Sposi that Mantegna painted frescoes of the first eight Roman emperors in lunettes that decorated the vault of the room. Just below the emperors were the walls frescoed with the famous scene of the Gonzaga family.[65]

Commissioned by Ludovico II in the early 1460s for his personal apartments, the paintings were located in the Castello di San Giorgio, a new wing of the Ducal Palace, the sprawling principal residence of the family located in the center of the city. Mantegna's fresco cycle, a masterpiece of early Renaissance wall painting and an "ideal celebration" of the Gonzaga family, was executed between 1465 and 1474.[66] It quickly drew praise as one of the most powerful examples of a collective Renaissance family portrait. From this vantage point, the images of the eight Roman emperors that adorn the ceiling seem out of place at first viewing. But placed in the context of the political myth of imperial succession advanced by the fifteenth-century Gonzaga lords, they make perfect sense. For the Roman emperors were the ancestors claimed by the dynasty and subsequently a natural part of the family portrait.[67]

Far from random ornamentation, these images of the Roman emperors, like the *Triumphs of the Caesar*, were strong iconographic statements

reference" to imperial Rome in the art collections and palace decoration, see Claudia Cieri Via, "Collezionismo e decorazione all Corte dei Gonzaga," in *La Corte di Mantova nell'età di Andrea Mantegna*, pp. 393–401. She writes: "Una continua corrispondenza fra scelta ideological e scelta culturale, funzionale alle ragioni di Stato, si produce in chiave auto-celebrativa con un preciso riferimento per lo più ai valori della Roma imperiale." P. 393.

[65] The restoration of the Camera degli Sposi in the early 1990s prompted insightful new scholarship, including the essays in *Mantegna's Camera degli Sposi*, ed. Michele Cordara (New York: Abbeville, 1993). See p. 57 for a vivid description of the portraits of the first eight Caesars that are noted as following the order of Suetonius's *Lives*. For a nuanced and sophisticated reading of the iconography of the room and how it functions, see especially Randolph Starn and Loren Partridge, *Arts of Power: Three Halls of State in Italy, 1300–1600* (Berkeley: University of California Press, 1992), chapter two. They note that the bust of Julius Caesar was directly above the portrait of Ludovico II. P. 131.

[66] Giovanni Rodella and Stefano L'Occaso, "'… questi logiamenti de castello siano forniti et adaptati …' Trasformazioni e interventi in Castello all'epoca del Mantegna," in *Andrea Mantegna e I Gonzaga*, ed. Filippo Trevisani (Verona: Mondadori Electa, 2006), pp.21–35. Quote from p. 23.

[67] Ronald Lightbown, *Mantegna* (Berkeley: University of California Press, 1986), p. 112. Commenting on the symbolism of the Caesars, the author claims that "The first eight Caesars are represented on the ceiling for a different reason: they appear as the founders of the Empire and so as the ultimate source of the Marchese's right to rule the Imperial fief of Mantua."

that reflected the political identity, sympathies, and connections that the Gonzaga family cultivated with both past and present Roman emperors. In the Camera degli Sposi, the emperors look down on the Gonzaga family almost like political patron saints who are giving their collective blessing to the gathering below.

Together with Mantegna's painted images of the emperors, the Gonzaga family also strengthened associations with the ancient Caesars through their activities as collectors of ancient sculpture and in the decoration of entire rooms and large halls in their palaces that were increasingly dominated by an imperial aesthetic. In the creation of this distinctive palace culture, leading women in the Gonzaga family also played a prominent role. More specifically, late in the fifteenth century the dynastic union of the Gonzaga and d'Este families brought one of the most refined collectors and art patrons of the entire period to Mantua, namely Isabella d'Este.

Francesco II Gonzaga (1466–1519), grandson of Ludovico II and head of the family from 1484 until 1519, was married to Isabella d'Este, princess of Ferrara, in 1490. Daughter of Alfonso d'Este, another famous patron and collector of Roman antiquities, she continued the tradition in Mantua, where she was joined and supported in these activities by her husband and her son, Federico. As a voracious collector of antiquities and modern art in the classical style, Isabella d'Este acquired one of the most notable art collections of the Renaissance.[68] The fame of her sculpture and medals, both ancient and contemporary, was widespread by the early sixteenth century. It attracted a regular stream of prominent visitors especially later in her life who sought an invitation to view the treasures and the famous apartments in which they were displayed.

On being widowed in 1519, Isabella had moved from her apartment in the Castello San Giorgio wing of the Ducal Palace near the Camera degli Sposi to two additional sets of rooms in the Corte Vecchia section of the palace, namely the Santa Croce apartment and the Grotta apartment, where her famous study or *studiolo* was built. She personally supervised the design and decoration of these apartments, where she demonstrated a fondness for imperial Roman iconography comparable to that of her ancestors and Gonzaga in-laws.[69]

---

[68] On the collection of Isabella d'Este, see especially Clifford M. Brown, *Per dare qualche splendore a la gloriosa città di Mantua: documents for the antiquarian collection of Isabella d'Este* (Rome: Bulzoni, 2002).

[69] Clifford M. Brown, "'Fruste et Strache nel Fabbricare,' Isabella d'Este's Apartments in the Corte Vecchia of the Ducal Palace in Mantua," in *La Corte di Mantova nell'età di Andrea Mantegna*, 1997, pp. 295–336.

In the Camera Imperiale of the Santa Croce apartment, for example, the large fireplace is topped with a Trajanic frieze modeled after an ancient fragment depicting Roman soldiers that is itself incorporated into the composition. The original sculpture may have come from Trajan's forum in Rome, where Isabella had spent considerable time.[70] Similarly, in the Grotta apartment, three antique marble heads, one of the emperor Augustus and the other two of Faustina and Lucilla, were displayed on top of the intarsia-decorated cabinets that presumably held part of her collection of gems, cameos, coins, and books.

The quality and fame of the bust of Augustus led an antiquities dealer and art agent of the later Duke Guglielmo (1538–1587) to advise his patron to collect similar heads of the other eleven emperors of Suetonius.[71] This was advice that the son and grandson of Isabella took to heart. By later in the century, there were more than thirty busts of Roman emperors displayed in the gallery of the ducal palace, including multiple copies of Julius Caesar, Marcus Aurelius, and Trajan.[72]

These acquisitions and others continued the precedent set by Ludovico II and further defined the Gonzaga court with an artistic and architectural aesthetic that harkened back to the Roman Empire. This development reached its apex with Federico II (1500–1540), whose court, although still a minor political power in Europe, became an ally of the first European ruler to actually have the power and empire that were equal to those of the ancient Caesars. Frequent military allies and servants of the Holy Roman Empire, the Gonzaga under Federico II became one of the most loyal Italian noble families in service to Charles V (1500–1557), the first modern emperor who could claim to equal the ancient Caesars in the size, wealth, and power of his empire. Life imitated art as Federico II followed the role imagined in the iconographic program cultivated by his ancestors over the preceding fifty years.

The imperial alliance was not inevitable, however, given the volatile political atmosphere of early sixteenth-century Italy that shaped Federico II's youth. Sent to Rome as a child in 1510 to ensure that his father would be

---

[70] Ibid., pp. 306–307.

[71] Ibid., p. 311.

[72] Federico Rausa, "'Li disegni delle statue et busti sono rotolate drento le stampe'. L'arredo di sculture antiche delle residenze dei Gonzaga nei disegni seicenteschi della Royal Library a Windson Castle," in Gonzaga: La Celeste Galeria, ed. Raffaella Morselli (Milan: Skira, 2002), pp. 67–91. The prominence of Roman emperors as a part of the Gonzaga sculpture collection is particularly evident in the table of the sculptures displayed in the main gallery of the palace provided here. Pp. 87–89.

loyal to Pope Julius II as he fought to expand the Papal State, Federico's forced sojourn in the papal court nonetheless provided him with the opportunity to experience the city at one of its most culturally dynamic moments. Bramante, Michelangelo, Raphael, and Giulio Romano were all at work for a new Julius, and together with the ancient ruins, they made a deep and lasting impression on the artistic tastes of the young Gonzaga heir.

So, too, did the rising power of the papacy, and shortly after taking over as head of the family on his father's death in 1519, Federico accepted a commission as a military captain in service of the pope. Initially, Rome was allied with France, and it appeared that Federico II would be fighting against the young king of Spain and heir to the Holy Roman Empire, Charles V. But Pope Leo X changed sides shortly before Francis I invaded Italy in 1521, and Federico ended up fighting on the side of the new emperor.[73] It was a fortunate twist of fate.

Federico fought in the Italian wars between Francis I and Charles V in 1522 to 1523, and he allowed his states to be used as a base of operations for the imperial troops in this period. But he was not drawn to the life of a captain for hire and was considered unreliable by Charles V in this regard. Still, he had the good fortune of having a younger brother, Ferrante, who filled this role and obligation for the family. Sent to the court of Charles V at the age of sixteen, Ferrante rose to be one of the most trusted captains of the emperor, eventually holding the positions of governor of Milan and viceroy of Sicily.[74]

In the meantime, Federico preferred cultivating the arts at home in Mantua. But in this realm, too, he provided excellent service to Charles V as he created art that furthered imperial imagery, ideas, and the concrete material expression of empire. He did so with the skill and taste befitting the son of Isabella d'Este and great-grandson of Ludovico II. Continuing in their footsteps as patron and collector, Federico II drew some of the greatest masters of his time into his service and commissioned from them painting, sculpture, and architecture that both continued and strengthened the imperial iconographic program of his ancestors. Because of his close political association with Charles V, moreover, the court at Mantua became one of the primary locations for the dissemination of this tradition.

Most important in this regard was the new Palazzo Te, Giulio Romano's architectural masterpiece built on the periphery of Mantua near the stables where the famous horses of the Gonzaga were raised. Begun in 1527,

---

[73] M. J. Rodríguez-Salgado, "Terracotta and Iron," pp. 32–37.
[74] Ibid., p. 39.

the palace was steeped in imperial Roman aesthetics both inside and out. Romano, the most famous student of Raphael, had grown up and studied in the Rome of Bramante and Michelangelo earlier in the century when the Vitruvian revival was already in full swing.[75] Although he introduced Mannerist architectural novelties in his building, there is no mistaking Palazzo Te as anything but a palace aiming to imitate ancient Roman grandeur and palace culture, if not always the formal rules and orders of Vitruvius. It was the first of its kind in Europe, and it made a deep impression on the artists and ruling class of its own day and beyond.[76] Sebastiano Serlio, author of one of the most influential architectural treatises of the age, the Vitruvian-inspired *Seven Books of Architecture*, called Palazzo Te "truly a paragon of architecture and painting for our times."[77]

The revival of Vitruvius through the study, editing, and increased dissemination of his major work, *On Architecture*, was another major component of the Imperial Renaissance that went hand in hand with the rise of Caesar and his writings. Petrarch, for example, had a copy of the manuscript with evidence of careful study.[78] As the only surviving writing on architecture from ancient Rome, *On Architecture*, together with drawings and study of the ancient ruins, was a critical source for the building revival of palaces, houses, villas, and temples that sought to imitate the aesthetics of the Roman Empire.

Although Vitruvius was known in the medieval period, he was not widely followed or imitated, a fact demonstrated by the evolution and popularity of the Gothic style and the virtual absence in Europe of any buildings prior to the fifteenth century that closely followed the models of ancient Rome.[79] This was also true of Mantua.

---

[75] Howard Burns, "'Quelle cose antique et moderne belle de Roma.' Giulio Romano, the theatre and the antique," *Giulio Romano Architect* (Cambridge: Cambridge University Press, 1998), pp. 129–142. The author notes that "Giulio certainly participated in the researches and discussions of the orders conducted by Raphael on the basis of his study of Vitruvius and the monuments." P. 136.

[76] For Giulio Romano and Palazzo Te, see especially Amadeo Belluzzi and Walter Capezzali, *Il Palazzo dei Lucidi Inganni: Palazzo Te a Mantova* (Florence: Ourubus, 1976); Amedeo Belluzzi and Kurt W. Forster, "Palazzo Te," in *Giulio Romano Architect* (Cambridge: Cambridge University Press, 1998), pp. 165–177; and by the same authors in the same volume, "Giulio Romano, architect at the court of the Gonzagas," pp. 90–128.

[77] Quoted in H. Burns, "Quelle cose antique et moderne belle de Roma," p. 138.

[78] Anthony Grafton, *Leon Battista Alberti* (Cambridge, MA: Harvard University Press, 2000), p. 269.

[79] Carole Herselle Krinsky, "Seventy-eight Vitruvius Manuscripts," *Journal of the Warburg and Courthauld Institutes*, 30, 1967, pp. 36–70. This study notes that there were at least twenty-seven complete or partial manuscripts of Vitruvius dating from the eighth to fourteenth

For advocates of Roman imperial renewal, however, reviving the knowledge of Vitruvius and the architecture of ancient Rome were crucial aspects and expressions of rebuilding real political power. Originally a military engineer for Caesar, Vitruvius wrote his treatise in the age of Augustus and dedicated his book to him. The function of buildings as an expression of imperial magnificence and expansion was emphasized from the opening dedication of *On Architecture* quoted in the introduction earlier.[80]

This close joining of political power and public buildings reflected an increasingly strong and pervasive component of the political mentality at the heart of Renaissance imperialism. Predictably, given their training by imperial humanists, the Gonzaga court was among the first to embrace and act on this Vitruvian ideal. Already in the fifteenth century, Ludovico II had commissioned Leon Battista Alberti to design the churches of San Sebastiano and Sant'Andrea. Alberti's treatise, *On the Art of Building*, was one of the earliest and most influential Renaissance architectural treatises that sought to revive ancient Roman building aesthetics. Critical of but deeply dependent on Vitruvius, Alberti had dedicated the book to his earlier patron, Leonello d'Este.[81] But it was in the court of Ludovico II Gonzaga that he found the cultivated patron who sponsored one of his most important architectural designs.

The church of Sant'Andrea was Alberti's last project and only begun after his death in 1472. The construction dragged out over more than a century and subsequently represents the collective effort of Ludovico's heirs, as well as the citizens of Mantua who helped fund the building. The design of the façade and Roman barrel vault of the nave, in particular, distinguished it as a powerful new expression of the revival of ancient Roman architectural forms.[82] More specifically, the façade was based on a "fusion of a Roman triumphal arch with an antique temple front."[83] Reminiscent of the ancient

---

centuries that survived in medieval libraries and fifty-one additional copies that date from the fourteenth to sixteenth centuries. All medieval manuscripts are presumed to have been derived from an eighth- or ninth-century archetype. P. 43. The basic difference between the medieval and Renaissance reception of Vitruvius is summed up here as follows: "The construction of churches and palaces in the new architectural style gave the architectural sections of the *Ten Books* an immediacy that they never had during the Middle Ages; the book surely reinforced the desire for Renaissance buildings, while the buildings stimulated interest in the book." P. 40.

[80] Vitruvius, *Ten Books of Architecture*, trans. Ingrid Rowland (Cambridge: Cambridge University Press, 1999), p. 21.

[81] Grafton, *Alberti*, p. 224.

[82] Eugene J. Johnson, *S. Andrea in Mantua* (University Park and London: The Pennsylvania State University Press, 1975).

[83] Ibid., p. 51.

Arch of Constantine in the Roman Forum, the arch that framed the entry to Sant'Andrea led into a spacious nave covered by a Roman barrel vault common in the ancient basilicas.

A bold departure from the prevailing Gothic style of church architecture, Sant'Andrea stood as testimony to the pioneering role played by the Gonzaga dukes in this genre of the classical revival.[84] As this new temple rose slowly in the center of Mantua, the Palazzo Te was rising on the outskirts of the city, albeit more quickly and dramatically as the first major palace inspired from the ground up by ancient Roman palace architecture. Originally planned as a pleasure palace for Federico II, in 1530 the building acquired "the new significance of the residence of the emperor."[85] It was in that year that Charles V visited the Gonzaga court after his coronation as Holy Roman Emperor in Bologna. His presence furthered the image of the building as an "imperial palace" that played a prominent political role as a vehicle and location for celebrating allegiances and imagined genealogies (Figure 1.3).[86]

For the emperor, the main initial purpose of the visit was to solidify his alliance with the Gonzaga, whose state played an important role in his broader Italian designs, more for its strategic location close to Milan than for its actual military power. Federico II, a capable and shrewd politician, understood this, and he sought to gain the ultimate favor for his pledge of faithful support, namely the title of Duke.

That Charles V would raise the Gonzaga into the first tier of European nobility with this act was not a foregone conclusion. Federico II had not been a particularly stable ally, and the two men had no personal bond. But that changed over the course of an almost month-long stay that was marked by lavish feasting, hunting, and the enjoyment of the artistic and architectural pleasures of the court. Both men were just thirty years old, and although there was a vast distance between them in terms of political power, Federico II enjoyed a serious cultural advantage. His court was one of the most celebrated locations of Renaissance art and architecture in all of Europe by 1530. Charles V may have been the emperor, but Federico II arguably lived

[84] Christoph Luitpold Frommel, *Architettura e commitenza da Alberti a Bramante* (Castello: Leo S. Olschi, 2006), pp. 368–369. The churches of San Sebastiano and Sant'Andrea represent the "birth of a completely new typology in the context of post-medieval sacred buildings," according to Frommel, who also notes that it was the Etruscan temple mentioned by Vitruvius that inspired Alberti's design of Sant'Andrea described here as a "pioneering experiment."

[85] Belluzzi and Capezzali, p. 34.

[86] Ibid., pp. 34–36.

1.3. Giulio Romano, Façade, Palazzo del Te, Mantua, Italy, 1525–1535. (Photograph: Scala/ Art Resource, NY.)

more like the ancient emperors in the opulence of his material life thanks to both his ancestors and his own refined taste.[87]

He also knew how to use these resources to his advantage both as a stage to display his own magnificence and as one to entertain and flatter his guest. Palazzo Te played a particularly important role in this regard. Early in his stay, Charles V was given a lengthy personal tour of the new palace with his host describing the meaning of the detailed frescoes that Giulio Romano and his workshop had painted in the first wing of the palace. He was especially fond of the cycle of twenty-two frescoes that decorate the Chamber of Psyche, where he also dined with Federico II attending to him (Figure 1.4).[88]

Afterward, the emperor was reported as having described Mantua as his favorite Italian city where he felt like he was truly at home.[89] All of this hospitality, together with lavish gifts of art and horses and vows of political

[87] M. J. Rodríguez-Salgado, pp. 43–45. The author notes that in *The Courtier*, Castiglione, himself a frequent servant of the Gonzaga, had highlighted the lavish court of Federico II, who he described as living more like the King of Italy than as the prince of a small state.

[88] *Palazzo Te Mantua*, ed. Ugo Bazzotti (Milan: Skira, 2007), p. 45.

[89] M. J. Rodríguez-Salgado, "Terracotta and Iron,", p. 44.

1.4. Giulio Romano, Garden Façade, Palazzo del Te, Mantua, Italy, 1525–1535. (Photograph: Scala/Art Resource, NY.)

fidelity, had its desired effect. In the most tangible and dramatic sign of the rise of the Gonzaga to the top echelon of European aristocracy, Charles V elevated Federico II to the level of Duke in 1530. At the same time, the emperor arranged for him to marry his aunt, Giulia d'Aragona, deepening the blood ties between the Gonzaga and Habsburg dynasties.[90] The Gonzaga had truly become part of an imperial family that rivaled the strength and grandeur of the ancient Caesars. It was a powerful myth that the walls of the Palazzo Te and the Palazzo Ducale served to both create and celebrate.

In Palazzo Te, the imperial motif and message are expressed most overtly in the Room of the Emperors, where portraits of Julius Caesar, Augustus, and others decorate the walls and ceilings. Although the artist responsible for the decoration is debated, both Romano and the Bolognese painter Francesco Primaticcio have been proposed as likely candidates. Primaticcio, who later worked on the palace of Francis I at Fontainebleau, took cartoons by Romano to Paris that included the ceiling painting of Caesar from Palazzo Te.[91]

[90] Leonardo Mazzoldi, *Mantova*, (Verona: Valdonega, 1961) vol. 2, p. 301.
[91] *Palazzo Te Mantua*, p. 61.

The ceiling painting was an important piece of political commentary as well as a compliment to Mantegna's *Triumphs* cycle hanging in the other palace across town. In the painting, Caesar is depicted refusing to open the letters of Pompey that were taken after his defeat. A major example of the personal qualities of Caesar that Petrarch had emphasized, it also cast both the present emperor and the Gonzaga by association as rulers who followed in the tradition of the ancient Caesars and held the same virtues.

This representational agenda also continued with the decoration of the other major residence of Federico II across town in the Ducal Palace where Charles V stayed during his visit in Mantua. In the case of his apartments located in the Corte Nuova section of the palace, the new duke deepened the ancient Roman decoration favored by his ancestors in all media.

He furthered the general opulence of the palace with new frescoes in the Apartment of Troy, where the Gonzaga family's connection to the Trojan founders of Rome was celebrated with a new fresco cycle by Giulio Romano. Similarly, he added to the collection of antique busts of ancient Romans in the Sala delle Teste. Most importantly, in 1533 he commissioned Titian to paint a series of the twelve Caesars of Suetonius that were hung in the Gabinetto dei Cesari.[92] Yet another major cycle of paintings by a great Renaissance master, they were both a continuation of Mantegna's *Triumphs* cycle and an expansion of the imperial theme to include the most famous pagan rulers of the Roman Empire.[93] When they were hung in the carefully prepared spaces that Romano crafted for them in 1537, Federico II could claim yet another contribution to the imperial iconography of the palace that rivaled even the great works of Mantegna. More broadly, Titian's emperors were also a striking sign that the Gonzaga court was northern Italy's most refined center of the revival of ancient imperial culture and political aspirations.

Combined with his new title of Duke, the building and artistic accomplishments achieved by Federico II represented a political peak for the Gonzaga dynasty. Although some of his successors may have harbored still greater aspirations, the reality is that the dynasty had reached its limit in terms of political power.

---

[92] For a provocative reconstruction of these paintings based on related documents and copies, see Frederick Hartt, *Giulio Romano* (New Haven, CT: Yale University Press, 1958), pp. 170–178.

[93] Claudia Cieri Via, "Collezionismo e decorazione all Corte dei Gonzaga," pp. 394–398. The connections between Vitruvian principles of decoration and the decoration of Federico's apartments are emphasized, as is the connection to the *Illustrious Men* literary tradition.

When Federico II waited on Charles V in Palazzo Te during his visit, it was an act of submission that underlined a number of important political facts about the Gonzaga specifically and the minor courts of Italy more generally: for all of the imperial artistic grandeur of their palaces and cities, they remained second-tier political players in Italy and third-tier political players in Europe. They simply did not have the economic or military strength to compete with Charles V, Francis I of France, Venice, or the papacy, the major Italian powers of the day.

They also had no historical claim on the legacy of actual imperial rule. Their cities and ancestors had always been servants of empire both ancient and medieval. Thus, the most they could hope for was to be tied by blood to the dominant dynasties of the period and to benefit from the economic benefits and military protection that came from their alliances.

Moreover, by the early sixteenth century, it was Rome that overtook the northern Italian cities as the artistic and political center of the Imperial Renaissance in Italy. Federico II's major architect, Giulio Romano, was Roman trained, and Federico II was himself a servant of the popes including Julius II, the Renaissance pope who most aspired to be a new Caesar. It was this prince of Rome who first placed a serious claim on being the legitimate heir of ancient Roman power, an ambition deepened by the artistic glory that was being literally and literarily exhumed from the ruins of the ancient city.

Renaissance Rome as New Imperial City: Phase One

Postponed by the French exile of the papacy in the fourteenth and early fifteenth centuries, the Roman Renaissance began to take root in earnest when Oddone Colonna, Pope Martin V (1417–1431), returned to Rome in 1420. The Colonna was one of medieval Rome's leading noble families. Their cardinals and senators already played the role of patrons of Petrarch in the fourteenth century, and Martin V was himself a well-educated man. His return to Rome initiated a long period of grace for scholars, architects, and artists who flocked to Rome in ever-greater numbers. As the century progressed, the papal princes increasingly sought to cultivate the memory and knowledge of ancient Roman grandeur and to imitate it in their literature, art, and architecture, much like their northern Italian counterparts.

This work progressed slowly during Martin V's reign because the pope found Rome in a sorry state of disrepair and poverty on his return. Much of his time and resources were devoted to cleaning up the streets and re-establishing the general rule of law. Still, the basic work of removing rogue buildings that had been built in the middle of ancient streets, piazzas, and monuments like the Coliseum was an essential part of urban renewal that pointed the way to a rejuvenated city. At the same time, Martin V did order important restorations like that of St. John Lateran with decorations by Gentile da Fabriano, and he initiated the building of the new Colonna family palace in the piazza Santissimi Apostoli.[94]

More importantly from the viewpoint of asserting temporal power, Martin V pursued a vigorous policy of reclaiming papal territories and prerogatives in the Papal State. A capable and shrewd prince, he built alliances and raised armies to defend and advance his territorial interests. In short, over the course of his fourteen years in power, he so successfully laid the foundation for a revival of temporal power for the papacy that he has been described as "the restorer and founder of Renaissance Rome as the capital of a Renaissance State."[95]

Building on this, Nicholas V (1447–1455) pursued an ambitious literary, artistic/architectural, and political agenda that furthered the cause of a more robust classical revival together with a stronger papal prince. In an era when cultural power and political power went hand in hand, he expanded the Vatican manuscript collection dramatically: by his death it had more than tripled in size and counted more than 1,150 volumes including more than 350 Greek manuscripts.[96] This constituted one of the largest collections in Europe at the time. It held important manuscripts including the works of Caesar, Vitruvius, Cicero, Livy, Suetonius, and Tacitus, the building blocks of Renaissance imperialism, all of which became more accessible to scholars thanks to the opening of a reading room that served as the de facto beginning of the Vatican Library.[97]

Rome under Nicholas V thus became a major location for the new scholarship as a notable group of humanist scholars collected, translated, and edited as many ancient Greek and Latin texts as they could find. Counted among them were Lorenzo Valla, George of Trebizond, Poggio Bracciolini, Flavio Biondo, and numerous humanists already noted for their work in

---

[94] Ludwig Von Pastor, *History of the Popes* (Nendeln: Kraus Reprint, 1969), vol. 1, pp. 208–282. Pastor's classic history of the papacy is still useful for its rich historical detail, if not for its political analysis.

[95] Peter Partner, *The Papal State Under Martin V* (London: British School at Rome, 1958), p. 68.

[96] Charles Stinger, *The Renaissance in Rome* (Indianapolis: Indiana University Press, 1998), p. 84.

[97] For the manuscript collection, see J. Bignami Odier, *La Bibliothèque Vaticane de Sixte IV à Pie XI* (Città del Vaticano, 1973); and Pastor, *History of the Popes*, vol. 2, pp. 207–214.

the northern Italian courts, most especially Leon Battista Alberti and Guarino Guarini.[98]

As in Ferrara and Mantua, their literary work was sometimes closely connected to the architectural and artistic renewal that was also gaining momentum under the patronage of Nicholas V. In 1453, for example, the pope restored the Aqua Virgo aqueduct that had been destroyed by the barbarian invasions in the sixth century. This promoted the increased settlement of the ancient center of Rome, and, like an ancient emperor, Nicholas V ensured that he would be remembered for his great public work by having a commemorative inscription carved on the restored Trevi Fountain. There he had himself described as "pontifex maximus," one of the titles traditionally claimed by Roman emperors. This title had not been used by popes since the fourth century, and it may have been Alberti, who was then working as a papal secretary in Rome, who composed the text of the inscription.[99]

Restoring the ancient Roman aqueducts and water supply to Rome became a common aspect of papal urban revival over the next two centuries, and they were celebrated with monumental fountains that most always included inscriptions paying tribute to the popes who built them. The large fountain on the Janiculum Hill that marked Paul V's restoration of the water supply to Rome's highest hill in the early seventeenth century is a later example of this same development that was central to the urban revival of Rome.

Nicholas V promoted other ambitious architectural projects, most importantly the plan to tear down and rebuild St. Peter's Basilica and to expand the Vatican palace. These were less successful in his lifetime but nonetheless demonstrated a growing papal ambition and appetite for monument building. They also set a precedent for his successors, who increasingly sought to surpass contemporary courts by imitating the monumental style of the ancient Roman emperors.[100]

This rising political confidence was encouraged by humanists like Flavio Biondo, who saw in the fall of the Byzantine empire an opportunity for the pope to consolidate power and claim the role and title of ideal emperor. He wrote, "Rome has jurisdiction over the many nations, for today the emperor is not the successor of Caesar, but the Vicar of the fisherman, Peter.

[98] Stinger, p. 284.

[99] See Anthony Grafton, "Historia and Istoria: Alberti's Terminology in Context," in *I Tatti Studies: Essays in the Renaissance*, Vol. 8, 1999, pp. 46–47 (pp. 37–68).

[100] For an excellent overview of the architectural patronage of Nicolas V, see Carol Westfall, *In this Most Perfect Paradise; Alberti, Nicholas V, and the Invention of Conscious Urban Planning* (University Park: Pennsylvania State University Press, 1974).

(His) imperium includes almost all of Europe, and (soon will extend to) Asia, Africa."[101]

For all of the success that Nicholas V enjoyed in enriching the intellectual life and reputation of Rome, as well as taking important steps in its urban revival, his pontificate was marked by political and military weakness. The fall of the Byzantine Empire to the Ottomans in 1453 under his watch demonstrated very clearly that western Europe, including the papacy, was fragmented and weak. Nicholas V tried to rally the Christian kingdoms to the aid of Christian Byzantium, but to no avail. Most disappointing to him was the fact that the Holy Roman Emperor, Frederick III, whom he had crowned as emperor in 1452, had failed to come through with the 30,000 men that he promised for the cause. When Nicholas V died in 1455, imperial revival in Europe was an unrealized dream and the imperial power of the Holy Roman Empire, a hollow fantasy. Although Petrarch had died disgusted at the Holy Roman Emperor's inability to unite Italy, Nicholas V had even greater cause for dismay.[102]

The pope who succeeded Nicholas V, Pius II, had himself written important texts against the Ottomans.[103] A celebrated humanist and imperial poet before he became pope, Pius II perpetuated and deepened the intellectual agenda of his predecessor.[104] As a major patron of imperial humanism, he ensured that the papal court continued to be a magnet for humanists of the highest caliber, but it was no ivory tower.[105] Rather, the humanists' work of reviving the knowledge, memory, and aesthetics of ancient Rome was increasingly and intimately tied to the political agenda of the pope.

More specifically, for Pius II, the major focus of his foreign policy was a continued attempt to forge a coalition of Christian princes against the looming threat of Ottoman aggression. This task was perceived by the pope

---

[101] Quoted in Marie Tanner, *Jerusalem on the Hill: Rome and the Vision of St. Peter's in the Renaissance* (London: Harvey Miller Publishers, 2010), p. 14.

[102] For a concise analysis of the political history of the reign of Nicholas V, see John B. Toews, "Formative Forces in the Pontificate of Nicholas V, 1447–1455," *Catholic Historical Review*, Vol. 54, No. 2 (Jul., 1968), pp. 261–284.

[103] Margaret Meserve, *Empires of Islam in Renaissance Historical Thought* (Cambridge, MA: Harvard University Press, 2008).

[104] Nicholas Weber, "Pope Pius II," in *The Catholic Encyclopedia* (New York: Robert Appleton Comp., 1911). Frederick III granted him the title of imperial poet in 1443.

[105] Cary N. Nederman, "Humanism and Empire: Aeneas Sylvius Piccolomini, Cicero, and the Imperial Ideal," in *The Historical Journal*, Vol. 36, No. 3 (Sep., 1993), pp. 499–515. The author specifically calls the humanism of Pius II imperial humanism and rightly argues that "We are justified in rejecting as a false dichotomy the distinction which has been repeatedly drawn within the scholarship on Aeneas between his renaissance humanist inclinations and his 'medieval', imperial propensities." P. 514.

to be comparable to the epic battles of Caesar himself, and one of the last writings of the humanist pope was a text titled *Commentaries on Memorable Things that Happened in [Pius's] Age*. It took the *Commentaries* of Caesar as a loose model and inspiration for recounting the deeds of his reign and casting himself, like Caesar, as a talented military commander and wise ruler.[106]

From this perspective, Rome and the papacy looked destined to play the leading role in the defense of Europe, and it was in this context that Flavio Biondo (1388–1463), the leading Roman humanist of his time, wrote *Rome Triumphant*, a rallying cry for Europe.[107] Biondo had already written two important studies on ancient Rome and Italy, *Roma Instaurata* and *Italia Illustrata*. These works provided the best compilation of ancient historical and geographical knowledge on ancient Rome and Italy to date. "Biondo elevated the study of ancient Roman history and antiquarianism to a high plane of sophistication," thereby providing essential knowledge for later scholars and proto-archeologists who sought to dig up better knowledge of Rome both in the ancient texts and soil of Rome.[108] *Rome Triumphant*, composed as the latter part of Biondo's Roman trilogy, focused on the triumphs of ancient Rome. It was dedicated to Pius II with the explicit hope that it would encourage the people of Italy, Germany, France, and Spain to imitate the valor and deeds of the ancient Romans in their fight against the Turk.[109]

Just as Petrarch had held up the example of the Caesars to imitate, Flavio Biondo, roughly a century later, held up the Roman Empire as the highest evolution of political life to both imitate and learn from. Biondo's collected work constituted the most detailed history of ancient Rome to date. Culminating in *Rome Triumphant*, it was a pillar of imperial humanism as it explicitly sought to use Roman history to instruct, admonish, and encourage contemporary readers to follow the example of the ancient Empire.

From Biondo's perspective, the Roman Empire attained the most perfect political ideal, uniting people through law, commerce, language, and letters. More specifically, Rome had civilized the largely illiterate peoples of

---

[106] For a good recent study comparing the text of Pius II with the *Commentaries* of Caesar, see Emily O'Brien, "Arms and Letters: Julius Caesar, the *Commentaries* of Pope Pius II, and the Politicization of Papal Imagery," in *Renaissance Quarterly*, Vol. LXII, No. 4 (Winter 2009), pp. 1057–1097.

[107] Flavio Biondo, *Roma Trionfante*, trans. Lucio Fauno (Venice: Michele Tramezzino, 1544). Printed text but with pagination as in folios. Unfoliated in forward material and author's preface.

[108] John D'Amico, *Renaissance Humanism in Papal Rome* (Baltimore: Johns Hopkins Press, 1983), p. 70.

[109] *Roma Trionfante*, from the unfoliated preface.

Germany, France, Spain, Africa, and Britain who had been divided not only by rivers, mountains, and seas but also by language and customs. Rome was the empire destined to bring order to these diverse peoples, uniting them through the Latin language, Roman law, and a common Roman currency. The good that resulted from the empire was so great that it seemed not human but divine.[110] From Biondo's perspective, "This great Empire was born, grew, and maintained itself through the great benefit and particular grace of God."[111]

For Biondo, the histories of the Republic and Empire generally merge into one large history. The history of the Republic gets the most attention in the first six books of the work, where Livy and Cicero are the most frequently mentioned authorities. In the last four chapters on the Empire, the *Lives of the Twelve Caesars* by Suetonius and the *Annals* of Tacitus are mentioned as ancient sources on the empire.

Both Republic and Empire, and many of the available ancient texts, were mined for the information they provide on the customs, religion, triumphs, military matters, patronage of letters, and other aspects of Roman accomplishment. The Republic was the primary source of information for examples of governance in which the work of the magistrate and senate was emphasized. But there was no great distinction or political judgment made by Biondo between Republic and Empire. When he briefly discussed the civil wars and Caesar, he noted the horror of Roman bloodshed, and he expressed doubt that Caesar was acting in the best interests of the Republic when he entered into the civil wars. Yet he also marveled over the many victories of Caesar. This was a book about Roman triumphs, after all.[112]

In the last section of the work, book ten, Biondo recounted some of the literal triumphs that were staged in Rome after the victories of various Caesars. Drawing on Pliny, he described the triumphs of Pompey in which elephants pulled silver carriages filled with the great plunder of war: three gold statues of the gods Minerva, Mars, and Apollo, thirty-three pearl crowns, golden vases, three gold tables, a large gold moon weighing 30 libre,

---

[110] Ibid., "conquistando I Romani la maggior parte de la terra; cosi la resero culta, e piena d'ogni costume buono & arte liberale; che le nationi, che per il tanti seni di mare, per li tanti monti, e fiumi, e per la differentia grande de le lingue, erano l'una da l'altra divise; vennero, mediante la lingua Latina, che a tutti si comunico'; e mediante I magistrate Romani a tutti communi; a diventare una istessa citta tutti; il quale beneficio, a chi'l va bene considerando, non pare humano, ma divino piu tosto."

[111] Ibid., unfoliated preface, "questo cosi grande Imperio nacque, accrebbe e si mantenne per gran beneficio, e gratia particolare d'Iddio."

[112] Ibid., ff. 257v–258r.

many gems, and a portrait of Pompey made of pearls were just the highlights of the vast wealth taken from the conquered territories.[113]

The triumphs of Julius Caesar, including one with forty elephants, were also briefly noted by Biondo, but the imperial triumph described with the most detail was that of Vespasian and Titus. Drawing on the long accounts given by the ancient author, Josephus, Biondo lingered over the spectacle in Rome that followed the conquest of Jerusalem. "There was not a man in Rome who stayed at home" on the day of that triumph, according to Biondo.[114] All of Rome turned out to see and hear Vespasian and Titus, who were dressed in silk and seated on ivory thrones in the midst of the Roman senate. After addressing the assembled legions and crowds and performing ritual sacrifices, they processed through the forum with all of the plunder of the conquest.

Biondo took obvious literary pleasure in describing the treasure laid out before the city. Never before had Rome seen so much gold, silver, ivory, and every other kind of precious material in a triumph. That which made for the "most beautiful spectacle" was the parading of the spoils taken from the temple in Jerusalem. There was a large gold table, golden candelabra, and "the most noble" of all the spoils, the scrolls of the Jewish law. All of this was the material display of "the greatness of the Roman Empire." A strong imperial nostalgia penetrated all of the passages on triumph, and it was almost as if the author wanted to tempt the reader with triumph, to make him desire the booty of war and to want to see the great displays and victory parades again.[115]

This, of course, was the point. Biondo, in all of his texts, promoted the idea that Rome was destined from its earliest pagan beginnings to be the sacred center of the world. By reconstructing the geography and rituals of imperial Rome, he and others intentionally sought to hasten the day when Rome would once again be preeminent. For most of these fifteenth-century humanists and popes, there was a self-conscious desire to be agents and witnesses of the greatness of ancient Rome reborn. Moreover, Biondo and others presented the popes as the true heirs of the Caesars and those best suited to lead the imperial revival.

But this remained a distant hope during the reign of Pius II and his fifteenth-century successors. The Ottoman advance continued, and the papacy remained unable to unite the Christian princes in any effective

---

[113] Ibid., ff. 367v–368r.
[114] Ibid., f. 369v, "non fu uomo in Roma, che restasse in casa."
[115] Ibid., ff. 369v–370v. These are the descriptions that have been connected to Mantegna's paintings for the Gonzaga.

response for another century. Still, the ideas of Biondo, as well as those of the other humanists at work in Rome, would have consequences. They planted important and powerful seeds in the minds of Romans that would eventually yield real fruit.

At the same time, the Imperial Renaissance continued to progress in Rome on other levels. The successful propagation of the broad humanist agenda in Rome was given institutional focus and strength in the new Roman Academy established by Pomponio Leto, Bartolomeo dei Sacchi, Giovanni Sulpizio da Veroli, and others in the mid–fifteenth century. It was formally sanctioned by Sixtus IV in 1478.[116] Its members often made their living as secretaries in the papal curia, wrote eloquent Latin poetry and letters, issued new editions of classical texts, and produced ancient Greek and Latin plays that were performed on the new impromptu stages of Rome fashioned using the architectural advice of Vitruvius.[117] Great imitators and admirers of the ancient empire, they continued to strengthen the intellectual foundations of an imperial revival.

So, too, did the introduction of the printing press that led to a dramatic increase in the diffusion of ancient texts including those central to Renaissance imperialism. First introduced at the Benedictine monastery in Subiaco just outside of Rome in 1464 where the first edition of Cicero's *De Oratore* was printed in 1465, the press was in Rome by 1467. The first edition of Caesar's *Commentaries* printed in Europe appeared in Rome in 1469 to be followed by the first edition of Suetonius's *Lives of the Twelve Caesars* in 1470 and the first edition of Vitruvius' *Ten Books of Architecture* in 1486.[118] In the case of Caesar's *Commentaries*, it was the humanist Giovanni Andrea Bussi who edited the *editione princeps*. As a former student of Vittorino de Feltre in Mantua alongside the children of the Gonzaga family, he was yet another point of connection between the humanism of the two courts.[119]

The introduction of the press had implications that went far beyond Rome, of course. Still, it is indicative of the importance attributed to the texts in Rome that they were first published there. Numerous editions that followed elsewhere attest to the broader popularity and diffusion of the

[116] Ingrid D. Rowland, *The Culture of the High Renaissance* (Cambridge: Cambridge University Press, 2000), pp. 18–25.

[117] Ibid., p. 34.

[118] John Edwyn Sandys, *A History of Classical Scholarship* (New York: Hafner, 1967), p. 103. Another major text for the imperial revival was the *Annals* of Tacitus, the first edition of which was published in Rome in 1515.

[119] D'Amico, p. 14.

ancient authors at the heart of imperial revival. More specifically, Caesar's *Commentaries* went to press sixteen times between 1467 and 1499, as did the work of Suetonius. Only Sallust and Valerius were more popular among ancient Roman historians. With an estimated press run numbering 1,000 copies, by 1500 knowledge about and by the ancient Caesars was more available than it had ever been, and this was just the beginning. Between 1500 and 1549, the *Commentaries* went to press an additional fifty-nine times, and from 1550 to 1599 Caesar rose to the rank of being the most popular of all ancient historians with fifty-nine more editions going to press. By the end of the seventeenth century, 189 editions of Caesar's work had been published, making it one of the most popular and widely circulating texts from ancient Rome in all of Europe.[120]

The writing of Vitruvius, too, was increasingly popular in the latter half of the fifteenth century, and Rome witnessed increasing progress in the parallel realm of architecture inspired by his text together with the ancient ruins. As in the Mantua of Ludovico II, the Vitruvian revival in Rome was initially indebted to Alberti, whose *On Architecture* was written there in 1450. It was first published under the patronage of Cardinal Raffaele Riario in 1482 in the papal court. The same cardinal sponsored the first printed edition of Vitruvius edited by Sulpizio da Veroli.[121]

The influence of Alberti led to the introduction of Vitruvian principles in various architectural projects in the age of Pius II and Paul II (1464–1471). The Palazzetto di Venezia, for example, part of the larger Palazzo di Venezia complex, was designed by Francesco del Borgo and begun around 1467. It imitated architectural features from the Coliseum also found in the work of Vitruvius.[122]

More overtly and dramatically tied to this tradition, however, was the new palace for the papal chancellery commissioned by Cardinal Riario, patron of the publication of both Alberti and Vitruvius. The nephew of Pope Sixtus IV (1471–1484) had substantial financial resources, and he put them to use in building a monumental palace whose clear purpose was to memorialize and put on display the grandeur of his family. Although the architect of the building remains unknown, contemporaries gave the cardinal himself a

---

[120] Peter Burke, "A Survey of the Popularity of Ancient Historians," *History and Theory* Vol. 5, No. 2, 1966, p. 137 (pp. 135–152).

[121] Rowland, p. 35.

[122] Frommel, p. 284. Specifically, the author notes that in the trabeation of the Ionic loggia of the Palazzetto Venezi, "Francesco del Borgo riesce a tradurre visivamente l'interpretazione di Vitruvio della treabazione del Colosseo."

major role in a plan celebrated for following the "principles of good design" of Vitruvius.[123]

Parallels have also been drawn between the Palazzo della Cancelleria and the Palazzo Ducale in Mantova. The uncle of Cardinal Riario, Girolamo, was the godfather of Ferrante Gonzaga, and he had chosen the Corte Vecchia in Mantua as the model for his palace in Imola. Both buildings represented "a synthesis of a civic palace and a Vitruvian forum," a fitting description of the Palazzo della Cancelleria as well.[124] In its monumental scale and materials, the palace evoked imperial Rome to a degree that was unparalleled in fifteenth-century Rome. Borrowing heavily from the Coliseum for everything from the travertine stone that covered its façade to the monumental dimensions of its design, it signaled that Rome had arrived as the new center of the classical revival.[125]

At the same time, the palace also served as a stage for a family with grand political designs that would match and even surpass the ambitions of Cardinal Riario. It was during the pontificate of Cardinal Riario's cousin, Guiliano della Rovere, Pope Julius II (1503–1513), that the Imperial Renaissance in Rome witnessed the development of a political program that sought to wed the maturing imperial humanism, iconography, and architecture of Rome with the military power and prowess of a new papal Caesar.

From the time of Martin V onward, the popes had been claiming more temporal authority and attempting to impose and consolidate their power in the Papal State. But the military power of the papacy was limited through most of the fifteenth century both because of financial and theological constraints. It was a basic fact of the papacy that its dual role as temporal prince and universal pastor required it to use care in wielding the sword. Most popes chose their battles carefully and preferred to have others fight them when possible.

This was not the case with the last pope of the century, Alexander VI (1492–1503), who joined fully in the political intrigue and battles of Italy at the beginning of an age of almost continuous warfare. His family, the Borgia, had its own raw imperial ambitions that drew classical inspiration not just from Rome but from fanciful associations with ancient Egypt. Although much of the humanist and artistic production of the Borgia pontificate

[123] Rowland, p. 39. According to the author, "The construction of the Palazzo Riario followed close on Sulpizio's Vitruvious text to offer living proof of the ancient author's currency." Frommel largely concurs with this view, noting the cardinal's great interest in Vitruvius and his attention to the Vitruvian orders. Frommel, p. 411.
[124] Frommel, p. 409.
[125] Rowland, pp. 38–39.

represented a digression from the more purely Roman-centered work of the previous decades, in the realm of political power, the decade of Alexander VI's rule gave new substance to papal ambitions for real power. He was determined to impose his rule on the traditional territories of the Papal State, many of which had enjoyed *de facto* political independence since at least the fourteenth century. To that end, he organized the most feared military that the Renaissance papacy had controlled to date.[126]

This drive for territorial expansion and military power was most dramatically embodied in the pope's own Caesar, Cesare Borgia. As the pope's son and military general, Cesare's ruthless and successful mission of subjugating independent-minded princes and towns in the Papal State was carried out with skill and brutality. His success famously won him Machiavelli's praise in *The Prince* where, in chapter seven, the Borgia Duke is recommended as a model for rulers. Using language that was extremely similar to that of apologists for Julius Caesar, Machiavelli excused Borgia's ruthless excesses, saying, "Since his courage was great and his purpose high, he could not conduct himself otherwise."[127]

The *Commentaries* of Caesar, as well as the earlier Renaissance biographies and images of him, had emphasized these same virtues, and it was predictable that Cesare Borgia and many other Renaissance rulers consciously sought to emulate the ancient Caesar in war and conquest. Although the brutality of the Borgia military campaigns shocked some contemporary observers, their determination to build a real state was not surprising when viewed in light of the political, literary, and artistic agenda of the previous decades in Italy. Martin V, Flavio Biondo, Nicholas V, and Pius II had all prepared the soil for the expansion of real papal political and military power. Alexander VI was simply following their lead in his attempt to restore ancient Roman and papal power, not to mention the fame and glory of his own family.

The victories of Cesare Borgia were thus celebrated with triumphs modeled after those of ancient Rome, and the celebrations of 1500 included images that recollected the victories of Julius Caesar.[128] This may not have been the kind of Roman triumph or papal power that Flavio Biondo hoped

---

[126] Niccolo Machiavelli, *The Legations*, trans. Allan Gilbert (Durham, NC: Duke University Press, 1965), vol. 1, pp. 120–169. Among the notable cities seized were Faenza, Pesaro, and Rimini, whose ruling families were exiled. Among the best primary sources detailing the campaigns and cunning of Cesare were the dispatches sent by Machiavelli during his diplomatic missions to the Duke in Imola and Rome from 1502 and 1503.

[127] Niccolo Machiavelli, *The Prince*, trans. Allan Gilbert (Durham, NC: Duke University Press, 1965), vol. 1, p. 34.

[128] Stinger, p. 242.

for, and they certainly did not include the kind of treasures brought back to Rome by Vespasian and Titus. But they demonstrated very clearly that Cardinal Rodrigo Borgia, as Alexander VI was known before he was pope, had been listening to and reading the literature of the Roman humanists during his decades in Rome prior to being elected pope. He and his courtiers knew exactly what they were doing in staging an imperial triumph that explicitly presented Alexander VI as an heir to the Caesars.

At the same time that new triumphs were being staged, another building was rising in Rome that furthered the Vitruvian project. On a smaller scale than the Palazzo della Cancelleria, but perhaps more evocative of classical forms, the Tempietto was located next to the church of San Pietro in Montorio on the edge of the Gianicolo Hill. Designed by Bramante circa 1502, it was a classical domed chapel that marked one of the spots where St. Peter was thought to have been martyred. For Renaissance Rome, the Tempietto's singular beauty and elegance was a powerful example of the revival of ancient Roman architectural splendor in yet another form. Indeed, it foreshadowed the greatest of all Roman Renaissance building projects, namely the building of new St. Peter's Basilica begun in 1506 with Bramante as its chief architect.[129]

The Tempietto also points to another rising imperial presence in Rome, namely the Spanish monarchy. It was king Ferdinand of Aragon who paid for the Tempietto, as well as the restoration of the church of San Pietro in Montorio next door. King of Naples and Sicily by 1504, Ferdinand was the new power in Italy at the beginning of the sixteenth century. Praised by Machiavelli as the most successful of the new monarchs of Europe, his rule established the foundations for the eventual Spanish domination of Rome and most of Italy. His patronage of the Tempietto, moreover, prefigured later Spanish patronage of Bramante's largest Roman project, new St. Peter's. Projects largely paid for by the imperial monarchs of Spain who sought to increase their reputations through their liberality, both buildings were subsequently monuments to the rising Spanish Empire in form and function.[130]

The growing influence of the Spanish monarch notwithstanding, in the age of Bramante it was Pope Julius II (1504–1513) who took center stage in

[129] Earl Rosenthal, "The Antecedents of Bramante's Tempietto," *Journal of the Society of Architectural Historians*, Vol. 23, No. 2 (May, 1964), pp. 55–74. He notes that the round peripteral temple described by Vitruvius was one of the antetypes for the Tempietto. Pp. 59–60.

[130] See Jack Freiberg, "Bramante's Tempietto and the Spanish Crown," *Memoires of the American Academy in Rome*, Vol. 50, 2005, pp. 151–205; and Thomas Dandelet, *Spanish Rome* (New Haven, CT: Yale University Press, 2001), pp. 1–3.

Rome as the new Caesar. The pope, whose chosen papal name intentionally came with clear imperial associations, expanded the territories of the Papal State through military conquests that surpassed even those of Cesare Borgia: Perugia, Bologna, Parma, Placentia, and Mirandola were taken by force, and through marriage he attached the duchy of Urbino to Rome. His pontificate embodied the full-blown secular ambitions of the Renaissance papacy, and he was the first pope whose building projects, military ambitions, artistic commissions, and personal self-fashioning so obviously and overtly evoked comparisons with and memories of the ancient emperors and city.[131]

In all of this he was supported by humanists in the papal court who promoted a view of imperial history that viewed the pope as the rightful heir of the ancient Empire. Raffael Maffei, for example, in his treatise titled the *Stromata*, advocated the position that after Constantine had handed over to the pope governance of the city of Rome, the empire had itself been made holy: "Therefore, the Church makes the empire, once the [source] of so much injury and obtained by tyranny, now a holy and just thing."[132]

Bolstered by such rhetoric, the *renovatio imperii* reached new heights in Julian Rome. More than any other ruler of his time, Julius II fully embraced as a politician and patron the values and ambitions of a prince steeped in the ideas of the Imperial Renaissance. Unabashedly drawing on the rituals and iconography of ancient Rome, Julius II presented himself to the world as a new Julius Caesar. His success in projecting that image was reflected in the writings of learned contemporaries like Erasmus, who unhappily noted after the famous conquest of Bologna in 1506 that "Pope Julius wages wars, conquers, triumphs, and acts wholly like Julius [Caesar]."[133]

That was exactly right. Returning to Rome as the conqueror in 1507, Julius made a carefully choreographed triumphal entry into the city following the ancient triumphal procession routes. Ephemeral triumphal arches were erected in his honor, and many other decorative trimmings of an ancient triumph were added to emphasize the parallels with ancient Roman victories. If there was any doubt left about the meaning of the event or the character of Julius II, the pope had a commemorative medal struck that was inscribed on one side with the name Julius Caesar Pont[ifex].[134]

---

[131] Stinger, pp. 269–291. The reign of Julius II is viewed as the apex of the Renovatio Imperii in Renaissance Rome, and Stinger provides a richly illustrated summary of the major aspects of the project that I follow here.

[132] John D'Amico, p. 208.

[133] Ibid., p. 236.

[134] Ibid., p. 236.

More lasting than the ephemeral constructions of his triumphal processions was the new processional street that Julius II had constructed along the Tiber on the side opposite the Vatican. The Via Giulia served the purpose of linking the Vatican to the major populated centers of the city at the same time that it created a large urban loop that the papacy used for its many processions. For Renaissance Rome, it was an important step in the recreation of a city of broad, straight thoroughfares that were increasingly used for rituals modeled on or inspired by those of ancient Rome. It also provided an example that was imitated many times over the course of the sixteenth century as new streets including the Via Sistina and the Via Felice connected the ancient center of imperial Rome as it was repopulated and reclaimed by an expanding population. By the time of Julius II, the population of Rome had doubled from the days of Martin V.[135]

For Julius II, the ambitious refashioning of Rome as an imperial capitol centered on his artistic program in the Vatican palace complex and St. Peter's Basilica. Inspired by imperial Roman palace decoration, Raphael of Urbino decorated the pope's apartment with the frescoes celebrating "The School of Athens." He also painted the new classical loggia of the Vatican palace with a decorative scheme inspired by the ancient frescoes from Hadrian's villa in Tivoli. Although any detailed analysis of Raphael's work exceeds the limits of this work, these two famous examples underline the fact that Julius II was determined to use all of his resources to create an imperial palace culture unrivaled in Europe.

And he succeeded in this, thanks in no small part to the presence of Michelangelo, then occupied with painting the Sistine Chapel and sculpting the marble ensemble best known for the monumental figure of Moses that was meant for the tomb of Julius II planned for the center of the new St. Peter's. Both projects represented a joining of imperial classical forms with Christian themes. The Sistine Chapel paintings, especially, announced to the world that Renaissance Rome was the leading European center of artistic production on a monumental scale.

This point was made even more dramatically by the announcement in 1506 of the most ambitious building project of the reign of Julius II, the construction of new St. Peter's. The decision to tear down the basilica that the first Christian emperor, Constantine, had built roughly 1,200 years earlier represented the height of the pope's imperial hubris as a builder. Unlike

---

[135] For a good general discussion of Roman population development in the sixteenth century, see Peter Partner, *Renaissance Rome, 1500–1559* (Berkeley: University of California Press, 1976), pp. 80–84.

the previous plan of Nicholas V, however, the ambition of Julius II was eventually realized. The appointment of Bramante as the architect of the new building indicated that the pope was aiming at a classically inspired domed temple along the lines of the Tempietto but on a vastly grander scale. The new St. Peter's was meant to be the largest and most magnificent church in Christendom, and it eventually became just that.[136]

Seen from the perspective of the revival of Vitruvian architecture and ideas in service of papal imperial ambition, the reign of Julius II and the project of New St. Peter's were decisive. An important new illustrated edition of Vitruvius was published by Fra Giocondo during his pontificate in 1511, and both the pope and Bramante were admirers of the ancient architect.[137] Although Bramante was not a strict adherent to every rule laid out by the ancient text, both he and the pope found inspiration for their vast building projects in his writing.[138] This was also true of Bramante's eventual successor as architect of the project, Michelangelo.

Julius II, for his part, also clearly embraced the strong relationship between good government and good architecture espoused by Vitruvius in the dedication of his book. Just as the emperor was praised for attending to the twin pillars of empire building, "the establishment of community life and of the body politic, but also for the construction of suitable public buildings," so too did Julius hope to be remembered for the interwoven projects of state building and monument building.[139]

---

[136] For the most recent literature on the phases of the building of St. Peter's, see the collection *Sankt Peter's Von Rom*, ed. Georg Satzinger and Sebastian Schutze (Bonn, 2008). For the history of the financing of the building that reveals much about the patronage and impact of political developments on the church, see in that volume Thomas Dandelet, "Financing New St. Peter's, 1506–1700."

[137] Vitruvius, *Ten Books on Architecture: The Corsini Incunabulum*, ed. Ingrid D. Rowland, p. 16. Rowland notes that "The pontificate of Julius II ensured that two factors would dominate the study of ancient architecture, virtually without alteration, for the next four decades: the authority of Bramante and the authority of Vitruvius."

[138] Ibid., p. 14. To quote Rowland: "In Bramante, the Pope found an ideal partner in his plans to rebuild Rome on a scale unimagined since antiquity, and together they found an inspiration for this kind of glorious urban renewal in the text of Vitruvius."

[139] Rowland, p. 4. On the influence of Vitruvius, she notes: "Vitruvius was not a great writer, but he was a thinker of uncommon clarity, and he had much to say not only to the rapidly developing literary and artistic culture of Imperial Rome under Augustus, but also to a whole series of later monarchs who nurtured high cultural aspirations: ... Louis XIV, who sponsored the great illustrated translation of Claude Perrault in 1673, and emphatically, the Popes of Renaissance Rome." She goes further to say that "*De Architectura* must be regarded as one of the most profoundly influential books to survive from antiquity, not for its technical information, but for the way in which it links good architecture with good government."

Although Julius II would never live to see even the basic outlines of the new St. Peter's take shape, he did set in motion what proved to be the largest and most expensive construction project in all of early modern Europe. It was building on a monumental scale that eventually resulted in Europe's most grandiose and expensive temple. But it was also a building that required a true empire to pay the huge bills, and the Papal State of Julius II and his immediate successors, even with its new territories, was not up to the task.

By 1527, in the aftermath of the sack of Rome, the building of the new St. Peter's and the new Rome were at a standstill, and the successors of Julius II were faced with the grim reality that it was much easier to tear down Constantine's old basilica than it was to build a new one. New Constantines were also in short supply, and the popes had to confront the fact that their own revenues would never suffice to build the new project. Indeed, the basilica had become a microcosm of the economic crisis facing the entire city. It also underscored the political limitations of the papacy.[140]

In many histories of Renaissance Rome, this is when the Renaissance ends. From this perspective, the Medici popes, Leo X and Clement VII (1523–1534) kept the dream of the *renovatio imperii* alive until the sack. But after 1527, Rome fell into the more austere age of the Counter Reformation. The reign of Paul III (1534–1549), who initiated the Council of Trent in 1548, was a transitional pontificate in this narrative because he, too, maintained the earlier Renaissance tastes and habits.

Seen from the vantage point of the revival of Empire, however, this Renaissance narrative ends much too quickly. In short, it neglects the deep continuities, indeed, the centrality, of the artistic and humanistic projects in Rome that furthered the imperial revival throughout the sixteenth century and beyond. Although the imperial Renaissance as a political revival headed by the pope as a new Caesar intent on territorial conquest did largely come to an end with the sack of Rome, the imperial Renaissance as a joint Constantinian venture of pope and imperial monarchy was just getting started. Catholic Reformation Rome did not displace this Renaissance. It merged with it. Indeed, the eventual success of the Catholic Reformation was the direct result of the papacy hitching its wagon to the new empires born of the Imperial Renaissance.

The reliance of the papacy on the military and financial aid of the rising power in the Italian peninsula, the Spanish monarchy, was already clear in

---

[140] Peter Partner, *Renaissance Rome* (Berkeley: University of California Press, 1976), p. 181. The author notes that "New St. Peter's was like a symbol of Roman urban progress. When St. Peter's grew, Rome grew; when the great church halted, so did the city."

1506 when Julius II used the soldiers of the Catholic King, Ferdinand, to conquer Bologna. This same dependency was again underlined in the following pontificate of Leo X. Although the Medici pope initially sided with the French monarch, Francis I, in the struggle for supremacy in Lombardy and Emilia Romagna, by 1520 Rome had entered into a secret alliance with the Holy Roman Emperor and King of Spain, Charles V. The victory of the papal-imperial alliance eventually left Milan as a fief of Charles V, and the papacy regained Parma and Piacenza.[141]

Regardless of the fear that Leo X had with being surrounded by an imperial monarch who ruled Sicily, Naples, and Milan, a growing political realism was taking root in the papal court and the rest of Italy. In the case of the papacy, this led Leo X and virtually all of his sixteenth-century successors to give up the ambition of Julius II to lead an imperial revival as papal Caesars. Rather, they increasingly acknowledged, if grudgingly, the political, military, and economic supremacy of the leading empire of the day, that of Charles V (1517–1558) and later his son Philip II (1558–1598).

This did not mean that they gave up their claims to spiritual supremacy over all of Christendom or temporal supremacy in the Papal State. On the contrary, they emphasized these aspects of their power all the more. But the early modern popes increasingly sought to cultivate the Constantinian imperial model whereby a Christian emperor, obedient to the popes just as Constantine had been, supported and protected papal Rome. On a temporal level, however, their state fell into the orbit of the Spanish imperial system in Italy.

The case of the construction of new St. Peter's illustrates this point. Although funding had dried up for the project by 1527, a deal was cut between Paul III Farnese and Charles V in 1537 that provided for renewed funding at a much higher and more consistent level. Details of this financing will be provided in the following chapter, but it is important to note here that this was the most extraordinary example of a Roman building project made possible by funding from the empire of Charles V.

This patronage also served Rome indirectly, especially to the extent that imperial military protection allowed the papacy to direct a far larger portion of its income to building up Rome. The other major example of this that constituted a secular counterpart to St. Peter's was the rebuilding of

---

[141] For the basic political narrative of this period, see the still-useful work of Leopold Von Ranke, *History of the Popes*, trans. E. Fowler (New York: Colonial Press, 1901), vol. 1, pp. 57–67.

the Capitoline Hill. This project had particular importance for the imperial revival in Rome, and it was again Michelangelo who was entrusted by Paul III with the job of designing the new buildings and piazza.

The ancient political center of Republican and Imperial Rome, the Capitoline in 1530 was a shadow of its former glory. The modest medieval town hall that stood at the center of the hill was not comparable to the great civic buildings of other Renaissance cities. Moreover, it was not easily accessible or suitable for the large processions and gatherings that marked civic ritual life in the sixteenth century. This inadequacy had been embarrassingly revealed when Charles V made his triumphal entry into the city in 1536 after his great victory in Tunis. Because there was no staircase able to accommodate the stream of horses, carriages, and soldiers, the procession had to make its way around the Capitoline Hill, thus depriving the Senator and civic government of Rome a chance to welcome and honor the emperor in the place most historically suited for such an occasion.[142]

Paul III (1534–1549) moved to correct this problem shortly after the visit. In a symbolically important act that emphasized the role of the Capitoline Hill as the center not just of the municipal government of papal Rome but as the center of Empire, the pope ordered the ancient bronze equestrian statue of Marcus Aurelius moved from the piazza in front of St. John Lateran, where it stood during the preceding centuries, to the Capitoline Hill in 1537. It was placed in the center of the piazza, directly in front of the Palazzo del Senatore. Later in the century, when the renovation of the piazza was complete, the statue stood at the center of a dramatic convex oval divided into twelve sections that gave the piazza its shape. It was designed in this fashion by Michelangelo to evoke the image of the legendary shields of Achilles and Alexander the Great that were transferred to the Roman Emperors. Thus, the equestrian statue of Marcus Aurelius was supported by the emperor's shield (Figure 1.5).[143]

In addition, Michelangelo designed facades for the Senator's palace, the Conservator's Palace and the New Palace that followed the colossal Order recommended by Vitruvius for palace architecture.[144] The palaces served to frame the statue on three sides while the open side facing the city led to a new monumental staircase that could accommodate the largest of processions. By

[142] James S. Ackerman, *The Architecture of Michelangelo* (Chicago: University of Chicago Press, 1986), pp. 152–153.

[143] Ibid., p. 169.

[144] Ibid., p. 154.

1.5. Replica of the Equestrian Statue of Emperor Marcus Aurelius, 1981 copy of 161–180 CE original. The original is in the Palazzo dei Conservatori, Rome, Italy. (Photograph: Ainari/Art Resource, NY.)

the late sixteenth century when it was finished, it was the greatest imperial space to be built in the Renaissance (Figure 1.6).[145]

But what empire, or empires, was it meant to serve and honor? Certainly it was meant to celebrate the ancient Roman Empire, standing as it did on the hill overlooking the ancient forum. The fact that Paul III chose to have the ancient equestrian statue brought there makes this much clear. Others have suggested that it also meant to honor Paul III as the successor of the emperor.[146] But the choice of the statue of Marcus Aurelius can also be interpreted as a sign of flattery to the emperor of the day, Charles V. He had been closely associated with Marcus Aurelius in the popular text written by Antonio de Guevara, *The Golden Book of Marcus Aurelius*. As a chaplain and courtier to the emperor, Guevara had dedicated the book to the emperor in the tradition of a mirror for princes, strongly advising Charles V to follow the example of Rome's philosopher emperor.

[145] *Vitruvius*, ed. Rowland, p. 2. Michelangelo's style, like that of Bramante and Romano, has often been described as Mannerist. But they remained Vitruvian in the broad sense described by Rowland: "Both Bramante and Michelangelo could invent strange new forms and still reconcile them to the limits of traditional classical aesthetics. Indeed, they recognized that, as Vitruvius insisted in his Book Six, flexibility was the very essence of architecture."
[146] Stinger, pp. 263–264.

1.6. Etienne Duperac, Engraving after Michelangelo Buonarroti's design for the Campidoglio, Capitoline Hill, Rome, Italy. (Photograph: Foto Marburg/Art Resource, NY.)

By association, the ancient statue could thus be seen as honoring the modern emperor as well. Placing it in the center of the piazza strongly implied that Charles V, as the successor of the ancient emperors, was a protector and patron of Rome just as they had been. The historical timing is critical to the interpretation because Paul III and Charles V had just reached the agreement that led to substantial Spanish funding for New St. Peter's. Although not abdicating papal sovereignty over his state, Paul III was pointing to a political reality of shared responsibility for the city that reflected the Constantinian model. He certainly could have ordered Michelangelo to cast a statue of himself for the spot, much like Julius II had done for the Piazza Maggiore of Bologna after his conquest of that city. But much had changed politically in the two decades since Julius II ruled.

Although the Capitoline restoration, the new St. Peter's, and the Farnese Palace embodied in their magnificence, size, and classical style the imperial ambitions of the Renaissance papacy, they also revealed that by the age of Paul III, those ambitions were increasingly joined with and dependent on the real political and economic power of the first modern emperor, Charles V (Figure 1.7).

Still, Papal Rome continued to be a central location and leader for the iconography and architectural models of empire as well as humanist scholarship

1.7. View of the Papal Basilica of Saint Peter, Vatican City, Rome, Italy. (Photograph: Album/Art Resource, NY.)

focused on the imperial theme. Throughout the sixteenth and seventeenth centuries, Rome maintained substantial cultural power, as well as its religious authority, even if earlier fantasies of being the leader of a temporal revival of empire came to an end. This was also true to varying degrees of other Italian states.

Although no Italian court ever became an imperial power in its own right, Italy provided the intellectual and cultural foundations for the empires that followed. Many of its leading artists, architects, intellectuals, noble families, and princes played central roles in the empires that did rise to fulfill the dream of full-scale imperial revival. This was true both of the territories that came under direct Spanish rule, Sicily, Naples, and Milan, as well as those that were informal client states of Spain, the papacy, Florence, Genoa, and Mantua. Italy subsequently remained a major player in the Imperial Renaissance throughout the early modern period and especially during the reigns of Charles V and his son Philip II.

Map 2.1. Europe.

2

THE RETURN OF CAESAR: THE HYBRID
EMPIRE OF CHARLES V, 1517 TO 1556

What security, what certainty was (Pope) Clement (VII) able to have that Caesar, not only in name and title Caesar, but (also in) theory, authority, and power similar to the ancient Caesars, did not aspire to restore to the imperial crown its pristine majesty and dignity?

Francesco Guicciardini describing the Holy Roman
Emperor Charles V in *The Political Discourses*[1]

Roughly two centuries after Petrarch had urged the Holy Roman Emperor Charles IV to imitate the ancient Caesars, there appeared on the European stage a new emperor, Charles V, who most closely resembled the Caesars of old in "theory, authority, and power." This was not a claim made lightly or rhetorically by a champion of an imperial revival as the elder Petrarch had been. Rather, it was the judgment of a former servant of the Florentine Republic who longed for its restoration, Francesco Guicciardini (1483–1540). As the author of *The History of Italy*, the *Political Discourses*, and *On the Discourses of Machiavelli,* among many other writings, the humanist-statesman was the principal sixteenth-century architect of the Italian national narrative that blamed foreigners like the kings of France and Spain for all of Italy's troubles after the French invasion of 1494.

He was also one of the central examples of a Renaissance historian who, following the ancient models of Livy, Tacitus, and others, embraced a hard-edged political realism in his analysis. His judgment of the power of Charles V was the result of more than three decades of political experience

---

[1] Francesco Guicciardini, *Discorsi Politici, in Opere Inedite di Francesco Guicciardini*, ed. Piero & Luigi Guicciardini (Florence: Barbara, Bianchi e comp., 1857), pp. 384. "Che securtà adunque, che certezza poteva avere Clemente, che Cesare, in chi non solo `e il nome e titulo Cesare, ma le ragioni, la autorità, la Potenza similie a quella delli antichi Cesari, non aspirassi a restituire la corona imperiale in quella prisitina sua maestà e dignità."

that spanned the period from 1512 to his death in 1540. His work included a term as ambassador to the Spanish court for the Republic of Florence (1512), courtier and military general for the Medici popes Leo X and Clement VII, governor of Modena for the Republic of Florence, and officeholder under the restored Medici government in the 1530s. His assessment and fear of the imperial power and agenda of Charles V was thus based on his first-hand knowledge of the emperor's actions and their consequences for Italy during the first half of his reign. It was also the result of a cold look at his vast political inheritance and pretensions in Italy.[2]

The grandson and heir of the Spanish monarchs, Ferdinand of Aragon and Isabella of Castile, and the Holy Roman Emperor and Empress, Maximilian I and Mary of Burgundy, Charles V inherited from them the largest collection of kingdoms and territories that any European monarch had ruled over since the time of Charlemagne. More specifically, the premature death of his father, Philip the Fair, in 1506 and the madness of his mother, Juana, daughter of Ferdinand and Isabella of Spain, left Charles, at the tender age of seventeen, ruler over the following territories: Castile and its New World possessions in the Caribbean, Aragon, Navarre, Naples, Sicily, the Balearic and Aeolian Islands, Sardinia, part of Burgundy, the Netherlands, and the Habsburg lands in Germany and Bohemia. To these he would add the duchy of Milan (1535), the former Aztec Empire in Mexico (1520), and the former Inca Empire in Peru (1534) in the course of his lifetime.[3]

The enormity of this collection of territories made it the object of much political reflection and anxiety in the first half of the sixteenth century. Comparisons with ancient Rome and the ancient Caesars by both friends and foes were inevitable. Guicciardini stated when referring to Charles V

---

[2] Ibid., p. 353. "Però se io temo che Cesare, quale io veddo che pretende al dominio di Italia, anzi forse alla monarchia de' christiani, e che non contento in Italia del regno di Napoli, ha ora occupato lo Stato di Milano, abbia a volere farsi signore di Firenze, farse padrone di Roma e di tanto Stato che tiene la Chiesa, e comandare a tutti con assoluta autorità, mi pare temerne più ragionevolmente che non fanno coloro che si assicurano del contrario."

[3] Among the many biographies of Charles V, see especially William Maltby, *The Reign of Charles V* (New York: Palgrave, 2002); Karl Brandi, *The Emperor Charles V*, trans. C. V. Wedgwood (London: J. Cape, 1960); Vicente de Cadenas y Vicent, *Carlos I de Castilla, señor de las Indias* (Madrid: Hidalguia, 1988); Manuel Fernández Alvarez, *Carlos V* (Madrid: Publicaciones Españolas, 1974); and Pierre Chaunu and Michèle Escamilla, *Charles Quint* (Fayard, 2000). See also the recent edited volumes: *Charles V, 1500–1558*, ed. Hugo Soly (Antwerp: Mercatorfonds, 1999); *Carlos V* (Granada: Universidad de Granada, 2000); and *L'Italia di Carlo V*, ed. Maria Visceglia (Rome: Viella, 2003).

that "the laws state that he is ruler (signore) of all the world; he has the example of the ancient Caesars."[4]

As a global emperor with legal claims to be "ruler of all the world," Charles V represented a central crossroads in the history of European politics: his empire, although rooted in the medieval European and Mediterranean worlds, took the first major steps on the new road toward the creation of modern European global empires. More concretely, his possessions constituted a new hybrid empire that was actually the fusion of three empires: two old empires that were rooted in medieval Europe and a new empire taking shape in the New World.

The Holy Roman Empire

The first of the old empires, the Holy Roman Empire, was ironically the weakest link in this Renaissance political hybrid and had the least in common with either ancient Rome or the emerging modern European empires. Although it gave Charles V the title of emperor and a collection of central European lands known formally as the Holy Roman Empire of the German nation, the political reality was that Charles V had the least amount of authority in the German lands, and they functioned least like an empire. In terms of the concrete ability to extract revenue, raise armies, and impose political allegiance and religious uniformity, Charles V was more truly a Caesar in his Spanish, Italian, and New World possessions than he was in Germany.

The fact that his title came through an election presided over by seven electors, six from German lands and one from Bohemia, underlined his dependence on them for political cooperation. He was able to collect far less income from these territories, and his legal jurisdiction was much more limited by local laws and feudal power than it was, for example, in the kingdom of Granada or any of the New World possessions. In short, Charles V was a dynastic monarch in the German lands where he held direct control, but in the imperial cities, German lands, and Bohemia ruled by the electors, he was a feudal overlord with far weaker jurisdiction. This was very far from the imperial power exercised by either the emperors of ancient Rome or by the "new princes" like his grandfather, king Ferdinand of Spain, whom Machiavelli had held up as a central example of powerful new monarchs in *The Prince*.

---

[4] Guicciardini, p. 388. The text reads: "poichè le leggi dicono che lui è signore di tutto il mondo: ha gli esempi degli antichi Cesari."

In contrast, Machiavelli provided one of the most concise descriptions of the limitations of imperial power in the Holy Roman Empire in the *Discourses*, where he wrote:

> And thus Germany is now divided between the Emperor, certain princes, the republics called free or imperial cities and the Swiss communities: and the reason why amongst these states with such a diversity of forms of government we see no wars, or only wars of short duration, is that this shadow of an Emperor, although having no direct power, yet has so much influence over them that, by interposing his authority as a conciliator and mediator, he quickly puts an end to any differences that occur between them.[5]

Even this critique of imperial power turned out to grant too much influence to the emperor during the reign of Charles V when many of the German princes, like Frederick of Saxony, revolted against his authority by supporting Martin Luther and his reformation after 1517, thereby further undermining imperial power in central Europe. Charles spent a vast amount of money and men trying to impose his rule on the German territories throughout his reign but with limited success. Although he won some important victories, he lost the war to keep Germany religiously united. The German lands thus represented the most bitter and costly political failure for Charles V. They also revealed the illusory nature of the Holy Roman Empire as an empire that was able to successfully project its power over both old and new territories.[6]

Indeed, for most of the sixteenth and seventeenth centuries, the Holy Roman Empire was consumed with internal religious wars and an external battle against the Ottoman Empire. The latter was constantly threatening to swallow up more and more of the territories of the Holy Roman Empire and subsequently demanding more of the military and financial resources of the emperors. These harsh political circumstances, combined with a lack of naval capabilities or ambitions, left the Germanic empire out of the picture of early modern imperial overseas expansion. In short, it was never a real empire by the classical or modern definitions of empire used here. Compared to Spain, France, Portugal, and Great Britain, it was a second-tier power that had no place in the game of modern empire building. It is primarily for this reason that this study will not include the Holy Roman Empire after the time of Charles V.

---

[5] N. Machiavelli, *The Discourses*, vol. 1, p. 379.

[6] For the failures of Charles V in Germany, see Thomas A. Brady, *German Histories in the Age of Reformations, 1400–1650* (Cambridge: Cambridge University Press, 2009), pp. 207–228.

Even in the time of Maximilian I and Charles V, it is only accurate to speak of an Imperial Renaissance in the Holy Roman Empire in a limited sense. Like the various Italian territories that had imperial aspirations, the Holy Roman Empire alone ultimately did not have the financial resources, military capabilities, or political cohesion needed to compete for global empires in the early modern period. Its zenith occurred in the early sixteenth century, but the fragmentation caused by the Reformation, combined with the constant warfare with the Ottomans, weakened it considerably between 1517 and 1555. Both of these factors also undermined any possibility of a coherent literary and/or artistic cultural program tied to the Italian Renaissance.

After the abdication of Charles V in 1555, which left the Holy Roman Empire and its title in the hands of his brother Ferdinand, this empire would continue to follow the definition of Machiavelli but with even less political cohesion and strength because of the division between Protestant and Catholic states in the German lands and Bohemia.

Charles V himself contributed to the weakening of the inheritance he had received from Maximilian by leaving to his son Philip II many lands that were originally ruled by Maximilian I and Mary of Burgundy, such as the Netherlands and Franche-Comte, and other traditional imperial fiefs such as the duchy of Milan. These lands became important parts of the Spanish Empire throughout the sixteenth and seventeenth centuries. Seen from the perspective of the dynastic politics of Ferdinand of Aragon and Maximilian I, Ferdinand won the gamble because it was the Spanish Empire, not the Holy Roman Empire, that became the dominant world power and modern global empire in the century after their deaths.

That said, the Holy Roman Empire did take part in some aspects of the imperial Renaissance for two primary reasons. First, on the theoretical level, the emperors were the presumed heirs of the Roman Empire dating back to the time of Charlemagne and the most natural political leaders to claim the mantle of the ancient Caesars. Second, on a practical political level, their relationship with the Northern Italian centers of the Imperial Renaissance as feudal overlords provided them close contact with major artistic and intellectual models.

Maximilian I, for example, had imitated Caesar in writing a history of his reign modeled after the *Commentaries* of Caesar. He also commissioned an unfinished series of illustrations entitled the *Triumph of Maximilian* (1516–1519) that was inspired by Mantegna's painted *Triumph of Caesar* in Mantua. The preeminent German Renaissance painter, Albrecht Durer, formed in part by travel and study in Northern Italy, drew a number of important sketches with strong classical themes, including a drawing of a triumphal arch, for the series. It serves as a modest example of imperial arts emerging in early sixteenth-century Germany.[7]

At the same time, the drawing also serves as a metaphor of the substantial difference between the conceptions of empire in Germany and Italy. Although the imagined arch followed ancient Roman triumphal arches in its general shape and conception, the details included a wide assortment of medieval images and decorative features that masked and overwhelmed the classical architectural elements of the arch. Images of everyone from Julius Caesar to Charlemagne to Frederick II were included on the structure that was topped with towers that look like they came from a medieval German cathedral. Like the Holy Roman Empire itself, Durer's arch thus obscured and transformed the classical ideal to a point at which the Roman past was hardly recognizable. At the same time, it was an imagined arch as opposed to a real construction built to mark a military victory. To push the metaphor one step further, the drawing was part of an imperial fantasy that was never finished.[8]

The Aragonese Mediterranean Empire

In contrast, the first real imperial triumphs modeled after ancient Roman celebrations took place in Italy in honor of Maximilian's grandson, Charles V. The primary triumphs, moreover, were not in any of the Italian cities claimed by the Holy Roman Empire but rather in Palermo, Messina, and Naples, cities that were part of Charles's Aragonese inheritance.[9] The papal cities of Bologna and Rome also staged major triumphs in the ancient style for Charles V in 1530 and 1536, respectively, and Florence, transformed from Republic to imperial duchy by Charles V and Cosimo de Medici, also put on perhaps the most elaborate of all classicized triumphs in 1536.

Fortunately for Charles V, the Mediterranean empire of the kingdom of Aragon proved to be a more reliable, resilient, and supportive part of

[7] See especially the classic work by Erwin Panofsky, *The Life and Art of Albrecht Durer* (Princeton, NJ: Princeton University Press, 2005) pp. 174–175; and K. Schutz, "Maximiliano y el arte," in *Los Reyes Católicos-Maximiliano I y los inicios de la Casa de Austria en España*, edited by Reyes y Mecenas (Madrid, 1992), pp. 233–251.

[8] Ibid., Panofsky, pp. 174–175. Panofsky sums up the limitations of the German Renaissance in the plastic arts concisely: "But the fact that most of Maximilian's enterprises existed, if at all, only on 'paper' is also characteristic of the German Renaissance as such. It illustrates the literary rather than the visual taste of an intelligentsia which felt more at home in the realm of words and ideas than in the world of forms and colors."

[9] Thomas DaCosta Kaufman, *Variations on the Imperial Theme: Studies in Ceremonial, Art, and Collecting in the Age of Maximilian II and Rudolf II* (New York: Garland Publishing, 1978), p. 11. Triumphs following the classical style in the Holy Roman Empire did not take place until the time of Rudolf (1576–1612).

his inheritance. This was a quintessential medieval Mediterranean empire, although it never claimed any imperial title or status. Still, it shared the features of other medieval merchant empires like Venice and Genoa that were described by sixteenth-century political writers like Giovanni Botero as "middle-sized" empires that owed their success to the fact that they were neither too large or two small.[10]

The Mediterranean possessions of Aragon included the island of Sicily, the Aeolian Islands, Sardinia, the Balearic Islands, and the kingdom of Naples. These territories brought Charles V considerable agricultural wealth, strategically important port cities like Palermo, Messina, and Naples, and the military and maritime talents of Italian soldiers and sailors.

The Italian states also provided a much closer link to ancient Rome and the ancient monuments and memories of the empire. In Naples, the fifteenth-century king Alfonso of Aragon cultivated a Renaissance court that was continued by the viceroys appointed by king Ferdinand and his successors. As an important part of the Roman Empire, Naples became a natural location for humanist reflections on antiquity as Petrarch's patron, king Robert of Naples, had already demonstrated in the fourteenth century. It would remain a center of reflection on the meaning of empire throughout the early modern period.

At the same time, direct rule over the kingdoms of Naples and Sicily also brought Charles V the responsibility of protecting their long and vulnerable coastlines from the constant threat posed by the Barbary pirates in North Africa and their sponsors, the Ottoman Empire. We have already seen in Chapter 1 that the rise of the Ottomans was the single largest spur to imperial aspirations in the West since at least the conquest of Constantinople in 1453.

But this threat was felt more acutely and widely by Charles V than by any of his predecessors simply because he had more territories that came under attack by the Ottoman emperors and their surrogates in North Africa. From Vienna to Sicily to Spain, the kingdoms of Charles V were subjected to attacks by the armies, navies, and pirates of the Ottomans. Some form of warfare against the Ottomans was thus a constant feature of his entire reign.

The Castilian Empire

More broadly, this was a continuation of the centuries-long struggle of the Christian West against Islam, a basic historic reality that was particularly fresh in Spain, where Charles V resided for ten out of the first twelve years – 1517

---

[10] Giovanni Botero, *Della Ragione di Stato* (Venice: Gioliti, 1598).

to 1520 and 1522 to 1529 – of his reign after coming into his political inheritance. Ferdinand and Isabella had only conquered Granada, the last Islamic kingdom of Spain, in 1492, and it was there that Charles V built his first and only major palace in the 1530s. It was a clear sign of the need he felt to put a decidedly Roman imperial stamp on the territory.[11]

It was as the king of Castile that Charles V was most truly an emperor in both a classical and a modern sense because it was under his rule that two previously sovereign empires, the Aztec and Inca empires of Mexico and Peru, respectively, were conquered and subjected to his rule by his Castilian subjects, Hernan Cortés and Francisco Pizarro. In Europe and Spain itself Charles was a dynastic monarch, someone who had inherited his kingdoms from the fusion of two major dynasties. It is important to note that the only new European territory that Charles V added to his inheritance was the duchy of Milan in 1535, a territory to which he had dynastic claims because his German ancestors had claimed it as an imperial fiefdom for centuries.

In relation to his European kingdoms, then, it is accurate to speak of Charles V as a dynastic or composite monarch. As with other monarchs who had acquired their territories through the successful marriage strategies and mergers of their ancestors, Charles V left intact many of the local laws and privileges of his distinct territories. There was no uniform imposition of law, taxation, military service requirements, or noble privileges and obligations. This composite nature of the economies, laws, and military policies of Charles V has often led historians to distinguish early modern empires from ancient Rome and to explicitly or implicitly judge his and other early modern empires as somehow lesser empires that were unable to exert the same level of control and uniformity that ancient Rome did.

Recent literature on ancient Rome, however, has pointed out that the Roman Empire, too, had a good deal of variation in the imposition of Roman law, economic policies, and military uniformity in its far-flung territories. Thus, making too great a distinction between ancient Roman imperialism and early modern imperialism, in this regard, at least, is misleading.

What Charles V shared with ancient Rome was the acquisition of vast new territories through military conquest and the imposition on these territories of a new language, law, religion, architectural and artistic tradition, economic and social system, and government backed up by a dominant military. In the New World, Charles V truly ruled as an emperor or imperial monarch, imposing generally uniform law, political structures, and military rule that

---

[11] For an excellent history of the Spanish kingdoms in the decades preceding Charles V, see John Edwards, *The Spain of the Catholic Monarchs, 1474–1520* (Oxford: Blackwell, 2000).

allowed him to extract treasure through plunder, taxation, and the extraction of natural resources, especially in the new viceroyalties of Mexico and Peru. This was the new imperial reality of the sixteenth century that legitimized comparisons between the empire of Charles V and ancient Rome, distinguished the new emperor from any of his medieval predecessors, and established a precedent for other envious early modern European monarchs.

Adding the Name of Caesar to Spanish King

The broad geographical and political boundaries of the hybrid empire of Charles V just established undoubtedly constituted great potential dynastic triumphs for his grandfathers, Maximilian and Ferdinand. They had both held together their territories and potentially enlarged them. But the actual shape of Charles V's empire ultimately depended on where their grandson decided to focus his political time, attention, and physical presence. Moreover, there was absolutely no guarantee that the young ruler would be successful in holding together the unruly group of territories. Challenges to his power were inevitable.

Although the monarchy of Charles V is described here as a hybrid of new and old forms of empire – as both a composite monarchy and imperial monarchy – he never used the terms "hybrid" or "composite" to describe his kingdoms. But he and his councilors did understand from an early point in his reign that they were far from united, and he clearly saw bringing them all together as part of his political mission. In 1520, shortly before leaving Spain for Germany, where he had just been elected Holy Roman Emperor, he explained his view of his territories to his concerned Castilian subjects, who were wary of sharing their king with the Germans. His reasons for leaving Spain to accept the title were clear:

> At last to me empire (imperium) has been conferred by the single consent of Germany with God, as I deem, willing and commanding. For truly he errs who reckons that by men or riches, by unlawful canvassing or stratagem the empire of the entire world is able to fall to anyone's lot. For from God himself alone is empire. Nor have I undertaken that charge of such great measure for my own sake. For well was I able to be content with the Spanish Empire (Hispano imperio) with the Balearics and Sardinia, with the Sicilian Kingdom, with a great part of Italy, Germany, and France and with another, as I might say, gold bearing world ... But here befalls a certain fatal necessity concerning matters which urges me to take sail. Furthermore decision must be taken out of proper respect for religion, whose enemy thus far has grown so that moreover neither the repose of

the commonwealth, nor the dignity of Spain nor finally the welfare of my kingdoms are able to tolerate such a threat. All these are hardly able to exist or be maintained unless I shall link Spain with Germany and add the name of Caesar to Spanish king.[12]

As this proclamation makes clear, Charles V and his political advisors favored the strategy of an imperial merger that would create a de facto mega-empire. They also understood from the beginning of his reign in 1517 that there were many opponents who threatened to undermine his rule. Both Francis I and the Ottomans loomed large as dark storm clouds that threatened to rain on his grand imperial parade, and a rebellious priest named Martin Luther was also cause for concern in Germany.

A struggle for power was not unexpected in the age of Machiavelli. The imperial election itself had been a hard-fought contest with Francis I that had cost Charles V an estimated 845,692 gold florins in payments to the electors and their councilors.[13] The emperor's assertion that it was God who granted empire notwithstanding, it was obvious that gold, successful lobbying, and savvy political advice and strategies played the dominant temporal roles in the attainment of the imperial title.

Charles V was surrounded from a very young age by a stable of formidable tutors, astute councilors, and savvy statesmen whose purpose was to groom him to rule his vast territories and to aid him in confronting the inevitable challenges to his power that arose. The most important of these men were steeped in Renaissance humanist learning. The lessons, books, and models that they provided for the young monarch were subsequently saturated with references to Roman antiquity and especially to the many lessons to be learned from the ancient Roman Empire. Their job, after all, was to ensure the new Caesar's success at ruling a vast empire, a new Rome. For humanists with imperial inclinations, the rule of Charles V was a bonanza, and they played a substantial role in shaping and reflecting his early political thinking and policies.

An early example of this was the creation of the device for the new monarch that emphasized the vastness of his realms. Crafted by an Italian humanist who was part of his court, the image depicted two columns meant to evoke the pillars of Hercules that once marked the end of the world from their position at the Straits of Gibraltar. But in the vast lands of Charles V, the

---

[12] Quote from John M. Headley, *The Emperor and His Chancellor* (New York: Cambridge University Press, 1983), pp. 10–11.

[13] Bruno Anatra, *Carlo V*, vol. 1, Fonti (Florence: La Nuova Italia, 1974) p. 39. Figures after F. Alvarez.

motto of Plus Ultra was paired with the columns to signify that his empire went beyond the pillars into a new world.[14]

This is not to say that all of the young prince's tutors fell neatly into the imperial tradition of Petrarch, Guarino, or Biondo. Most famously, Adrian of Utrecht, future pope Adrian VI (1522–1523), was an Erasmian humanist whose influence on Charles V has been analyzed at length. Erasmus himself had consistently vied for the attention and patronage of Charles V as well and dedicated his *Education of a Christian Prince* to him. This text, with its emphasis on peace making as one of the principal duties of the prince, was an important element of the Christian humanism of the Netherlands, where Charles V spent his formative years. When he and his Flemish councilors moved to Spain in 1517, this intellectual tradition went with them and enjoyed the protection and support of the king and his court.[15]

The Christian humanism of Erasmus undoubtedly had an early influence on the language and princely role that Charles V held vis-à-vis his responsibilities toward the Church as reflected in the 1520 speech quoted earlier. The views found in the *Education of a Christian Prince* stood squarely in the long "Mirror for Princes" literary tradition that stretched back to the medieval period. Like similar late-medieval works by Dante and Marsilio of Padua, all of these texts, to varying degrees, advocated a Christianized Ciceronian ideal of the generous, just, loved prince who was motivated by the classical virtues of wisdom, temperance, fortitude, justice, and Christian faith.[16]

Applied to the Christian Emperor, the vision of Erasmus saw Holy Roman Emperor and Pope ruling over Christendom side by side, each respecting the special realms of authority of the other. Specifically, the emperors granted spiritual supremacy to the popes and served as protectors of the Church and the popes respected and backed up the temporal supremacy of the emperor and other princes. Erasmus and his followers had no time for the imperial papacy of Julius II and wanted the popes out of the business of waging war, a view that certainly appealed to Charles V.

The single strongest sign of the ascendancy of this view in the court of Charles V in the 1520s was the election of Adrian of Utrecht as pope in 1522. There was strong lobbying for Adrian on the part of Charles V among the College of Cardinals, in part because the young monarch was pushing for a

---

[14] Earl Rosenthal, "Non plus Ultra, and the Columnar Device of Emperor Charles V," *Journal of the Warburg and Courthald Institutes*, Vol. 34, 1971, pp. 204–228.

[15] The classic work on Erasmus in Spain remains Marcel Bataillon, *Erasme et l'Espagne* (Barcelona: Critica, 1978).

[16] Examples included Bartolomeo Sacchi's *The Prince*, written for the Duke of Mantua (1471), and Giovanni Pontano's *The Prince*, written for Ferdinand of Naples (1468).

reform of the Church along the lines favored by Adrian, Erasmus, and others. At the same time, Charles V also wanted a political ally in Rome to help him consolidate his authority in Italy and throughout his realms.

But Pope Adrian VI died after less than two short years, and his death coincided with the decline of Erasmian influence and thinking in the court of Charles V more generally. By 1522, Charles had faced rebellions in Castile, war in Italy with the French, the rebellions of Martin Luther supported by the Duke of Saxony in Germany, and continued Ottoman aggression. In this world, Erasmian idealism, with its pacifist inclinations and suspected affinities with Luther, was of increasingly limited use and popularity. Although the Christian view of monarchy it extolled still provided good rhetorical value that the emperor would use throughout his career, continuous war and/or rebellion on multiple fronts required that Charles V take up the sword to maintain and expand his power. In short, Machiavellian realism, not Erasmian idealism, was the dominant, if veiled, political ideology of the king. This was clear from the earliest days of his rule.

Machiavelli and Charles V as the Imperial Prince

In May of 1519, Charles V wrote to Fabrizio Colonna, head of the powerful Roman imperialist noble family already prominent in the time of Petrarch, with an important request. It had come to the young monarch's attention that one of his Spanish subjects, Diego de las Casas from Seville, was in Rome and that with much skill and money he was engaging in various negotiations that were "of a bad quality, very offensive to our God and to our service."[17] Thus, the king was calling on Fabrizio, the famous condottiere who had served his grandfather, Ferdinand, so well, and toward whom he felt "full trust and true love," to act against las Casas in the following manner: he was to kidnap him, using "much secrecy and dissimulation," spirit him out of Rome to one of the Colonna castles in Naples, and then arrange to have him sent to Barcelona, where the king could administer proper justice. The king instructed Fabrizio to keep track of all of his expenses, which would be repaid, and he further assured him that if he took care of this important business, the king would be sure to take care of him.[18]

The letter, even if composed with the help and hand of one of the king's advisors, is striking for the calculating and ruthless political portrait it paints

[17] Biblioteca Santa Scholastica, Archivio Colonna, Personaggi Illustri, Busta AG, letter 2082. The text reads: "de mala qualidad, mucho en offensa de dios nuestro y del servico nuestro."
[18] Ibid.

of Charles V. No student of Erasmus here. Rather, he appears as the good student of Machiavelli that at least one of his first biographers claims he was. In the 1561 Italian version of the *Imperial History* by Pedro Mexia, the relatively brief sketch of Charles V added by the Italian translator, Ludovico Dolce, claims that although the emperor was not a particularly good student, he did have three favorite books, including *The Prince* of Machiavelli, that he used for political guidance.[19]

Machiavelli, like Guicciardini, was a humanist historian, child and servant of the Florentine Republic, and Italian patriot. He, too, mourned the passing of the Florentine Republic much as he mourned the fall of the Roman Republic. He was thus no fan of Caesar and carried on the opinion of Bruni and Poggio and all the others who saw him as a tyrant who deprived Rome of her liberty and was justifiably assassinated for it.

Still, Machiavelli praised Caesar for his military skills and the acquisition of power, and he wrote his book for a Medici prince, not a Republic, who he hoped would restore Italy's independence. Although he was clearly not an imperial humanist in the style of Biondo or Guarino, he nonetheless wrote an instructional text, perhaps *the* text, for absolutist princes who wanted to acquire and hold power. And the political reality, as Charles V revealed, was that the advice Machiavelli offered, not only in *The Prince* but also in the *Discourses* and *The Art of War*, served as important political guidance for emperors with global ambitions, as well as for local Italian princes. Charles V, in fact, was the most successful European ruler of his generation in Machiavellian terms: he won unprecedented glory and fame through the consolidation, expansion, presentation, and maintenance of his power, with the exception of the German lands.

By 1521, Charles V had a new political councilor, the Italian Mercurino Gattinara, who knew his Machiavelli and his ancient Roman history well. Under his tutelage, Italy became a central focus of imperial strategy and consolidation because it was seen as the key to the strength of the empire. Gattinara, like his contemporaries Machiavelli and Guicciardini, also dreamed of an Italy united under one prince, but in his case that prince was the emperor Charles V.[20]

---

[19] Pedro Mexia, *Le Vite di Tutti Gl'Imperadori da Giulio Cesare insino a Massimiliano*, trans. Lodovico Dolce (Venice: Olivier Alberti, 1597), p. 525v. Giralomo Bardi Fiorentino, in the sixth edition of the work, added the lives of Ferdinando I, Massimiliano II, and Ridolfo. The biography of Charles V was added in the 1561 Italian version by Ludovico Dolce.

[20] The best work on Gattinara remains John M. Headley, *The Emperor and His Chancellor*. The book constitutes in its own right an important chapter in the Imperial Renaissance.

The chancellor subsequently pushed for a vigorous engagement with Italian affairs that led the armies of Charles V into numerous decisive Italian wars in the 1520s. Scoring victories against France, the papacy, Florence, and Milan in 1521, 1525, and 1527, Charles was the dominant monarch in the peninsula by 1530. Moreover, together with his formal rule over Naples and Sicily, Charles V was on his way to gaining the informal control and allegiance of the majority of other Italian states: Genoa joined the imperial party when Andrea Doria abandoned the French during the wars of 1527; in Florence the Medici were installed by his general in 1527 and owed their power to his armies; and in the Papal State from Rome to Bologna, the defeat of the Medici pope, Clement VII, in 1527 ushered in a long period of imperial and Spanish domination. Only the Republic of Venice consistently maintained a strong, independent state in the following centuries.

The Imperial Renaissance in Italy, with intellectual and aesthetic roots two centuries deep, thus witnessed the beginning of a full political flowering and realization that resulted from being under the overt, or de facto, rule of a real emperor or imperial monarch. This was not something celebrated by many Italians, but it was a political reality recognized by the most astute among them. Guicciardini, in a bitter lament to Clement VII opposing the draft terms of the treaty of Bologna in 1529 that he felt gave too much to Charles V, complained that "in effect it makes him a universal lord and all the rest servants."[21]

The critique, moreover, did not end there. For Guicciardini, Charles V, like Julius Caesar, clearly deserved the name tyrant. This became clear in his response to the *Discourses* of Machiavelli, in which he generally agrees with his fellow Florentine's judgment that "As much as the founders of a republic or kingdom are praiseworthy even more are the founders of tyrannies hateful." Guicciardini argued that because the historical cases differ, it was necessary to look at the particulars and especially to judge if a tyrant who occupies a "free country" (*patria libera*) had any valid justification for doing so. Caesar, in his view, clearly did not, instead being motivated by the "ambition to dominate." Men like him were thus "inhumane and detestable."[22]

Similarly, he recalled from his own experience the case of the change in government in Florence in 1526 and 1527 in which a tyranny was imposed on the Florentines by the general of Charles V, the prince of Orange. This

---

[21] Guicciardini, p. 375. The text reads, "e in effetto a fare lui signore universale, e tutti li altri servi."

[22] Guicciardini, p. 23, *Considerazioni sui Discorsi del Machiavelli*, "E questa sorte di uomini, tra' quali fu Cesare, pieno di molte altre virtù, ma oppresso dalla ambizione del dominare, sono certo inumanissimi e destabili."

reminded him of the actions of the ancient Caesar, who merited the fullness of reprehension for his actions. The conflation of the action of the old and new Caesars made it clear that Charles V deserved the same.[23]

As these charges revealed, being compared too closely with Julius Caesar came with the potential cost of being named a tyrant. But for the humanists that surrounded the young emperor, there were many other imperial role models to choose from as the work of Antonio Guevara vividly demonstrated.

Marcus Aurelius as Ideal Emperor in the Spanish Renaissance

The first major example of imperial humanism emerging in the Spain of Charles V was *The Golden Book of Marcus Aurelius (1528)* and the *Mirror of Princes (1529)* by Antonio de Guevara, a Franciscan bishop, imperial councilor, and royal historian. Originally dedicated to Charles V, the two books, often printed together under the single title *The Golden Book*, had the specific purpose of providing advice for ordering the young emperor's states and life. As the product of an influential courtier, they had the full support of the emperor. Although frequently neglected by historians, they reveal the political mentalities and image of imperial rule cultivated by Charles V as much or more than any early text written in his vast realms.[24]

First published in Seville in 1528 and 1529, the two books were translated into numerous languages and published repeatedly during the sixteenth and seventeenth centuries. More specifically, there were fifty Spanish editions between 1528 and 1698; thirty-three Italian editions between 1542 and 1663; fifteen French editions between 1530 and 1593; eleven Dutch editions between 1565 and 1640; six English editions between 1534 and 1566; and three German editions between 1607 and 1610. Forty additional editions of the *Relox de principes* in various languages prior to 1700 brought the total number of editions published between 1527 and 1700 to roughly 158.[25] In short, these were two of the most successful books, judged by their

---

[23] Ibid., p. 24. "Chi adunque è autore nella patria libera di una tiranide, e lo fa per appetite di dominare, merita soma reprensione; e di questi fu Cesare."

[24] Guevara's text is never mentioned in many studies of the Spanish Empire, including Anthony Pagden's *Lord of All the World*, John Elliott's *Imperial Spain*, or in Henry Kamen's *Empire*. This is a noticeable gap in the historical literature that this study aims to fill. The neglect of Guevara points more broadly to the fact that the political history of the Spanish Empire has seldom been marked by the full integration of humanist historical production into its analysis.

[25] Antonio Palau y Dulcet, *Manual del Librero Hispanoamericano* (Barcelona: Libreria Palau, 1953), vol. 6, pp. 441–455.

publishing and translation history, written in Spain or any other part of the empire of Charles V during his reign.[26]

The extraordinary dissemination of the text in Spain, other parts of the empire, and Europe demonstrates the popularity of the political lessons and model of imperial rule contained in the book. As a variation on the earlier Renaissance theme of using the examples and writing of the Roman emperors as political models, it represented a continuation of the imperial humanism of Petrarch, Guarino, Biondo, and others. At the same time, it drew on the Christian mirror-of-princes tradition, including the writings of Erasmus. The final product was a synthesis of imperial humanist and Christian humanist thought that painted the picture of a stoic Roman emperor with many implicit Christian virtues.[27]

But Guevara's text also provided some stark contrasts with earlier imperial and Christian humanist writings in subject matter, form, and scholarly integrity, contrasts that reveal much about the different political environment of the early sixteenth century. Unlike earlier writers who wrote for relatively weak princes and for whom the example of Julius Caesar provided a necessary example of robust military power, Guevara wrote for an already powerful monarch who needed the wisdom to know how to use his power.[28]

By the time Guevara was writing his text, Charles V had established his military credentials. In addition to the Italian victories already noted, he had put down the Communero revolt in Spain in 1521, and his subjects in the New World had conquered the Aztec Empire. It was in this context of the rising military power of the Empire and the need to control it that Guevara chose Marcus Aurelius, not Julius Caesar, as his favored imperial model. He needed a Roman emperor who was free of some of the less attractive aspects of Julius Caesar and especially from the charge of tyranny. So, too, the memories of other contemporary Caesars like Julius II and Cesare Borgia were also fresh in Guevara's mind, and he was obviously not going to use them as models for Charles V.

At the same time, Guevara distinguished himself from the Erasmian tradition in both content and form by choosing a pagan role model as the primary source of political council and the primary, as opposed to secondary,

---

[26] Augustus Pallotta, "Reappraising Croce's Influence on Hispanic Studies in Italy: The Case of Guevara and Mexia," *Modern Language Studies*, Vol. 22, No. 3 (Summer, 1992), pp. 44–52.

[27] Augustin Redondo, *Antonio de Guevara et L'Espagne de Son Temps* (Geneva: Droz, 1976). This is the most expansive intellectual biography of Guevara to date, but the tendency to view him through an Erasmian lens distracts from other major humanist influences on his work, most especially those from Italy.

[28] For the broader European context of the text, see Simon A. Vosters, *Antonio de Guevara y Europa* (Salamanca: Ediciones Universidad Salamanca, 2009).

source of the text itself. More specifically, Guevara's *Golden Book* privileges the letters of Marcus Aurelius as the source for the political council that was offered to the emperor. They make up the heart of Guevara's text, and the author offers his gloss as the secondary level of council.

More accurately, it was Guevara's imagined view of the emperor and his person or voice that gave authority to the text that Guevara alone could not have hoped for. In a shrewd if deceptive literary move, Guevara presented his book as a combination of authentic but previously unknown letters of Marcus Aurelius and his own commentaries on related issues. He also added various opinions and texts from numerous other relevant ancient authors ranging from Plato and Plutarch to the author of the *Historia Augusta*, available in a newly edited version by Erasmus in 1518.[29]

The letters, as he presented them, were translations of a Greek manuscript authored by Marcus Aurelius that came from the library of none other than Lorenzo the Magnificent in Florence. This is a strong example of the reliance of Spanish Renaissance authors on Italian sources, even if they had to forge them, and it underlines the deepening connections both real and imagined of Spanish and Italian humanistic culture. It is also the most famous example of a Spanish author playing the forgery game that was so common in the Renaissance and that so often focused on the creation of ancient imperial documents such as the *Acts of Cesar* or the *Last Will of Cesar*.[30]

There is no evidence that Guevara had access to authentic texts by Marcus Aurelius. The first Renaissance editions of Greek manuscripts of the *Meditations* of Marcus Aurelius are those of the codex Palatino edited by Xilandro in Zurich in 1559 (the manuscript is now lost) and the fourteenth-century manuscript preserved in the Vatican Library to which Guevara had no known access.[31]

Guevara had critics in his own day who accused him of fabricating the letters of the ancient emperor. His rebuttal, apparently successful if the repeated publication of the book is any measure, was that he was actually indebted to

---

[29] The fifteenth-century Spanish humanist Alfonso de Palencia (1424–1492) had translated Plutarch into Castilian. He is an excellent example of an early humanist bridge between Italy and Spain who lived in Italy between 1447 and 1453, knew Leonardo Bruni, and wrote a history of Spain modeled on Livy's *Decades*.

[30] Anthony Grafton, *Forgers and Critics. Creativity and Duplicity in Western Scholarship* (Princeton, NJ: Princeton University Press, 1990). Grafton points out that the nostalgia for antiquity led to a "rich production" of forgeries such as the estimated 10,576 forged inscriptions from the great *Corpus Latino* and the *Last Testament of Caesar*. See pp. 26–31 in the Italian version, *Falsari e critici* (Einaudi, 1996).

[31] Marco Aurelio, *I ricordi*, trans. Francesco Cazzamini-Mussi, ed. Carlo Carena (Torino: Einaudi, 2003), p. xxi. The Vatican manuscript is cited as Mss. Vat. 1950.

his critics even if their intentions were not good. In his opinion, if he had actually written a work of such importance and "gravitas," drawing only on his own knowledge, the ancient Romans themselves would have erected a statue of him in Rome.[32] He goes on to rhetorically ask if it is really that difficult to believe in the discovery of an unknown ancient text in an age that witnessed the discovery of an entire new world.[33] In Guevara's case, at least, one of the consequences of empire was an increase in literary hubris and historical fabrication.

With this illustrious if fake ancient and contemporary Italian pedigree bolstering its authority, the imaginative forgery produced by Guevara began with a lengthy prologue written to Charles V that served to justify his choice of Marcus Aurelius as imperial model. As one of the most successful and revered emperors of Rome, Marcus Aurelius (ruled 161–180) was a perfect choice for a Renaissance audience. An important stoic philosopher, he wrote the *Meditations*, a text noted for the political ideals of duty and service. At the same time, he was successful on the battlefield. Guevara thus urged Charles V to imitate this "very wise" and "very powerful prince" and to take him as his primary model for ruling his empire. For Guevara and the many translators who dedicated new edition after new edition to rulers from all over Europe, the example of Marcus Aurelius was eminently worth following: "everything that Marcus Aurelius said and did is worth knowing and necessary to imitate." More specifically, the young Holy Roman Emperor and king of Spain was urged to take Marcus Aurelius as a "father in matters of governance," as an example for the virtues that marked his personal life, as a "teacher for his learning," and as a "competitor in his deeds."[34]

[32] Guevara, *Libro di Marco Aurelio con L'Horologio de Prencipi* (Venezia: Pietro Ricciardi, 1606), C5v. "Quelli che dicono, come io solo ho composto questa dottrina, mi fanno essere a loro obligato, benche l'intentione, con la quale dicono non sia buona, perche se fuisse cosi in effetto, ch'io havesse per mia scientia scritto tante sententie, et di tanta gravita, gli antichi Romani mi havrebbono rizzato una statua in Roma."

[33] Ibid., "Vediamo a nostro tempo quello, che non mai habbiamo veduto, vediamo cose non piu udite, et esperimentiamo un nuovo mondo, et poi vogliamo maravigliarci, che hora da nuovo si trovi un libro. Quantunque io habaia trovato M. Aurelio con molta diligentia, et sia stato studioso a tradurlo: non percio `e cosa giusta, ch'io sia lodato da i savi, ne accusato da gli invidiosi."

[34] Antonio de Guevara, *Marco Aurelio con el Relox de principes* (Seville: Cromberger, 1534). (BNM) The title page has no author or publication material, but inside the front cover someone has penciled in Antonio de Guevara Seville, 1534 (iiir.). The text reads, "todo lo que dixo y hizo Marco Aurelio es digno de saberse y necessario de imitar." And later, on the fifth page of a nonpaginated section titled the "Prologo sobre la obra" that followed the "Prologo General": "Nuestro Marco Aurelio fue philosopho muy sabio y principe muy poderoso; y por esta causa es razon que sea mas creydo que otro porque como principe contara los trabajos; y como philosopho dara los remedios. A este sabio philosopho y noble

Marcus Aurelius as political father and model for the king of Spain was made all the more appealing by Guevara through the creation of the ancient emperor's supposed Spanish lineage. Emphasizing the central role played by the Spanish-born emperors of ancient Rome from Spain – Trajan, Hadrian, and Theodosius – Guevara cultivated this increasingly common trope among Spanish humanist historians and chroniclers.[35] Writers such as Florian de Ocampo and Ambrosio Morales, to name the most famous, elaborated at length on this theme as they created the literary and historical foundations to support the contemporary political reality of a Spanish emperor or imperial monarch ruling over the new Roman Empire.

Guevara, then, was one of the first and most successful Spanish authors to begin building an imperial literary edifice that mirrored real imperial political power. His success was a literary reflection of the expansion of the imperial humanism of Flavio Biondo that presented the Roman Empire and its good emperors like Marcus Aurelius as the apex of political development in the ancient world and as the role models for Renaissance empires and emperors.

Charles V and the "Empire of the World"

The Imperial Coronation in Bologna, 1529 to 1530

A central moment in the construction of a classicized imperial persona for Charles V in a different medium was the triumphal procession and ceremonies held in Bologna in 1530 for his imperial coronation. Italian Renaissance monarchs like king Alfonso of Naples and Julius II had begun to imitate classical triumphs through the use of ephemeral constructions of triumphal arches and other devices in the middle of the fifteenth century. They had the same classical texts to instruct them that inspired the written *Trionfi* of Flavio Biondo and the painted *Triumph of Caesar* by Mantegna or the drawings of Durer. What they did not have was a real empire to celebrate, a fact that undermined the political substance, if not drama, of the triumphs they performed.

---

emperador tome vuestra magestad por ayo en su mocedad; por padre en su governacion; por adalid en sus guerras; por guion en sus jornadas; por amigo en sus trabajos: por exemplo en sus virtudes; por maestro en sus sciencias: por balanco en sus desseos: y por competidor en sus hazanas."

[35] Pierre Chaunu and Michèle Escamilla, *Charles Quint* (Fayard, 2000), pp. 265–266. The authors note that Guevara accompanied Charles V to Tunis and to Italy after the victories of 1535, and in this context they also point out that he was instrumental in fashioning the emperor as the new Trajan, although they curiously never mention his text.

With Charles V, however, political ritual mirrored political reality for the first time in many centuries. Put another way, the majesty of ritual pageantry in the antique imperial style was backed up by imperial political power and military victories in a way that it had not been since the time of the ancient Caesars.

After thirteen years of governing, with a string of military victories to his credit, Charles V had reached a political maturity and level of power unseen since antiquity. After his famous victory over Francis I at Pavia in 1525 and the occupation of the duchy of Milan shortly thereafter, Guicciardini wrote that "there is no doubt whatsoever that the power of Caesar, when he defeated and imprisoned the king of France, became most formidable in all of Italy."[36]

The triumphal entry into Bologna in 1529 for the imperial coronation was the first major triumph that marked the emperor's domination of Italy. It also had the effect of being an active part of that process. Not "just ritual" or hollow pageantry, the coronation and accompanying processions and celebrations were a part of imperial political strategy. Again, the master analyst, Guicciardini, forecast the coming of Charles V to Italy to claim the imperial crown even before it even happened in 1528. As he explained in a letter to pope Clement VII: "He will want to come to Rome for the imperial crown: it would be foolish not to expect it ... because with this trip he will double his power and reputation."[37]

Charles V had already received the first of the imperial crowns in 1520 in Aachen, an event that provided important comparisons and contrasts to the later Bologna ceremonies. On the one hand, the first coronation also brought him great reputation. But the means of attaining that crown, as well as the imagery and place of the event itself, underlined the medieval roots of the title. Held in the location of Charlemagne's court, the ceremonies were dominated by ritual acts such as the handing over of Charlemagne's sword to the new emperor. The crown and title of emperor had been purchased at a very high price, and the well-paid imperial electors played a central role in the ceremonies that emphasized their power as well.[38] This was a celebration of the old medieval empire, not the new.

---

[36] Guicciardini, *Discorsi*, p. 381. "E non è dubio alcuno che la Potenza de Cesare quando ebbe vinto e fatto prigione il re di Francia diventò formidolosa a tutta Italia."

[37] Ibid., p. 377. "Se sarà in Italia, vorrà andare a Roma per la corona dello imperio: sarà pazzia non lo aspettare, perchè volendo rompere seco, era meglio farlo innanzi venissi in Italia, che poi che con questa venuta arà duplicato le forze e la reputazione."

[38] De Cadenas y Vicent, pp. 172–174. One of the best primary accounts of the first coronation came from Castiglione, then papal ambassador, who wrote back to the pope with a description of the ceremonies.

Charles had arrived for the ceremonies with a relatively modest military presence of around 5,000 soldiers including 3,000 infantry and 1,200 men of arms in his personal guard. This was far from an imposing or threatening force – certainly not a victorious army celebrating a real triumph – and it reflected the still-untried military power of the new emperor. The fact that the Communero rebellion in Spain broke out in the same year as the coronation revealed that the title of Holy Roman Emperor alone did little to guarantee loyalty or increase real political power.[39]

The coronation that took place in Bologna, on the other hand, was all about projecting an image of real military and imperial might that had been won on the battlefields of Italy over the previous decade. Held in the second city of the Papal State, in part out of fear that the emperor might sack Rome again if it were held there, it was one of the major gatherings of the era as testified to by the many treatises and artistic productions dedicated to preserving its memory.[40]

Rather than one event, it was a series of events that began with the entry of Charles V into Bologna in November of 1529 for the official signing of the treaty of Bologna.[41] A dramatic contrast to the Aachen entry in both size and imagery, it was a fully classicized imperial military event that celebrated a victorious emperor and his armies. In addition to the Italian victories, word had reached the pope in October of 1529 of the victory of imperial forces over the Ottomans who had attacked Vienna, which added yet more luster to the event.[42]

The imperial parade entered Bologna from the west at the Porta San Felice led by 200 Burgundian men of arms announced by a group of trumpets. Numerous pieces of artillery pulled by German horses came next, followed by 4,000 German infantry and a squadron of men of arms including 600 Flemish and Burgundian soldiers. Then came the cavalry and the emperor himself riding a white horse and dressed in armor including a helmet topped by an imperial eagle. He carried a scepter in his right hand. Behind him were

[39] Pedro Mexia, *Historia Del Emperador Carlos V*, ed. Juan de Mata Carriazo (Madrid: Espasa-Calpe, 1945), pp. 197–200.
[40] The literature on the Bologna coronation is substantial. Vicente de Cadenas y Vicent, *Doble Coronacion de Carlos V en Bologna* (Madrid: Hidalguia, 1985) includes many of the primary accounts of the coronation and the events leading up to it. See also *La Imagen Triunfal del Emperador* (Madrid: Sociedad Estatal para la Commemoracion de los Centenarios de Felipe II y Carlos V, 2000).
[41] Among the historical accounts by contemporary historians are those of Pedro Mexia and Paolo Giovio. Pedro Mexia, *Historia Del Emperador Carlos V*, pp. 536–538; Paolo Giovio, *Storia*, trans. Lodovico Domenichi (Giovan Maria Bonelli: Venice, 1560), vol. 2, pp. 128–131.
[42] De Cadenas y Vicent, Vicente, p. 96.

two more large groups of high-ranking nobles, grandees, and knights, and finally 3,000 more Spanish infantry that were very well armed. In short, the emperor entered Bologna with the equivalent of two Roman legions that Paolo Giovio described as "quanto terribile per lo splendor dell'armi, et per la bravura dell'aspetto."[43]

The Porta San Felice had been decorated with portraits of the ancient emperors including Caesar, Augustus, Vespasian, and Trajan, and an ephemeral triumphal arch had also been erected outside of the gate. Charles V was met by fourteen Bolognese gentlemen, and once inside the gates by the bishop and clergy who were signing the Te Deus laudamus. As the procession moved down the Via Felice to the Piazza Maggiore where the pope was waiting, two gentlemen on either side of the emperor tossed out gold and silver coins from two large bags. Two additional triumphal arches along the route were decorated with later emperors including Constantine and Charlemagne.[44]

Once inside the Piazza Maggiore, the emperor processed to a raised platform, where pope Clement VII awaited him. After kissing the pope's feet and hand, the emperor and pope exchanged pleasant words and then went to their neighboring apartments in the Palazzo Acursio.

For the next three months, the emperor and pope lived side by side in the *palazzo publico* of Bologna while their respective political councilors worked on issues of mutual concern. The coronation, held in February of 1530, was a double coronation: Charles V received the iron crown as king of the Lombards on February 22 in the cathedral of St. Peter and the gold crown of Holy Roman Emperor on February 24 in the basilica of San Petronio.

Both rituals were fusions of Christian and imperial imagery. The first witnessed Charles V being anointed with the holy chrism usually reserved for use in the sacraments of baptism, confirmation, and ordination. He was then dressed in a large imperial mantle of gold brocade on purple.[45]

At this point, the pope and cardinals processed into the church and took their places and Mass was said. Afterward, the pope was given the crown itself, said a number of prayers over it, and then gave it to Cardinal Farnese, who placed it on the emperor's head. Charles V then approached the pope to render his obedience, and the pope, after embracing the emperor, gave a short speech that emphasized the obligations that came with the crown. First and foremost, the iron crown symbolized the emperor's right and

[43] Paolo Giovio, *Storia*, vol. 2, p. 128.
[44] Bonner Mithell, *The Majesty of the State* (Florence: Olshcki, 1986) p. 140.
[45] De Cadenas y Vicent, pp. 232–239.

responsibility to wield the iron sword against the infidel and other enemies of the Church.

> Your Holy Majesty and my son; God has conceded this gift of the great imperial dignity to you above all others; and this is the crown of iron, that God wants to be yours, so that with iron the enemies and infidel against the holy mother church are castigated and scattered; thus your majesty has to take up iron, that is arms, against the infidel and others who are against the holy mother Church; thus as your majesty is the leading king and Emperor of the Christians, so your majesty has to scatter all of the enemies of the Holy Faith and elevate the Christian name for the praise of God and of your majesty.[46]

The emperor responded that the only reason he had risked the dangerous sea voyage to come to Italy was to pacify Christianity and to make "good war" against the infidel Turks in order to advance Christianity. This reasoning certainly conformed to the role of emperors that various imperial humanists had been advocating for the past century, even if political realists like Guicciardini thought the trip was all about building power and reputation in Italy and Europe. As the successful defense of Vienna in 1532 and future victory against the Barbary pirates in 1535 were to prove, these agendas went hand in hand for Charles V.

The second coronation in the church of San Petronio was the central ritual for which all of the previous processions, feasting, and first coronation served as an elaborate prelude. Security was tight. On the day of the coronation, the plaza in front of the church was filled with 2,000 Spanish soldiers, and another 400 German soldiers guarded the temporary bridge that connected the church and palace where the pope and emperor resided. Two hundred additional soldiers were stationed at all of the gates leading into the cities, whose bridges were raised.[47]

The emperor was accompanied to the church by a large gathering of ranking noblemen from throughout his realms, four of whom carried the main symbols of his power: sword, scepter, orb, and crown. After processing into the

[46] Ibid., p. 232–233. The text reads: "Sacra M.ta et Figliol mio, Dio ha concesso questa gratia a voi più che altra persona di questa grande dignità imperiale, et questa si `e la Corona di Ferro, la quale Dio vuole che vostra M.ta si quella, si come cole Ferro se castiga et scaccia li Inimici et Infedeli contra la s.ta Matre Chiesa et tutta la Christianità, cosi vostra M.ta ha da pigliare il ferro cioè l'armi contro delli Infedeli et altri contra la S.ta Matre Chiesa, acciò che la M.ta vostra si come primo Re et Imperatore di christiani, vostra M.ta habbia ad scacciare tutti li Inimici della sua S.ta Fede et inalciare il nome christiano a laude a Dio et di vostra M.ta."

[47] Ibid., pp. 233–234.

church, saying a prayer at the main altar, and bowing to the pope, who was already seated, the emperor took his seat on an elevated platform on the left side of the church. Both pope and emperor were dressed in elaborate robes for the occasion, which began with a mass presided over by the pope.

After opening prayers, the coronation proceeded with the bestowing of the four symbols of power by the pope on the emperor. After the granting of scepter and sword with language reminiscent of the earlier coronation, the pope put the orb in the emperor's hands and proclaimed that God had bestowed on him the right to govern and reign over the whole world. The crowning with the golden imperial crown followed with the pope proclaiming that this was "the principle crown of the empire of the world," as he placed it on the head of the kneeling emperor.[48]

As a final material sign of the imperial might and glory just conferred, the cardinals Farnese and Ancona draped a new mantle on the emperor's shoulders that was covered with so many diamonds, pearls, rubies, and emeralds that is was reputed to be worth 500,000 gold ducats.[49]

Thus adorned in all of the material majesty that the Renaissance decorative arts could muster, Charles V listened as the pope finished saying the mass. Finally, the whole crowd left the church to begin a triumphal procession through the streets of Bologna. The pope and emperor rode side by side, the first mounted on a donkey and the second on a Spanish white horse, and more gold and silver coins were thrown to the crowds as the four-month stay of Charles V in Bologna came to its ritual climax.[50]

The impact of the triumphal entry, numerous feasts and festivals put on over the course of the winter, and the coronation rituals on the collective political imagination of the Italian ruling class gathered in Bologna would be hard to overestimate. Guicciardini, not surprisingly, was right when he complained to the pope that the coronation would vastly increase the emperor's power and reputation in Italy. In part, this was because it gave Charles V the opportunity to increase the loyalty of old allies and to attract new clients through the display of his vast wealth and military power. These were the keys to his imperial success. With unmatched patronage power, Charles V made good use of his time in Italy to distribute gifts, jobs, and titles to various Italian nobles, clergy, and artists.

He also benefited from his time in Italy in another important regard, namely becoming acquainted with central locations and artists of the

---

[48] Ibid., p. 236. "'e la prima corona dell'Imperio del Mondo."
[49] Ibid.
[50] Ibid., p. 237.

imperial Renaissance. His long Italian sojourn stretched into April of 1530, and it was during this period that the emperor met Titian, the painter who would define his painted image like no other artist. Tragically, a painting done by Titian at that time of Charles V in his imperial dress on his white horse was lost in a later fire. Still, many of Titian's portraits of the emperor remain, as he became his favorite painter.[51]

Also important for the development of the emperor's imperial aesthetics was time spent in Mantua. As described, Charles V stayed with Federico Gonzaga from March 26 to April 18 of 1530, where he was feted at Palazzo Te and the old palace in the center of town.[52] Giulio Romano had erected a copy of Trajan's column from Rome in the piazza San Pietro in honor of the emperor's visit, but rather than tell the story of Trajan's victory as the original did, Romano's column was decorated with paintings celebrating Charles, "the dominator of the world."[53] Mantua, in short, provided an immersion in the iconography of the imperial Renaissance and a theater in which everyone could play their appropriate roles.

Through a combination of this personal experience, as well as the influence of many Italian and Spanish advisors, the aesthetics of the imperial Renaissance in Italy increasingly became the preferred style of Charles V. The 1530 trip was formative in this regard, and having tasted the pleasures of Italy, the emperor was eager to build his own imperial palace, as his building program back in Spain most dramatically revealed.

The Roman Imperial Palace of Charles V in Granada

As important as the Bologna triumphs were as events that staged and bolstered the imperial persona of the emperor, they were ephemeral. Although memorialized in many treatises, some drawings and a few sculptural programs, their ability to serve as a continuous reminder of the emperor's presence was limited.[54] But this was not the case with another medium that the emperor and his court used to create and project an image of power and grandeur, namely the imperial palace.

---

[51] Ibid., p. 122.
[52] Ibid., p. 252.
[53] B. Mitchell, p. 147.
[54] For the major example of a sculptural program that memorialized the Bologna triumph, see *La Imagen Triunfal del Emperado (2000)*, where the sculptures on the frieze of the town hall of Taragona in Spain are studied in detail. This is the only sculptural cycle of its kind based on the events in Bologna.

2.1. Pedro Machuca and Luigi Machuca, Façade, Palace of Charles V, Granada, Spain, 1526–1550. (Photograph: SEF/Art Resource, NY.)

The emperor had established his major residence in Granada after moving there with his new bride, Isabella of Portugal, in 1526. During the first years, the couple lived in the old Nasrid palace in the center of the Alhambra fortress complex on the hill that overlooked the city. It had been the favored residence of his grandparents after they conquered the last Islamic kingdom of Spain in 1492.

Between 1528 and 1533, Charles V and Isabella were content to do some modest remodeling by adding a few rooms on the north side of the old palace. But on returning to Spain from his Italian and German travels between 1529 and 1533, Charles began building an entirely new palace that eventually became the major architectural symbol of his reign. It was distinguished by the classical style of a Roman imperial palace and proclaimed loudly in stone that Spain, following Italy, was a new center of a classical Roman architectural revival (Figure 2.1).[55]

At the same time, the palace was the most dramatic material sign that by 1533 Charles V was actively deepening his associations with and imitation

[55] Earl E Rosenthal, *The Palace of Charles V in Granada* (Princeton, NJ: Princeton University Press, 1985), p. xv. He describes the palace as "a rare iconographical type: the regal or imperial palace." This study remains the most expansive work on the palace. While rich in archival detail and formal architectural analysis, the study lacks adequate attention to the impact on the building of the Italian connections and travels of Charles V between 1529 and 1530.

of the ancient Roman emperors. To imperial devices, triumphs, paintings, and literary models he now added palace architecture, a development that also represented a new level of maturity for the imperial Renaissance more generally. With the palace in Granada, imperial Roman architecture and real imperial power merged with a fullness that Western Europe had not witnessed since antiquity.

This is not a surprising development when seen in light of the artistic and architectural tradition of the imperial Renaissance in Northern Italy and Rome. More specifically, Charles V, who spent weeks in Mantua in 1530 enjoying Giulio Romano's newly built Palazzo Te with Duke Federico Gonzaga, had first-hand knowledge of the imperial architectural revival through his Italian sojourn. It is subsequently in the context of his Italian travels of 1529 to 1530 and the imperial coronations of 1530 first and foremost that the decision to build the imperial palace following the colossal order of ancient Roman architecture must be viewed.

Although one early design for the palace dates to 1528, ground was not being cleared for the new palace until 1533, and the first reference to funding for the building comes in a letter of Charles V from 1534. It notes that that the emperor had granted the sum of 50,000 ducats for its construction.[56] Major decisions on the plan of the building thus took place when Charles was back on the ground in Spain, and it is inconceivable that the emperor did not play a major role in choosing and approving the final design for the building.[57] He did so, moreover, with Italian models and memories clearly in mind.

This was also the case for the architect chosen to design the building, Pedro Machuca, and the governor of the Alhambra, Luis Hurtado de Mendoza.[58]

---

[56] Besides Rosenthal on these points, see Cammy Brothers, "The Renaissance Reception of the Alhambra: The Letters of Andrea Navagero and the Palace of Charles V," in *Muqarnas*, Vol. 11, 1994, pp. 79–102. The letter from Charles noting the funding of the building is found in Rosenthal, document 5, pp. 266–267 and also cited by Brothers, p. 84.

[57] Rosenthal downplays the role that Charles V played in the conception of the building, giving the lion's share of credit to the presumed architect, Pedro Machuca, and the governor of the Alhambra, Luis Hurtado de Mendoza. He, and Brothers to a lesser extent, point to the long absences of Charles V from Spain. However, Charles was in Spain for seven out of ten years during the first decade when construction was underway, 1533 to 1543: Charles V was in Spain from September of 1517 to May of 1520; July of 1522 to July of 1529; April of 1533 to May of 1535; December of 1536 to November of 1539; December of 1541 to April of 1543; and September of 1556 to September of 1558, when he died. See Vicente de Cadenas y Vicent, *Diario del Emperador Carlos V* (Madrid: Hidalguia, 1992).

[58] E. Rosenthal, pp. 7–9. Luis Hurtado de Mendoza's family had been governors of the Alhambra since the conquest in 1492. See also Helen Nader, *The Mendoza Family in the Spanish Renaissance* (New Brunswick, NJ, 1979). Following Nader closely, Rosenthal states

Machuca spent the formative years of his youth in the Rome of Julius II, Bramante, Michelangelo, Raphael, and Giulio Romano. There he had ample opportunity to study both the ancient buildings of Rome and their early Renaissance imitations like the Tempietto, the palace of the Cancelleria, and the Vatican palace.[59]

In addition, by the time Machuca went to work on the Granada palace, he also most likely had access to some of the work of Vitruvius thanks to the translations and publications of the Milanese architect Cesare Cesariano, who was named Charles V's official architect in Milan in 1527 to 1528. Thus, through exposure to and study of both the example of ancient and Renaissance architectural examples and the theory of ancient architecture, he became well versed in the colossal order of the ancient imperial style that he applied with vigor to the imperial palace in Granada.[60]

The imposing square palace started by Machuca, if not brought to completion by him on his death in 1550, was an imperial triumph in stone. The Doric-order pilasters of the first story, common to ancient imperial palaces, project strength, as does the rusticated façade. The two-story main entrance with its fluted columns topped by a broad arch evokes the image of a triumphal arch. This leads into a striking interior oval courtyard. Unique in its size and application to Renaissance palace architecture, this space nonetheless followed earlier Italian examples such as the house of Mantegna in Mantua. It also followed the d'Este palace in Ferrara in the use of busts of ancient Roman emperors in its wall decoration.[61]

Never really needed as a living space as attested to by the fact that neither Charles V or any of the other Hapsburg or Bourbon kings of Spain ever resided there for any length of time, the palace was primarily a monument to the Roman imperial power of Charles V. It proclaimed definitively that

that the Mendoza "consciously cast themselves and their ancestors as the spiritual heirs of the ancient Romans in Spain – men of arms and letters." P. 247.

[59] C. Brothers, p. 86. Brothers suggests that Luis Mendoza had the most influence on the building, noting that his cousin, Rodrigo de Vivar y Mendoza, in 1508 had brought back to Spain from Rome the *Codex Escurialensis*, a book of drawings of ancient architecture perhaps by Giuliano da Sangallo.

[60] E. Rosenthal, *The Palace of Charles V*, pp. 234–237. Rosenthal notes that Machuca's "attention was focused on Italy," and especially the "Roman School" prior to 1520. He also suggests that he had access to the work of Cesariano, who translated part of Vitruvius in 1521, and Serlio's translation of the fourth book of Vitruvius from 1537. Manfredo Tafuri, *L'architettura del manierismo nel cinquecento europeo* (Rome: Officina Edizioni, 1966), pp. 194–195. Tafuri notes that Cesare Cesariano (1483–1543) was named an official architect of Charles V in Milan in 1527–1528.

[61] Ibid. For the thick description of the architectural details of the palace, see especially Rosenthal. A more succinct version is provided by C. Brothers.

the Alhambra, and Granada and Spain more generally, had returned to their ancient Roman roots. Even though the ruins of the ancient empire, like the Roman theatre near Seville, reminded Spaniards that they had once been a part of ancient Rome, the new palace stated with renewed classical architectural drama that they were now ruled by an emperor equal to the ancient rulers of Roman Spain.[62]

Although the Nasrid palace was preserved, the new Roman palace, by its size and the monumental orders it deployed, was a building that dominated the sight, literally cast a shadow on the old palace, and pronounced permanency. It was the architecture of imperial conquest that served multiple purposes: to celebrate victories already won, to definitively claim the territory for the victors, and to announce to foes, especially the Ottomans or their agents in Spain or Africa, that the new Roman emperor, the only true heir to ancient Rome, was now permanently back in lands that Islam had once claimed.

This last point, the most compelling strategic explanation for the location of the palace, was given added urgency by a revolt of the Islamic subjects of Charles V in the kingdom of Granada in 1526. In addition, in 1529 the eastern coast of Spain near Valencia had been raided by the Barbary pirates, and many Spaniards had been seized for the slave markets of North Africa.[63] In this political context, the palace served as added assurance to his Spanish subjects that their new Roman emperor was dedicated to protecting the gains of the *reconquista*, the Christian war against the Islamic rulers of Spain that had lasted for almost eight centuries and only ended with the capture of Granada in 1492.

Caesar and the Art of War

As the examples of Flavio Biondo and Pius II demonstrated in the mid-fifteenth century, a strong and recurring theme for popes and imperial

---

[62] Ibid., p. 248. Rosenthal provides one of the best descriptions of the relationship between imperial architecture and the imperial image of Charles V. It also applies more broadly to imperial monarchs throughout the period. P. 248, "By the early sixteenth century the classical style itself had gained metaphoric value in that it was associated with the ancient Romans, and when used for princely residences or honorific entries, it identified a ruler with the Roman emperors, whose skill in both administration and war was legendary ... contemporaries seem to have accepted architecture as the best evidence of the heroic qualities of ancient Rome. Hence, the Roman style, when used for the palace of a Renaissance prince, attributed to him the heroic virtues associated with Roman emperors – magnificence, majesty, courage, clemency, magnanimity, justice, and prudence, together with invincibility; and, in addition, the style was inevitably reminiscent of the stability and durability of the empire."

[63] John Lynch, *Spain Under the Habsburgs* (Oxford: Blackwell, 1981), vol. 1, p. 95.

humanists from the fifteenth century onward was the need to revive ancient Roman imperial military strength in order to combat the Ottoman threat. Clement VII, too, had made clear in his speeches in Bologna in 1530 that this remained a central motif in the sixteenth century.

With Charles V, this Italian imperial humanist rhetoric merged with the traditional Spanish language and agenda of the *reconquista* to create a powerful new variation on the theme. The emperor began to act on the rhetoric shortly after his coronation when he raised an army led by Spanish captains that joined the forces of his brother, Ferdinand, in the defense of Vienna against an Ottoman attack in 1532. Even though it was successful, this was a defensive action that fell far short of the dreams of an imperial military revival with enough strength to take the fight to the enemy as the ancient Caesars had once done.

But the revolt of 1526 in Granada, the attacks on Spain in 1529, and the fall of Tunis to the Barbary pirates in 1534 pushed Charles V to go on the offensive against the Ottomans for the first time. It proved to be a decisive moment in the military career of the emperor, because it witnessed the new Caesar imitating the original Caesar as he led his soldiers in the thick of a successful African battle.

War was a central reality and defining feature of Renaissance imperialism in the reign of Charles V and beyond. As the dominant theme of the *Commentaries* of Caesar, most especially, war was presented as the main vehicle to honor, fame, and glory for the new and aspiring emperors and imperial monarchs of the early modern period.

This was also the clear message of Machiavelli's *Art of War*, in which Caesar, if condemned for robbing the Republic of its liberty, was nonetheless presented as a major historical example of a successful practitioner of war. The ability to wage war, moreover, further legitimized power because it was a fundamental and core right of the modern state in the brave new world of Machiavelli.[64]

It was as one of history's most successful military strategists and fierce warriors, first and foremost, that Caesar was presented to Renaissance readers. Imitating him in this realm subsequently became an essential aspect of imperial rule. But Caesar was obviously not an easy act to follow because of the large number of his military victories and the geographical expanse of his conquests. It was one thing to imitate the imperial symbols and artistic

---

[64] Niccolò Machiavelli, *The Art of War*, trans. Christopher Lynch (Chicago: University of Chicago Press, 2003). Caesar's skill in war is praised more than a dozen times in Machiavelli's text, where both he and Pompey are described as able but not good men, p. 15.

trappings of empire. It was quite another matter to imitate the military might and success of Caesar and the ancient empire.

By 1535, however, the armies of Charles V had already won a series of impressive victories that put him on that path. To briefly summarize, by the young age of 35, Charles V could count important battles against the French at Pavia, the *Communero* and Islamic revolts in Spain, the French and papacy in 1527, and the Ottomans in Vienna in 1532.

This was a solid record, but it lacked one important element, namely the personal participation of the emperor in battle. This changed with the conquest of Tunis in 1535 when Charles put his life on the line as he led his men in battle. Together with all of the previous victories of his armies, this personal victory at Tunis cemented the emperor's reputation as a new Caesar in both word and deed.

These historical parallels were emphasized by contemporary imperial humanists such as the Italian historian Paolo Giovio, who recorded his version of the African campaign based on personal interviews he had with the emperor after the battle.[65] Giovio is the central example of an Italian humanist from the reign of Charles V who stood in the tradition of Petrarch, Biondo, and the Roman imperial humanists of the late fifteenth century. Like them, he found work in the papal court as a courtier for cardinals and eventually two popes, Leo X and Clement VII. He was in Rome from 1512, moved in the circles of the Roman Academy and the curia, and was named a professor of the University of Rome. A doctor by training, he had wide humanist interests and began writing his *History* as early as 1515.[66]

As a servant of two Medici popes and as someone who survived the sack of Rome, Giovio was not a natural supporter of the imperial cause. The first volume of his history, which covers the period up to 1527, shares much in common with Guicciardini's lament about the loss of Italian liberty in the face of foreign invasions. But Giovio was not a Republican in his political sympathies, a fact he made clear while in Florence as a representative of Leo X between 1516 and 1523. During this period he had the chance to meet and talk with Guicciardini, and certainly knew the Republican perspectives of many Florentines. But as the servant of the papal monarch, he advocated a strong prince as the best hope for restoring Italian liberty.[67]

---

[65] Paolo Giovio, *Historie del suo tempo*, vol. 2, p. 373. See also Barbara Agosti, *Paolo Giovio* (Florence: L. S. Olschki, 2008).

[66] T. C. Price Zimmermann, *Paolo Giovio: The Historian and the Crisis of Sixteenth-Century Italy* (Princeton, NJ: Princeton University Press, 1995), pp. 14–15.

[67] Ibid., p. 32.

Although he had the pope and not Charles V in mind as that prince prior to 1527, he was a political survivor and realist. By 1530, when he attended the coronation in Bologna, he had begun to develop a positive imperial image for Charles V, perhaps because he had been named *conte palatino* by the emperor. This patronage favor granted to him as part of the papal court in Bologna gave him the right to place the columns of Hercules from the imperial device on his own family coat of arms. Shortly thereafter, in 1532, he dedicated his treatise *Commentario delle cose de turchi* to Charles V.[68]

The text was clearly meant as a primer for Charles V, who, Giovio already assumed, was preparing to battle the Turk. His short history of the Ottomans is subsequently meant to help the emperor understand the nature and strength of his enemy. Besides a condensed chronicle of the rise of the Ottomans and their major military victories, Giovio also adds some later commentary on the advantages the Turkish soldiers have over the Christians including diet, discipline, and fierceness in battle.[69]

At the same time, Giovio uses the text to encourage Charles V to take up the fight "because God wants to guide the course of the universe towards the ancient monarchy to make your majesty, with only one victory, in effect like Caesar Augustus."[70] Writing as someone already incorporated into the growing circle of Italian clients of Charles V, Giovio's history of the battle for Tunis subsequently cast the emperor in a heroic light that evoked images of ancient Roman victories. His task was made easy by the facts of the story and the words of the emperor himself, who explained to Giovio that he had gone to battle for the sake of maintaining his reputation and with the hope of acquiring fame through a noble victory.[71]

With these ancient Roman motives, in 1535 the emperor gathered an impressive fleet and army from various parts of his empire. The specific target was Tunis, the new stronghold of Kheirredin Barbarossa. More generally, Charles V was fighting to halt the spread of Ottoman influence by depriving it of its major outpost in the central Mediterranean. At the same time,

---

[68] Ibid., p. 111.

[69] Paulo Giovio, *Commentario de le Cose De' Turchi, di Paulo Giovio, Vescovo di Nocera, a Carlo Quinto Imperadore Augusto* (Rome: Antonio Blado d'Asola, 1532). I consulted a copy found in a bound volume of numerous printed sixteenth-century texts. Biblioteca Universitaria Bologna (A.5.Tab.1.M.2.) 201(31) ff. 271–316.

[70] Ibid., f. 309r. The text reads: "V.M. à sotto il suo sceptro piu regni che nessuno altro Imperadore occidentale habia mai havuto, cosi Solimanno di potentia, et amplitudine d'Imperio avanza tutti quelli re esterni di che se l'ha memoria per l'historie, et par'che Dio voglia condurre le cose del'universo alla antica Monarchia per far V.M. con una sola vittoria, cosi in effetto come un Cesar Augusto."

[71] Giovio, *Historie*, p. 374.

he wanted to avenge the damage done to his reputation and honor by the recent enemy attacks on his kingdoms.

Barbarossa, who had recently been named the head of the Ottoman fleet, headed a potent naval force that threatened all of the Mediterranean territories of Charles V from the kingdom of Naples to Sicily to Sardinia to Spain itself. Using a form of naval guerilla warfare that persisted in the Mediterranean throughout the early modern period, Barbarossa and his men engaged in surprise attacks on coastal cities with the goal of capturing slaves that they sold or held for ransom in the African slave markets. This struck fear in the hearts of coastal dwellers, who lived under the constant threat of sudden raids. More imminently, there were rumors in 1534 that the Ottomans were preparing a fleet to sail against Sicily and Naples the following summer.[72]

The imperial forces raised for the Tunis campaign were formidable: roughly 140 vessels carrying as many as 30,000 soldiers. More specifically, the Italian contingent led by Andrea Doria counted thirty-eight ships that carried 13,000 soldiers, 8,000 German and 5,000 Italian. Another twenty-five Portuguese ships commanded by the brother of Queen Isabella joined them with 2,000 men, as did sixty other galleys from Flanders with an unspecified number of men. Charles V sailed from Barcelona with a fleet of nineteen ships that carried 8,000 Spanish infantry, 700 cavalry, and a great number of canon.[73]

Equal in size to ancient Roman navies but more powerful because of the Renaissance innovation of heavy canon, the imperial forces arrived off the coast of Africa in mid-June and first attacked the port of Goletta. After a few days of heavy fighting, the city fell and Charles V had his first African victory. Giovio recounts a telling encounter between the king of Tunis, Muley Hassan, who had lost his kingdom to Barbarossa in 1534, and Charles V following the victory. After the African king pledged his obedience and service to the emperor, Charles V replied that he had come to Africa to avenge the attacks that Barbarossa had made against his kingdoms for some time and to get rid of the corsairs that were the worst and most harmful men in the world. But then he embraced the king, exhibiting great clemency and ordering all of his men to do the same.[74]

The portrait drawn here with its emphasis on the virtues of clemency, honor, and justice could have come straight out of Petrarch's portrait of Julius Caesar or out of the *Commentaries* themselves. Giovio obviously knew

---

[72] Ibid., p. 354.
[73] Ibid., pp. 357–359.
[74] Ibid., pp. 368–370.

his imperial rhetoric well, and he applied it again to descriptions of the next phase of the battle that witnessed the conquest of Tunis.

Charles V famously led the assault in person, riding in the midst of his men next to the imperial standard with a look of "joy and confidence" on his face.[75] He then raised his voice in a great battle cry, according to Giovio, and threw himself into the fight "against the barbarians, in a manner that not only embraced the role of a spirited captain but also of a most valiant soldier, and he then acquired the honor of the civil (iron) crown." The literary echoes of the role of Caesar in battle could not have been stronger.[76]

The victory of the forces of Charles V at Tunis freed thousands of Christian slaves who joined in the fight, captured more than eighty enemy ships, and forced Barbarossa to flee to Algeria.[77] In the short term, it restored Muley Hassan to his throne, and the fortress of Goletta was left the in the hands of 1,000 Spanish soldiers who were supplied and paid by the Tunisian king as part of the agreement. Barbarossa and the Barbary pirates were thus deprived of one of their most important bases in the central Mediterranean, and an important blow was struck against the Ottomans.

The victory added military luster and substance to the imperial image of Charles V in all of Europe in a way that none of his many earlier victories had. Here, clearly, was the emperor of Petrarch's and Pius II's and Biondo's dreams, a new Caesar in image and deed winning victories against the new Carthaginians. As important as literary and artistic production were in paving the way for a Renaissance of Empire, the realization of such a dream ultimately depended on military force and victories. Triumphs and palaces were important signs, but it was Charles V as a successful warrior in the style of Caesar that truly established his imperial power, fame, and reputation.

In the Italian context, it was the history of Giovio in both form and content that best reflected this point of view. As a dense historical narrative that focused on politics and battles, Giovio's history sought to imitate the style of Livy, implying by its form that the exploits of his own day were of comparable importance and greatness to those of antiquity. To this end, the regular appearance of Charles V was an important element of the story, and he gave his imperial authority to the text with personal interjections and admonitions to Giovio to write about his battles.[78]

[75] Ibid., p. 375.
[76] Ibid., pp. 371–372: "In quell'assalto l'Imp. in persona, ... spinse in tal modo contra i Barbari, che fece l'ufficio non pur di Capitano animoso, ma ancora de valentissimo soldato, et acquistó ancora l'onore della corona civile."
[77] Lynch, p. 86; and Braudel.
[78] Giovio, *Historie*, p. 693.

That the military victories of Charles V were viewed as equal to those of ancient Rome was underscored by the Italian triumphs that followed his Tunis victory. The first of these were celebrated in Palermo and Messina in September and October of 1536, respectively. Those in Messina were the most lavish and began outside the city gates, where an ephemeral triumphal arch with two Victories welcomed the emperor. Two chariots came out to accompany the imperial entourage, including one drawn by captured Moors that carried a large golden trophy. The other carriage was large enough to carry twenty-four actors dressed in classical attire who surrounded a large globe on which stood a boy representing the emperor. A "truly imperial thing," it was as if one of the panels from Mantegna's *Triumph of Caesar* was being brought to life.[79]

The imperial theme continued when Charles V reached Naples in November, where he was greeted by yet more triumphal arches decorated with images of Caesar, Scipio, and Alexander the Great. Caesar, most noticeably, was shown proclaiming to Charles that "You are the greatest hero of our Rome."[80]

This great outpouring of heavily classicized processions and decoration also included festivities staged for the emperor in smaller Southern cities like Cosenza, Cava, Salerno, and Capua. All of these towns erected various ephemeral statues or arches in the ancient style decorated with inscriptions celebrating the age of a new *Pax Romana*. In Capua, a host of colossal statues representing the emperors Julius Caesar, Augustus, Vespasian, and Constantine lined the route of the new Caesar's procession.[81] Combined, all of these ceremonies revealed the quickly expanding revival of classical imperial imagery, allegory, and ritual even to the more minor cities of Italy. After a lengthy stay in Naples, the emperor made his way north to Rome in early 1536, where Pope Paul III welcomed him with the most symbolically important triumph of all. What a difference a decade made. The same emperor whose troops had sacked the city in 1527 was given the most magnificent triumphal procession witnessed in Renaissance Rome to date. Planned to imitate those of the ancient emperors, the procession went down the ancient *via triumphalis* to the Arch of Constantine. It then passed the Arch of Titus at the beginning of the ancient Forum, moved down the *via sacris* through the forum to the Arch of Septimius Severus and then to the Capitoline Hill. The ghost of Biondo would certainly have applauded the sight.[82]

[79] Bonner Mitchell, *The Majesty of State* (Florence: Olschki, 1986), pp. 152–154.

[80] Ibid., p. 158.

[81] Ibid., pp. 154–159.

[82] Ibid., pp. 160–166.

To the monuments of ancient empire were added ephemeral constructions for the triumph as it made its way from the forum to Piazza San Marco. There Antonio da Sangallo the younger had constructed a celebrated wooden triumphal arch dedicated to Charles V Augustus, Emperor of the Romans, as its main inscription read. When the procession finally made its way across the Tiber to St. Peter's, it found yet more imperial images at the main door of the Vatican that had been decorated with statues of the emperors Augustus and Constantine.[83]

Greeted by Paul III at the steps of St. Peter's, the emperor presented himself as the protector of Christendom that Pius II and every other pope following him had hoped for. Here, finally, was a flesh-and-blood Roman emperor to accompany the freshly painted Constantine of Giulio Romano in the Vatican palace. It was a Constantinian model of the relationship between pope and emperor that Clement VII had urged in his Bologna coronation speech of 1530. But it was with Charles V and Paul III that this idea gained substance in the form of military protection and economic patronage on an imperial scale.

The pope had given his strong support to the emperor's Tunis campaign when he granted an increased subsidy from the Spanish clergy in the amount of 252,000 ducats.[84] At the same time, the emperor's ambassador in Rome negotiated a renewal of the crusade indulgence that eventually included negotiations over the bull of St. Peter's that the pope was pushing anew to fund the church. The settlement that was agreed on in 1537 stipulated that the bull of St. Peter's would be attached to the bull of the crusade indulgence, and no separate income from that indulgence would go to Rome. Rather, 20,000 ducats would be paid annually to the Fabbrica of St. Peter's from the crusade indulgence that was normally reviewed and renewed by the pope every three years. In the final formula worked out in 1538, it was determined that 100,000 ducats would be paid to the Fabbrica every six years.[85]

This was a mutually beneficial arrangement that in the first six-year period from 1538 to 1542 brought to Charles V 730,000 ducats for his defense budget and to St. Peter's, 100,000 ducats.[86] The impact on the construction of New St. Peter's was dramatic. Payments from the crusade indulgence began to arrive in Rome in 1540, and during the next two years more than 62,000

[83] Ibid., p. 164.
[84] Dandelet, *Spanish Rome*, p. 45.
[85] Jose Goñi Gaztimbide, *Historia de la bula de Cruzada en España* (Vitoria, 1958), pp. 484–490.
[86] Tarsicio de Ascona, "Reforma del episcopado y del clero de España en tiempo de los Reyes Catolicos y de Carlos V (1475–1558)," in *Historia de la iglesia en España*, vol. III-1, p. 191.

ducats flowed into the papal coffers for the building.[87] This was suddenly real money on a consistent level, and it constituted 63 percent of the total income for the Fabbrica.[88]

In addition to this large sum, there was another source of income from the emperor's state closest to the Papal State, namely Naples. As part of the broader negotiations with Charles V in 1537, the papacy was allowed to collect various *esatione* from Naples that included a portion of pious bequests and money from the sale of the indulgence. This revenue totaled 6,000 scudi, or 6 percent of the total for the period from 1529 to 1542, and thus brought the total contributions to the Fabbrica from the emperor's lands to roughly 69 percent.[89]

In the next seven years of Paul III's pontificate, this pattern once again repeated itself with the crusade indulgence being renewed and the Fabbrica receiving its determined share. The total paid to St. Peter's from Spanish-ruled lands was 107,646 scudi, or 64 percent of the total.[90]

The year 1546 marked perhaps the most important watershed moment in the history of the new basilica. It was in that year that Paul III appointed Michelangelo as the chief architect of the building, and for the next eighteen years, sixteenth-century Rome's greatest artist worked first to demolish the work of his predecessor, Antonio da Sangallo, and then to begin the work that would largely determine the future design of the building. By his death in 1564, Michelangelo had built the supporting walls for the great dome of the church and roughly three quarters of the supporting drum was complete.

Significantly, it was again funding from Spanish-ruled lands in the age of Charles V that made up the majority of financing during this critical period. The reign of Julius III (1550–1555) witnessed the continuation of the crusade indulgence funding for New St. Peter's, as well as increased funding from revenues in Naples. Thus, between March of 1549 and March of 1556, 110,545 scudi were paid to the Fabbrica from the crusade indulgence and another 30,747 scudi came in from Naples.[91] Work on the church subsequently proceeded at a brisk pace as hundreds of masons, laborers, stonecutters, and others began to give material substance to the vision of Michelangelo, an imperial architectural vision paid for largely with money from the empire of Charles V.

---

[87] A.F.S.P., Arm. 24, F, 4, ff. 7v–10r.
[88] Ibid., f. 11v.
[89] Ibid., ff. 5v–pr.
[90] A.F.S.P., Arm. 24, F, 21, ff. 1v–10v.
[91] A.F.S.P., Arm. 25, C, 45, ff. 2r–26r.

New St. Peter's has not usually been noted as one of the imperial building projects of Charles V, but it was money that would have normally gone to his treasury that made rapid progress on the building possible in its most important phase. Far more money went to St. Peter's than to any of his other building projects, including the palace in Granada. Charles V, in short, was the primary economic patron of Michelangelo as he built the largest and most important temple of rising imperial Catholicism. Although the dramatic dome and bold classical façade of the church gradually emerged as Europe's greatest example of the imperial Renaissance in stone and marble, at its economic foundation, New St. Peter's was a monument to the imperial financial patronage of Charles V and his Spanish successors.

Charles V and Global Empire

The Age of Plunder

The triumphs of 1536 came less than a century after Mantegna and Flavio Biondo conjured the powerful memory of ancient Roman triumphs. Together they ritually announced to Europe that the military revival of ancient imperial power was now at hand. The previous two centuries had provided the literary blueprint and symbolic foundations for the revival, but it was the victories and conquests of Charles V and his armies that demonstrated the resurrection of real imperial power on a military and economic level.

Much of this was made possible, moreover, by the treasure that came from two other imperial conquests that were far more important to the history of empire than the victory at Tunis, namely the conquests of Mexico (1520) and Peru (1533–1535). Although the enormous plunder of those conquests was not literally paraded through Palermo, Naples, Rome, or Florence in 1536, it was present in the form of the men and arms for which it had paid. This was also true of all of the Italian victories that the armies of Charles V had won from 1520 onward, and all of his many additional military campaigns up to his abdication in 1555.

The empire of Charles V truly became a modern global imperial colossus when his Castilian subjects, Cortés and Pizarro, conquered the Aztec and Inca Empires in 1520 and 1534, respectively. It was then that Castilian soldiers, acting in the name of Charles I of Castile, fulfilled a basic requirement of one contemporary definition of empire used here: they conquered and submitted to their emperor's rule one or more previously sovereign states. All of the other territories of Charles V had come to him by inheritance, or, in the case of Milan, through ancient dynastic claims enforced in battle. But the conquests of Mexico and Peru constituted a radically different imperial moment marked by unprecedented plunder of the resources of the new territories together with the subjugation, suffering, and death of the conquered peoples.

The earlier Spanish domination and virtual annihilation of the native Arawak people in the Caribbean islands after the Columbian discoveries in 1492 were the first dramatic step in Spanish expansion in the Americas. But this early phase proved to be far less beneficial economically than originally hoped. The conquest of Granada increased the wealth, and arguably the reputation, of the Catholic Kings far more than their New World possessions.

But the conquests of Mexico and Peru were another story. Their acquisition for the empire of Charles V marked the emergence and recognition of a new imperial age on an epic scale. Signs of this were already present in 1520 when Charles V was presented with some of the Aztec treasure sent to him by Cortés shortly after the new emperor's first coronation in Aachen. These included the famous two large disks, one a large sun made of gold and the other a moon, described by the secretary and chronicler of Cortés, Francisco Lopez de Gomara. They were part of a shipment of treasure that served as an early sign of a flood of precious bullion that would transform the economies of Europe in ways completely unforeseen over the next 150 years.[92]

Unlike Europe, where the power of the emperor was more constrained by different privileges and laws in his composite states, in the Americas, the first generation of conquistadors engaged in outright plunder. In the Caribbean, the treasure was thin, but they took the land and enslaved the people. In Mexico and Peru they claimed enormous quantities of gold and silver while also claiming the land and exploiting the labor of the subjected peoples.

Ferdinand and Isabella initially allowed the conquistadors to set up an encomienda system on conquered lands in the Caribbean that often mirrored the economic system imposed on conquered Granada in 1492. In this system, the conquistadors claimed the rights over the labor of the conquered Indians to work on the encomendero's share of the conquered lands.[93] This resulted in tax revenue for the monarchy, but the amounts were not on a scale to considerably shift the economic balance of power in Europe.

---

[92] For the most recent and comprehensive study of New World treasure and the Spanish Empire in the early modern period, see John J. TePaske, *A New World of Gold and Silver*, ed. Kendall W. Brown (Leiden: Brill, 2010).

[93] On the encomienda system, see especially Silvio Zavala, *La Encomienda Indiana* (Mexico, 1973).

That changed dramatically with the conquests of Mexico and Peru. Treasure began to flow back to Seville and the royal coffers in unprecedented quantities between 1520 and 1535, the same years that the imperial armies were winning one battle after another in Europe and the Mediterranean. More specifically, in the period between 1516 and 1535, roughly 4,500,000 gold ducats from the New World had expanded the treasury of the young emperor.[94]

Not surprisingly, the great majority of the unexpected bonanza was quickly used for war. In the period between 1516 and 1535, New World bullion accounted for roughly 25 percent of the total war budget, an amount equivalent to the emperor's revenues from his Italian kingdoms of Naples and Sicily that were used for the same cause.[95]

The flow of New World gold and silver increased dramatically in the following two decades. Between 1536 and 1556, more than 31,000,000 gold ducats bolstered the treasury of Charles V.[96] The percentage of the war budget paid for with American gold and silver increased even further. The military strength of Old World Empire, in short, was directly related to New World treasure. The central focus of the imperial project in the Americas from the perspective of the court of Charles V was subsequently the extraction of as much treasure as possible to fund his never-ending wars.

This was raw and exploitative imperialism, and the early recognition of the financial importance of Mexico and Peru led the emperor and his government in Spain to impose a more uniform imperial program on the new territories. The old conquistadors like Cortés were brought home and granted titles, and powerful viceroys, imitating those of Naples and Sicily, were appointed to rule in the emperor's place. Courts were established, judges were appointed, and permanent armies were maintained to back up imperial power. The Church, completely under the power of the emperor because he, like Ferdinand, had been granted the right of the *patronato real* for all New World conquests, constituted another branch of monarchical power. So, too, did the new tribunals of the Spanish Inquisition that were eventually established in Mexico and Peru.

This form of imperialism fundamentally transformed the polity, language, law, economy, religion, social system, and military of the subject states over the next century. Dominant military power – canon, steel swords and armor, and armored cavalry – gave the Spaniards the physical means to do so. The

---

[94] Bruno Anatra, *Carlo V, I Fonti*, p. 72.
[95] James Tracy, *Charles V, Impresario of War* (Cambridge: Cambridge University Press, 2002), p. 182.
[96] Ibid.

memories, models, and ideas from Roman antiquity, together with ubiquitous religious language drawn straight from the *reconquista*, gave them the rhetorical firepower they needed to justify their conquest and the extraordinary amount of human suffering and death that it brought with it.

At its root, the ideology of conquest in the New World grew straight out of the ideas and culture of the Imperial Renaissance in Italy. Alexander VI, in his act of investiture of 1493, already put this stamp on the discoveries when he gave the kings of Castile and Leon what Las Casas described as "supreme and sovereign empire and lordship of that whole universal world of the Indies, establishing them as emperors over many kings."[97] Cortés, moreover, exhorted his men to follow the example of the ancient Romans when preparing to conquer Mexico. According to his follower and historian, Bernal Diaz, all of the men "responded that we would follow his orders, that the die was cast for good fortune, as Caesar said at the Rubicon."[98]

Even though the example of the Roman Empire was used as a point of comparison and contrast for the New World Empire, there were also important differences between the earlier writers and those of the sixteenth century. Although fourteenth- and fifteenth-century Renaissance writers had presented ancient models to learn from and imitate with a whimsical eye toward the future revival of empire, in the age of Charles V, writers had a real empire as the subject of reflection. Moreover, for many of the writers, the New World colonies looked far more like the ancient barbarian lands of Gaul, Britain, or Germany than their other "barbarians," the Ottomans. They subsequently also had a new "enemy" to define and understand. At the same time, the magnitude of their conquest led them to sometimes boast that they and their emperor had surpassed the ancient Romans and that their victories were greater than even those of Caesar.

These parallels often increased the importance of the ancient texts as they continued to be the dominant tools used to make sense of, justify, and explain the New World Empire. In this astonishing moment that the historian Francisco Lopez de Gomara described as one of the most important events in world history, surpassed only by the Creation and Incarnation, ancient Rome was a critical point of comparison and contrast. Indeed, it took on a new immediacy vis-à-vis the New World, where authors like Cortés, Sepúlveda, and Gomara all looked on the Spanish conquest using a

---

[97] On this theme, see especially David A. Lupher, *Romans in the New World* (Ann Arbor: University of Michigan Press, 2009), pp. 128–130.

[98] Quoted in John Hale, *The Civilization of Europe in the Renaissance* (New York: Atheneum, 1994), pp. 192–193.

Roman mirror. How could it have been any other way in the early sixteenth century when the major point of historical reference for European humanists was ancient Rome?[99]

Imperial Scholasticism

Imperial humanism was anything but static, however, and the American conquests led to a new wave of literary production, especially in the realms of history writing and political treatises that focused on the fresh ethical questions raised by the conquests of Mexico and Peru. These led to major new developments in imperial humanism that included but also went well beyond evoking the memories of Caesar in war, the triumphs of ancient Rome, or the glories of ancient art and architecture.

Rather, imperial humanists, seeking to justify the American conquests, turned to one of the other major streams of Renaissance thought, scholasticism, for the moral justification of imperial conquest. The critical figure for this development in the age of Charles V was Juan Ginés de Sepúlveda (1489–1573), a royal historian and chaplain since 1536, when Sepúlveda had met the emperor in Rome and joined his court.

Raised near Cordoba, where he studied Latin and Greek during grammar school, Sepúlveda's academic training and profile embodied the thick intellectual exchange and convergence of Spain and Italy in the late fifteenth and early sixteenth centuries. His university training took place first at the new university in Alcala de Henares, a school that embraced the Italian curricular innovation of the *studia humanitatis* with its focus on grammar, rhetoric, history, poetry, and moral philosophy.

In 1510, the year Sepúlveda arrived in Alcala, Spain's most gifted humanist, Antonio Nebrija, had joined the faculty to teach rhetoric and lead the team that produced the famous Complutensian Polyglot bible. Nebrija had been trained at the Spanish College in Bologna and, on returning to Spain, had written the most important Latin grammar produced in Renaissance Iberia. An example of another form of imperial humanism, a Castilian edition of Nebrija's grammar was dedicated to Queen Isabella with the reminder that language, in this case classical Latin, was an essential tool of empire.

Sepúlveda followed in Nebrija's footsteps when he went to the Spanish College in Bologna to pursue doctoral studies between 1515 and 1523. He had earned another degree in theology in Siguenza after his years in Alcala

---

[99] The Roman theme in colonial Latin American history writing is also treated by Sabine MacCormack, *On the Wings of Time* (Princeton, NJ: Princeton University Press, 2007).

and was also ordained in that period. With solid Greek translation skills, Sepúlveda turned his attention to Aristotle during his time in Bologna. He studied with Pietro Pomponazzi, among others, and was also introduced into a broad and influential Italian circle that included Cardinal Giulio de Medici (the future Pope Clement VII), Alberto Pio (the Prince of Carpi), Hercules Gonzaga, and Adrian of Utrecht (the future pope Adrian VI).[100]

These contacts provided Sepúlveda with an essential patronage network, and after receiving his doctorate in 1523 he moved to Rome where he spent most of the next thirteen years. It was thus in the epicenter of the imperial Renaissance that Sepúlveda first began his real career. Like his Italian counterpart, Giovio, he found work in the papal curia, where he held the title of translator and commentator on Aristotle from 1526 to 1536. It was there that he published a translation of the Commentary of Alejandro de Afrodisia on the *Metaphysics* of Aristotle under the patronage of Clement VII in 1527.[101]

Sepúlveda's academic writing took a political turn in the aftermath of the sack of Rome in 1527, and in 1529 he wrote his first text, *Ad Carolum V, ut bellum suscipiat in Turcas*, that directly linked him to the long line of imperial humanists going back to Pius II. Dedicated to Charles V, it was an admonition to the emperor to lead a war against the Turk. Like so many of the earlier humanists who tried to inspire the monarchs and emperors of their day to take the fight to the modern Carthaginians, Sepúlveda also used classical parallels and images of the ancient Caesars as models for his emperor.

Unlike so many of his earlier predecessors, however, Sepúlveda had the good fortune of seeing his advice acted on successfully when Charles V triumphed in Tunis in 1535. By the following year when the emperor visited Rome, moreover, Sepúlveda had also written another treatise, *Demócrates Primero*, that justified warfare generally by using the war against the Ottomans as a central example. It was also the foundation for his later writings that justified the Spanish war against the American Indians. More immediately, in 1536, it added to the probable reasons that Charles V appointed him as one of his official royal historians.

If there was ever any doubt, the emperor's embrace of Sepúlveda, even if he had been a courtier of Clement VII, also represented another triumph of imperial humanism over Erasmian humanism in his court. Sepúlveda had composed his first just war treatise in response to a student protest at the

[100] *Diccionario de historia eclesiastica de España*, ed. Quintin Aldea Vaquero, Tomas Marin Martinez, and Jose Vives Gatell (Madrid: Instituto Enrique Florez, 1972), vol. IV, S–Z, pp. 2433–2437.
[101] Ibid.

Spanish College in Bologna where students were arguing that all war was against Christianity. They were apparently inspired by the pacifist treatise of Erasmus, and Sepúlveda aimed to set them straight.[102]

Charles V, perpetually at war throughout the first two decades of his rule, obviously had need of an academic proponent of just war in his court. Moreover, the fact that Sepúlveda was eventually appointed to tutor the prince, Philip II, revealed the extent to which the general intellectual pedigree and positions of the author of *Democrates Primero* were trusted. In short, Sepúlveda's broad worldview, shaped by two decades of immersion in humanist and Aristotelian thought and tempered by the political realities of Italy between 1517 and 1536, reflected the mentalities of the court. His was a virulent ideology of empire, forged in the military struggles of Europe and the Mediterranean world, and it was Sepúlveda who became the most visible and strident advocate for its application to the conquest of the New World.

By the time Sepúlveda became an official part of the court in 1536, two basic realities of the New World Empire were very clear: (1) it brought immense wealth for the emperor that was indispensable for his military needs, and (2) the seizing of that wealth from the native people and their subsequent subjugation brought strong moral challenges that had to be answered. It fell to Sepúlveda, above all others, to respond to the moral challenges, especially those so lucidly and convincingly laid out by Bartolomé de las Casas.

Las Casas (1474–1566), educated in a grammar school of his native Seville and later in the cathedral school of Granada, was the son of a merchant who had traveled to the New World with Columbus on his second voyage. After a brief career as a soldier in Granada, the younger Las Casas also went to Santo Domingo in 1502, where he was given land and Indian slaves by the governor, Diego Colón. Ordained a priest sometime between 1510 and 1512, Las Casas was increasingly troubled by the harsh treatment of the Indians, and he renounced his own Indian servants in 1514. After this "conversion," he turned his attention to trying to defend the Indians by both exposing and criticizing what he saw as an unjustified Spanish war against the native people. Increasingly, he condemned the illegitimate theft of their land and property, the killing of large numbers of Indians, and the enslavement of many others.[103]

Using considerable rhetorical skills that were themselves the product of a modest Renaissance education, Las Casas waged a persistent literary

[102] Ibid.
[103] *Diccionario de historia eclesiastica de España*, ed. Quintin Aldea Vaquero, Tomas Marin Martinez, and Jose Vives Gatell (Madrid: Instituto Enrique Flores, 1972), vol. I, pp. 374–376.

campaign against the conquistadors and their supporters in Iberia starting in 1516 with treatises addressed to Charles V and then a personal visit to the court in 1517. For the following thirty years as a Dominican priest and bishop of Nicaragua and Chiapas, he wrote letters and treatises condemning the conquistadors and especially the encomienda system. Most famously, in 1543 he wrote the important treatise, *A Brief Account of the Destruction of the Indies*, which he dedicated to the future king Philip II. It was published in 1552.[104]

Las Casas was shrewd. He was careful to distinguish between the atrocities of the conquistadors and the rights of the emperor. He maintained the right of the soldiers and governors, for example, to use force to protect missionaries in their work of converting the Indians, which he supported as a bishop himself. In that sense, at least, his work was also a part of the imperial project. But he cast Charles V as the protector of the Indians against the early conquistadors and argued that Christian ethics and theology demanded that the emperor protect the property and political rights of the Native Americans.

Charles V was not deaf to these arguments or unaware of the damage to his reputation that Spanish atrocities in the New World could cause. He was well informed of the theological and legal debates swirling around the ethical issues born of the conquest and especially the treatment and status of the Indians. Most importantly, Spanish theologians of the Salamanca school, led by Francisco della Vitoria, a Dominican professor at Salamanca, crafted the first sophisticated natural law argument in favor of the natural rights and sovereignty of the Indians.

Partially in response to this theological pressure, in 1542, the Council of the Indies, with the support of Charles V, passed the New Laws. These laws technically paved the way for the restoration to the Indians of their land and property and acknowledged their status as free subjects of the emperor. Most dramatically, they were supposed to eliminate the encomienda system that Las Casas harshly condemned. They did this primarily by denying the original encomenderos the right to pass their lands on to their heirs. This last provision, although certainly favoring the Indians, also served the political purpose of undermining the emergence of a powerful new class of landowners in the New World.

Like virtually all of the reforms urged by Las Casas and passed by Charles V, however, these laws were changed in the face of protest, watered down, or

---

[104] The collected works of Bartolomé de las Casas fill fourteen volumes. For the most recent complete edition, see Fray Bartolomé de las Casas, *Obras Completas*, ed. Paolino Castañeda Delgado (Madrid: Allianza Editorial, 1990).

simply not enforced effectively during his reign. Even though they did provide an effective tool to promote the appearance of imperial and Christian justice, they had a limited impact in the 1540s and 1550s. Most significantly, they did not go so far as to legitimize the strongest and core criticism of Las Casas that the wars of conquest were unjustifiable.

The views of Las Casas were, after all, a clear challenge not just to the conquistadors but to a large percentage of the whole imperial project. Most obviously, Las Casas did not approve of the plunder of Cortés or Pizarro, which included the many millions of ducats mentioned earlier that went into the imperial coffers. Certainly Charles V did not move to give back any of the treasure that was fueling his armies. That plundering continued, of course, in the 1540s, as did war against any native rebellions. If the moral admonitions of Las Casas had won the day, the plunder and war would have ended or been sharply reduced and revenues from the New World would have dried up. But they did not.

At its most base economic level, millions of ducats for the emperor and many millions more for his subjects were at stake in the debate over whether the war against the Indians of the New World was justified. In the 1540s, the expensive wars of Charles V continued, especially in Germany, making the debate all the more important for the immediate military budget.

Sepúlveda, the royal historian, arguing a position that was initially supported by the government of Charles V through various highly ranked Councils in Spain, entered into the argument with his treatise of 1545 to 1550, *Democrates secundus, Concerning the Just Cause of the War*.[105] In it, he directly argued that the Spanish war against the American Indians was a just war. Drawing on the works of Aristotle in his *Politics* and more broadly on Thomistic reasoning and natural law, the treatise uses scholasticism as its philosophical foundation. At the same time, it incorporated a strong humanist argument into the text, using the Roman Empire as a parallel example. Thus, scholastic reasoning was bolstered by the persuasive power of Roman historical precedent to form a virulent new literary strain of Renaissance imperialism.[106]

---

[105] Anthony Pagden, *La caduta dell'uomo naturale*, trans. Igor Legati (Torino: Einaudi, 1989), p. 142. It is suggested that Fernando de Valdés, the cardinal archbishop of Seville and president of the Council of Castile, encouraged Sepúlveda to write the treatise.

[106] Ibid., pp. 141–154. Pagden's portrait of Sepúlveda depicts him as far from the "enlightened humanist" described by many historians, and his scholastic credentials are also questioned. Following Marcel Bataillon, Pagden also sees Sepúlveda as a rigid theological conservative who prefigures Trent. Another French scholar, Henry Méchoulan, called Sepúlveda an antihumanist in his *L'Antihumanisme de J. G. Sepúlveda* (Paris, 1974). The most important Spanish scholar of Sepúlveda, Angel Losada, argues against this depiction and describes him

Scholasticism has long been recognized as one of the major schools of Renaissance thinking together with humanism and Platonism. The revival of Aristotle's work stretched back to the twelfth-century Renaissance, when many of the philosopher's works were reintroduced into Europe. In the following century, St. Thomas Aquinas fully applied Aristotelian analytical categories and methods to Christian systematic theology, which resulted in his great theological work, the *Summa Theologica*, perhaps the most influential compilation of Catholic doctrine of all time. In the centuries that followed, the Dominican brothers of St. Thomas, many of them teachers or schoolmen, embraced his theology. Scholasticism, the theology of these schoolmen, or Thomists, thus grew to be the dominant theological school in European universities.

Scholasticism was first fully employed in the service of Renaissance Empire with Sepúlveda and a number of other Spanish Thomists who followed him. In Sepúlveda's case, moreover, his training and scholarship on Aristotle joined with his study of patristic scholarship, ancient history, and general humanistic training. In short, he embraced a synthesis of scholastic and humanist learning that provided him with the academic tools to create the arguments he needed to engage in the realm of contemporary politics and the biggest issue of his day.

Central to his treatise justifying the war against the Indians, the taking of their property and land, and the imposition of Spanish political imperium over them was the Aristotelian concept of natural law, especially in the realm of political order.[107] More specifically, Sepúlveda argued that the most applicable just cause of the war against "those barbarians vulgarly called Indians" that was directly derived from natural and divine law was the following: "that those whose natural condition is such that they must obey others, if they refuse to be governed and there is no other recourse, they should be dominated by arms; thus such a war is just according to the opinion of the most eminent philosophers."[108]

---

as a true humanist (*verdadero humanista*), and especially notes his history of Charles V as an example of his humanist erudition. Fray Bartolomé de las Casas, *Obras Completas*, vol. 9, ed. Angel Losada (Madrid: Alianza Editorial, 1990), pp. 15–17.

[107] Juan Ginés de Sepúlveda, *Obras Completas III: Democrates Segundo*, trans. A. Coroleu Lletget (Salamanca: Europa Atres Gráficas, 1997), vol. III, pp. 47–48. Numerous definitions of natural law were given by Sepúlveda in his treatise citing both Christian and pagan authors, among whom Aristotle was his favorite.

[108] Ibid., "Hay además, otras causas que justifican las guerras, no de tanta aplicación ni tan frecuentes; no obstante tenidas por muy justas y se fundan en el Derecho natural y divino. Una de ellas, la más applicable a esos bárbaros llamados vulgarmente indios, de cuya defensa pareces haberte encagado, es la siguiente: que aquéllos cuya condición natural es tal que

To illustrate this philosophical claim that "the dominion of the prudent, good, and humane, over the opposite is just and natural," Sepúlveda turned to the example of the Roman Empire. It was the basic reality of Roman moral superiority that justified ancient Roman domination, something that was acknowledged by both St. Thomas Aquinas and St. Augustine, who wrote that "God conceded to the Romans a very expansive and glorious empire to impede the great evil that spread among many peoples." Sepúlveda elaborated on the concept by stating that the Romans, who were always considered virtuous and prudent, by imposing their good laws, were able to change the customs of the barbarians by suppressing and correcting their many vices.[109]

At its heart, Sepúlveda's argument was that all of the evidence from participants in the conquest revealed the native peoples of the Americas to be what Aristotle called natural slaves and what St. Augustine called barbarians. Sepúlveda had met Cortés when both were in the south of Spain in the late 1540s, and he also had at his disposal reports from early chronicles of the conquest that described the habits and customs of the Aztecs, in particular.

Focusing his attention first and foremost on Aztec religious practices to demonstrate their "primitive condition," Sepúlveda lingered long over the ritual of human sacrifice, the opening of the victim's chest to extract the human heart, and the eating of their flesh. He then concluded that "These are crimes that surpass all human evil; they are considered by the philosophers among the most ferocious and abominable perversities."[110] Can there be any doubt, he continued, that such a barbarous people had been conquered by such an "excellent, pious and just king as Ferdinand was and Caesar Charles now is" with the greatest right and for their own good? More specifically, Sepúlveda argued that after receiving "our government, our letters, laws, and ethics shaped by Christianity," their primitive condition

---

deban obedecer a otros, si rehúsan su gobierno y no queda otro recurso, sean dominados por las armas; pues tal guerra es justa según opinión de los más eminentes filiósofos." P. 53.

[109] Ibid., p. 63. "Quede, pues, sentado, conforme a la autoridad de los sabios más eminentes, que es justo y natural el dominio de los prudentes, buenos, y humanos sobre los contrarios, pues no de otro motivo justificó el imperio legítimo de los romanos sobre los demás pueblos, según el testimonio de Santo Tomás en el libro Del régimen del principe, siguiendo a San Agustin, quien al referirse al imperio de los romanos en el libro quinto de *La Ciudad de Dios* dijo: `Dios concedío a los romanos un imperio muy dilitado y glorioso para impedir los males graves que cundian en muchos pueblos que en busca de la gloria tenian ansias de riqueza y otros muchos vicios, es decir, para que, con la buena legislación que seguian y la virtud en que sobresalian, cambiasen las bárbaras costumbres y suprimiesen y corrigiesen los vicios de muchos pueblos bárbaros."

[110] Ibid., p. 68. The text reads, "Crimenes son estos que al sobrepasar toda humana maldad son considerados por los filósofos entre las más feroces y abominables perversidades."

had been transformed so much so that the comparison between their later and previous state was like that between men and beasts.[111]

In contrast to the "barbarians," Sepúlveda argued that the cultural superiority of the Spaniards that entitled them to rule over the inferior Indians was revealed in their letters, laws, and government. Looking for authority in antiquity like the humanist he was, Sepúlveda pointed to the long and illustrious string of Spanish philosophers like Seneca, Lucian, St. Isidore, Averroes, and King Alfonso as examples of illustrious philosophers. In matters of government and war, the Spanish warriors, already famous in the ancient Roman Empire as more formidable than the Romans themselves, were linked to those of his own day and especially to the likes of the great captain, Gonzalvo de Cordoba, and the armies of Charles V. The emperor, above all others, was the commander who had won great glory in Milan, Naples, Tunis, France, Belgium, and Germany, not to mention in the New World, where the far larger forces of the Indians "had run away yelling like women" when faced with a small force of Spaniards.[112]

This last harsh judgment of Sepúlveda revealed the sharp polemical edge that characterized much of the *Democrates secundus*. It left little or no room for acknowledging the accomplishments of the Native Americans in the realms of architecture, astronomy, or art. It was writing that conquered, a literary sword that sought to cut the heart out of the opposing view of Las Casas and others who depicted the Indians as having the marks of high civilization and thus the right to political sovereignty.

Although the text initially passed the scrutiny of the censors and was approved for publication, the treatise was challenged by members of the Council of the Indies, and probably Las Casas, who successfully sought to have its publication blocked at both the universities of Salamanca and Alcalá. Sepúlveda responded by writing a condensed version of the treatise, the *Apologia*, that was published in Rome in 1550. He also wrote to the imperial

---

[111] Ibid., p. 68. The text reads, "Asi pues, ¿dudaremos en afirmar que estas gentes tan incultas, tan bárbaras, contaminadas con tan nefandos sacrificios e impias religiones, han sido conquistados por rey tan excelente, piadoso y justo como fue Fernando y lo es ahora César Carlos, y por una nación excelente en todo género de virtudes con el mejor derecho y mayor beneficio para los indios? Antes le la llegada de los cristianos tenían la naturaleza, costumbres, religion y práctica de nefandos sacrificios que hemos explicado; ahora, al recibir con nuestro gobierno nuestras letras, leyes, y moral, imbuidos de la religión Cristiana, quienes se han mostrado dóciles a los sacerdotes que les hemos mandado, tanto se diferencian de su primitive condición como los civilizados de los bárbaros ... en una palabra y para decirlo de una vez, casi cuanto los hombres de las bestias."

[112] Ibid., p. 66. "Y muchas veces miles y miles de ellos se han dispersado huyendo como mujeres al ser derotados por un reducido número de españoles."

court then in Germany asking for the emperor's intervention and pointing out that a majority of theologians and ministers had approved of his
treatise.[113]

What followed was the famous gathering in Valladolid of a *Junta* of theologians, canon lawyers, and civil lawyers summoned by Charles V to analyze
the two writers' views and render an opinion for the emperor's benefit. Las
Casas wrote his own *Apologia* for the event that included a summary of his
argument and a preface dedicated to the future Philip II.

The summary, in particular, was a virulent polemic against Sepúlveda that
depicted him as an advocate of the conquistadors who sought to subvert the
New Laws of 1542. He was cast as a doctor whose writing was "adorned with
flowers of eloquences" but whose erudition in this case was very weak.[114]
The thinly veiled jab at humanist eloquence as "flowery," together with the
attack on Sepúlveda's "erudition," or scholastic reasoning, provided an effective rhetorical frame for undermining his work in the face of the Junta made
up of scholastic theologians with few humanist inclinations.

In contrast, the *Apologia* of Las Casas used formal scholastic reasoning,
together with extensive quotations from the Bible, to make a point-by-point
rebuttal of the argument made in Sepúlveda's treatise by the same name.
At its core, the argument of Las Casas denied that the Indians were natural
slaves, even if they fit Aristotle's definition, and that the Spanish had a superior civilization. The Indians were God's children with their own natural
rights, and the laws of the gospel, most especially charity and love, tran-
scended those of Aristotle. The Spanish conquest and war was thus not a just
war. The obligation of the emperor was subsequently to restore the Indians'
original liberty and property and to protect them from the conquistadors as
his children and subjects.[115]

By 1548, Las Casas was back in Iberia and had considerable influence
among his fellow Dominicans and other theologians in Salamanca. These
included Melchor Cano, Diego de Covarrubias, and Bartolomé de Carranza,
who were part of the *Junta*. As students of Francisco della Vitoria, all of these
men were first and foremost scholastic theologians, steeped in the language
and methods of Thomistic reasoning.

---

[113] Fray Bartolomé de las Casas, *Obras Completas*, vol. 9, ed. Angel Losada (Madrid: Allianza
   Editorial, 1990), pp. 11–15. Losada's edition of Las Casas benefits from his mastery of the
   corpus of Sepúlveda's work as well.
[114] Ibid., p. 53. The text of Sepúlveda is described as "adornado con flores de eloquencia," and
   he is described as "poco brilla por su erudición."
[115] For a good account of the debate, see Lewis Hanke, *All Mankind Is One* (Dekalb: Northern
   Illinois University Press, 1974).

Although Sepúlveda, like them, drew on scholastic methods and expansive knowledge of Aristotelian principles, he was not a part of their school. His humanistic argument also depended on the historical precedent of the Roman Empire and was not entirely consistent with their form of academic discourse. Moreover, Sepúlveda suspected they disagreed with his central argument, as did Las Casas, that the war of conquest was justified because the Indians met the Aristotelian definition of natural slaves.[116]

Whatever the cause, in the end, Sepúlveda lost the publication battle as the *Junta* upheld the ban on his treatise. Las Casas and his supporters on the Junta had successfully suppressed the most dangerous justification of the conquest and enslavement of the Indians. Moreover, their criticisms successfully planted the seeds for a growing tradition of anti-conquest and anti-imperial literature most famously represented outside of Spain by the Black Legend. Over the course of the sixteenth century, moreover, this theological tradition gained more authority in Spain and eventually altered the imperial conversation, a theme taken up in the next chapter.

But on the larger and central question of whether the Spanish war of conquest was justified, no judgment was rendered in Valladolid. In fact, the specific reasons for the Junta's decision are not known because the final opinions were not published or preserved.[117] This could be because they did not conform to the perspective of the emperor, who generally used the tool of the Junta "to legitimate, and not to judge" various pressing issues of the day.[118] From this perspective, because the Junta did not legitimate Sepúlveda's views, the lack of any published commentary points to the de facto support of many of those views on the part of the emperor.

As a shrewd and calculating ruler, Charles V could not afford to alienate the dominant theological school in Spain, especially at the moment when he was consumed with fighting the Protestants in the German lands. He subsequently did not push for the publication of Sepúlveda's treatise and supported the ban. It was the emperor at his Machiavellian best, cloaking himself with the rhetoric of Christian prince and defender of the Indians, whose new laws of 1542 aimed to put a stop to the abuses of the conquistadors. Thus distancing himself from the atrocities and epic bloodletting of the conquest, he could nonetheless claim the glory and fame that came from claiming vast new territories for Christendom.

---

[116] Pagden, p. 143.
[117] Losada, p. 19.
[118] Pagden, pp. 26–27.

But in the realm of policy toward the Indians, the deliberations in Valladolid brought about no dramatic changes. The conquest was implicitly, if not explicitly, accepted as a just war by the court of Charles V and the majority of the ruling class. It was a *fait accompli* never to be fully reversed or officially renounced as an unjustified war by the Habsburg imperial monarchs.

For all practical purposes, the second just war treatise of Sepúlveda, the official historian of the emperor, constituted the most concise imperial manifesto of the age of conquest vis-à-vis the New World. He may have lost the publication battle, but his views reflected the reality of a war of conquest already won. Gold and silver continued to be extracted in ever-larger quantities with forced Indian labor. Much of the land taken by the conquistadors remained in their hands as the Spanish assimilated the new territories ever more into their Empire. And, through violence and disease, the deaths of millions of Native Americans continued to decimate the indigenous populations. In the century that followed the conquest of Cortés, the population of Mexico alone was reduced from an estimated 20 million to just 1.9 million largely because of the ravages of European diseases.[119] This was the most brutal cost of the freshly realized dreams of imperial revival.

For many critics of Sepúlveda, both past and present, he represented the dark side of the Renaissance: a scholar who used his intellectual tools and position in the service of tyranny. But seen in the context of the imperial Renaissance, he was the loyal intellectual servant of the new Caesar for whom many of his predecessors had long been hoping. His treatise on the just war of the soldiers of Charles V against the Indians was a logical extension of his earlier just war treatise written with the Ottoman enemy in mind. It was also just one small piece of a larger scholarly and iconographic agenda that was focused on exalting Charles V as the new Caesar and Spain as the new Roman Empire.

The Imperial Image of Charles V

In this endeavor Sepúlveda was joined by many contemporary writers and artists who saw the conquest of Mexico and Peru as part of the magnificence of the imperial march in the emperor's first decades in power. Images of the conquered Indians together with Africans and Turks were included in the ephemeral imagery of the triumphs of 1536, for example, and in the

[119] Jarred Diamond, p. 199.

triumphal entry of Charles V into Milan in 1541.[120] At the same time, they were incorporated into the histories of his reign as a constant feature of the imperial narrative that was not silenced by the religious censors and theologians in Spain. In the words of the royal historian Florian de Ocampo, writing in the prologue of his well-received *History of Spain*, the emperor's "wars against the Indians" were one of his major accomplishments that contributed to his fame and glory.[121]

Illustrating this point, moreover, was a popular series of engravings by Martin Heermskerk titled *The Victories of Charles V.* Dedicated to Philip II in 1566 and first printed in the Netherlands, this series went to press seven times over the next century. Composed of twelve illustrations described as "paternal triumphs," the victories celebrated included those at Pavia (1525), Rome (1527), Vienna (1529), Tunis (1535), Muhlberg (1547), and the undated victory against the Indians.[122]

The image titled "The imperial troops bring civilization to the Indians" followed the image of "Charles V and Suleiman" and came before "The fall of Tunis." It was thus joined with the victories against the other "barbarians" in Africa and Istanbul. As if to underline the point, the image depicted largely naked Indians in front of cave dwellings roasting a Spanish soldier over a fire.

Certainly a curious image to celebrate a victory, it makes perfect sense as an illustration of Sepúlveda's critical section in *Demócrates Segundo*, where he cited human sacrifice and cannibalism as his central justification for calling the Indians natural slaves and the war against them justified.[123]

Although *The Victories of Charles V* serve as a good example of the propagation of a heroic image of the emperor in a popular medium, elite forms of the imperial arts more traditionally associated with the Renaissance, sculpture and painting, also served to do the same thing in a more dramatic and lasting fashion. Just as the ancient Roman emperors had used images of

---

[120] Bonner Mitchell, p. 175. The triumphal arch erected in the piazza del Duomo in Milan featured an equestrian statue of Charles V major on the top of the arch. Under the horse's feet were a Moor and an American Indian.

[121] Ambrosio Morales Florian de Ocampo, *Coronica General de España*, ed. B. Cano (Madrid: Quiroga, 1791), vol. 1, p. xx. "Y comenzó á obrar aquella Guerra tan larga de los Moros, y despues las empresas que tomó contra los Indios, y la conquista de Italia y de Africa, que fueron mucho famosas y senaladas, no contentandose con mandar á todos los primero la mandaba, sino ensanchando su imperio, y pasandolo mucho mas adelante."

[122] Bart Rosier, "The Victories of Charles V: A Series of Prints by Maarten Van Heemskerck, 1555–56," in *Simiolus: Netherlands Quarterly for the History of Art*, Vol. 20, No. 1 (1990–1991), pp. 24–38, 24.

[123] Ibid., p. 30.

themselves to promote their image, authority, and power in stone, paint, and metal, so too did Charles V. Drawing on the rich precedents of the Italian courts, in particular, he used his immense wealth to hire some of the best artists that Europe had produced since antiquity. Two artists above all others, Leone Leoni and Titian, were entrusted with the important task of fashioning his personal image through painting and sculpture.[124]

It is revealing that Charles V began to pay more attention to the artistic representations of himself and his family that would define his image and theirs for posterity in the same years that both the debate over the conquest and his conflict with the Protestants in Germany were at their height. Leaving little room for doubt about his own political models and self-perception in works that he personally commissioned, Charles V chose to have himself repeatedly depicted in the classical Roman imperial style in both bronze and marble statues, as well as in the famous painted portrait by Titian that celebrated his victory of the Protestant princes in 1547.[125]

Building on the revival of monumental bronze sculpture that emerged in northern Italy in the fifteenth century, especially in the workshop of Donatello, Leone Leoni, above all others, practiced this art in the service of the empire of Charles V. Born in Arezzo in 1509, his early formation took place in the fertile Renaissance milieu of Venice and its environs in the late 1520s, where he moved in the circles of Titian, the principal portrait painter for Charles V. Leoni first cast medals in the ancient Roman style for the humanist Pietro Bembo in this period and then moved to Rome, where he became the engraver for the papal treasury under Clement VII and Paul III.[126]

Roughly a decade in Rome gave Leoni plenty of time to study the great works of Roman antiquity and the imperial Renaissance, especially those of Michelangelo, whom he knew and admired. At the same time, the contemporary events of the day, like the triumphal entry of Charles V into Rome in 1536, made it clear where the political winds were blowing. Like Giovio and Sepúlveda, with whom he certainly brushed shoulders as a fellow employee of the Roman court, his future was also with the empire, not the papacy. But it was the images, ideas, and examples of imperial Rome, both past

---

[124] For a recent synthesis of various aspects of the "fashioning" of *Charles V* over the centuries, see Peter Burke, "Presenting and Re-presenting Charles V," in *Charles V*, ed. Hugo Soly, (Antwerp: Mercatorfonds, 1999), pp. 393–475.

[125] Fernando Checa Cremades, *Carlos V, La Imagen del Poder en el Rinacimiento* (Madrid, El Viso, 1999), p. 15. This work provides the most comprehensive study of the artistic production of the reign of Charles V.

[126] Eugène Plon, *Leone Leoni et Pompeo Leoni* (Paris: E. Plon, 1887), p. 3.

and present, acquired during the formative years in Rome, which exercised the most powerful influence on Leoni's work as official sculptor for the emperor.

First appointed the master engraver of coins for the imperial treasury in Milan in 1542, an office he held for all but three of the next forty-seven years, Leoni had even greater ambitions. In 1546, he first proposed to the new governor of Milan, Ferrante Gonzaga, a large equestrian statue of Charles V to be placed in a central location in Milan. He noted that the ancient emperors had their statues modeled after their live image, and he proposed the same thing for the statue of Charles V. He went further to describe his projected image of the emperor as being that of a warrior who was commanding and exhorting his army into battle.[127]

It is almost certain that Leoni had the ancient Roman statue of Marcus Aurelius in mind as his model for this sculpture. He was particularly found of the ancient work and in 1549 traveled to Paris to secure the mold of this sculpture, which he used to cast a plaster copy that he placed in the central courtyard of his own house.[128]

Although the equestrian statue of Charles V was never realized, many other portrait statues of the emperor and his family were commissioned by the emperor from Leoni starting in 1549. Charles V was at the height of his power at this point but also aging quickly and in ill health. Thinking of his personal legacy, he began the task of creating a lasting image of himself and his family for his present heirs and future generations.

The emperor was very much in control of his own image at this point, and he ordered his main artists, Titian and Leoni, to his court so they could work from his live image. Titian was the primary agent of fashioning his image in painting, and Leoni was also ordered by the king to follow Titian's image of him in his engravings for coins and medals. But for the larger sculptures, Leoni had the benefit of spending time with the subjects of his work because he was ordered to the imperial court in Brussels in 1549. Working out of an apartment near the emperor's, Leoni wrote about the long hours spent talking with Charles V during 1549, and it was in that year that he

---

[127] Ibid., p. 38.

[128] Ibid., pp. 48–49. The correspondence of Leoni from 1549 tells the fascinating tale of the twelve molds of ancient Roman sculptures done by Primatice at the order of Francis I. These were used to cast copies that, according to Vasari, the king wanted "to make a second Rome at Fontainebleu." Among the subjects were the Laocoon, Venus, Apollo, Tiber, the Satyrs, Arian, and presumably Marcus Aurelius. Supporting the idea that the mold used was one of those in Paris is Leoni's letter to Ferrante Gonzaga describing the special trip to Paris to try and buy the molds after the death of Francis I.

cast his first major imperial bust of the emperor, as well as busts of Philip II and the "two queens" of Charles V, his only wife Isabella and sister Mary of Hungary.[129]

The bronze bust was one of the first imperial portrait busts of the Renaissance and signaled that Renaissance imperial artists had reached another peak in the climb to imitate the ancient Romans. A similar move had taken place in the client court of Cosimo de Medici, where Benvenuto Cellini had also created imperial images of his patron that were revolutionary for their day. Even though Cosimo was a worthy captain whose artists may have had imperial aspirations for their master, Leoni worked for the real thing. By 1550, many feared the power of Charles and were plotting to undermine it, but no one could deny that his empire was as vast and powerful as that of ancient Rome. The bronze bust represented a real emperor with wide-ranging imperial power.

The success of these images bolstered Leoni's reputation further, and in 1551 he was ordered to the emperor's court again, this time in Augsburg. Titian was also there in 1551, another clear sign that the emperor was increasingly preoccupied with his artistic legacy in these years. A good salesman, Leoni made use of this visit to show the emperor sketches that he had done for numerous additional sculptures of the imperial family, many of which would be realized over the next four years.

By 1552, the work of Leoni had won him the title of knight and an annual pension of 150 ducats for life. Moreover, he had the right to pass the title on to his son, Pompeo, who he had introduced to Charles V in 1549 in Brussels. It was a long way from being a galley slave only ten years earlier, and the social promotion apparently inspired the artist to work harder, because he finished eight large sculptures, four in marble and four in bronze, over the next four years.[130]

Among these was his most famous, the *Furor*, a bronze metaphor of Renaissance imperial might. Inspired by a verse from Virgil, the larger-than-life statue has Charles depicted as a conquering Roman general in imperial dress standing over a prostrate man who was meant to represent all of the collected enemies of peace and virtue. Leoni wrote that in keeping with the emperor's "modesty," he chose not to identify the conquered subject as any one province or defeated prince but rather as the general forces of disorder and violence in the world (Figure 2.2).

[129] Ibid., pp. 44–49.
[130] Ibid., pp. 92–96.

2.2. Leone Leoni, Charles V and the Fury, 1551–1553. (Museo Nacional del Prado, Madrid.
Ref. E00273.)

Although the original idea for this work came from Leoni, Charles V had seen the sketches, made unspecified suggestions for changes, and approved the final plan. This was also true of the life-size sculptures of the emperor, the queen, and Philip II that the sculptor also finished in this period in both marble and/or bronze.

In 1556, Leoni was ordered to bring all of his work to the imperial court in Brussels, where he and his work were warmly received. His son, Pompeo, was entrusted with the task of escorting the work to Spain in that same year because Charles V wanted his new acquisitions with him in Spain on his return in that same year. Once there, they became part of a growing repertoire of paintings and sculpture in the royal collection that were united by the imperial theme. Joined with the sculptures of ancient Roman emperors, the new sculptures of Leoni emphasized and celebrated the connections and continuities of Charles V with the emperors of ancient Rome on yet another level.

Transitions: 1549 to 1558

The extraordinary military successes of Charles V during the first thirty years of his reign and the overall rise of his empire were seen by friends and foes alike as remarkable. The early judgments and fears of Guicciardini that a new Caesar was rising were confirmed by his consolidation of power in Italy, Spain, the Netherlands, and the New World during his first three decades in power. Literary and artistic production, joined with real military power and the treasure of New World conquest, bolstered this view and provided the material evidence that a new empire to rival ancient Rome had risen. Ancient empire was reborn.

But in the 1540s, the emperor suffered a number of setbacks such as the failed naval campaign against Algeria in 1541. More seriously, he became increasingly stuck in the quagmire of Germany, where rebellious Protestant princes increasingly consumed his time and resources. The most vivid illustration of this was the fact that from 1543 to 1556, Charles V resided almost exclusively in Germany and the Netherlands largely to try and bring the German lands more firmly under imperial control.[131]

It was the clear hope and desire of Charles V to pass on the title of Holy Roman Emperor to his son Philip II, together with his German possessions

---

[131] Vicente de Cadenas y Vicent, *Diario del Emperador Carlos V* (Madrid: Hidalguia, 1992). In the period from 1517 to 1558, Charles V spent nineteen years in Spain, eighteen years in the German lands and the Netherlands, and roughly three years in Italy. Checa Cremades notes that the emperor lived in his Brussels palace more than in any other royal residence. P. 138.

and revenues. And it was inevitable that he would do everything in his power to protect this German inheritance. This was the product of both an ancient and medieval political instinct to protect and pass down royal title, property, and privilege.

But the German electors had a different idea. When the election of a new Holy Roman Emperor was held, they denied the crown to Philip II, instead choosing his uncle Ferdinand for the imperial title. This proved to be a major defeat for Charles V and his plans to pass on that symbolically important part of his inheritance to his son. From 1557 onward, the Holy Roman Empire and emperor would once again be distinct and independent, as well as weak, divided, and a second-tier power in Europe. Philip II would have many titles, but not that of emperor.

This was a stinging rebuke to Charles V, but in 1550 he received a serious consolation prize from another part of his empire that served as a strong sign of where the strength and future of his empire, and that of his son, lay. It was in that year that the Spanish Captain Lagasca, who he had sent to Peru in 1546 to mediate in the civil war between Pizarro and Almagro and to impose a new government and political order, returned to Spain. A critical part of his mission was to escort Peruvian conquest treasure safely back to Spain, a task he successfully carried out that brought Charles V 1.5 million gold ducats in 1550. The emperor ordered Lagasca to come to Augsburg in that same year to give him a full account of Peruvian affairs. As a sign of his pleasure with the good news, he rewarded him with the bishopric of Valencia that included an annual income of 20,000 ducats.[132]

The good news and treasure from the Spanish part of his empire did not end the bad news from Germany, where warfare with the Protestant princes continued. When it finally ended with the Peace of Augsburg in 1555, a peace that included the famous provision to let the individual princes decide which religious confession their subjects would follow, it was yet another bitter German cup for the emperor to drink. The many years and enormous amounts of treasure and blood that he had spent trying to maintain religious unity in the German lands had come to naught.

Not surprisingly, the old gout-ridden emperor decided to spend his last years in Spain, where he had enjoyed his greatest successes and support. In 1556, he began to abdicate his realms in favor of his son in the Netherlands and then made the trip back to Spain in 1557 to retire at the monastery in Yuste. But peace was elusive. The various challenges that immediately

---

[132] Gomara, Francesco Lopez de, *Historia dell nuove Indie*, trans. Agostino di Cravalie (Venice: Francesco Lorenzini da Turino, 1560), pp. 264r–265r.

confronted Philip II from Pope Paul IV Caraffa and the French deprived the emperor of his sought-after tranquility and often left him an angry old man up to his death in 1558.

Still, the legacy that Charles V left to Philip II was monumental, and those who judge that the emperor's reign ended with failure are only partially correct. The enormity of the empire that he passed on to his son, first and foremost, represented a resounding success. Yes, the German lands and imperial title were gone, but this loss was not completely negative. The German lands had drained money and men from other parts of the empire for decades. Philip II was free of that burden and thus able to direct resources to other challenges that emerged early in his reign in Spain, Flanders, and Italy. At the same time, Charles V had added the far more important territories of Mexico and Peru to his possessions, and the income that they produced for the monarchy continued to grow. Moreover, Charles V added the Duchy of Milan to his son's Italian inheritance. Together with a stable Naples and Sicily, it ensured Philip II dominance in Italy. So, too, the fact that Charles V had brought the new Duchy of Florence and the Republic of Genoa firmly in the Spanish camp as client states. In short, Charles V left to Philip II the largest global empire that had ever existed, no small feat.

Time would prove that there was another latent, potential inheritance formed in the dynastic alliances created early in the reign of Charles V that provided for yet another dramatic addition to the empire of Philip II. When the Spanish king, son of the Portuguese princess, Isabel, claimed the Portuguese Empire in 1580 on the death of its childless king Sebastian, it represented both the greatest dynastic victory of Charles V and another enormous territorial gift to his son.

Charles V understood his accomplishments and the parallels that they drew with those of the ancient Caesars. Like Julius Caesar, he had been constantly on the move for forty years, battling to ensure both the preservation and expansion of his realms. In one of his abdication speeches of 1556 he recounted his many travels: he had been nine times in Germany, six in Spain, seven in Italy, ten in Flanders, four times in peace and war in France, twice in England, and twice in Africa. In total he had made forty different excursions that included eight sea voyages in the Mediterranean and four in the Spanish Ocean (Atlantic).[133]

Besides this concise summary of his military career, Charles V also meant to leave a written account of his career that imitated in some measure the commentaries of Caesar. Dictated to one of his secretaries, Guillaume Van

---

[133] Cadenas y Vicent, *Diario del Emperador Carlos V*, p. 7.

Male, the work was not published until the early seventeenth century, and its exact authorship is contested.

Still, it is a compelling literary monument to his military accomplishments in the ancient style. Begun in the same period that he was commissioning his imperial Roman portraits in bronze and marble from Leoni, it was natural for Charles V to imitate the first Caesar in recording his deeds. Certainly the intent of the eventual author of the *Memoirs* saw it that way, because he had urged the emperor to call his work *The Commentaries* in direct imitation of Julius Caesar.[134]

The original *Commentaries* had continued to grow in popularity through-out the reign of Charles V, yet another example of the rising tide of empire. In the period from 1500 to 1549, no fewer than fifty-nine new editions were published, making Caesar the fourth most popular ancient historian in Europe in those decades. Reflecting the continuity of the imperial theme and imperial power in the age of Philip II, moreover, from 1550 to 1599 yet another fifty-nine editions were published, raising Caesar to the rank of the number-one ancient historian for that period. It was a telling sign of the times.[135]

[134] Kervyn de Lettenhove, *Commentaires de Charles Quint* (Paris: Firmin-Didot, 1862), p. xiv.
[135] P. Burke, "A Survey of the Popularity of Ancient Historians," p. 137.

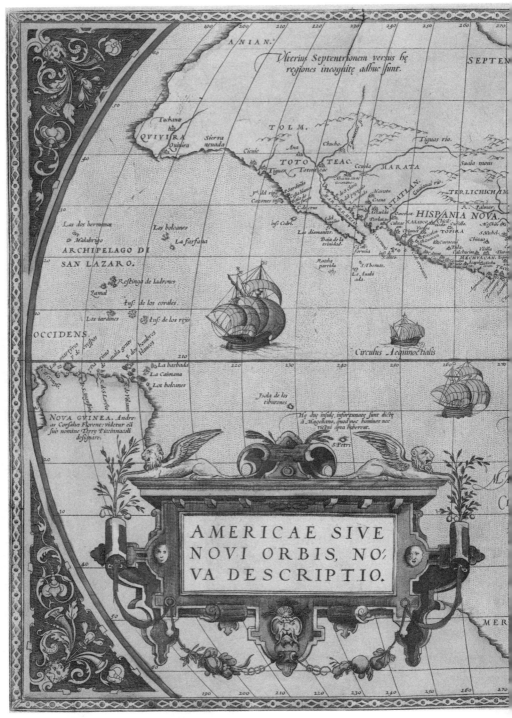

Map 3.1. Americas.

3

THE SPANISH EMPIRE, APEX OF THE IMPERIAL RENAISSANCE

This book recounts the lives of the emperors, a topic that could not be more appropriate, your Majesty being the son of the Emperor and the descendant of the emperors whose deeds are written about here ... remember the deeds and examples of the good (emperors), not only to imitate them, but to move beyond them.

From Pedro Mexia's dedication to Philip II of Spain in the
Historia Imperial y Cesarea, 1547[1]

Charles V left his son with large shoes to fill on his abdication, but he had also prepared Philip II for his role as well as he could. Unlike the old emperor, who had come into his political inheritance at the tender age of seventeen, his son had the advantage of a much longer period of formation. Philip II was almost thirty when his father began handing over pieces of his empire. In the years leading up to that time, he benefited from a humanist education with a host of personal tutors including Cristóbal Calvete de Estrella, Honorato Juan, and Juan Gines Sepúlveda, who was entrusted with the prince's instruction in history.[2] A good deal of travel throughout his future realms in Italy and the Low Countries between 1548 and 1554, a brief stint as king of England between 1556 and 1558, and the personal instructions

---

[1] Pedro Mexia, *Historia Imperial y Cesarea* (Seville: Dominico de Robertis, 1547), p. *ii rv, The opening quote is taken from the following passages of the dedication: "lo que este libro tracta, son vidas de emperadores abreviadas, que no pudo venire cosa mas aproposito, siendo vuestra Alteza hijo de Emperador y desciendo de tantos y tales Emperadores cuyos hechos en summa aqui se escriven terna memoria de los hechos y exemplos de los buenos, no solamente para imitarlos, pero para adelantar se y hazelles ventaja en las virtudes y excelencias, y esto sera conseguir yo el ultimo fin y desseo que he tenido en esta obra."

[2] Joseph Pérez, *L'Espagne de Philippe II* (Paris: Fayard, 1999), pp. 24–25. The author notes that both Petrarch and Vitruvius were among the authors read by Philip II as a student.

and example of his father in those same years rounded out his political education.[3]

On both the intellectual and cultural levels, he was steeped in the ideas and images of the classical Roman revival that had deepened and spread in the age of Charles V, especially in Spain and Italy. From the beginning of his adult life, his own image was fashioned in the ancient imperial style by the same primary artists who created the images of Charles V in marble, in bronze, and on canvas: Leone and Pompeo Leoni and Titian. He was trained from the beginning to rule an empire.

To this end, in the realms of politics and the art of war, Philip II had a range of texts, classical and contemporary, at his disposal, as well as the paternal example of Charles V. Following him and the model of the ancient Caesars, he demonstrated a strong appetite for fame and glory. War and international political contest were a constant part of his reign for forty years. His war machine, unmatched in size, constituted the most concrete manifestation of power known in the early modern world. The king built it up and used it constantly to both defend and expand his territories. Fueled by the unprecedented resources of the New World, the armies and navies of the Catholic King waged war on a virtually perpetual basis. In the forty-one years that he ruled, 1557 to 1598, only six months were completely free of war by some estimates.[4] To judge by Machiavelli's proposition that the ability to wage war was central to the meaning and validation of the prince's power – that military power and war were constitutive of political power – Philip II was the consummate Renaissance prince.

Shrewder and more ruthless than his father, he combined sharp political realism, opportunism, and a skillful Machiavellian control and manipulation of Roman Catholicism to maintain and expand his power both at home and abroad. He became, over the course of his lifetime, the ruler of the largest global empire that the world had ever known. In size, military power, economic strength, and global influence, this was the apex of Renaissance Empire.

---

[3] An excellent recent summary of the historiography on his reign can be found in Manuel Fernández Álvarez, *Felipe II y su Tiempo* (Madrid: Editorial Espasa Calpe, 1998), pp. 19–36. See also *Felipe II y el Mediterráneo*, ed. Ernest Belenguer Cebrià, 4 volumes (Madrid: Closas-Orcoyen, S. L., 1999); and *Filippo II e il Mediterraneo*, ed. L. Lotti and R. Villari (Rome: Laterza, 2003); Joseph Pérez, *L'Espagne de Philippe II* (Paris: Fayard, 1999); Henry Kamen, *Philip II* (New Haven, CT: Yale University Press, 1997); and Geoffrey Parker, *Philip II* (Chicago: Open Court, 1995).

[4] Geoffrey Parker, *The Grand Strategy of Philip II* (New Haven, CT: Yale University Press, 1998), p. 2.

The mature imperial humanism of the mid-sixteenth century provided the intellectual blueprint for ruling this behemoth, a fact that is fundamental to understanding the political strategies and policies of Philip II. Although some recent studies have depicted the king as having no strategy and others have attributed to him an anachronistic "grand strategy," the true key to the political philosophy and practices of Philip II is the imperial humanist literature that provided the models that he imitated in maintaining and expanding his own empire.[5]

Besides Guevara and the earlier Italian authors, Philip II was the recipient at the age of eighteen of a far more expansive political guide book from the royal historian Pedro Mexia.[6] One of the later royal historians appointed in the age of Charles V, Mexia shared with his predecessor the distinction of writing a text that was popular both in Spain and abroad. Eight Castilian editions of his *Historia Imperial y Cesarea* were printed between 1545 and 1665 in Seville, Madrid, Basel, and Antwerp. The Italian translation by Ludovico Dolce was even more successful. Between 1558 and 1688 at least seventeen Italian editions were printed in Venice, some of which included the additional lives of Charles V, Maximilian II, and Ferdinand. A German translation was printed in Basel in 1564, and two English translations by William Traheron and Edward Grimestone were published in London in 1604 and 1623, respectively. In total, at least twenty-eight editions were printed in the sixteenth and seventeenth centuries, making it the most successful of the Spanish imperial histories after that of Guevara.[7]

It surpassed Guevara, however, in the influence and reputation that it enjoyed in Spain, where it was considered a fundamental work by the educated class in the latter half of the sixteenth century. Viewed as free of the lies and exaggerations of chivalric literature, the *Historia Imperial* was considered by some contemporaries to be the first general work of humanist history written in Castilian.[8]

---

[5] G. Parker, p. 1. He writes that "The assumption that the king lacked a `blueprint for empire' underlies most writing about the general policy aims of Habsburg Spain." Arguing against this tendency in recent biographies like that of Henry Kamen, Parker analyzes many details of Spanish policy through the modern prism of "Grand Strategy." Noticeably absent in his work is any analysis of the humanist histories that provided the intellectual foundations for the political strategies of the monarch.

[6] Mexia's text as an important source for understanding the political formation of Philip II has been largely neglected. Neither Henry Kamen's *Empire* nor Geoffrey Parker's *The Grand Strategy of Philip II* mention Mexia or his text in their expansive works. Anthony Pagden briefly mentions Mexia's enthusiasm for the ancient Roman Empire as the greatest of all empires but does not analyze his text in any further detail. See his *Lords of All the World*, pp. 40–42.

[7] Palau y Dulcet, Vol. IX, pp. 177–179.

[8] Ibid., p. 177. Palau y Dulcet writes that "Toda la cultura española de la segunda mitad del XVI la tuvo por obra fundamental."

Its popularity was not due to its brevity. The *Historia Imperial y Cesarea*, a chronologically ordered compilation of brief lives of more than 120 Roman emperors from the time of Julius Caesar through the life of the grandfather of Charles V, Maximilian I, was a lengthy work of more than 800 pages.[9] It aimed to provide Prince Philip with a cornucopia of political and moral lessons as a primer specifically dedicated to the descendant of the emperors. As the author stated clearly in the dedication to Philip, he hoped that the young prince would learn from the examples of good emperors whose deeds and virtues he was advised to follow and exceed.[10]

For further justification, Mexia pointed to the authority of Aristotle and Cicero, who both praised the usefulness and indispensability of history in political and public life. How else, he asked, could the prince know about the "clemency of Caesar" or the "justice and goodwill of Trajan" if not from history? It was historical knowledge of the deeds that brought fame and glory to earlier men that inspired the imitation of their accomplishments. Thus Alexander the Great was inspired by the tales of Achilles as told by Homer, and Caesar was inspired by Alexander as told by his historians.[11]

Mexia embraced to the full the humanist view of history as the teacher of life.[12] He included with each of his lives a list of the ancient sources consulted for his own text. His references to these sources were included in the margins of the text, and their prominence in the work underlined the author's overt preoccupation with displaying his humanist credentials by going directly *ad fontes*, to the ancient sources. Loosely imitating classical works on the lives of emperors like those of Plutarch and Suetonius, as well as those of Renaissance predecessors like Petrarch, the work of Mexia followed the general shape of a collection of illustrious lives. Although it did not provide the level of detail of the ancient works, it did cover more ground chronologically as it surveyed more than 1,500 years of imperial history. The period from Caesar to Charlemagne, 100 BC to 814 AD, is covered in the first 250 folios and the remaining 700 years in 173 folios.

The length and large number of lives, together with a novel analytical perspective, distinguishes Mexia's work from earlier examples of imperial humanism. Most noticeably, it is characterized by a merging of imperial models from both pagan and Christian antiquity, as well as the medieval emperors.

---

[9] Pedro Mexia, *Historia Imperial y Cesarea*, 1547. All of the following references are taken from this edition, which was numbered as folios.

[10] Ibid., f. iir.

[11] Ibid., f. iiirv.

[12] For more on the text as a model and point of reflection for the contemporary empire, see Mariarosa Scaramuzza Vidoni, *Retorica e narrazione nella "Historia Imperial" di Pedro Mexía* (Rome: Bulzoni, 1989), pp. 91–121.

Although Petrarch and many other earlier Renaissance writers emphasized the gap between the ancient and medieval Caesars – and between the Roman and Holy Roman Empires – Mexia sought to keep them united in a narrative sequence. He thus perpetuated a medieval myth of Roman imperial continuity that was common to the Holy Roman Emperors. This was not surprising given his primary patron, Charles V.[13]

Mexia began his work with a glowing portrait of Julius Caesar that was one of his longer lives at twelve folios. It avoided any serious criticism of Caesar, most noticeably the common charge that Caesar unjustifiably seized power and imposed tyranny. At his most negative, Mexia claimed that the cause of the civil wars was the envy, ambition, thirst for power, and inability to share rule that characterized both Caesar and Pompey. This fault he viewed as almost inevitable with rulers of their stature, and it brought no serious criticism or rebuke.

Rather, Mexia's life of Caesar was a celebration of his accomplishments and a heroic portrait of the founder of what the author described as the ancient world's greatest empire. Caesar was the incomparable captain, the head, and the foundation of that empire. The most impressive fact about his life, in Mexia's opinion, was the short time it took him to reduce the great Roman Republic that had lasted for 500 years to the "rule of one." Moreover, the empire he founded, unlike that of his closest competitor, Alexander the Great, had lasted longer, was more powerful, and was larger.[14] Indeed, according to Mexia's perspective, the Roman Empire had lasted for 2,300 years, "and it lives still today the Empire and the Roman name."[15]

Within this gilded frame, Mexia's life of Caesar recounts his victories in the Gallic wars, which established him as the greatest military captain of antiquity; the details of the Civil War, in which his virtues as a strategist, soldier, and gracious victor were emphasized; the unprecedented four triumphs that celebrated his victories; the many honors and titles that were conferred on him after his assumption of the title of dictator; and the many "great works" that he began as soon as peace was established.

As in Petrarch's account of the assassination of Caesar, Mexia's version condemned the cowardice and betrayal of the assassins. But his final judgment on Caesar was filled with the highest praise: he was "the most powerful,

[13] A. Pagden, *Lords of All the World*, pp. 41–42. He notes the tendency of Mexia and others to compare the age of Augustus, especially, with that of Charles V.
[14] Mexia, f. 1v, "el señorio y imperio de los Romanos que es la quarta monarchia, notariamente se aventaja a todos en tiempo, y en grandeza, y poder."
[15] Ibid., f. 1v, "porque a pocos menos de dos mil y trezientos años, que se fundo Roma, y vive oy el imperio y nombre Romano."

the strongest, the wisest and (most) fortunate Captain" that the world both before and after had ever seen who surpassed in "virtue and valor" every natural human condition.[16]

This archetype set the tone for the treatment of the good emperors that followed and for Mexia's general set of assumptions about empire. Struggle and conquest brought fame and glory. The most successful and important emperors all engaged in the contest as they fought for the highest political prize, empire. War narratives were thus the major components of the individual lives that united the larger work.

For example, Mexia's treatment of Octavian, or Caesar Augustus (63 BC–14 AD), dedicated ten out of twelve folios to a narration of the battles that Octavian fought to secure his place as Caesar's successor in the face of Marc Anthony's challenge. The story climaxed, as it did in the case of Julius Caesar, with an account of the three triumphs celebrated in Rome for Octavian's major victories, including the final subjugation of Egypt.

In a common literary pattern, the life of Augustus ended with a summary of his accomplishments and final judgment on his reign. First and foremost, he was credited with finishing the task of firmly establishing the imperial monarchy. He always used his power prudently and justly and, in the final analysis, "was one of the best princes that the world has ever had."[17]

This high praise was due not only to his military victories but also to his success in governing the empire and for establishing the famous pax romana. Spanning a period of more than fifty years, the reign of Augustus was a model of good government. Mexia elaborated on this theme for prince Philip, who was also faced with the challenge of preserving a vast empire.

Once victory was won, Augustus sent skilled governors and administrators to the provinces while also attending diligently to the administration of justice, to matters of religion, and to the building of public buildings. "He passed excellent laws and ordinances reforming and emending abuses and bad customs. He built in Rome and abroad great and sumptuous buildings,

---

[16] Ibid., f. 12v, Caesar is praised as "el mas poderoso, y el mas valeroso y valiente, sabio, y venturoso principe y capitan, que sin duda ninguna hasta el ha avido en el mundo: y aun no se si despues, en valor, y poder humano: por que contadas y consideradas bien las excellencias y gracias y habilidades, el animo invincible, el effuerzo incomparable, las victorias y batallas que vencio, las provincias y reyes, y naciones que domo y sojuzgo, los avisos y ardides que uso para ello, su magnanimidad, su clemencia, y liberalidad con los vencidos y vencedores, los pensamientos tan altos y propositos que tenia quando fue muerto hallar se ha por cierto que en ninguna de las cosas dichas, ni en otras que se podrian dezir del, le aya hecho ventaja capitan, ni rey alguno."

[17] Ibid., f. 23r. The full text reads, "y fue uno de los mejores principes, que ha avido en el mundo."

he granted many favors to all classes of people. He entertained the people with festivals and games of various kinds."[18] From the vantage point of the Spanish Empire in 1547, this read like a blueprint for its project in Europe and the New World in the second half of the sixteenth century.[19] All the attributes and lessons of Augustus were applicable to sixteenth-century imperial rule.

In addition to those of Julius Caesar and Augustus, Mexia gave at least a dozen expansive imperial lives that provided positive examples worthy of both admiration and imitation, including the "Spanish" emperors Hadrian and Trajan, who added to the qualities of Caesar and Augustus the additional advantage of being from Spain. Besides them, it was the first Christian emperor from antiquity, Constantine the Great (272–337), who received the most praise and attention from Mexia because of the distinct religious contribution that he brought to the table.

Unlike the best pagan emperors, Constantine provided a model for religious behavior and actions toward the Church. This was particularly relevant in the 1530s and 1540s when Charles V was engaged in battles with the Protestant princes in Germany. The revival of interest in Constantine, an important development in the Renaissance of Empire, grew noticeably in the early sixteenth century, helped along by new editions of the *Ecclesiastical History* of Eusebius. Mexia's biography constituted an important chapter in this history because it appeared as part of the long march of Roman emperors as opposed to having it treated as an isolated chapter in Church history.

In this literary context, it was natural that many of the virtues attributed to Trajan, Hadrian, and Augustus were also applied to Constantine. He was courageous and powerful in war but also wise and prudent in times of peace. He ruled with justice, eliminated many bad laws and made new ones, and also revived learning in both the sciences and the liberal arts.[20] He himself dedicated much time to reading and writing and engaged in learned conversations with the ambassadors that visited his court. In addition, Constantine

---

[18] Ibid., f. 24v. "Hizo ordenancas y leyes maravillosas, en reformacion y emmienda de los abusos y malas costumbres. Edifico en Roma y fuera della grandes y suntuosos edificios, hizo grandes liberalidades y Mercedes a todos los estados de gentes. Alegro el pueblo con fiestas, y juegos de diversas maneras."

[19] Ibid., f. 23v. Octavian was credited with "criando y embiando pretores, y proconsules; y otros governadores, varones excelentes que la rigiessen y administrassen, y el mismo aviso y diligencia tuvo en lo tocante a la justicia, y costumbres, y religion; y en los edificios publicos."

[20] Ibid., f. 144r. "Fue efforcado y venturoso en la guerra, assi era prudentissimo y sabio en la paz, y hizo y ordeno leyes nuevas ... y trabajo mucho en perficionar todas las artes ... principalmente las liberales artes y estudios y sciencias."

followed the examples of many of the Caesars in being a generous benefac-
tor of temple building, but in his case it was Christian churches that received
his patronage and endowments.

   This was no small difference, and for Mexia the age of Constantine represented a golden age when the "good and Christian emperor" bestowed
on the empire a time of "universal peace." He was loved and admired by all
of his subjects, feared by the barbarians, and the "holy faith" was honored
and embraced by everyone. The age of martyrs was ended, good bishops
were appointed to put the Church in order, and holy monks and hermits
built monasteries and worked miracles in life and death as reported by
Cassiodorus. For all of this Constantine was given the name Constantine
the Great, which he richly deserved.[21] All of the succeeding emperors were
implicitly or explicitly measured against his example.

Philip II as Augustus

Imperial Inheritance as Triumph and Challenge, 1545 to 1577

The composite portrait offered to Philip II by Mexia as a guide was welcomed by the emperor, the young prince, and their ministers. In the royal
privilege granting publication rights for the book in 1545, Prince Philip
stated that members of the Emperor's council who had seen the book
judged that it was useful and beneficial for the general good of society.[22]
More personally, over the next five decades, Philip II found many occasions
to draw on the language and examples of the text, and his political vision
and agenda resonated powerfully with many of the imperial examples provided by Mexia. The critical key to understanding the reign of Philip II, like
that of his father, is to recognize that from the beginning of his life it was the
political models of the ancient Caesars that fueled his ambitions and drove
him to imitate and surpass ancient Roman imperial glory. And although it
was Charles V and his empire that first gave political and material substance
to this Renaissance dream, it was Philip II and his empire that made the
dream stick and ensured its survival for another two centuries in some shape
or form. To use the ancient analogy cited by contemporaries around 1550,
Charles V was Julius Caesar while Philip II was Augustus.

---

[21] Ibid., f. 146r.
[22] Ibid., p. *iv, "Porque aviendo se visto la dicha obra por algunos del consejo de su Magestad,
   parescio que de imprimirse no solamente no se seguiria inconviniente, pero utilidad y beneficio tuvimos lo por bien, y por las presente os damos licencia."

Philip II was first and foremost an imperial monarch, not a national or composite monarch, and secular political concerns and priorities trumped religious concerns throughout his reign. This is not to say that Spain, and especially Castile, was not a vitally important part of his empire, or that Catholicism was not a critical part of his imperial identity. But they were both subservient to the dominant goals that drove Philip II throughout his life: the preservation and expansion of his empire.

In 1545, the eighteen-year-old prince was regent of his father's Spanish kingdoms. He had assumed that role in 1543 at the age of sixteen when Charles V left Spain for Germany, and for the next five years he governed with the help of senior statesmen appointed by the emperor. He had also married Maria of Portugal in 1543 and was both father and widower by 1545, his young wife having died from the complications of childbirth.[23]

At the age of twenty-one, after what constituted a five-year Spanish apprenticeship in the art of ruling, Philip II was instructed by his father to join him at the imperial court in Brussels. There he was to be introduced to his future subjects in the Low Countries and discuss plans for the succession. His itinerary was planned to take him through Italy first, where he visited Genoa, Milan, Mantua, and various other cites including the battleground of Pavia, where his father's armies had won the famous battle of 1525.[24]

Philip's Italian tour of 1548 was an early rite of possession, even if it was not until 1550 that he was officially made Duke of Milan. The trip was centered on the Milan visit because Philip had already been told by his father that the duchy was to be part of his inheritance. The kingdoms of Naples and Sicily would come to him later, but his entry into Milan and the celebrations held during his stay there had the clear political function of reminding Italians of his imminent inheritance of those territories as well.

Philip had first visited Genoa, where Andrea Doria hosted him in the family palace. Elaborate classical structures had been built for the visit, which was the prince's baptism in Italian classicized pageantry. During the entry, the main triumphal arch near San Ciro was decorated with paintings and inscriptions praising the victories of Charles V around the globe. Philip II was also included in the decorations in the form of an equestrian statue of himself placed between Jupiter and Apollo.[25]

---

[23] A useful summary of the king's youth and formation can be found in Henry Kamen, *Philip of Spain* (New Haven, CT: Yale University Press, 1997), pp. 4–20.

[24] Ibid., p. 47.

[25] Bonner Mitchell, pp. 181–182.

These celebrations, as well as those in Milan a few weeks later, presented Philip II as the emperor's son and heir to a global empire of which Italy was a central part. The festivities strengthened and reaffirmed his ties to the powerful noble families in the imperial orbit: the Doria in Genoa, the Gonzaga in Mantua, and Cosimo de Medici in Florence among others. All of them were present to pay homage to Prince Philip as the designated heir to the most powerful empire of their age, and, more locally, as the prince who would soon be the dominant force in Italy.

The Italian sojourn also gave the young prince his first major exposure to the imperial aesthetics and artists of northern Italy. Like his father, he favored the imperial style of the high Renaissance throughout his reign in painting, sculpture, and architecture, a fact underlined by his decades-long patronage of Titian and Leone. He met and was painted by Titian for the first time in Milan in 1548 to 1549. Two years later he commissioned numerous additional works from the old Venetian master when both were in Augsburg in 1551, where the emperor was holding court. Over the next twenty-five years, Titan remained the most important court painter for Philip II even if it was from the comfort of his Venetian studio.[26] In these same years, Philip II met Leone Leoni (Figure 3.1), first in 1549 in Brussels, where the sculptor cast a bronze bust of Philip in the imperial style, and then again in Augsburg in 1551, when Leoni first designed a life-size sculpture of the prince in bronze, which he delivered to the court in Brussels in 1556.[27]

The theme of imperial continuity and succession and the comparisons it evoked with ancient Rome were promoted by Leoni. In 1550, he proposed to cast a medal with Charles V and Philip II on one side "as was done by another sculptor for Caesar and Augustus."[28] Obviously viewed as a flattering and noble comparison by Leoni, the idea that Charles V and his son represented a new imperial moment comparable to that of Julius and Augustus Caesar was not a view celebrated by other European princes. But it was consistent with the plans of Charles V in 1550 to hand on the great majority of his empire, including its title, to his son.

---

[26] Marie Tanner, *The Last Descendant of Aeneas* (New Haven, CT: Yale University Press, 1993), p. 145. Among the many commissions that Titian received from Philip II, Tanner notes "a series of mythic paintings that extolled Hapsburg destiny in the manner of the ancient Caesars." Tanner also looks at a broader range of imperial iconography cultivated by Philip II, who, she argues, "took as the chief tenet of his monarchy his right to restore the universal rule of the Roman Empire from East to West." P. 143.

[27] Plon, pp. 43–46; pp. 69–70. Although the senior Leoni never went to Spain to work for Philip II, his son, Pompeo, spent years in the Spanish court, where he continued the artistic style and legacy of his father as the primary sculptor of the king for the El Escorial.

[28] Ibid., pp. 69–70.

3.1. Leone Leoni, Philip II, 1553. (Museo Nacional del Prado, Madrid. Ref. E00272.)

This represented a change of plan where the title of emperor was concerned because Charles V had previously agreed to leave that to his brother Ferdinand. When Ferdinand resisted the change, the two brothers hammered out the Habsburg Family Compact of 1551 that left Ferdinand with the title until he died. He promised to then support Philip II's claim to the title with the German electors.[29]

But this resistance was only the beginning, and the Habsburg plan was rejected by Henry II of France and the Protestant princes of Germany, who declared war on Charles V in 1552. For the next three years, the old emperor was forced to spend millions of ducats – 11 million from the Spanish kingdoms alone – to defend his reputation and German territories.[30] More than a continuation of the religious wars in Germany, the wars of 1552 to 1555 were a preemptive strike by France and the Protestant princes against the imperial colossus that Philip II was about to inherit.

And they did succeed in denying the imperial title to Philip II. Ferdinand and his heirs continued to claim that title for centuries to come. But the opposition of France and the German Protestants did not stop the emergence of Philip II as a ruler who was far more powerful than any Holy Roman Emperor had ever been, including Charlemagne and Charles V. Henry II, in particular, understood this, and he mounted his next challenge directly against the young monarch.

When Philip II formally took full power in 1556, he was immediately confronted with both internal and external challenges to his rule that were reminiscent of his father's early years. Specifically, during his first decade in power he had to defend his inheritance against a papal–French alliance in Italy; a rebellion of the Moors in southern Spain; Ottoman attacks and threats in the Mediterranean world, especially Malta in 1565; and rebellion in the Netherlands. Like Augustus Caesar, Philip II's first decade in power was all about holding on to his inheritance, and he was tenacious, fierce, and unyielding in its defense throughout his life.

The first confrontation came from France and Rome, where Pope Paul IV Caraffa, a Neapolitan by birth, entered into a secret treaty with the French monarch, Henry II, to drive the Spanish out of Italy.[31] A native of Naples, Paul IV harbored a strong dislike for the Spanish, and he agreed to let Henry II claim both Naples and Milan for his sons should he succeed in driving them out of Italy. As some of the wealthiest parts of the Spanish Empire and

---

[29] Patrick Williams, *Philip II* (New York: Palgrave, 2001), p. 19.

[30] Ibid., p. 20.

[31] Brandi, p. 632.

important sources of revenue, grain, and military recruits, Philip II was not about to give them up. The Italian possessions also gave Philip II deep claims on the role of heir to the Roman emperors both medieval and ancient. Title or no title, he was the ruler who ruled over the majority of Italy, and in concrete political terms, as Charles V reminded his son in one of his political testaments, Italy was the key to his strength.[32]

In the confrontation with Rome, Philip II had the advantage of a superior and well-disciplined army under the command of the Duke of Alba. He took charge of the military forces in the Kingdom of Naples and marched easily into the Papal State in the spring of 1556. Demonstrating great control of his troops as they massed outside Rome, the Duke sent couriers into the city urging the pope to negotiate a peaceful settlement.[33] Abandoned by the French and facing certain defeat, the pope agreed to Alba's terms of peace that left the King of Spain more powerful than ever in Italy.

The pope agreed never "to make war, or offend the king and his states, nor to favor or help any prince or anyone else who wanted to," and to refrain from building new fortifications.[34] These conditions ensured that Rome would be militarily weak and dependent on an alliance with the Spanish Empire for protection, a position that played nicely into Philip II's emerging Constantinian image. It was the true beginning of the Spanish domination of Rome that would last for the next century.

Although Alba's victory was the local and immediate cause of this subjugation, it was Philip II's personal victory over the French at the famous battle of St. Quentin in 1557 that constituted the more important victory for the eventual transformation of the political landscape of Italy. As the first and only battle that Philip II was ever present for, the defeat of Henry II at St. Quentin was a major victory for the young king and a demonstration of the superior resources that his vast inheritance could supply. Counting almost 80,000 men from various parts of his empire, his army easily routed the French, who simply could not sustain a war on two fronts.[35]

The most important result of Philip II's victory at St. Quentin was that it signaled the end of more than sixty years of war in Italy between the French and Spanish monarchies. In the treaty of Cateau-Cambresis of 1559 that marked the end of the war, France formally acknowledged Philip II's

---

[32] See Dandelet, *Spanish Rome*, pp. 53–57, for details on the Caraffa War.

[33] See especially the letters written by the Duke in Grottaferrata and Ostia from October 24 to December 2 of 1556. Duque de Alba, *Epistolario del III Duque de Alba Don Fernando Alvarez de Toledo* (Madrid, 1952), Vol. I, 1536–67, pp. 434–446.

[34] Ibid., f. 163r.

[35] P. Williams, *Philip II*, p. 95.

rightful claim to Naples and Milan. Thus began a century of relative peace in Italy, the age of the Pax Hispanica. Italy, the birthplace of the Imperial Renaissance, was merged more deeply than ever with the Spanish empire as the two Mediterranean peninsulas enjoyed a growing and vibrant traffic of people, commerce, ideas, and aesthetics.

The Italian possessions came with a cost as well, first among them defense of the expansive coastlines from the Ottoman threat. The great nemesis of Charles V, Suleiman the Magnificent, was still in power in Istanbul when Philip II first occupied the throne in Spain. Besides supporting the Islamic pirates who sailed from various ports in North Africa to make raids against the Italian and Spanish coastlines, he was capable of sending his own slaving expeditions into the central and western Mediterranean to menace Spanish possessions. One such raid on Menorca in 1558 resulted in thousands of subjects of the Spanish king being sold into slavery.[36]

It was during the reigns of Suleiman the Magnificent (1520–1566) and his successor Selim (1566–1575) that Ottoman naval power and the power of their Barbary allies were at their peak. Fernand Braudel went so far as to call the constant corsair threat during this period a "reign of terror from Gibraltar to Sicily." Marked by pirate raids and incursions that left coastal towns burned and looted and tens of thousands of Spaniards and Italians killed or sold into slavery, the impact of this conflict on the collective mentality of Philip II's subjects and the king cannot be underestimated.[37]

Spanish Sicily and the Aeolian Islands provided a particularly strong example of the threat. They suffered a number of large-scale attacks in the middle of the sixteenth century, including a full-scale attack on the island of Lipari by a large fleet of thirty triremes led by Barbarossa in 1544. After sacking the island and killing or carrying off the entire population of 11,000 people as slaves, the city of Patti on the north coast of Sicily was also attacked.[38]

Another series of major raids occurred in 1560 and 1561 after the loss of the Spanish fortress at Goletta: the Ottoman surrogate, Dragut, took the entire Spanish fleet of seven galleys after a surprise attack in the summer of 1561, and the large fleet of victorious corsairs then sacked Aeolian and Sicilian towns at will.[39] Corsair slaving raids on coastal villages continued

[36] Fernand Braudel, *The Mediterranean and the Mediterranean World in the Age of Philip II*, trans. Sian Reynolds (New York: Harper Collins), 1973, Vol. 2, p. 993.
[37] Ibid.
[38] Filippo Irato, *Patti nella Storia* (Messina: Pungitopo, 2004), pp. 94–102.
[39] Braudel, Vol. 2, p. 984.

throughout the late sixteenth and seventeenth centuries. Sicily alone was attacked an estimated 136 times between 1570 and 1606.[40]

Faced with this constant threat and assault on his reputation, Philip had assembled a force of roughly 100 ships and 12,000 men to sail on the forces of the pirate leader, Dragut, in Tripoli in 1559. But Suleiman had sent reinforcements that surprised the Spanish, who ended up losing the battle and many ships. A remnant of the Spanish force that took refuge in a fortress in Malta also eventually fell to an Ottoman siege, and thousands of soldiers were taken back to Istanbul as slaves.[41]

This was a grim beginning for Philip II's defense of his Mediterranean possessions, and it was only made worse by yet another naval loss to Dragut in 1562 that further weakened the Spanish navy force in the Mediterranean. But the heavy loss of ships, men, and reputation did not lead the young king to resignation on the seas. Rather, Philip II made an important innovation that his father had never made: he embarked on a systematic naval buildup that included the establishment of a permanent force of 100 ships for the western and central Mediterranean. Shipyards in Sicily, Barcelona, and Naples got busy building ships that were eventually stationed in Cartagena, Messina, Naples, and Genoa.[42]

Philip II received additional confirmation of the need for a permanent Mediterranean navy in 1565 when Suleiman unleashed a furious assault on the island of Malta. The knights of Malta were to the Ottomans what the Barbary pirates were to the Spanish kings. Since their eviction from Rhodes by the sultan in 1522 and relocation in Malta in 1530 under the protection of Charles V, they had dedicated themselves to raiding Ottoman outposts and North African ports and seizing any Islamic ships they could get their hands on. Suleiman was subsequently determined to deliver a fatal blow to the knights and to seize Malta as yet another important step and prize in his western imperial expansion.

Because of its proximity to Spanish Sicily and Naples, control of Malta was strategically critical for Philip II, and he subsequently ordered his Sicilian viceroy, Don Garcia de Toledo, to organize a fleet to relieve the embattled knights. The Spanish fleet of 100 galleys carrying 12,000 fresh soldiers arrived four months after the siege of the island had begun and quickly defeated the Turkish forces, who suffered large losses. The Ottoman ships that did make

[40] Robert C. Davis, *Christian Slaves and Muslim Masters* (New York: Palgrave), 2003, p. 8. Numbers after the work of Giuseppe Bonaffini, *La Sicilia e i Barbereschi. Incursioni corsare e riscatto degli schiavi (1570–1606)*, Palermo, 1983.

[41] P. Williams, pp. 98–99.

[42] Ibid., p. 100.

it back carried the grim news of the loss of as many as 30,000 out of 36,000 men.[43]

The successful defense of Malta was arguably a victory equal to that of Philip II in 1559 in terms of what it did to protect his Italian inheritance. But it was a greater victory for his imperial reputation in Europe and Italy, because it revealed him to be living up to the old (largely Italian) humanistic program of reviving ancient Roman military power to crush the Ottoman threat.

Philip II was also the recipient of new histories on the Ottomans that had the purpose of informing him of the nature of one of his major enemies. The first work of the royal historian, Antonio Herrera de Tordesillas, for example, was a history of the Ottoman Empire that he wrote in 1565, the same year as the siege of Malta.[44] It represented yet another line of humanist continuity between the fifteenth and sixteenth centuries that underlined the role of the Ottoman threat as a constant spur to the Renaissance of Empire in the West in terms of both literary production and real military power.

The difference between the earlier period and the age of Philip II, however, was the increasingly common clash of large navies that could involve as many as 100,000 men and 500 or more ships. The Mediterranean Sea was an increasingly major theatre of large-scale imperial contest in the middle of the sixteenth century with the Ottomans sending out large armadas almost every summer. When it came to naval power, Philip II was playing a game of catch-up in the early decades of his reign. He had no choice but to build and maintain a strong navy to defend his Mediterranean territories as well as the constant flow of goods, gold, information, and soldiers that circulated in the Western Mediterranean between his Spanish and Italian possessions.

At the same time, the fight against the Ottomans also had a more local dimension for the Catholic King because they were feared to be inciting revolt on the part of the old Morisco population of Granada. The Alpujaras revolt, which took its name after the hills where many of the Morisco rebels lived, was caused more by the strident attempts of the king, acting through the Church and his governor, to force the Morisco population to give up their local culture and identity than it was by any secret Ottoman plot. No matter the cause, only a few years after the defense of Malta, in 1568, Philip II

---

[43] Ibid., pp. 100–101.

[44] BNM, Mss. 3624: Antonio Herrera y Tordesillas, *La Chroníca de los Turcos*, 1565. The title page noted that Herrera's text followed the work of Juan Maria Vicentino, a *chronista* of Suleiman. Herrera also described himself as the chronísta of Philip II, to whom the work is dedicated.

was faced with another Islamic challenge to his inheritance, this time quite literally in the shadow of his father's imperial palace in Granada.[45]

Philip II appointed his brother, Don Juan of Austria, as the commander in charge of suppressing the revolt of the Moriscos, but he took a personal interest and role in the fight, traveling to Seville to be near the action. When the rebels, who had been aided by 4,000 North African allies, were defeated and exiled in chains from Granada in 1570, it was yet another victory for the king.[46]

It was also an important blow against the Islamic threat, at least in the eyes of the king and many of his subjects. Like the defense of Malta, it allowed Philip II to again claim the title of defender of Christendom. In this case, he also tied himself to his many Spanish ancestors who had led the *reconquista*, including the conquerors of Granada, his great-grandparents, Ferdinand and Isabella.

But just as Philip II was expelling the last remnant of Islamic Spain in the kingdom of Granada, Sultan Selim II was reasserting his power over the eastern Mediterranean. He was dedicated to perpetuating the bellicose policies of his father and had built another large navy that once again threatened Christian coastlines throughout the Mediterranean. His conquest of the last Venetian stronghold of Cyprus, Famagosta, in August of 1571, and the infamous torture and execution of the Venetian governor, Marcantonio Bragadin, underlined Selim II's intention of continuing Ottoman expansion with the characteristic Ottoman ferocity that had sown fear in Europe for more than a century.[47]

The battle between the two emperors and their allies reached a new crescendo in the autumn of 1571. In October of that year, a fleet of more than 300 ships from the Holy League of Spain, Venice, and the papacy met an Ottoman fleet, including their Barbary and Algerian allies, of roughly the same size in the Gulf of Lepanto off the west coast of Greece. The ensuing clash of roughly 85,000 men from the Holy League and roughly 75,000 from the Turkish navy constituted one of the largest naval battles in the Mediterranean Sea in the entire early modern period.

The Spanish Empire was the largest contributor of money, ships, and men to the League, and Philip II's admiral and brother, Don Juan of Austria, subsequently led their forces. With participants like Don Juan, Ali Pasha,

---

[45] Kamen, *Philip of Spain*, pp. 128–31.
[46] P. Williams, pp. 102–106.
[47] See Cecilia Gibellini, *L'immagine di Lepanto* (Venice: Marsilio, 2008), pp. 29–39, for a description of the literary response to the fall of Cyprus.

Alessandro Farnese, and Marc Antonio Colonna and a young unknown soldier who would become more famous than all of them, Miguel Cervantes,
the clash had all the ingredients of the epic battle that it quickly became for
the victors.[48]

Building on their initial advantage of better and more numerous canons that inflicted serious damage on the Ottoman forces, the soldiers of
the League overwhelmed the Ottomans during five hours of hand-to-hand
combat. The resulting bloodshed left an estimated 30,000 Turks dead and
8,000 more taken as slaves. In addition, 12,000 Christian slaves that were
chained to the Ottoman oars were set free.

The forces of the League had lost close to 8,000 men, but they had also
captured 200 Ottoman ships and lost only 15 galleys.[49] By all measures it
was a dramatic victory for the League and celebrated as such from Venice to
Rome to Madrid.

Here, at long last, was the kind of victory that the imperial humanists had
been dreaming of for more than a century.

Accordingly, artists and writers set to work to give the battle its appropriate Renaissance frame. Vasari created historical narrative paintings of the
battle in the Sala Reggia for Pius V. Titian painted an allegorical celebration
of it that prominently displayed Philip II lifting his infant son Ferdinand
toward the opening heavens that put the palm of victory in his young hand.
Poets throughout Italy and Spain wrote new epic poems comparing it to
ancient victories, and Cervantes famously described it as the battle that shat-
tered the myth of Ottoman naval invincibility. Theatres were built that could
be flooded so that the battle could be reenacted on an annual basis. And this
was the tip of the representational iceberg.[50]

Even if the Ottomans were able to quickly rebuild their navy and recap-
ture Tunis in 1574, they never again sent a large fleet against Malta or to
directly attack Spain or Italy. Lepanto had been a wake-up call for the
Ottomans that Spanish naval power was formidable. New World treasure
allowed Philip II to spend vast sums on his navy, and competition with the
Ottomans for control of the Mediterranean led to a major expansion of the
Spanish Empire's naval power and capabilities that brought them to a rough
parity with the Ottomans.

Neither the Spanish nor Ottoman Empire ever equaled the ancient Roman
accomplishment of making the Mediterranean a Spanish or Ottoman lake.

---

[48] Jack Beeching, *The Galleys at Lepanto* (London: Hutchinson, 1982), p. 192.
[49] P. Williams, pp. 108–110.
[50] Dandelet, *Spanish Rome*, pp. 71–73.

By 1580, however, they had reached a cold truce that effectively divided the great body of water and its surrounding territories into two large spheres of political influence that they largely controlled. Pirates from both sides still raided the opponent's coastlines for the rich booty of slaves, but Lepanto signaled the end of Ottoman expansion beyond Crete, and it led them to sign secret treaties with Philip II that allowed both empires to turn their attention to other problems.[51]

This was enough for Philip II, whose willingness to negotiate with the Ottomans after 1574 revealed a healthy sense of political pragmatism about his Mediterranean limits. He was no blind crusader driven by Messianic illusions who dreamt of conquering Jerusalem. Besides, he had other major problems on his hands, namely another internal revolt in the Netherlands.

The Dutch Challenge

In 1567, the Florentine merchant and writer Lodovico Guicciardini dedicated a book to Philip II titled *A Description of All the Low Countries*.[52] It was an accomplished piece of scholarship that drew on ancient, medieval, and contemporary sources with the aim of describing the geography, resources, customs, people, economy, and cities of the Netherlands. Above all else, it served as a vivid and detailed reminder to Philip II of the richness of the territory that Guicciardini described as "a most important member of your entire empire."[53]

Just as Philip II's portrait at the beginning of the book was given a classical frame, Guicciardini's picture of the Netherlands was also placed in the frame of empires past and present. From the beginning of his description of Belgium, for example, he pointed out that he was following Caesar's

[51] For details on the treaty negotiations, see my article "Between Empires: Spanish Sicily and the Contest for the Central Mediterranean in the Late Sixteenth Century," in *Spagna e l'Oriente Islamico* (Istanbul, 2007), Note 8.

[52] For biographical information on Lodovico Guicciardini, see D. Aristodemo, "Lodovico Guicciardini," in *Dizionario Biografico degli Italiani* (Roma: Romagraf, 2003), Vol. 61, pp. 121–127. A nephew of Francesco, Lodovico had lived for many years in Antwerp working with his merchant brothers. Following in his famous uncle's footsteps, he had already published a history of the Low Countries from roughly 1500 to 1560 that largely focused on political and military events. D. Aristodemo edited a modern edition of the text in 1994.

[53] Lodovico Guicciardini, *Descrittione di Tutti Paesi Bassi, Altrimenti detti Germania Inferiore* (Anversa: Guglielmo Silvio, 1567). In the unpaginated dedication, the author called his work "un ritratto al naturale di questi suoi bellissimi, et nobilissimi paesi Bassi, accioche ella riveduto, et riconosciuto, a parte a parte per iscritto, et in pittura, un membro tanto importante di tutto il suo Imperio."

description of ancient Gaul: "Julius Caesar, (that excellent author, whom we intend to follow in this material as much as we are able) in his *Commentaries* divides Gaul into three parts."[54] More importantly, he also wove Charles V and Philip II into the picture, underlining their place in the history of the various lands. In his lengthy description of Antwerp, for example, he wrote a detailed account of Philip II's triumphal entry into the city in 1549, including his speech.[55]

It is easy to imagine that Philip II experienced some nostalgia when he read the book, or at least glanced at its many maps of the regions and cities, as well as engravings of notable churches and civic buildings. He had spent a number of years in the Low Countries, and Guicciardini's book could only have reinforced the monarch's pride of possession as well as his determination to maintain his rule. It is possible that this was part of the goal of Guicciardini, who rightly feared that the iconoclastic riots and rebellion of the lower nobility in 1566 were only the beginning of a long and destabilizing wave of civic disturbances that would be bad for his business.

The narrative provided by Guicciardini corresponded with Philip II's views of his rights and responsibilities vis-à-vis the Low Countries. He was the rightful ruler by dynastic inheritance, and it fell to him and those he appointed, in this case his aunt Margaret, who was the acting governor of the Low Countries, to impose law and order. The growing resistance to his government on the part of the nobility and Dutch Protestants was viewed as treason, plain and simple, and could not be tolerated. When it came to the governance of his own lands, Philip II was not open for negotiations. His was a rule of one, and the challenge to his imperial authority from his own subjects led the Catholic King to respond to the growing rebellion in those regions with an iron fist.

What began as Calvinist religious rebellion with the iconoclast riots of 1566 merged with the growing discontent of the nobility over bad governance and slights to their privileges and status. When some of them rebelled in 1567, the monarch's response was to send the Duke of Alba with an army of 10,000 men to crush the revolt. The subsequent execution of an estimated 1,000 subjects of the king – including the public beheading of two noblemen of the highest rank, Egmont and Hornes, who had been his councilors – ushered in a period of war and bloodshed that would last until

---

[54] Ibid., p. 1. In his introduction to his description of Belgium he notes: "Dicendo che Giulio Cesare (il quale ottimo autore, in quell tanto, che di questa material si potrà, intendiamo di seguitare) divide nelli suoi Comentarii, tutta la universal Gallia in tre parti; Belgica, Celtica, et Aquitania."

[55] Ibid., pp. 85–88.

the king's death in 1598.[56] He would pass the hostilities on to his son rather than negotiate any settlement or truce with the rebel provinces. To the end, he refused to yield any single piece of his inheritance, although by 1598 the Northern provinces of the Netherlands were effectively operating as an independent country.

The wars in the Netherlands have received enormous amounts of attention from historians, and many have asked why Philip II was so tenacious and unbending in a series of conflicts that cost his treasury tens of millions of ducats.[57] How to understand a political policy that so clearly went against the best interests of the larger empire in terms of the money and men that it drained away from so many other endeavors?

The answer has often been religion: Philip II had to defend Catholicism against the Calvinist rebels and their eventual Protestant allies in England and France. Just as religion was an obvious part of the explanation for the relentless wars of Charles V in Germany a generation earlier, so too did the Reformation play a role in the wars of Flanders. Philip II made much of his role as defender of the faith in his own correspondence justifying his bellicose policies.

But many of the Dutch rebels were not Protestant, and in the first brutal suppression executed by the Duke of Alba in 1567 to 1568, many of those executed, including the leading noblemen, were Catholics. Their offense was rebellion, not heresy, but that brought them little mercy. The fact is that Philip II responded to rebellion whenever and wherever it occurred in his realms with the same harsh treatment. Whether Catholic bread rioters in Naples or unhappy Catholic Aragonese nobles in 1591, rebellion was met with a strong show of force and the harshest forms of execution. In short, the twin political goals of defending his territories and enforcing the obedience of his subjects were preeminent. Enforcing Catholic orthodoxy was simply a part of enforcing his broader authority.

The repeated attempts to suppress dissent in the Low Countries came with a high cost not just in terms of money and men but also in terms of reputation. A central lesson of imperial humanists since the time of Petrarch had been that the good emperors, from Julius Caesar forward, strove not only for the glory of conquest but also for the honor that came from wise governance and the generous application of the virtues of mercy and clemency toward one's enemies. Emperors who forgot this

[56] For a good synthesis of Alba's repression, see Jonathan I. Israel, *The Dutch Republic* (Oxford: Oxford University Press, 1998), pp. 155–168.

[57] For details on the cost of the wars in Flanders in terms of both money and men, see G. Parker, *The Grand Strategy*, pp. 115–146.

lesson quickly devolved into despots and tyrants, always the dark side of imperial rule.

If any one conflict led to the charge of tyranny against Philip II, it was the war in Flanders. The propaganda campaign of the Dutch rebels, and later the English and French, against the king proved that the knowledge of the ancient Roman Empire could also provide excellent grist for the mill of the anti-imperialists. Philip II regularly found himself tagged as a tyrant every bit as bad as Tiberius, Nero, and Caligula. The famous Black Legend that grew up in Protestant Europe against the king showed that imperial comparisons could cut both ways, but Philip II understood this and fought back against the dark image that aimed to ruin his royal reputation. Selective grants of amnesty issued by Philip II early in the conflict, for example, were worded to underline the king's virtues of clemency toward his subjects.[58]

More substantially, the royal historian, Antonio Herrera y Tordesillas, with the support and encouragement of Philip II, wrote a history of Flanders during the king's reign. It cast the monarch as fully justified in defending his territories from the rebels. Indeed, it praised his tenacity in pursuing the struggle and cast the king as driven by political duty to preserve the territories of his ancestors.[59]

The battle in the Low Countries was but one part of Philip II's epic struggle to defend his empire and spread the faith from this official point of view. Herrera also wrote separate volumes on the wars in France, the conquest of the New World, and the history of Milan under Charles V and Philip II. Together these works constituted the most expansive historical apologetics and imperial history written during the reign of Philip II and Philip III.[60]

From the vantage point of the New World and Italy, in particular, the image of Philip II as a ruler who successfully defended his inheritance and ruled following the model of the good Caesars was easier to justify for writers like Herrera y Tordesillas. In those territories Spanish imperial power was consolidated during Philip II's reign. Generally good governance on the part of a series of viceroys and governors served to more fully integrate those important territories into the imperial system.

Subsequently, both became increasingly vital parts of the Spanish Empire as the New World provided an ever-growing supply of silver for Philip II's

---

[58] See, for example, *Il Perdono Generale Che Il Re Filippo Concede a Tutti Paesi, Stati, et Luochi di Fiandra* (Bologna: Alessandro Benacci, 1574), un-paginated. The king wrote that the amnesty he was granting in 1574 was following his natural inclination, clemency and piety: "nostra naturale inclinatione, clemenza, et pieta."

[59] Antonio de Herrera y Tordesillas, *Comentarios de las alteraciones de Flandes* (Madrid, 1600).

[60] Richard Kagan, *Clio and the Crown* (Baltimore: The Johns Hopkins University Press, 2009). See especially chapter 5, "Defending Imperium," pp. 150–200.

military. Italy, for its part, provided not only skilled soldiers and captains but also a steady supply of artists and humanists who built up the king's icono-graphic and literary reputation. The skillful domination of Rome and the papacy, moreover, allowed Philip II to control the Church throughout his lands and to extract large amounts of revenue from it. More often than not, the papacy also supported the king's imperial rights and rule in territories both old and new, still an important political factor in the sixteenth century. In return, Philip II supported traditional papal claims to spiritual supremacy and played the role of generous patron and protector of Rome.

The New World in the Age of Philip II

The Age of Imperial Consolidation and Exploitation

In November of 1569, the new Spanish viceroy of Peru, Francisco de Toledo, made his official entry into Lima to take up his duties. It was an entry fash-ioned as triumph complete with a city gate decorated to look like a trium-phal arch and a large contingent of soldiers dressed in special red, yellow, and black uniforms for the occasion. After the king's official order granting him his office had been read, the doors of the gate were opened to allow his entry to take possession of the city.[61]

Over the next thirteen years, Toledo gave military and material sub-stance to the ritual image of his reign as a triumph in the ancient style. The royal official most responsible for the increased production of the mines of Potosí, he presided over the first phase of an unequaled silver boom. The city of Potosí itself became a living metaphor of Spanish imperial expan-sion as it grew to be a large boom town of more than 120,000 people, equal in size to Seville or Rome. Throughout the reign of Philip II, it produced a steady stream of treasure to fill the galleons that sailed back to Spain each year like great triumphal carriages filled with the continuing spoils of conquest.

If the age of Ferdinand and Isabella was one of discovery and conquest and the era of Charles V one of conquest and plunder, the reign of Philip II was the period of increased colonization, consolidation of power, and the systematic economic exploitation of the New World colonies on an unprecedented level. The driving goal that united imperial policy was the

---

[61] Alejandro Osorio, "La entrada del virrey y el ejercicio de poder en la Lima del siglo XVII," *Historia Mexicana*, Vol. 55, No. 3, 2006, pp. 767–831. Toledo's entry is described on pages 769–770.

extraction of as much raw wealth as possible from the colonies in the form of silver, gold, and taxation on the land and trade of the New World.

Revenue from the New World was an increasingly critical source of income that allowed Philip II to expand and maintain his military edge in Europe. By 1557, when Philip II took power, the amount of income from the king's various economic claims in the Americas had grown to 1,200,000 ducats or around 11 percent of his total income. This represented a rapid growth from the 250,000 ducats that Charles V was getting from the New World annually in the 1530s and 1540s. The king understood well that the Americas represented the growth area of his budget, and he subsequently sought to maximize royal revenues from the colonies.[62]

Guided by this economic project, the king's agenda in the New World also sought to transform the social and cultural fabric of the conquered lands through increased colonization. The Spaniards believed in their cultural superiority, and they subsequently sought to impose it on the Americas. This meant building cities and towns that imitated those of Europe with their central town squares surrounded by a courthouse, viceroy's palace, and church. By the 1570s there were 192 distinctly Spanish cities and towns in the Americas.[63] It also meant building universities to perpetuate humanist and scholastic learning, not to mention Latin and Spanish as the main languages of the ruling class. Finally, it meant erasing pre–Columbian religious beliefs, rituals, buildings, and the priestly class and replacing them with Spanish Catholicism. Spanish imperialism in the age of Philip II sought nothing short of remaking the New World in the image of the Old World with a few adjustments that actually increased the king's power. The result was the most pervasive and expansive example of political domination, economic exploitation, and cultural conquest since the time of the Roman Empire.

Building on the foundations laid by Charles V, Philip II and his ministers developed and strengthened the major institutions of government already in place and created new ones as well. Using the Council of the Indies as his main advisory body in Spain, the king governed through his viceroys in Mexico and Peru. Royal correspondence with these men was thick as Philip II sought to ensure that his priorities were carried out. The viceroys, in turn, presided over a growing network of *corregidores*, or regional governors,

---

[62] Lyle N. McAlister, *Spain and Portugal in the New World, 1492–1700* (Minneapolis: University of Minnesota Press, 1984), pp. 186–187. Besides the 20 percent of all mineral rights claimed by the crown, the main sources of royal income in the reign of Philip II were Indian tribute, the customs duty on European imports, investments in business ventures, the diezmo, or tithe, and the cruzada indulgence.

[63] Ibid., p. 144.

to enforce their policies outside of the capital cities of Mexico and Lima. Together with a growing number of *Audiencias*, or courts, they imposed royal policy and administered justice.

By most accounts, Spanish rule in the Americas, benefiting from experience in Iberia and Italy, was largely successful at reordering society and controlling both the settlers and native peoples alike. Together with the secular branches of government, the Inquisition in both Mexico and Peru enforced religious discipline, as did the growing network of bishoprics and religious orders, including the Jesuits, who also established colleges and eventually universities. At the same time, new law codes, building on that of 1542, strengthened royal power by limiting the rights of the *encomenderos* and increasing the monarchy's control over Indian labor. Thus, Philip II replicated the major administrative, legal, and ecclesiastical structures of his European territories to control both the conquered societies of the New World and the estimated 220,000 Europeans who lived in the New World by the latter half of the sixteenth century.[64]

The additional piece of imperial government that was expanded in this period was the military. Philip II built up a standing navy to protect both the coasts and treasure fleet that brought back the bullion that was such a critical part of the royal treasury. With the Caribbean islands particularly vulnerable to a growing number of British and then Dutch pirates, he also ordered built a string of fortifications for Santo Domingo, Florida, and on the Central American coast in the important coastal city of Cartagena from which the treasure fleet sailed. In yet another Italian contribution to the Spanish empire, the engineer and architect Bautista Antonelli entered into the service of Philip II in 1570 and was sent to the New World to build Renaissance fortifications much like those that his family had built in Italy.[65]

The economic success of Philip II's New World policies and imperial strategy was dramatic. The traditional one fifth of mineral rights in all of its territories that were claimed by the crown put more than 71 million ducats into the royal coffers in the period between 1561 and 1600.[66] This was a tremendous amount of income that was simply not available to any other European monarchy. It goes a long way toward explaining how Philip II was

[64] Ibid., pp. 111–117. Incomplete documentation for Spanish emigration to the New World limits our precise knowledge of population numbers, but McAlister, following Peter Boyd-Bowman, puts our best estimate at 226,870 emigrants in the period from 1493 to 1579. By 1570, the estimates project the European population to have been around 220,000 people.

[65] On B. Antonelli and New World fortifications, see *Historia del arte hispano-americano* (Barcelona: Salvat, 1955), Vol. 1, pp. 494–516.

[66] P. Williams, pp. 83–85.

able to fight multiple-front wars, build up his navy, and fund the expensive fortifications in the New World.

Mexican and Peruvian silver grew in importance as a part of royal finances over the reign of Philip II by virtue of the continual and extraordinary growth in the amount of silver extracted. The discovery of the great silver mines at Zacatecas (1546), Potosi (1545), and Guanajuato (1558) had all occurred before or at the very beginning of Philip II's reign. But it was the introduction in 1557 of the mercury amalgamation process that allowed the silver to be separated from other minerals much more efficiently. Introduced in Potosi in 1572 by the viceroy Francisco de Toledo, this process led to the tripling of the amount of income from the mines over the forty years of Philip's reign. Annual royal income from American silver production went from an average of roughly 700,000 ducats annually in the first decade of his rule to more than 2,800,000 ducats annually in the last decade of his reign.[67]

Besides the effective harnessing of new mining technology, the other major factor in the increase of American silver imports into Spain for both the crown and other investors was the introduction of the *mita* in Peru. This system of forced Indian labor, also introduced by the Francisco de Toledo in the 1570s, required the various Inca communities of Peru to provide a rotating population of 13,500 men per year to work in the mines.[68] This forced Native American labor was perhaps the most obvious example of the overt exploitation of the conquered people of the Americas.

One of the main aims of the New Laws of 1542, as well as additional legal reforms promoted by Philip II that were not finally codified until the later seventeenth century, was to provide more protection for the Indians from the abuses of the *encomenderos*. The monarchy also sought to phase out, or modify, the *encomienda* system by reclaiming lands and their Indian subjects when an *encomendero* died or sold his lands. Through this means, as well as original claims from the earliest days of the conquest, the king, acting through his viceroys, became the major owner of Indian labor who benefited from it on a scale never reached by any of the conquistadors.[69]

---

[67] Ibid., p. 84.

[68] Good details on the functioning and evolution of the *mita* system can be found in Thierry Saignes, "Notes on the Regional Contribution to the *Mita* in Potosí in the Early Seventeenth Century," in *Bulletin of Latin American Research*, Vol. 4, No. 1, 1985, pp. 65–76; Enrique Tandeter, "Forced and Free Labor in Late Colonial Potosí," *Past and Present*, No. 93 (Nov., 1981), pp. 98–136; and Jeffrey A. Cole, "An Abolitionism Born of Frustration: The Conde de Lemos and the Potosí Mita, 1667–73," *Hispanic American Historical Review*, Vol. 63, No. 2, 1983, pp. 307–333.

[69] On the evolution of the *encomienda* system, see L. McAlister, pp. 156–157.

The exploitation of Native American labor in the mines with the support and encouragement of the crown was the clearest proof of this. So, too, was the gradual transformation of the New World agricultural economy and the Indians' role in it. Early Spanish practices took advantage of the existing tribute system that used the native noble class to collect tribute from the native population that farmed the land. By the end of the sixteenth century, however, most of the best arable land in Mexico was owned, controlled, and farmed by Spanish *encomenderos* and the crown using Indian labor.[70]

Philip II, like his predecessors, justified his policies toward the conquered societies of the New World largely through his role as protector and patron of the Church. The original papal proclamation of Alexander VI from 1493 granting the Spanish monarchs dominion over the New World had emphasized their obligation to evangelize the conquered peoples. It also gave them the power and means to do so through the granting of the *patronato real*. This was the most prized gift that a pope could grant a monarch because it effectively gave him control over all of the clergy. He had authority over the appointment of bishops, Inquisitors, university professors, and the activities of all of the religious orders.[71]

The role came with responsibilities as well. The papal bull of Paul III in 1537 had recognized the full humanity of the Indians and repeated the obligations of Charles V to evangelize his newly conquered subjects. This meant building up and supporting the Church in all of its institutional manifestations, a process that was just getting started in the age of Charles V but that accelerated rapidly under Philip II.

Fully aware of the central importance of religion to his political identity, reputation, and the maintenance and increase of his power, the Catholic King took seriously his role as primary patron of the Church in the New World. Substantial royal support and patronage led to widespread building and endowments of churches, convents, monasteries, schools, hospitals, and orphanages. They became the material proof that the king was living up to his part of the papal bargain that acknowledged his right to the fruits of the conquered lands so long as he evangelized the Indians. At the same time,

[70] Hanns J. Prem, "Spanish Colonization and Indian Property in Central Mexico, 1521–1620," *Annals of the Association of American Geographers*, Vol. 82, No. 3, 1992, pp. 444–459. The article points out that the process of dispossessing the Indians of their property in the rich agricultural areas of Mexico accelerated in the second half of the second century to a point where most arable land was in the hands of Spaniards by 1600. The policies of Philip II played a direct role in the process.

[71] W. Eugene Shiels, *King and Church: The Rise and Fall of the Patronato Real* (Chicago: Loyola University Press, 1961).

successful evangelization, or at least the appearance of it, was the strongest tool against the critics of Spanish imperialism in the New World.

When Philip II came to power, the great debates of 1551 to 1552 between Las Casas and his former tutor, Sepúlveda, were still fresh. Although Charles V, in deference to the powerful Salamanca school of theologians, had upheld the ban on the publication of Sepúlveda's *Apology*, he had not supported the arguments of Las Casas or his dark version of the conquest. Neither did Philip II.

Philip II, in fact, moved to push the Franciscans and Dominicans, the most ardent defenders of Indian rights, to the periphery of New Spain during his reign. The diocesan clergy and Jesuits took over the work of conversion and instruction in the settled territories, and they largely supported the crown. Although there were plenty of disputes over ecclesiastical jurisdiction, nobody rose to contest the right of the Spanish monarch and his subjects to rule and exploit the land as Las Casas had done.

At the same time, Philip II also eventually moved to push the argument of Las Casas to the periphery of the conversation on the Indies. More specifically, he sponsored or supported historians who wrote against the harsh condemnation of the early conquistadors by Las Casas. The view that was clearly favored by the king was that of Sepúlveda with its Aristotelian defense of the conquest based on the view that the Indians were natural slaves because of their lack of some basic marks of civilization as well as their practice of human sacrifice. Philip II, like most of the ruling class in Spain, clearly believed that the Spaniards possessed a superior level of civilization and had the right by natural law to rule over the Indians. Unlike his father, he sponsored no continuing debate on the topic, and the leading humanist historians of his era moved decidedly in defense of the conquest.

This was the case with the Jesuit Juan de Mariana, who dedicated his *General History of Spain* to Philip II in 1592. The work was a particularly important and singular example of imperial humanist history because it united in one work the entire span of Spanish imperial history from the age of the Roman Empire to the time of the Spanish conquest of the Indies. Unlike the unfinished history of Spain by Florian d'Ocampo and Ambrosio Morales, the work of Mariana went through the age of Ferdinand and Isabella, thus providing a narrative continuity between the ancient and new empires that most defined Spain.[72]

---

[72] Juan de Mariana, *Historia General de España* (Madrid: Andres Garcia de la Iglesia, 1669). The date of this edition is taken from the printing licenses. Quotes from the text are from this later edition.

The original work of 1592 was written in Latin because, as Mariana explained, he wanted the history of Spain to be known by other Europeans who did not understand Castilian. This goal was met to judge by the foreign editions of the work published in Germany (1605–1606) and the Netherlands (1633). In 1601 Mariana dedicated a Castilian version to Philip III with the explanation that because of the "little knowledge" of Latin in Spain, he did the translation so that Spaniards could read about their own history. The vernacular version enjoyed greater success. It went to press twenty-three times over the next two centuries, and there were an additional five French editions published between 1628 and 1725 and one English edition from 1699. The text subsequently joined the works of Guevara and Mexia as one of the most successful Spanish histories of the sixteenth century.[73]

It was an accomplished work of high Renaissance learning that drew on the increasingly familiar list of ancient and medieval sources, both pagan and Christian, to chart the long march through the entire political history of the peninsula. After going rapidly through the earliest history of Iberia, where documentation was thin and less reliable, the history quickly moves to the Carthaginian and Roman contest for the peninsula. The Roman period is predictably the first to receive more detailed attention, and Mariana covers the entire span from the Republic to the last Roman emperors in roughly 100 pages.[74]

Following Mexia in his favorable treatment of the early emperors, Mariana also gives Constantine high praise. He was a particularly easy and apt point of comparison for the Spanish monarchs, and increasingly in the later years of his rule, Philip II was compared to Constantine because of his patronage and perceived protection of the Church both in the Old World and the New. This was a role that he inherited, moreover, from his great grandparents, Isabella and Ferdinand, who represented the culmination of Mariana's history.

Mariana acknowledged that the Roman and medieval periods in Spain were fragmented and often colored by the weakness and failings of rulers, most especially the loss of the peninsula to the Moors. But he ultimately aimed to celebrate the successes of Spain, and the most glorious of all accomplishments for him was the discovery of the Indies under Ferdinand and Isabella. "The most memorable enterprise that ever occurred in Spain, of

---

[73] Palau y Dulcet, Vol. 8, pp. 196–198.

[74] Mariana, *Historia General.* Part of book two and all of books three and four are dedicated to the ancient Roman period or pp. 53–155 in Vol. 1 of the 1669 edition.

the greatest honor and benefit, was the discovery of the West Indies, which are called, with good reason, the New World, because of their greatness."[75]

Mariana's views on the Indians looked much like those of Sepúlveda as he noted the marks that revealed them to lack civilization: they did not have letters; they did not use money; they did not know how to build ships beyond simple canoes; they did not have linen or wool or silk; they married multiple women and practiced sodomy. Worst of all, "they sacrificed slaves and men captured in war in such a great number that is taken as certain that in the city of Mexico alone 20,000 were (sacrificed) each year, whose flesh they ate without any disgust."[76]

From this perspective, the subjugation of the Indians by the Spanish was a great favor that God performed for the peoples of the Americas. It was the divine plan that the Spanish would find and conquer them and that they would generously share in the great abundance of gold and silver that they diligently mined.[77] Most importantly, they received from the Spaniards the knowledge to leave the life of savages and live as Christians. For this reason, it was more a gift to subject them to Spanish rule than it would have been to leave them free.[78]

Mariana's text thus set the tone for other Spanish histories of the conquest including that of the royal historian of the Indies, Antonio Herrera y Tordesillas, who depicted Philip II as building on the great triumph of his ancestors.[79] Viewed in this historical frame, the successful colonization of the land, the development and imposition of the Spanish system of government, effective military defense, and religious domination of the conquered peoples of the New World all revealed the reign of Philip II to be a great success.

But by a number of other measures, especially the demographic impact on the conquered, the reign of Philip II was one of the darkest periods of colonization and Renaissance Empire. The social dislocation of the Indians,

---

[75] Ibid., Vol. 2, p. 407. The original text reads, "La empresa mas memorable, de mayor honra y provecho, que jamas sucedio en España, fue el descubrimiento de las Indias Occidentales: las quales con razon por su grandeza llama el Nuevo Mundo."

[76] Ibid., Vol. 2, p. 409. The text reads, "Sacrificavan hombres cautivados en guerra, y esclavos en numero tan grande que se tiene por cierto, en sola la ciudad de Mexico passavan de veinte mil por año, cuya carne comian sin asco ninguno."

[77] Ibid., Vol. 2, p. 409. Mariana describes the divine plan for the Indies as follows: "Gran bien le hizo Dios, y gracia en traellos a poder de Christianos, y para que los buscassen, y conquistassen, repartir con ellos con larga mano el oro, y la plata en tanta abundancia."

[78] Ibid., "Sobre todo dalles su conocimiento, para que dexada la vida de salvages viviessen Christianamente. Mas merced fue sugetallos, que si continuaran en su libertad."

[79] Herrera y Tordesillas, Antonio, *Historia General de los Hechos de los Castellanos en las Islas y Tierra Firme del Mar Oceano* (Madrid: Juan Flamenco, 1601).

their forced labor in the mines and on the land, and the ravages of European diseases decimated their populations. Although the exact population numbers are a matter of scholarly debate, some estimates project that the indigenous population of the Spanish American colonies fell by a staggering 90 percent over the course of the sixteenth century. If the high estimate of the original population of Spanish America in 1492, 90 million, is assumed, then the population loss was more than 80 million people. If the lower estimate of roughly 50 million is used, the loss is still a dramatic 45 million people.[80]

This was not a story that received much official attention after the time of Las Casas. It clearly never made its way into histories that passed the censors' scrutiny, and it never had a major impact on official policy decisions in the age of Philip II. This is not surprising when viewed in the literary mirror of the imperial Renaissance. There was no room, no precedent, no method for incorporating the deaths of millions over an entire century into the heroic narrative of empire. The genre did not allow for it. Philip II and the humanist historians of his day subsequently turned a blind eye to the epic dying that was going on in the New World. They favored instead their own imperial epic presenting the discovery and conquest as the greatest accomplishment of the Spanish Empire that Philip II had effectively completed.

It was a feat, moreover, that was seen as entitling the king to his just economic reward. Up to the last decade of his rule when he needed more revenue for his last great fight with the king of France, Philip II successfully pushed to extract more wealth from the New World and especially the mines at Potosí. This was the primary objective of his colonial policy from beginning to end,[81] and no treasure fleet ever failed to bring back to Spain the bounty of American silver in the period from 1557 to 1598.

El Escorial and Philip II as the New Constantine

Philip II lost little time in putting some of his American treasure to work building a monumental new palace complex outside of Madrid. The king was the largest single owner of Indian labor in the New World, and he dedicated 20,000 ducats that he received annually from the sale of his Indian

---

[80] McAlister, L., pp. 83–85 and 119–121. McAlister provides a concise summary of the scholarly debates and estimates of the Indian population before the conquest and in the later sixteenth century.

[81] For Philip II's final great push to squeeze even more wealth from Peru, see C. B. Kroeber, "The Mobilization of Philip II's Revenues in Peru, 1590–1596," *The Economic History Review*, New Series, Vol. 10, No. 3, 1958, pp. 439–449.

labor rights to the building of El Escorial.[82] Over the twenty years that it took to compete the building, this accounted for roughly 80 percent of the total cost of the building, calculated at more than 5,000,000 ducats.[83]

A project that spanned the years from 1563 to 1584, not counting another fifteen years to finish the interior decoration on the church, it was a work of colossal Vitruvian dimensions that combined the artistic and architectural genius of the Italian and Spanish Imperial Renaissance with the treasure of the New World. It dwarfed his father's palace in Granada from only a generation earlier, and unlike that building, it became the favorite residence of the king and the center of his considerable patronage and personal attention. The palace of Charles V was a strong symbol of imperial aspirations when it was first begun, but El Escorial was a powerful statement of the full realization and stabilization of that Empire with its center in Iberia.

The declared intention and inspiration of the building was to celebrate Philip II's victory at St. Quentin on the feast of St. Lawrence in 1557. But the building was far more than that, embodying like no other Spanish building of the late sixteenth century the triumph and style of Philip II's imperial monarchy. Like the palace of Charles V in Granada, El Escorial was first and foremost inspired by the monumental orders of imperial classicism exported from Rome to Spain. In the case of El Escorial, however, the architectural genealogy is much clearer than that of the Granada palace: Juan Bautista de Toledo, the original and arguably most influential architect of the building, was a disciple of Michelangelo and his chief assistant in the building of New St. Peter's from 1546 to 1548.[84]

A mathematician and architect shaped by the broad revival of Vitruvius then in full flower, Toledo was called by the king to Madrid in 1559 from Naples, where he had been working for the Spanish viceroy, Pedro de Toledo, on various projects. Named the first "royal architect" by Philip II, he set to work on designs that were eventually submitted for review to the Academy of Florence, then presided over by Giorgio Vasari. Various other architects including Michelangelo provided drawings for parts of the palace, and in 1573 Andrea Palladio, among others, submitted potential plans for the church of San Lorenzo that was the center piece of the complex.[85]

---

[82] P. Williams, p. 56.
[83] Ibid., pp. 56–59.
[84] For the connection of Toledo to Italy and Michelangelo, see George Kubler, *La Obra del Escorial* (Madrid: Allianza, 1983), pp. 42–45; Catherine Wilkinson Zerner, *Juan de Herrera* (New Haven, CT: Yale University Press, 1993), p. 7; and José Javier Rivera Blanco, *Juan Bautista de Toledo y Felipe II, La Implantación del classicismo en España* (Valladolid, 1984).
[85] Ibid., Kubler, p. 73.

Although Toledo died in 1567 before much work could be done on the building, his plans exercised a strong influence on his successor, Juan de Herrera. Described by some art historians as "Spain's first great classicist," Herrera had been the apprentice of Toledo since 1563. He was an old servant of Philip II who had traveled with him to Milan, Genoa, and Mantua in 1548. In 1553 he was again in Italy as a soldier in the service of the Gonzaga family and subsequently had numerous occasions to become familiar with Palazzo Te and the aesthetics of the Imperial Renaissance in Italy.[86]

Under the watchful and enthusiastic eye of Philip II, with whom he met regularly to discuss the design and progress on the building, Herrera presided over a building project that employed 1,000 men for a period of twenty years. Largely completed by 1584, the palace-church-library-monastery-mausoleum was the most ambitious example of a distinct architectural form of Spanish imperial classicism. Herrera, for his part, was credited by some in the ensuing centuries as the architect who ensured through his work on El Escorial and other buildings that "the pure and excellent taste for ancient Roman architecture extended itself through all the provinces" of Spain.[87]

This would have pleased Herrera, a self-trained draftsman with little formal training in architecture who learned the trade as an apprentice under Toledo. Although El Escorial was part of the broader Vitruvian revival, Herrera was not bound to a strict interpretation or application of the ancient master's lessons any more than numerous other Renaissance architects in the sixteenth century, including Giulio Romano and Michelangelo. Herrera employed the classical orders throughout the building, albeit with personal adjustments in scale and ornamentation that belied the notion that a completely "pure" classicism guided his work. Moreover, the lack of decoration and ornament on both the interior and exterior of the building and his departure from the use of organic metaphors common among Italian Renaissance architects reveal Herrera to have developed a distinctive plain style that marks the entire El Escorial.[88]

Still, Herrera's work is an unmistakable variation on the theme of the classical orders of architecture employed on a monumental scale. The Doric columns that grace the façade of the palace's main entrance and the façade of the church; the soaring Roman barrel vault of the church supported by Doric pilasters; the retable of the main altar delineated by four stories of

---

86 Wilkinson Zerner, pp. viii–2.
87 Ibid., p. 28. The quote is from the *Noticias de los Arquitectos y Arquitectura de España desde su Restauración* by Eugenio Llaguno y Amirola and Juan Augustín Ceán Bermúdez, 1798.
88 Ibid., pp. 30–37.

3.2. Spanish School, view of El Escorial, Seventeenth Century. (Photograph: Album/Art Resource, NY.)

columns, each representing one of the classical orders; the graceful dome, inspired by both the pantheon and St. Peter's; all of these features mark El Escorial as a classically inspired building after the Roman style both ancient and Renaissance (Figure 3.2).

At the same time, there are obvious features of El Escorial that set it apart from the main precedent of the imperial palace in Spain, that of Charles V. With its Flemish-inspired towers and austere, unadorned exterior, the first impression that it gives is not of an Italian Renaissance palace transplanted in Spain. The palace in Granada projected the secular power and image of a Roman emperor first and foremost as it successfully sought to make a strong political and cultural statement. By way of contrast, El Escorial projected by size, grandeur, decoration, and use the power of an imperial Spanish Catholic monarch. Religious symbolism and use were absent in Granada. In El Escorial, they were pervasive.

Although the use of the classical orders in both Granada and El Escorial represents the continuities between the imperial Renaissance in early and later sixteenth-century Spain, the differences in religious function of the two complexes reveal substantial transformations in the image of the Spanish monarchy in the latter period. From the beginning, Philip II planned El Escorial as a royal complex that included a monastery, a large church, a library, a mausoleum, and a palace for himself and his family. In the case of Granada, Charles V had a cathedral-mausoleum project in the city, but it was separate from his palace, which was meant primarily to house his own family and court. What model or models inspired Philip II?

In merging the ecclesiastical and royal buildings at El Escorial and by giving the Church of Saint Lawrence such a dominant and central position in the complex, Philip II was most closely following the model of the Vatican and papal monarchy. Famously few documents exist that allow us to know the king's exact models, inspirations, or intentions for the design of El Escorial. Smaller precedents existed in Leon for a royal mausoleum and palace complex; in Madrid the monarchs kept an apartment in the monastery and church of San Jeronimo; and Charles V had retired at Yuste combining his imperial residence with a monastery.

But in terms of scale, aesthetics, and function, the El Escorial complex most closely compared with the Vatican in the latter half of the sixteenth century. If Philip II was competing with any other monarch, it was the papal prince. Both complexes had buildings to house the communities of religious to serve them and their churches in life and to pray for them after their deaths; substantial libraries and art collections; monumental Renaissance churches decorated with fine paintings and sculpture that enjoyed pride of place; mausoleums for their predecessors and themselves; sumptuous palace quarters graced by substantial collections of Renaissance art and decoration celebrating the deeds of the respective monarchies; and spacious interior courtyards as well as exterior gardens.

Philip II closely followed Roman affairs, and he continued the practice begun by Charles V of sending part of the receipts from the sale of the crusade indulgence in Spanish lands for the building of New St. Peter's. In fact, virtually the same amount that Philip received from the sale of Indian labor dedicated to El Escorial, 20,000 ducats annually, was dedicated to New St. Peter's from the crusade indulgence revenues in Spain. El Escorial and New St. Peter's were the biggest building projects in Europe in the latter half of the sixteenth century, and only St. Peter's would eventually exceed the cost of building and decorating the church of St. Lawrence. They were intimately related by architectural genealogies as well as patronage, and it is in this comparative context that the El Escorial is best understood.

It is particularly from the perspective of patronage that Philip II can be seen playing the imperial role that the papacy and its major humanist historian of the late sixteenth century gave to him, namely that of the new Constantine. In his *Ecclesiastical History* of 1593, Cesare Baronio dedicated volume three of his twelve-volume history to Philip II. It is a 684-page volume devoted exclusively to the history of Constantine, and in the four-page dedication the author makes clear parallels between the role of Constantine as great protector and propagator of the Church and the similar contemporary role of Philip II. Baronio presented the work with the suggestion that Constantine provided a good example for Christian monarchs, from which much could be learned. The message could not have been clearer: Baronio, faithful member of the papal court, clearly sought to present the papacy's version of Constantinian history, its preferred political myth, to the Spanish king as a model and reminder of the best kind of monarchical behavior.[89]

This idea also had an artistic parallel in El Escorial in the form of a painting by El Greco titled *The Vision of Philip II*. As Philip gazes heavenward, his eyes focus on the golden letters I H S prominently displayed in the heavens at the top of the painting. An abbreviation for the Latin phrase *in hoc signo*, or "in this sign," the image clearly evoked the vision of Constantine before the battle at the Milvian bridge. The church historian Eusebius famously reported that the emperor saw the symbols of Christ and heard a voice saying, "In this sign you shall conquer." In El Greco's rendering, Philip II has clearly become the new Constantine, and it does not take much political imagination to understand the paintings as a celebration of Philip II's many conquests.

Closer to the source itself, the first historian of the Escorial, José Sigüenza, made explicit connections between the church that Constantine dedicated to the martyr Lawrence and the church that Philip II built in honor of the same saint. A more recent historian of the building has seen this as evidence that "in court circles the new monument to Lawrence was seen as a material bridge linking the achievements and ambitions of the first and last legitimate universal Christian sovereigns."[90]

El Escorial is thus best understood as a palace complex for a new Constantine. Philip II did not need to leave detailed written testimony to explain his intentions. The building that he so carefully supervised speaks clearly for him in form, function, and aesthetics. It was the palace of the century's most powerful Catholic imperial monarch, of the new Constantine. Philip II did not want to be another pope or a priest king as some have proposed. But his style of governance and attitudes toward the Church came close to an eastern Byzantine model that gave the emperor extraordinary power in ecclesiastical affairs. This model became increasingly popular as the Renaissance of Empire matured in the sixteenth century. It was embraced by Catholic and Protestant imperial monarchs alike

---

[89] Cesare Baronio, *Annales Ecclesiastici*, Vol. 3 (Antwerp: Plantiniana, 1593).
[90] Tanner, p. 162.

as the following chapters will reveal, although with differing historical and theological interpretations.[91]

The Renaissance of Empire in Italy in the Age of Philip II

At the same time that the Italian artist, Pompeo Leoni, was fashioning the image of the new Constantines, Philip II and Charles V, in gilded bronze for the altar of the El Escorial, there were Spanish and Italian humanists at work in Italy who continued to use the lives, images, and works of pagan emperors as instructive parallels for Philip II.

Alfonso Chacón was among the most important Spanish humanists of classical and Christian antiquity who worked in Rome in the late sixteenth century. As a student of Ambrosio Morales, he provided continuity with the humanist historians in Spain and represented the maturation of Spanish humanism. But as a Spaniard working in Rome, Chacón was a prime example of the relatively new phenomenon of a Spanish humanist who, following the tradition of Flavio Biondo, made a serious contribution to the literature of the Imperial Renaissance in Rome itself. His works included *De antiquitatibus Romani, Historica Descriptio Urbis Romae*, and, most importantly, *Historia iutruisque belli datici a Traiano Caesare gesti quae in columna euisdem Romae visuntur, collecta*.[92]

This last work was the first detailed humanist study of Trajan's column, among the best preserved and most important of Rome's ancient monuments. Building on the flattering portraits of Trajan produced by Mexia and others, Chacón expanded the analysis of Trajan's virtues as a triumphant warrior with his study. The famous relief sculptures that wind their way up Trajan's column in a corkscrew pattern tell the story of the Spanish Roman emperor's victory over the Germanic tribe of the Dacians. Using illustrations of the column that fold out like a great Renaissance pop-up book, the historian described the various stages of the battle as well as details like the weaponry and clothing of the soldiers.

---

[91] Henry Kamen, *The Escorial: Art and Power in the Renaissance* (New Haven, CT: Yale University Press, 2010). This study takes issue with the political interpretation of Tanner based on the lack of direct documentation from Philip II himself that specifically stated the symbolic intentions of his architectural or iconographic program. Given the famous fact that the king personally directed the architects and artists of his most important building project meeting with them regularly, the lack of written instructions is not hard to explain. Moreover, viewed in the context of the imperial revival of which it was so clearly a part, the Constantinian interpretation of the building is all the more convincing.

[92] Dandelet, *Spanish Rome*, p. 82.

Not surprisingly, Chacón dedicated the work to Philip II, calling the Spanish king the successor of Trajan because both were Spanish, both were kings of Spain, and both ruled a good portion of the world.[93] He sent a copy of the book for the new library in El Escorial confidant that Philip II knew, like the ancient Romans, that a wise ruler conquered and defended his realms with books as well as arms.[94]

Chacón's work highlighted two interwoven facts: by the latter half of the sixteenth century, the Renaissance of Empire that had begun more than a century earlier in Italy was in full bloom, and it was Philip II who played the role of the new emperor in the minds and literary formulations of many humanists at work in Rome and Italy more generally. This was obviously not the Renaissance of Empire that Julius II had in mind at the beginning of the century. But Spanish arms and Spanish gold in the age of Philip II made the armies and treasury of Julius II and the popes that followed him look quaint by comparison.

Although both Ferdinand and Charles V had established the pattern of Spanish and imperial patronage of Rome, it was in the age of Philip II, Philip III, and Philip IV that Spanish economic contributions to Rome reached their peak. Through a combination of ecclesiastical taxes from Spanish imperial lands, pensions from Spanish churches, direct gifts, and a variety of other subsidies, the Spanish Empire pumped millions of ducats into the city of Rome. The kings of Spain truly became the new Constantines as both protectors and patrons of Rome in the period between 1560 and 1700.

More generally, the Spanish monarchy was the dominant power in the Italian peninsula in this period. The defeat of the French and papacy in 1557 proved to be a decisive victory for Philip II and his successors in Italy. For the next 140 years, their formal rule over Milan, Naples, Sicily, and Sardinia would remain intact, if sometimes contested. At the same time, the Spanish kings usually maintained informal sway over the Papal State, the Duchies of Florence, Savoy, and the Republic of Genoa. All were client states of the

---

[93] Alfonso Chacón, *Historia Ceu Verissima a Columniis multorum vindicata* (Rome, 1576) F. Zanetti, p. 1r. The text reads in part, "Praesertim cum iure quodam tibi eam vendices, qui multis nominibus successor Traiani Caesaris fuisti. Hispanus ille, Hispanus + tu: ille Italicae ortus, tu Hispali urbe illi proxima genitus: Rex ille Hispaniarum, tu regnum idem moderaris: ille medietati orbis praesuit, medietas etiam tibi sub est: ille inter ethnicos principes optimus, tu inter Christianos censeris."

[94] Ibid., 1v. The text reads in part, "ingentem gloriam et famam ea in resupra cunctos Hispaniarum reyes conciliaturus, qui non solum armis religionem Christianum tueri, sed et libris, ubique terrarum et locorum conquistis, ut propria instrumenta, quibus adversus fidei nostrae hostes pugnetur affatim et benignissime ministres."

Spanish empire to one extent or another. Only Venice, among the major Italian states, remained truly independent.

No Italian or European power raised any major military challenge in Italy in the era of Philip II after 1559, and the four decades of peninsular peace that followed allowed him to hold and consolidate his power in Italy to an extent that made him the most powerful single ruler in Italy since the fall of the Roman Empire. Although his formal states provided him with revenues to build his military, both they and the informal states provided him with the invaluable resource of soldiers and captains who played leading roles in his wars. This skillful exploitation of the financial and human resources of Spanish Italy, together with consistent political control, constituted his major success on the Eastern edge of his Empire.[95]

The period of the Spanish Peace, in stark distinction to the situation in Flanders, was largely due to the Spanish monarchy's successful cultivation of a large number of powerful Italian noble families that became the political glue that held Spanish Italy together. Unlike their Northern European counterparts, families like the Gonzaga, Medici, Doria, Farnese, and Colonna produced numerous generations of viceroys, admirals, generals, and military governors who served the Spanish Empire. They frequently sought out the king as the godfather of their children, asked for his approval of their marriages, and sent their young sons to serve at the Spanish court and to study at Spanish universities. Some achieved the highest status granted to the Spanish nobility, that of grandees of Spain. All of these noble families, and dozens of others, had deep affinities with the ancient Roman revival. Much more than any other European group, they actively cultivated the images and associations of their families with ancient Rome. Thus, taking up their place as soldiers and statesmen in service of the world's new imperial power was a comfortable fit with their political imagination.

Increasingly giving their sons names like Marcantonio, Vespasiano, Giulio Cesare, and Cesare, they embraced the identity and ideals of the imperial revival like no other Europeans. With the best artists and architects of the age at their disposal, they far exceeded their Spanish counterparts as the most active agents and beneficiaries of the spread of the material culture of Renaissance imperialism. Revenues that they generated directly or indirectly from their role as servants of empire were spent lavishly on the arts as their courts were fashioned in an increasingly imperial image. The examples

---

[95] For a recent collection of essays on the broad theme of the Spanish in Italy in the early modern period, see *Spain in Italy: Politics, Religion and Society, 1500–1700*, ed. Thomas Dandelet and John Marino (Leiden: Brill, 2007).

of the court of Ferrante Gonzaga at Guastala, of Vespasiano Gonzaga in
Sabbioneta, and the Villa Imperiale at Pesaro, built by Leonora Gonzaga,
sister of Ferrante and Duke Federico, for her husband, Francesco Maria della
Rovere, the Duke of Urbino, stand out as central examples.

The Imperial Renaissance in Florence

The deepening embrace of imperial aesthetics was also increasingly evident
in the new court of the Medici dukes. Alessandro de Medici (r. 1530–1536),
the first duke of Florence, owed his power and title to Charles V, whose
armies had put down the last Republican revolt against the Medici in 1529
and then given him the title of Duke in 1532. In raw political terms, it was
the title and the betrothal in 1536 of Alessandro to Margherita of Austria, the
natural daughter of the emperor, which signaled the beginning of the imperial phase in Florentine Renaissance history.[96]

A tangible if ephemeral sign of this was the classicizing festivities staged
by Alessandro for Charles V in 1536 after the victory at Tunis. As with the
celebrations in the cities further south, those in Florence included triumphal arches decorated with the imperial eagle and pictures celebrating the
victory at Tunis. Giorgio Vasari was one of the major artists working for the
occasion, and he had produced a series of paintings of the conquest of Tunis
for the occasion. Another artist, Il Tibolo, had attempted to create a wood
equestrian statue for the occasion, but it was never finished, a sign, perhaps, of the still uncertain future of the imperial phase in Florence.[97] When
Alessandro was assassinated a few months after the visit of Charles V, it fell to
his successor, Cosimo I, to bring political stability to the new Duchy.

Cosimo I (r. 1536–1574) proved up to the task, and he became the most
important protagonist of the transformation of Florence from a center of the
Republican Renaissance to a center of the Imperial Renaissance. Cosimo
I clearly understood himself as political client and servant of the emperor.
Operating under the imperial umbrella in Italy, he remained a loyal servant
of both Charles V and Philip II throughout his reign, even as he worked successfully to advance his own status in Italy.

In the field of creating a distinctly imperial iconography, Florence in his
age played an important and sometimes leading role. The major artists of his
court – Giorgio Vasari, Benvenuto Cellini, Bronzino, Pontormo, Bandinelli,

---

[96] On the transition to the duchy, see Erich Cochrane, *Florence in the Forgotten Centuries:
1527–1800* (Chicago: Chicago University Press, 1973), chapter 1.

[97] R. Strong, p. 84.

and Vincenzo Dati – all put a decidedly imperial stamp on Florence. But their work also exercised a strong influence beyond Florence as other artists found inspiration in some of their innovations.

Cosimo's artists initially embraced the new theme for the ephemeral constructions that they erected for the wedding celebration of Cosimo to Eleonora de Toledo in 1539. The wedding was arranged by Charles V to create new bonds between the Spanish noble house of Toledo and the Florentine Duke and, by implication, between Spanish Naples and Florence. Like the entry of 1536, these events included triumphal arches, equestrian monuments, and other images that increasingly appeared as part of the pre-scribed repertoire of classicized Renaissance political celebrations.[98] Explicit references to Charles V made it clear to all observers that the wedding was done with the emperor's blessing and literally under the sign of the eagle. More than just a marriage, it was a ritual that furthered the integration of Florence into the Spanish imperial system in Italy.

Cosimo I, for his part, sought to make permanent the transformation of Florence from a Republic to a principality under his rule. Arts and letters played a central role in this transformation. Because Cosimo's power was so directly tied to the power of the new empires of his day, it was almost inevi-table that he sought to create a personal image that was linked to the history of empire. Thus, much like the Gonzaga and d'Este families had cultivated imperial associations through the historical texts they patronized and the decoration of their city and palaces, so too did Cosimo I.[99]

The transformation of Florentine history, for example, was undertaken by the humanist Filippo de Nerli, who crafted an historical narrative of the four centuries leading up to the rule of Cosimo I that depicted his rule as the culmination of Florentine political development. From this perspective, Florence was the new Rome and Cosimo I the new Augustus.[100] This narra-tive was accompanied by the ambitions of artists such as Giorgio Vasari, who also dreamt of seeing his Florence surpass the age of Augustus.[101]

It followed that the Duke of Florence went further than his predecessors in having his own image sculpted in bronze and marble posing as an ancient

[98] See AnnaMaria Testaverde Matteini, "La decorazione festivi e l'itinerario di 'rifondazi-one' della città negli ingressi trionfali a Firenze tra XV e XVI secolo," in *Mitteilungen des Kunsthistorischen Institutes in Florenz*, 32. Bd. H. 3, 1988, pp. 323–352.

[99] On the theme of ritual and empire in the age of the Medici dukes, see David Rosenthal, "The Genealogy of Empires: Ritual Politics and State Building in Early Modern Florence," *I Tatti Studies: Essays in the Renaissance*, Vol. 8, 1999, pp. 197–234 (Florence: Leo S. Olschki, 1999).

[100] E. Cochrane, p. 86.

[101] Ibid., p. 91.

Roman nobleman or general. This was the case first with the marble bust of the Duke sculpted by Baccio Bandinelli around 1544 and then more dramatically in the large bronze bust done by Benvenuto Cellini at roughly the same time. Michelangelo had sculpted a portrait bust of Brutus a few years earlier that was considered a symbol of republicanism. By contrast, the busts of Cosimo I in the Florentine imperial style were the exact opposite.[102] Rather than being primarily biographical or historical images meant to preserve an accurate portrait of the duke, their major purpose was political and ideological. They established Cosimo I as an imperial figure.[103]

They were important for both their artistic quality and the sense of political strength and permanence they projected, not to mention the central role they played in Renaissance imperial iconography. Prefiguring and perhaps serving as models for the busts of Charles V and Philip II done by Leone Leoni a decade later, they put Florence in a leading role in this realm.

So, too, did the major artistic project of Cosimo's reign, namely the new decoration of the Palazzo della Signoria or Palazzo Vecchio. Formerly the seat of the Republican government, this symbol of Republican Florence became the Duke's palace and seat of government in the age of Cosimo I and Eleonora. If the strong political statement of moving from the old Medici palace to the Palazzo Vecchio in 1537 needed any explanation or clarification, Cosimo I was intent on providing it with the extensive painting cycles and sculptures that he commissioned for his new home.[104]

The paintings and sculpture ordered and carefully supervised by the Duke served two overarching and interwoven purposes. First, there were historical paintings and portraits commemorating the long line of Medici patriarchs, princes, and popes from the fifteenth century onward. Second, Medici history, and particularly that of Cosimo, was closely associated with the history of ancient Rome with allegorical paintings explicitly tying the founding of Florence to the age of Augustus.[105] This was a crucial piece of historical revision. It contrasted sharply with the dominant historical interpretation of

[102] Irving Lavin, "On Illusion and Allusion in Italian Sixteenth-Century Portrait Busts," in *Proceedings of the American Philosophical Society*, Vol. 119, No. 5, October 1975, pp. 353–362. See especially pp. 357–361 where Lavin describes the "mode of characterization" used in the busts of Cosimo as the Florentine imperial convention.

[103] Kurt Forster, "Metaphors of Rule. Political Ideology and History in the Portraits of Cosimo I de' Medici," in *Mitteilungen des Kunsthistorischen Institutes in Florenz*, 15. Bd., H 1, 1971, pp. 65–104.

[104] For the symbolism of the Sala Grande decoration, see Starn and Partridge, *Arts of Power*, chapter 3, pp. 151–212.

[105] K. Forster, pp. 98–99. Forster, after the interpretation of Nicolai Rubinstein, on the meaning of Vasari's painting "The Foundation of Florence."

Republican Florence advocated by Leonardo Bruni since the early fifteenth century. Bruni had famously located the foundation of Florence in the age of the ancient Roman Republic, a critical piece of Florentine political identity for the Republican Renaissance.

For Cosimo I, on the other hand, the foundation by Augustus became central to his own image as he increasingly had himself associated with that emperor in the new painted imagery of the Palazzo Vecchio. This was political propaganda, of course, but it was increasingly common propaganda in the Italian courts that fell under the umbrella of Charles V and Philip II. And it had the long precedent of the Renaissance in Ferrara, Mantua, and Rome, among other lesser locations, to draw from.

Cosimo I and his artists capitalized on this tradition to the fullest extent. Bronzino, Francesco Salviati, and, above all others, Giorgio Vasari completely transformed the apartments and great hall of the Palazzo Vecchio. Vasari and Salviati were immersed in the iconography and style of the papal version of the imperial Renaissance from years spent working in Rome. Vasari, the most famous disciple of Michelangelo, had made his own contribution to the style in the frescoes of the Cancelleria palace. Salviati, for his part, had painted the frescoes for the Palazzo Farnese that celebrated the Farnese family myth. Both he and Vasari had first-hand knowledge of Giulio Romano's Constantine cycle in the Vatican palace that was a foundational work for history painting that advocated a strong political ideology. Like Giulio Romano, they embraced "the turn to politically motivated use of Roman Imperial models" for the paintings of the Palazzo Vecchio.[106]

Central examples of this in Vasari's paintings include the use of the reliefs on the Arch of Constantine in Rome as models for a portrait of Cosimo I in the palace. Similarly, these reliefs provide the inspiration for the composition of the "Foundation of Florence" on the ceiling of the Salone dei Cinquecento that depicts the emperor Augustus founding the city.[107]

Besides the use of these ancient motifs, Vasari and Cosimo I also included references to the modern imperial connections of the house of Medici. In the Sala degli Elementi, for example, Vasari had painted a golden fleece, a symbol of the honor that was bestowed on Cosimo I by Charles V. According to at least one explanation tied to Vasari himself, Cosimo was made a knight of the Golden Fleece as a sign of and reward for the "faithful spirit and great strength" with which the Duke had served the empire.[108] This was service

---

[106] Ibid., pp. 94–96. The quote is from page 96.
[107] Ibid., p. 100.
[108] This was the explanation given in the treatise titled *Ragionamenti del Signor Giorgio Vasari sopra le invenzoni da lui dipinte in Firenze nel Palazzo Vecchio con D. Francesco Medici* (Pisa:

that continued in the age of Philip II, and as a sign of his fealty to the young monarch, Cosimo I sent his young son Francesco to live at court with Philip II from 1561 to 1562.

Twenty years later, another son of Cosimo I, Pietro, also traveled to Iberia at the head of an army of 4,500 Italian soldiers ordered by Philip II to aid in his greatest conquest. Like many other Italian noble families, the Medici frequently sent their sons to war in the service of Philip II. As the clearest sign that their dedication to empire was not limited to ritual triumphs and romantic artistic imitations of ancient Rome in their palaces, they also put themselves and their sons on the front lines of battle to prove their worthiness to claim the costume of ancient Roman warriors. They were a critical part of the Spanish Empire's defense of its territories as the case of Alessandro Farnese in Flanders starkly demonstrated. And they also played a critical role in Philip II's greatest victory and expansion of his empire, the conquest of Portugal.

Philip II and the Conquest of the Portuguese Empire

On August 29, 1580, Philip II dictated a five-page letter to his military commander in Milan, Don Zanchio di Guevara et Padiglia. A masterpiece of brevity and understatement, it concisely summarized the conquest of Portugal that had taken place over the previous four days. Although the king had not participated directly in the conquest, remaining at a safe distance near the Spanish–Portuguese border in Badajos, he wrote his letter in the form of a military history, presenting himself as the leader and strategist who had organized and directed the actions of his army and navy.[109]

The lightening-fast conquest of Portugal was Philip II's most important victory. It overshadowed any previous European military success in many decades, if not centuries, measured by the size and wealth of the prize. As an imperial conquest, it rivaled that of Mexico and Peru by Charles V and subsequently elevated Philip II to a level of political accomplishment that was comparable to that of his father. In the language of the Caesars, as well as Machiavelli, it brought him the most sought-after trophies of any ancient or Renaissance ruler: fame, honor, and increased reputation.

Capurro, 1823), p. 13. The treatise, presented as a work by Vasari himself, has also been attributed to his nephew, who first had it published in 1588, decades after his death.

[109] "Copia D'una Lettera Scritta da S.M. Catholica, al S. Castellano di Milano nella quale s'intende l'acquisto del Regno di Portogallo, con gli avisi, et relationi di quanto è successo in quell'impresa" (Milan and Ferrara: Baldini, 1580).

This was a fact that the king clearly appreciated. The letter to his Italian commander had the distinct feel of a description of a military campaign modeled after Caesar's *Commentaries* as it coolly described the logistics, central people, and chronology of events that led to the victory. Philip II was careful to note the role played by the military forces from Sicily, Naples, and Lombardy in the conquest. The three Italian *tercios* comprised roughly one third of the estimated 25,000 soldiers who had taken part in the victory. To their credit, the king emphasized that his troops had been well disciplined and had not sacked the city.[110] Although the soldiers did sack the suburbs of Lisbon, contemporary observers agreed that the loss of life was very low. By one contemporary account, only 1,000 Portuguese soldiers and 100 men from the Spanish forces lost their lives.[111]

Philip II had good reason to celebrate. The victory expanded his territories dramatically and left him with an empire that was far larger than that of Charles V. More dramatically, it was larger than any other empire in history in terms of territory and global reach. The Portuguese "inheritance" that Philip took possession of, thanks to his father's wise marriage to the Portuguese princess, Isabella, forty-four years earlier more than made up for the loss of the German lands and imperial title. In this sense, it was also a victory for the old emperor, who would surely have applauded his son. At the same time, the merging of Portugal with the other Iberian kingdoms meant that Iberia was united under one ruler for the first time since the fall of ancient Rome, a fact that gave Philip II a strong Spanish claim to be the most authentic successor of the ancient Caesars in political power.

The exceptional speed of the victory, minimal loss of life, and minor damage inflicted on the city of Lisbon reinforced the message propagated by Philip II that he was a beneficent king who had only claimed what was rightfully his by the laws of dynastic inheritance. His was not a violent conquest of a foreign people but rather the just occupation of the throne that was his right by blood. It was old-fashioned imperial expansion through dynastic claims.

The event that precipitated this development was the death of Philip II's cousin and nephew, King Sebastian, the last direct male heir to that throne, who was killed during an ill-fated battle in North Africa in 1578. The

---

[110] Ibid., A2.

[111] Gerolamo (Jeronimo) de Franchi Conestaggio, *Dell'Unione del Regno di Portogallo alla Corona di Castiglia* (Genoa: Giralomo Bartoli, 1585), p. 177. Conestaggio was a Genovese merchant who had previously lived in Antwerp and had close ties to the Spanish ambassador in Lisbon. His account is among the best of the contemporary histories of the conquest of Portugal, and the work itself is an excellent example of humanist historiography.

Catholic King claimed that as the oldest of the male grandchildren of King Manuel, he had the right by blood to claim the throne. He also had an army of lawyers and theologians to back up this interpretation and a real army to enforce their legal judgment.[112] His only major competitor, his illegitimate cousin Sebastian, was unable to sustain a real challenge. Quickly defeated in battle, he disappeared from Portugal never to resurface again.

The Portuguese Empire was, together with the Spanish Empire, the other major European power that had grown into a global power in the late fifteenth and early sixteenth centuries. A number of Atlantic islands – the Azores and Madeira especially – had been conquered and colonized in the early fifteenth century. Using African slaves bought at Portuguese trading forts on the West African coast, Madeira produced substantial sugar and provided a colonial laboratory for later American plantation practices.

American territories were added to the Portuguese Empire in 1500 when the explorer Pedro Alvares Cabral claimed Brazil for the Portuguese crown. Lacking the large bullion deposits that the Spanish were quick to discover in Mexico and Peru, Brazil developed much later and never provided the same mineral bonanza that Mexico and Peru gave to Spain. It was nonetheless rich in natural resources, and by the mid-sixteenth century, the Portuguese were extracting substantial amounts of wood and sugar from the New World.

The more important early source of imperial wealth for the Portuguese came from new Indian Ocean possessions taken in the decades after 1488, the year the Portuguese explorer Bartolomeu Dias had rounded the Cape of Good Hope. Later voyages by Vasco de Gama in 1498, Cabral in 1501, and Antonio de Abreu in 1511 led to the eventual establishment of trading fortresses/factories in Cochin, Goa, Calicut, Ormuz, Madagascar, Ceylon, Macau, and the Moluccas. These territories allowed the Portuguese to dominate the lucrative spice trade with Europe. Far more than the sugar plantations or wood harvested in Brazil in the sixteenth century, the spice trade brought the Portuguese monarchs substantial new wealth. By claiming a monopoly on the spice trade, the monarchs brought in as much as three million *cruzados* per year by the mid-sixteenth century, wealth that Philip II would add to his own treasure after 1580.[113]

---

[112] Ibid., p. 77–81. Philip II ordered official opinions from his stable of lawyers as well as from the theology faculty at Alcala. They supported the king's claims, not surprisingly.

[113] A. R. Disney, *A History of Portugal and the Portuguese Empire* (Cambridge: Cambridge University Press, 2009), Vol. 2, pp. 149–156. The spice of most importance for the Portuguese was black pepper, which generated as much as 95 percent of revenue from the spice trade. The income of 2,000,000 cruzados from the annual Macau-Nagasaki voyages was estimated as twice that of crown revenue from the Goa-Lisboa route at its height by the 1580s. p. 156.

But the Portuguese empire was a much less developed Renaissance empire than that of Spain. Weaker levels of contact with Italy and the Italian Renaissance explain a large part of this difference in the realms of cultural production and intellectual life. Still, the Portuguese monarchs did appreciate the value of Italian humanists, artists, and architects as they acquired works of art directly or appropriated and imitated the literary and artistic styles of the Italian Renaissance.[114] But the Imperial Renaissance in Portugal on the level of intellectual production, art, and architecture was a shadow of that in Spain for various reasons.

First among these was the fact that the kings of Spain in the late fifteenth and sixteenth centuries were also kings of Naples and Sicily. This created a far thicker traffic of people, ideas, and new cultural models between Italy and Castile. Ferdinand of Aragon lived for years in Naples, had many Italian servants in his court, and brought Italian humanists to Spain to educate his own children and those of the court. His strong ties to the Rome of Pope Alexander Borgia, the creation of the first permanent ambassador there, and strong commercial ties with Italy all led to far more Italian influence in Spain than in Portugal.

Even more importantly, the joining of the Spanish crown with the Holy Roman Empire in the person of Charles V gave Spain something Portugal never had: a real emperor who brought with him all of the humanist expectations and images of a Roman imperial revival. Although the Portuguese monarchs appreciated some Italian architectural innovations, none presumed to build a palace like that in Granada, not to mention El Escorial. There were no Portuguese parallels to the Spanish architects who had lived in Rome and worked with Giulio Romano and Michelangelo.

The kings of Portugal did hire Italian humanists to translate Portuguese chronicles into Latin to give them added gravitas as early as 1510. They also supported new historians like Joao de Barros, who wrote a history of the Portuguese discoveries that was translated into Italian and dedicated to the Duke of Mantua in 1559.[115] But they could not compare with the number or quality of Spanish royal historians in the tradition of Nebrija, Ocampo, Sepúlveda, Mexia, Morales, Mariana, and Chácon. Perhaps because they did not have the same ideological roots as the heirs of empire in Spain, they simply did not invest in or desire the letters and arts of the imperial Renaissance on the same level as their Spanish neighbors did.

---

[114] For an excellent collection of essays on ties between Portugal and Italy, see *Cultural Links Between Portugal and Italy in the Renaissance*, ed. K. J. P. Lowe (Oxford: Oxford University Press, 2000).

[115] Joao de Barros, *Dell'Asia*, Venice, 1561. The Italian translation was by Alfonso Ulloa and the text was dedicated to Guglielmo, Duke of Mantova.

Portugal's differences with Spain extended further in the political nature of their empire. The Spanish conquistadors saw themselves as "Romans in the New World" and the protagonists of an epic conquest that was equal to or greater than that of ancient empires. Their monarchs successfully imposed significant aspects of their social, political, economic, cultural, and religious systems on the new territories. Capitalizing on their military advantage, they exploited native labor to extract as much raw wealth as possible from their colonies.

The Portuguese, by contrast, set up trading fortresses in India and the Spice Islands using the model they had developed along the West African coast in the fifteenth century. They did not conquer vast territories and established monarchies or empires, and they initially did not carry out an expansive imperial project like that of the Spanish. Rather, they focused on extracting wealth through trade. In Africa, this came from trade in slaves and gold, and in the Indian Ocean region it came from dominating the spice trade, especially that of black pepper. In both areas, the actual amount of territory that they claimed was small compared to the Spanish territorial conquests.

Similarly, the extent of colonization was much more limited in the Portuguese territories. In part this was because the Portuguese did not have the same population surplus that the Spanish did in the sixteenth century. Spain's population grew from an estimated 3.8 million in 1528 to 6.6 million in 1591, a 73.6 percent increase.[116] Portugal had less than half that number and subsequently did not have much excess population.[117] The estimated number of emigrants to their trading fortresses was small. The number of Portuguese residents in the entire *Estado da India* reached a peak in 1600 at about 5,500 people.[118]

The differences in Portuguese and Spanish imperialism were most stark in the New World. In Brazil, the Portuguese had claimed a large new territory, but it was a land without advanced societies like those Mexico and Peru. No major gold or silver deposits were discovered until late in the seventeenth century, and colonization was fragmented, slow, and sporadic.

This meant both a more modest measure of fame and, more concretely, a smaller increase in revenue and military power compared to the Spanish. Although the Portuguese navy was among the largest and strongest in the world in the sixteenth century, it never reached the size of Spain's. As for its

---

[116] Annie Molinié-Bertrand, *Au siècle d'or L'Espagne et ses homes: La population de Royaume de Castille au XVIe siècle* (Paris: Econimica, 1985).

[117] A. R. Disney, Vol. 2, p. 280. The population was estimated at 2.8 million at the end of the eighteenth century.

[118] A. R. Disney, Vol. 2, p. 148.

army, the fact that Portugal fought virtually no European land battles after the early sixteenth century left it far less experienced and formidable as a military force.

Spain's constant participation in the wars of reconquest under Ferdinand and Isabella and the endless European wars of Charles V and Philip II provided a steady stream of experienced soldiers and captains for the New World colonies. This was not the case in Portugal, and the subsequent imposition of Portuguese control in Brazil was slow in part because of fewer experienced and capable military governors.

Besides these differences, the most dramatic contrast between the Spanish and Portuguese empires in the New World was gold and silver. While the Spanish flotillas were carrying back ever-greater quantities of gold and silver worth millions of ducats throughout the sixteenth century, Portuguese ships were carrying back wood and sugar worth a small fraction for the monarchs and merchants of Portugal. Far fewer Portuguese traveled to Brazil given the perception of limited opportunities to strike it rich, and the project and scope of colonization were subsequently much more limited.

An eighteenth-century French historian summarized the differences in a way that reflected the early modern imperialist perspective well:

> "The conquests of the Portuguese in the New World are not as pleasing on a broad view as the conquests of Mexico and Peru. In the latter we see a single Conqueror who ... successfully conquers a mighty State in a short space of time with a few men to establish himself solidly on the ruins of a great Empire. As in the epic Poem, it appears as a single action embellished by a few Episodes. With the former on the contrary, it is a long period of years, a multitude of different lands, an infinite number of actions, many Chiefs who succeed one another with different ideas, an assemblage of disparate things which have neither unity or sequence, and a kind of chaos from which a single whole emerges only because it is the same nation which acts everywhere and to which all is related."[119]

One of the many chiefs in the succession mentioned in this passage was Philip II, who ritually claimed Lisbon and the Portuguese empire as his own in 1580. Predictably, he did so with a triumphal procession complete with arches and sumptuous ephemeral constructions in the ancient style.[120] Looking very much like another single conqueror who successfully conquered "a mighty State in a short space of time," to quote the historian

---

[119] Quoted in L. McAlister, p. 250.
[120] Contestaggio, ff. 205v–206r. A brief description is given of the entry noting the triumphal arches.

above, the Catholic King's victory had an undeniable epic quality that other major European powers resented and feared. The imperial merger meant yet another increase in his power in terms of both wealth and military might. Philip II had seldom hesitated to use both against his foes, and the Portuguese victory inevitably increased his political and military hubris.

It is not difficult to see why. Viewed from the perspective of global imperial geography, the conquest of the Portuguese empire added substantial African and especially Asian territories to the Spanish Empire, thereby making it more truly global. The only previous imperial expansion that Philip II could claim was the conquest of the Philippine Islands by the Spanish adventurer Legazpi in 1570. The Philippines eventually became an important center of the silver and silk trade between Mexico and China and gave the Spanish Empire an important connection to Asia. But the Philippines paled in comparison to the Portuguese trading colonies and their network of military and trading outposts, which constituted a far greater imperial expansion for the Spanish monarch and placed the Spanish Empire directly in the midst of Asia. In later decades it would be the Pacific-Asian frontier that lured future imperial adventures even as the reality of imperial limitations began to appear.

Imperial Limits: The Wars against England and France

From 1580 to 1583, Philip II remained in Lisbon. His decision served both to assure his new subjects of his dedication to being their king and to solidify his power. Taking care to defeat the remaining pockets of resistance in the Azores as well as closer to home in places like the University of Coimbra, the king also demonstrated that he new well how to use soft power. With deep reserves of royal treasure and patronage, he distributed offices and royal privileges to the nobility, dowries to poor women, and endowments to various churches and monasteries. He also commissioned a new palace to be built, bringing Herrera from Spain to oversee the project. It stood as a clear and visible reminder of his royal presence in the city even when he decided to move back to Spain. In short, in Lisbon the king followed the script of the beneficent emperor cultivating goodwill by distributing favors and charity and creating visible signs of his power.[121]

It was a strategy that worked, at least in the short term. When Philip II decided to return to Castile in 1584, his newest subjects were generally tranquil and resigned to being under his rule. This was the peak of Philip

---

[121] A. R. Disney, Vol. 1, pp. 191–209.

II's accomplishments as an empire builder, and it aptly coincided with the completion of the major architectural symbol of his rule, El Escorial. For the remaining fourteen years of his life, Philip resided primarily in his new palace, where he could carefully supervise the completion and decoration of the church and his final resting place.

But this was not an early retirement. The Catholic King continued to rule through his pen. More precisely, it was the pens of his secretaries, to whom he dictated thousands of letters that went out to his viceroys, governors, ambassadors, and governing councils. Ever the chief bureaucrat of his expansive imperial administration, the old monarch remained the commander in chief as well, and he continued to pursue a vigorous military policy in Europe.

In the Netherlands, England, and France, Philip II pressed on with an interventionist agenda that was as aggressive as or more so than his policies of the previous three decades. In England, the old monarch aimed to strike a crippling military blow to Elizabeth and her Protestant Dutch allies with his planned naval invasion of 1588. In France, he intervened on the part of the Catholic League against the Protestant pretender to the throne, Henry of Navarre. It seemed obvious to present observers that his motive was nothing less than to place one of his own descendants on the French throne.[122]

Thus, the political agenda of Philip II continued to be driven by the desire to preserve and defend his inheritance while also expanding it when the occasion presented itself. This was especially true in the context of the great game and gamble of creating dynastic alliances with an eye toward future expansion. It may appear astonishing that the king aimed to put one of his heirs on the French throne. But it was completely consistent with the strategy that Philip II had pursued with great success over a lifetime. Charles V had raised his son to be a military ruler jealous of his possessions and reputation and driven by an appetite for victory. The lessons taught by tutors like Sepúlveda and Mexia had most celebrated the emperors who expanded empire and won fame and glory. This was the imperial script that Philip II had been handed, and he followed it faithfully.

It is a mistake to see the old monarch as driven by Messianic delusions. Certainly Philip II, like his father and great-grandfather Ferdinand, regularly described his motives using the language of defending or spreading the true and only faith of Roman Catholicism. But as Portugal had clearly demonstrated, Philip II and his own lawyers were quick to label the succession

[122] Anthoine de Bandole, *Les Paralleles de Cesar et de Henry IIII* (Paris: Jean Richer, 1609), p. 19.

question a secular matter regulated by secular law. Similarly in the case of France, the Catholic King frequently cited the Protestantism of Henry of Navarre as the pretext for sending soldiers and money to aid the League in France. But Philip II fought hard against papal attempts to reconcile Henry to the Church, a move that paved the way for Navarre's legitimate succession. On the Ottoman front, too, Philip II's policies were guided by reason of state as he signed secret treaties, hardly the actions of a Messianic monarch who many urged to sail on Jerusalem. All of these examples revealed clearly that Philip II put his political interests before religious principle. It was a defining characteristic of his entire reign.

Although shrewd realism served Philip II well through most of his reign, his political fortunes began to change in his last decade in power. The failure of the Great Armada against England in 1588, the de facto independence of the United Provinces in the Netherlands, and the absolution and crowning of Henry IV as king of France in 1595 all pointed to the limits to Spanish power. The king of France and the queen of England both had their own growing imperial agendas in the Atlantic world, as did the Dutch Protestants. Closer to home in Castile, Mother Nature added to the king's woes with a series of bad harvests followed by famine and plague in the 1590s that reduced the population of Spain by an estimated 10 percent. Economically, the king's treasury was also strained under the chronic military burden.

Thus, by the time of the king's death in 1598, it was already clear that the next king would have many challenges in maintaining control of a global colossus. But there was no denying the accomplishment of Philip II and the continuing power of the Spanish Empire. He had set the standard for imperial monarchy in the sixteenth century. Future pretenders to the title in both France and England would imitate many aspects of his reign. His competitors resented and feared him, but they also wanted what he had.

A contemporary French critic of Spain in the decade after Philip II's death summed up Spain's perceived dominance well with the following complaint: the kings of Spain had "Navarre in their hands, Portugal in their claws, Italy in tutelage, Germany under lease, England in their nets, the Indies in their coffers, Flanders under their lance, and Poland at their call."[123] The old king would have been happy to hear this political judgment from his enemies a decade after his death, even if it was exaggerated French polemic.

---

[123] Ibid., p. 12. The text reads, "Tiennent la Navarre en leurs mains, le Portugal en leurs griffes, l'Italie en tutelle, l'Allemagne en lesse, l'Angleterre aus filets, les Indes dans leur coffres, la Flandres sous leur verge, et la Pologne a leurs voeux."

Philip III, Tacitus, and the Arts of Imperial Maintenance

When Philip III took power in 1598 at the young age of twenty, many wondered whether he was up to the task. He was fonder of hunting than of long hours at his desk managing the affairs of his sprawling inheritance and delegated a great deal of power to his favorite, the Duke of Lerma, and to the councils that exercised growing influence during his twenty-two-year reign. This was not necessarily a bad thing for the empire.[124]

Like Lerma, who had been the viceroy of Valencia, many of the men who sat on the primary councils of state, war, the Indies, Italy, Portugal, finance, and the Inquisition were experienced governors and military men. They benefited from this experience as well as excellent educations, and all of them were steeped in the political practices, ideas, and aesthetics of empire. A contemporary described the council of state as being composed of "great men, all very well qualified, each of them worthy of governing the whole world."[125] It followed that they were committed, first and foremost, to preserving the vast empire to which they owed their status and position. They also relished the new opportunity to take a more active role in governing than they had been allowed during the days of Philip II.

The councils represented the political coming of age of the Spanish ruling class in the form of an increasingly robust and active imperial administration. Their largely effective management goes a long way to explaining the preservation of the Spanish Empire during the reign of Philip III. But they still served very much at the pleasure of the king, and not surprisingly they generally followed his bidding. The fact that Philip III chose to delegate many acts of governance to his councils did not mean that he gave up his royal prerogative. He followed a clear agenda marked by the traditional imperial priorities of maintaining and expanding his inheritance. In his first decade in power, this meant supporting a number of costly military adventures, and the young king was determined to win a measure of fame on the battlefield much like his father and grandfather.

War against England and the Netherlands subsequently resumed. As part of the hostilities, an armada was sent to aid the Irish in their battle against

---

[124] Recent studies on the reign of Philip III that share this view of the young king and his government include Alfredo Alvar Ezquerra, *El Duque de Lerma* (Madrid: La Esfera de los Libros, 2010); Patrick Williams, *The Great Favourite: The Duke of Lerma and the Court and Government of Philip III* (New York: Palgrave, 2006); and Antonio Feros, *Kingship and Favoritism in the Spain of Philip III, 1598–1621* (Cambridge: Cambridge University Press, 2000).

[125] Jerónimo de Sepúlveda quoted by Patrick Williams, "Philip III and the Restoration of Spanish Government, 1598–1603," in *The English Historical Review*, Vol. 88, No. 349, Oct., 1973, pp. 751–769. Quote from p. 766.

England in 1601. A few years later, an army of 30,000 was raised in Italy to aid the pope in the face of a potential war with Venice and France in 1607 during the Interdict crisis. Closer to home, an increasingly aggressive policy toward the Morisco population of southern Spain led to the radical measure of their total expulsion in 1609.

Together with this bold and bellicose agenda both at home and abroad, Philip III also sought glory in imperial expansion. Most noticeably, he supported the Pacific Ocean expedition led by the Portuguese explorer, Pedro Fernández de Quirós. He had convinced the king that another great continent existed in the Pacific Ocean to the west of Peru, which he aimed to claim for Philip III. The young monarch's formal approval of the voyage in 1603 was supported by his council of state, although not by the council of the Indies that continued the conservative approach to further exploration that marked the later years of Philip II's reign. The voyage in search of Australia thus took place in 1605 to 1606 because of royal enthusiasm for yet another potential imperial gain.[126]

All of these examples amply demonstrate that Philip III made a good effort to win fame and glory in the most traditional of ways: through military victory and imperial expansion. The dreams of Caesar continued, fueled by the New World treasure that kept the king's military power potent. But unlike his father, grandfather, or great grandfather, Philip III had little luck in battle on land or at sea. No great victories were claimed, and no new discoveries or conquests were forthcoming.

Rather, the new king and his councilors had to settle for a peace treaty with the English in 1604, a truce with the Dutch in 1609, and a stalemate with the Venetians and French in Italy. The voyage of Quirós came close but ultimately failed to reach Australia. In addition, the Spanish were confronted with the reality that in 1607 both the English and French had established colonies in Jamestown and Quebec, respectively. This clearly challenged the Spanish position held since 1494 that they had exclusive rights to settle the New World. It was increasingly obvious, however, that they did not have the money or military reach to defend the vast expanses of North America from British and French settlement.[127]

---

[126] Kevin Sheehan, "Voyaging in the Spanish Baroque: Science and Patronage in the Pacific Voyage of Pedro Fernández de Quirós, 1605–1606," *Science in the Spanish and Portuguese Empires*, ed. Daniela Bleichmanr, Paula de Vos, Kristine Huffine, and Kevin Sheehan (Stanford, CA: Stanford University Press, 2009), pp. 20–22.

[127] For a revealing study of Spanish reactions to Jamestown, see William S. Goldman, "Spain and the Founding of Jamestown," *The William and Mary Quarterly*, Vol. 68, No. 3 (July 2011), pp. 427–450.

None of these developments fit well, if at all, with the imperial model and policies of the previous century. The commentary provided by Guevara and Mexia, not to mention Caesar, provided few lessons for negotiating the increasing complexities of global imperial contest. But that did not mean that imperial humanism had run its course or exhausted its potential resources for political council and reflection.

In fact, it was in the age of Philip III that a new chapter in imperial humanism came into full bloom. Although previous princes, kings, and emperors took the writings and biographies of the Caesars as guides, Philip III, his councilors, and the other aspiring imperial monarchs of his generation increasingly turned to imperial Rome's greatest historian, Cornelius Tacitus (circa 55 – circa 117), for council. A Roman governor of Asia Minor under Trajan in 112 AD, he had written two primary histories, the *Annals* that covered the period from the death of Augustus in 14 AD to the death of Nero in 66 AD and the *Histories* that continued the *Annals*, covering the period from 69 to 70 AD.

The revival of Tacitus constitutes yet another constitutive element of Renaissance imperialism, but it was a later development as revealed by the publishing history of the *Annals and Histories*. Although the first printed edition of books 11 through 16 of the *Annals* were published in 1470 in Venice, the first edition of the entire edition of the *Annals and Histories* only appeared in 1515 in Rome.[128] Moreover, the popularity of these works lagged far behind that of other ancient historians with only seventeen editions being printed in the first century of the press. Ranking thirteenth among ancient historians between 1450 and 1550, the *Annals* and *Histories* became more popular in the age of Philip II with thirty-two new editions going to press and the work's ranking rising to number six. But it was only in the first half of the seventeenth century that the popularity of Tacitus reached a peak with sixty-seven editions raising the *Annals and Histories* to the number-one rank among all ancient historians.[129]

In a related development, a growing body of literature that focused on the political uses of Tacitus began to flourish in the 1580s thanks in large part to the appearance of the best translation and edition of the *Annals* to date by Justus Lipsius.[130] The publication of his version of the

---

[128] J. Sandys, p. 108.

[129] P. Burke, "Popularity of Ancient Historians," p. 137.

[130] An early essay on the reception of Tacitus that makes this point is Arnaldo Momigliano, "The First Political Commentary on Tacitus," in *The Journal of Roman Studies*, Vol. 37, Parts 1 and 2, 1947, pp. 91–101. He states that "It is a fact that the whole of the literature specifically illustrating Tacitus' political thought is later than 1580 and somewhat influenced by Lipsius." P. 92.

Annals with commentaries in 1574 and 1581, respectively, marked a new appreciation and use of Tacitus that had been largely suppressed in earlier decades. In part this was because of the association of Tacitus with tyranny promoted by earlier Republican authors like Guicciardini, who, in his *Ricordi*, claimed that Tacitus "teaches tyrants the ways of founding a tyranny."[131] Similarly, many later authors negatively associated Tacitus with Machiavellian political analysis even as they increasingly read and used both for their writings.[132]

Such was the case with Giovanni Botero in his famous *Reason of State*, first published in 1589. In his dedication to the archbishop of Salzburg, he noted his surprise at finding Machiavelli and Tacitus often mentioned in discussions on the reason of state in the courts of Italy and northern Europe that he had frequently visited.[133]

At the same time, he condemned Machiavelli for having little conscience and Tacitus for admiring the example of Tiberius, the tyrant, and offering it "almost as the norm and ideal of that which one must do in the administration and governing of the state."[134]

Ironically, it was Botero who first fully articulated how the view of governing found in Tacitus could be applied to the European politics of his own day. In other words, it was Botero who explained his own political world through a secular reason of state. As in ancient Rome, the justification for the actions of modern governments and princes could be interpreted in the framework of how they served the interests of their state, as opposed to some higher spiritual or moral purpose.

This was not a view of politics that Botero championed. As a priest, he condemned it. But this is precisely why it was also easily published and translated in Spain at a time when the Tacitus of Lipsius was still banned. Botero was translated by the royal historian Antonio de Herrera y Tordesillas in 1592, and reason of state subsequently became a part of the intellectual world of

---

[131] Mark Morford, "Tacitean *Prudentia* and the Doctrines of Justus Lipsius," in *Tacitus and the Tacitean Tradition*, ed. T. J. Luce and A. J. Woodman (Princeton, NJ: Princeton University Press), 1993, pp. 129–151. The full quote from Guicciardini reads, "Tacitus very well teaches those who live under a tyrant how to live and conduct themselves prudently, just as he teaches tyrants the ways of founding a tyranny." P. 144, note 49.

[132] On Tacitism in Renaissance Italy, see especially *Tacito e tacitismi in Italia da Machiavelli a Vico*, ed. Silvio Suppa (Naples: Archivio della Ragion di Stato, 2003).

[133] Kenneth C. Schellhase, *Tacitus in Renaissance Political Thought* (Chicago, University of Chicago Press, 1976), p. 124.

[134] Giovanni Botero, *Della Ragion di Stato* (Venice: Gioliti, 1589), p. ★iiv. "Si che io me meravigliavo grandemente, che un'Autore cosi empio, e le maniere cosi malvagie d'un tiranno fossero stimate tanto, che si tenessero quasi per norma, e per idea di quel, che si deve fare nell'amministratione, e nel governo de gli Stati."

the court and governing class. But the full-blown use of Tacitus as a tool of governing and political reflection did not begin until the age of Philip III.

In 1614, the Spanish humanist and *licenciado*, Baltasar Alamos de Barrientos, published his major life work, the Spanish translation of the works of Tacitus. Dedicated to the Duke of Lerma, *Tacito Español* was the first translation of Tacitus to be published in Spain, and it came complete with a royal privilege that reserved all publication rights to the author for a period of twenty years. With the royal imprimatur and censor approvals by the royal counselor, Antonio de Covarruvias, and the royal historian, Luis Cabrera de Cordova, Barrientos's text was a translation produced at and for the center of Spanish power. Its popularity at the upper echelons of the government revealed the important role that Tacitus and the example of the Roman empire continued to play as a source of political council and reflection.[135]

This was clearly the intention and purpose of Barrientos. His translation included expansive marginal notes, or aphorisms, that were explicitly meant to draw political lessons from the history of the first century of the Roman Empire.[136] The dedication to the Duke of Lerma stressed that while

> in the time of the Republic the histories of Republics are good and necessary, … in the time of Princes those of Monarchy [are necessary] to understand its condition, and that of its dependents, and to benefit from this knowledge in order to acquire and conserve, and not to lose [the empire].[137]

This concisely summed up the new view on Tacitus that allowed him to be embraced so enthusiastically in the courts of Paris and Madrid in the seventeenth century. Tacitus was seen as a handbook for imperial acquisition and preservation.

---

[135] *Tacito Español*, Ilustrado con Aforismos por don Baltasar Alamos de Barrientos. Dirigido a Don Francisco Gomez de Sandoval y Rojas Duque de Lerma Marques de Denia (Madrid, Luis Sanchez), 1614.

[136] Previous scholarship on *Tacito Español* includes J. A. Maravall, "La corriénte doctrinal del tacitismo politico en España," in *Cuadernos Hispanoamericanos*, Vol. 240, pp. 645–667, 1969; and José Fernández-Santamaria, "Baltasar Alamos de Barrientos' Ciencia de Contigentes: A Spanish View of Statecraft as Science during the Baroque," in *Bibliotheque d'Humanisme et Renaissance*, Vol. 41, No. 2, 1979, pp. 293–304. My own views differ considerably from both of these authors insofar as I consider Barrientos and Spanish tacitism as a continuation of a long Renaissance intellectual tradition and not a Baroque innovation, as they call it.

[137] Ibid., f. +1v, The text reads in part:

> "En tiempo de Republica son buenas, y necessarias las historias de Republicas; y conocer por ellas el natural, y costumbres del vulgo: y en tiempo de Principes las de la Monarquia, para entender su condicion, y la de sus dependientes; y valerse deste conocimiento: para adquirir, para conservarse, y para no perderse."

It was in his aphorisms that Barrientos elaborated on these lessons: no fewer than seventy-five were dedicated to the theme of empire. Among these, the selection of the "rules, lessons, and sentences" that focused on the example of Caesar Augustus dominated the group. The aphorisms were the most popular part of Barrientos's work abroad: they were translated into Italian and included with Italian translations of Tacitus in no fewer than five editions published between 1618 and 1665.[138]

For Barrientos, the writings of Tacitus were likened to "precious jewels of the prudence of state."[139] He stressed that he wanted Spain to benefit from "this master of the conservation and growth (advancement) of its monarchy."[140] He also pointed to earlier Spanish statesmen who were devotees of Tacitus such as the ambassador Don Diego de Mendoza and Cardinal Moron, the "great spirit of the Roman court in the time of Pius IV and Pius V" who "always carried [Tacitus] with him."[141]

The new Latin editions available in Italy in the early sixteenth century led to its popularity among princes such as Pope Paul III and Duke Cosimo de Medici.[142] But no Spanish press published Tacitus until the translation of Barrientos appeared. The flurry of Tacitism in the late sixteenth century in France, the Netherlands, and Italy was kept at bay by Philip II, perhaps because he did not want too many people reflecting on tyranny. The first edition of Lipsius, after all, was dedicated to the Dutch Protestants fighting the Catholic King, and it was meant to instruct them in how to resist tyranny. But there was a sea change in the age of Philip III.

The new translation by Barrientos acknowledged the debt to Lipsius by including a two-page passage by the author in the front material of his translation titled the *Vida, Oficios, y Escritcos [Life, Offices, and Writings]* of Cayo Cornelio Tacito.[143] Lipsius had famously stressed the applicability of Roman history to the political life of his own day, and he praised Tacitus as the greatest of all ancient Roman historians, especially because of his political

---

[138] Antonio Palau y Dulcet, *Manual Del Librero Hispanoamericano*, second edition, Barcelona, 1970, Vol. 22, pp. 375–76.

[139] *Tacito Espanol.*, f.+4r, "los escritos de Tacito, piedras finas y verdaderas de la prudencia de estado."

[140] Ibid., "Aviendo yo conocido esto; y deseando que pues la demas naciones le posseian en sus lenguas; tuviesse tambien la nuestra en la suya este maestro de la consevacion, y aumento de su Monarquia."

[141] Ibid.

[142] Schellhase, p. 121.

[143] For a good example of recent work on Tacitus and Lipsius, see Mark Morford, "Tacitean *Prudentia* and the Doctrines of Justus Lipsius," in *Tacitus and the Tacitean Tradition*, ed. T. J. Luce and A. J. Woodman (Princeton, NJ: Princeton University Press), 1993, pp. 129–151.

usefulness. Barrientos followed Lipsius in this and also contrasted Tacitus with Livy, who was seen as being entertaining to read but not of nearly as much use because he wrote about the Roman Republic.

Lipsius, like Barrientos, had a passion for imperial Rome: "How beautiful the Roman Empire," Lipsius exclaimed in a letter written to a student. But because he originally wrote for a Dutch Protestant government, he emphasized the negative lessons of imperial government and its inclination toward tyranny. In his 1581 commentaries on the *Annals*, dedicated to the Dutch government, he used the Spanish Empire as a major example of contemporary imperial tyranny.[144]

Barrientos's translation and aphorisms, on the other hand, treated the *Annals and Histories* of Tacitus as providing largely positive lessons about and for empires and emperors new and old. As one of the censors, the royal historian and first biographer of Philip II, Luis Cabrera de Cordoba, noted in support of Barrientos's work, it promoted the "glory of the Spaniards and the Romans."[145]

Barrientos was particularly interested in the lessons to be learned from Tacitus for a *new* prince. He began working on the text very early in the reign of Philip III, even though it was not finished until 1614. Subsequently, the purposes of the imperial aphorisms revolved around three central themes: (1) the superiority of monarchical government to republican government, (2) the dangers and pitfalls of ruling an empire, and (3) how to conserve an empire.

Among the basic and foundational lessons was that empire was the superior form of government and the successor to Republican government in a mature and successful political system. This was because "The body of the Republic is one, and its members cannot come apart without its irreparable damage, so as not to either divide or give itself to many; and so it is governed better by the spirit and understanding of one alone; and thus the government of the monarchy is better."[146]

This lesson is gleaned from a speech in the *Annals* by Sallustius Crispus, one of the counselors to the new emperor Tiberius, who advised him against

---

[144] Morford, p. 133. Lipsius had said of Rome, "Oh great and glorious Empire" in a letter to a student, and also held up Tacitus as a source of encouragement and examples. Also p. 138, where Morford points out that in 1581 Lipsius dedicated a new commentary on *Annals* to States of Holland, where he commented on evils of Spanish rule at some length.

[145] Barrientos, from front material "Aprovacion de Luis Cabrera de Cordova," not paginated.

[146] P. 13, Aphorismo H.95: "El cuerpo de la Republica es uno solo, y no se pueden apartar sus miembros sin daño irreparable suyo; y por esto ni dividirse, ni darse a muchos; y assi se rige mejor por el animo y entendimiento de uno solo: y por esto es mejor govierno el de la Monarquia."

trying to justify to the Senate the murder of the grandson of Augustus, Postumus Agrippa, because "the condition of holding empire is that an account cannot be balanced unless it is rendered to one person."[147] The spin that Barrientos gave to this text and the political lesson rendered from it was obviously stretching the original context and meaning, to say the least. But it was typical of the work of Barrientos and numerous other interpreters of Tacitus that they could use him for various purposes, including advancing the virtues of empire or harshly criticizing it as a political system.

For Barrientos, the lessons of imperial Rome clearly pointed to not just the superiority but also the necessity of the government of one alone as the remedy for a divided Republic full of discord.[148] He drew this and many other lessons especially from the life of Caesar Augustus, or more precisely from his accomplishments as they were related by Tacitus in the context of the discussions that took place on the emperor's death.

It was during the age of Augustus, as Tacitus related, that:

> The ocean and remote rivers were the boundaries of the empire; the legions, provinces, fleets, and all things were linked together; there was law for the citizens; there was respect shown to the allies. The capital had been embellished on a grand scale; only in a few instances had he resorted to force; simply to secure general tranquility.[149]

This Augustan example, the gold standard of empire, was clearly worthy of imitation and envy, and Barrientos pointed especially to the fact that "the legions, provinces, fleets, and all things were linked together," as being essential to the "conservation of great empires."[150]

Finally, Barrientos also found the last advice of Augustus to be worth careful consideration: namely the emperor's admonition to his successor to honor the established boundaries of the empire and to *not* try to expand it. The corresponding aphorism noted that "the new prince who fears any diminution of his Empire that would be blamed on him ... abstains from foreign wars and does not try to expand the Empire."[151]

These last pieces of political counsel from Barrientos came at the end of a long string of costly wars and at least one failed attempt at expanding the

---

[147] *Complete Works of Tacitus*, trans. John Church and William Jackson Brodribb, ed. Moses Hadas (New York: Random House), 1942, p. 7.

[148] Barrientos, p. 10, aphorismo D. 67.

[149] *Complete Works*, p. 10.

[150] Barrientos, p. 10. Barrientos calls these characteristics of the empire under Augustus "Puntos en que consiste la conservacion de los grandes Imperios."

[151] Ibid., p. 13, aphorism B. 89.

empire. By 1614, the councils of Philip III were increasingly pushing the king to avoid war, negotiate peace, and not spend money on more expeditions. In 1609, the twelve-year truce had been signed with the Dutch Protestants. A second attempt by Pedro Fernández de Quirós to get funding from the crown for yet another Spanish expedition in search of Australia was refused. The hawkish party in the government that urged action against the English in Jamestown was not followed. In short, precisely the kind of political realism and caution urged by Barrientos increasingly reflected the policies of the Spanish government in the second half of the king's reign.

The general peace, or *pax hispanica*, that followed in the years between 1609 and 1620 was seen by many as the major accomplishment of Philip III. In part, it was the reading of Tacitus offered by Barrientos and others that supported the political turn already taken by 1609. Peacemaking was the new priority guided by the Augustan model with its emphasis on the political virtues of prudence, knowledge, and moderation. The king could see himself reflected in this mirror and still claim his role as successful heir and ruler of the world's largest empire.

Philip III will never be confused with the emperor Augustus. But the more pragmatic policies that he and his government eventually pursued preserved the global empire that he had inherited, an undeniable accomplishment in and of itself. It was not something that his successor, Philip IV, would be able to claim.

4

THE RENAISSANCE OF EMPIRE
IN FRANCE

But change only the name of Caesar to Henry, the names of Ariovistus and of Vercingetorix to the leaders of the League; the name of those who fought against Caesar to Spaniards, Italians, Savoyards, Lorrainers, and others that were joined against Henry: who have made resolutions, plots, revolts, and efforts against the two; the speed, the valor, the struggles, the work and the success of the two, and you will see the life of the one fully reflected in the image of the other, so that one is able to look at one and see both.

Anthoine de Bandole, *Les Paralleles de Cesar et de Henry IIII*, 1609[1]

In 1616, a large bronze equestrian monument of Philip III arrived in Madrid after the long voyage from Florence. It was a gift ordered by Archduke Ferdinand de Medici from the workshop of Giambologna a decade earlier that was eventually placed in the center of the Plaza Mayor in Madrid.[2] The monument connected Spain's monarchy to the long genealogy of equestrian monuments stretching back to Donatello's Gattamelata, the sculpture of Borsa d'Este in Ferrara, and the ancient Marcus Aurelius moved to Michelangelo's new Capitoline Hill by Paul III. It also had three contemporary siblings, including the two statues that Ferdinand had commissioned of Cosimo I and himself for the Piazza della Signoria and the Piazza della Santissima Annunziata in Florence, respectively.[3] Leone Leoni would have

---

[1] Anthoine de Bandole, *Les Paralleles de Cesar et de Henry III* (Paris: Jean Richer, 1609), p. 45. "Mais changeons seulement le nom de Cesar `a Henry, les noms d'Arioviste et de Vercingentorix aus Chefs de la Ligue: la nom de ceux qui se liguerent contre Cesar, aux Espagnols, Italiens, Savoyards, Lorrains, et autres qui se sont bandez contre Henry: Qu'on marquee les resolutions, les motions, les revoltes, et efforts contre ces deux; la promptitude, la vaillance, les hazards, les travaux, et les succez de ces deux; et l'on verra la vie de l'un tellement peinte dans le tableau de l'autre, qu'on n'en peut voir un qu'en les voyant tous deux."
[2] For notes on the commission, see Charles Avery, *Giambologna. The Complete Sculpture* (London: Phaidon Press, 1993), p. 258.
[3] Ibid.

been pleased that the project he first proposed for Charles V in Milan was at least realized for his grandson in Madrid. In the case of Philip III, the statue was an acknowledgement of a real empire that the Medici dukes still had to please. But it was not the first equestrian monument to be erected in a European capital in that decade.

Rather, it was in 1614 that an equestrian monument of Henry IV of France, also executed by the workshop of Giambologna, arrived in Paris and was soon placed in a prominent position on the Pont Neuf, the bridge constructed by the king overlooking the still unfinished Louvre Palace. It, too, had been commissioned by Archduke Ferdinand de Medici on the request of his niece, Maria de' Medici, Queen of France and wife of Henry IV. That the Archduke sent statues to the kings of both Spain and France signaled a fundamental realignment in European politics once the French wars of religion were concluded and the newly converted Catholic, Henry of Navarre, had been crowned as king Henry IV in 1595. Like many rulers in Europe, the Florentine prince hoped that a revived France would provide a counterbalance to Spanish hegemony. His marriage in 1589 to Christina di Lorena, the daughter of Charles III, the Duke of Lorraine, had already signaled that the Medici were moving to strengthen ties outside of the direct Habsburg orbit. More dramatically, Ferdinand's decision to have his niece, Maria de Medici, marry Henry IV in 1600 demonstrated his determination to revive the traditional alliance between Florence and France.[4]

The assassination of the king in 1610, however, represented a setback to hopes for a strong French revival. Still, the equestrian statue accurately embodied the imperial image and aspirations that Henry IV and his predecessors had been fashioning for the past century. Unlike the statue of Philip III that celebrated an empire then at its peak, that of Henry IV served as a symbol of dreams that remained largely unrealized. Blocked in the sixteenth century by a combination of Habsburg competitors, internal religious and civil war, and weak or short-lived kings, French political ambitions for empire finally came to fruition with the reign of Louis XIV in the last half of the seventeenth century. But the Renaissance roots of that ambition were two centuries old and reached deep into Italy.

Early Renaissance Images of the French Imperial Monarchy

The kings of France had embraced the imagery and texts of the imperial Renaissance at an early stage as they cultivated both their connections with

---

[4] E. Cochrane, p. 101.

ancient Rome and related claims on contemporary Italy. Already in the late fifteenth century, Charles VIII and his court had demonstrated an attachment to the revival of Caesar. The king most famous for invading Italy in 1494 had visited Florence on his march south in that year, and no less a humanist than Marsilio Ficino had written a laudatory piece that compared him with his ancestor, Caesar, among others.[5]

This was not the first comparison of the two. The young king who impressively swept down into Italy with an army of 25,000 men had received the first French translation of the *Commentaries* of Caesar from Robert Gaguin (1443–1502) in 1485.[6] Gaguin's translation of the seven books of the *Commentaries on the Gallic Wars* was first published in Paris in 1488 by Antoine Verard, and it was the basis for many later translations.[7]

Various new editions of the *Commentaries*, including the six books of the *Civil Wars*, went to press repeatedly in France: six editions from the sixteenth century and another twelve editions from the seventeenth century are preserved in the National Library in Paris alone. Three additional editions appeared in the age of Napoleon. French translations of his works were printed at least sixty times in the early modern period.[8]

Indeed, of all the European monarchs, the French demonstrated the strongest personal attachment to the works and example of Julius Caesar: Henry IV translated the first two books of the *Commentaries*, Louis XIII translated the last two books, and Louis XIV again translated the first book in 1651. Spending time with Caesar in their youth was a veritable rite of passage for the French kings of the Renaissance.[9]

Although Charles VIII produced no translation himself, he was an obvious fan of Caesar who had ordered Gaguin to translate the work. It was a commission with a practical aim. Gaguin, a doctor of law, priest, and leading French humanist of the late fifteenth century, pointed to the real purpose

---

[5] On the theme of imperial symbolism in the reign of Charles VIII, see Robert W. Scheller, "Imperial Themes in Art and Literature of the Early French Renaissance: The Period of Charles VIII," in *Simiolus: Netherlands Quarterly for the History of Art*, Vol. 12, No. 1 (1981–1982), pp. 5–69. See pp. 6–8 for a summary of Ficino's eulogy.

[6] *La Guerre des Gaules par Napoleon III, Histoire de Jules Cesar* (Paris: Editions Errance, 2001), p. 3 of preface, and Scheller, p. 14. New editions of Caesar and Seutonius were also published in Lyon in 1500 and 1508 by Baldassarre de Gabbiano. For more on his press and the connection to Aldo Manuzio in Venice, see Franco Simone, *Umanesimo Rinascimento Barocco in Francia* (Milano: Mursia, 1968), p. 63.

[7] *Les Commentaires de Julius Cesar*, trans. Robert Gaguin (Paris: Anthoine Verad, 1488).

[8] Andrew Pettegree, *The Book in the Renaissance* (New Haven: Yale University Press, 2011), p. 199.

[9] *La Guerre des Gaules par Napoleon III*, p. 3.

in the dedication of the first French edition, where he noted that a prince needed two things above all else: the prudence to conduct the affairs of state well and the power to wage war valiantly and with courage when necessary.[10] It was to this end that he offered the king the writings and example of Caesar with the hope that in reading his work, Charles VIII would learn from the first emperor's incomparable virtue and diligence.[11]

With no word of criticism or reflections on tyranny, Gaguin continued the Petrarchan revival and rehabilitation of Caesar as a model for the modern prince. This was not the only historical example offered to Charles VIII or his successors by their humanist courtiers. Lives of Charlemagne, like the version Gaguin had given to Charles VIII prior to translating Caesar, continued to be popular in France as they had been in the medieval period. But Caesar's star was on the rise, and France's growing contact with Italy in the decades following 1494 only increased knowledge of and attraction to the ideas and images of the imperial Roman revival. When Charles VIII returned to France after his Italian campaign in 1495, he brought with him books, paintings, and sculpture to serve as models back home, and he also recruited twenty Italian artists to work for him in France. It was a modest beginning but one that has been credited with assuring that the Renaissance took root in France.[12]

Although the early death of Charles VIII in 1498 limited the impact that he had as a patron and protagonist of the arts and letters, he continued to play a role in the growing myth of the imperial French monarchy that developed over the next two centuries. His year in Italy had been marked by rumors that Pope Alexander VI had crowned him emperor of Constantinople in 1495 in the hopes that he would lead a new crusade. In a related vein, various cities had given him welcomes using some classical images and titles that associated him with the ancient empire. But few original sources from the visit refer to any real claims to an imperial title on the part of Charles VIII.

On the other hand, by the late sixteenth century, French historians of his reign had rewritten the history of 1495 to include a majestic imperial entry into Naples that presented the king as a true emperor. According to the history of Brantôme, for example, the king entered Naples holding an

---

[10] *Les Commentaires*, p. aii v.

[11] Ibid., *p.* aiii r. "mais a tant je fairay affin que vous oyez parler le principal acteur Jules Cesar duquel en lissant vous congnoistrez la vertu et incomparable diligence plus que en nul autre empereur ou chef de guerre."

[12] M. Eugène Müntz, *La Renaissance en Italie et en France a L'Époque de Charles VIII* (Paris: Firmin-Didot, 1885), p. 515. For Muntz, the Italian artists and objects acquired by the king "assurent à la Renaissance un triomphe decisive et durable dans notres pays."

orb of gold in his right hand, and his great imperial scepter in his left hand, and on his head he had a costly gold imperial crown, set with many precious stones, imitating in this lofty way the emperor of Constantinople, a dignity which had just been conferred on him by the pope, and all the people acclaimed him with one voice as most august emperor.[13]

A fictional account that literally dressed the king of France with all of the signs and symbols of imperial rule, this text resonated with many other real images and objects from the early sixteenth century that built up the imperial theme and iconography of the French monarchy. In 1502, for example, medals had been created for the successor of Charles VIII that proclaimed, "Every nation rejoices under the reign of the second Caesar, the fortunate Louis XII."[14] Strong associations between the new king and the Caesars were also created by the images accompanying various texts, including a 1510 edition of the *Chronicles of Monstrelet* produced in Genoa by the French scribe Antoine Bardin. More specifically, the frontispiece for one of the volumes is an image of an enthroned Louis XII framed by an elaborate border that includes nine medallions with busts of the good Roman emperors. The author explicitly compares the French king with these ancient Romans in the introduction of the text, where he is celebrated for exhibiting all of their combined virtues.[15]

In another realm of royal symbolism, it was also in Louis XII's reign (1498–1515) that the image of a an imperial crown began to appear in royal ceremonials, such as the king's entry into Paris in 1498, and in text illuminations such as those for Petrarch's *Trionfi*, a new translation of which was dedicated to the monarch early in his reign. In what has been described as "Frances' nationalization of an imperial symbol of power," the usurpation of the imperial crown reserved only for the Holy Roman Emperors was a largely symbolic salvo signaling that the contest for imperial reputation and power was heating up.[16]

This competition manifested itself more concretely in the long string of wars that marked the reign of Louis XII, beginning with his conquest of Milan in 1499 and again after the rebellion of 1500. This was the king's greatest acquisition, and it was in northern Italy that Louis XII counted

[13] Quoted from Scheller, "Imperial Themes," p. 64.

[14] Robert W. Scheller, "French Royal Symbolism in the Age of Louis XIII," in *Simiolus: Netherlands Quarterly for the History of Art*, Vol. 13, No. 2 (1983), pp. 75–141.

[15] Robert W. Scheller, "Louis XII and Italy 1499–1508," in *Simiolus: Netherlands Quarterly for the History of Art*, Vol. 15, No. 1 (1985), pp. 26–29.

[16] Scheller, "French Royal Symbolism." On the "imperial monarchy" and imperial crown, see especially pp. 101–110.

his major victories, including the famous defeat of the Venetians in 1509 at Agnadello.[17]

In the south of Italy, however, Louis XII was not so fortunate. A major war with Ferdinand of Spain for control of the kingdom of Naples raged in 1503 to 1504. It ended with a bitter loss for the French in 1504 that marked the beginning of two centuries of Spanish imperial domination of southern Italy. Later in the decade, in 1512, another contest with Ferdinand for control of the kingdom of Navarre ended in defeat, and that kingdom was claimed for Ferdinand's successors for the next two centuries. To make matters worse, war on the northern front with Henry VIII led to the loss of Tournai to the English in 1513. Finally, Louis lost control of Milan in the face of a league formed against him that restored the Sforza to power in 1513. Even the constant stream of royal pageants and propaganda back in France had a hard time covering up this dismal record.[18]

By the time Louis XII died in 1515, his early aspirations had come up short in the areas that mattered most: increased reputation, glory, and above all else, real territories. In all of these realms, it was Ferdinand, Machiavelli's model new prince, who was on the rise while France faced increasing setbacks. In the same decades that Columbus claimed the New World for Castile and the first steps of Spanish colonization began, the French could count only a few voyages of exploration in North America.

But the next king, Francis I (1515–1547), engaged in imperial contest at a level far surpassing that of his predecessors. This became clear from the very beginning of his reign, and it was again in Italy that the king sought to make his mark. Immediately on assuming power in 1515, Francis I led a large army into Italy. Like Louis XII in 1499, he won his first campaign, this time with the celebrated victory at Marignano. A battle famous for the size of the armies and canons used by the French to dominate the field, it brought the monarch a large measure of fame and glory.[19]

Chroniclers and poets alike proclaimed that such a victory had not been won since the time of Julius Caesar. Louise de Savoie, mother of the king,

---

[17] For the most famous primary account of the French invasion in 1494, see Francesco Guicciardini, *The History of Italy*, trans. Sidney Alexander (Princeton: Princeton University Press, 1984), pp. 32–75. Also see David Abulafia, *The French Descent into Renaissance Italy*, 1494–95 (Aldershot: Ashgate, 1995).

[18] On royal ritual display in the age of Louis XII, see Michael Sherman, "Pomp and Circumstances: Pageantry, Politics, and Propaganda in France during the Reign of Louis XII, 1498–1515," in *The Sixteenth Century Journal*, Vol. 9, No. 4 (Winter, 1978), pp. 13–32.

[19] Machiavelli, *Discourses*, 2.18, p. 376. Machiavelli estimated the French infantry at 40,000, the cavalry at 20,000, and the number of canon at 100. He put the number of Swiss infantry at 26,000.

went further to describe her son as the "glorious and triumphant second Caesar subjugator of the Helvetians (Swiss)" in her *Journal*.[20] On the one hand, these references were a continuation of the growing uses of Caesar as a point of comparison for the French monarchs since the late fifteenth century and a continuation of romantic references to Caesar scattered throughout medieval chivalric literature.

But the reign of Francis I was also a watershed for the imperial theme and the French monarchy because it constituted a major departure from these earlier traditions in two primary ways. First, from the time of Francis I onward, the comparisons of the French monarchs with the ancient Caesars became a constant and expanding theme in monarchical literature. The secular Caesars, and especially Julius Caesar, were fully embraced as models and predecessors for the French kings on a scale not seen previously. Second, in the world of artistic representation, it was with the court of Francis I that the full range of Renaissance artistic production was harnessed to project an imperial image of the French monarch. To paraphrase a contemporary study, the image of the victorious ancient emperors was "reintegrated" with that of the French kings using the antique style of the Renaissance under Francis I.[21]

A central example of the integration of text and image came in the form of a new edition of Caesar's *Commentaries on the Gallic Wars* produced in 1519 to 1520 by the Franciscan François Demoulins and illustrated by a team of painters including Jean Clouet and Godefroy le Batave. The work was commissioned by Francis I to celebrate the victory at Marignano, and it reached a new height of political association of the ancient Caesar with a Renaissance prince. On the level of images, a portrait medal of the French king painted by Jean Clouet was paired with an image of Caesar. It is the earliest portrait of Francis.[22] On the textual level, the author chose to give Francis I a prominent role in the text by presenting the *Commentaries* in the form of a dialogue between Caesar and Francis I wherein Caesar answers questions posed to him by Francis I about the strategies of war, the philosophy of rule,

---

[20] Janet Cox-Rearick, *The Collection of Francis I: Royal Treasures* (Antwerp: Fonds Mercator Paribas, 1995), p. 4.

[21] Anne-Marie Lecoq, *François I imaginaire* (Paris: Macula, 1987), pp. 215–257. This work provides the best study to date of the imperial theme in literature and art for Francis I. The author writes that the reference to Caesar "prend dans la littérature monarchique la dimension d'un leitmotiv" in the age of Francis I, and she also notes that it is at this time that "les arts figuratifs amorcent, à l'usage du roi de France, la `réintégration' de l'*imperator* victorieux dans son apparence antique" p. 217.

[22] J. Cox-Rearick, p. 5. Referring to Francis I, this work describes the imperial theme as "omnipresent in his personal imagery."

and military leadership. It is the *Commentaries* as a guide for princes with the old master providing instruction in his own voice.[23]

With marginal notes explaining various details in the text, this three-volume manuscript was the most expansive version of the *Commentaries* to date. Numerous additional illustrations underlined the close association between Francis I and Caesar, as they were shown embracing one another in the gardens of the chateau of Cognac and walking arm in arm in the forest of Fontainebleau. If there is any doubt that Francis I is the true heir of Caesar, another image shows Caesar handing the king of France "the sword and the ancient herald's wand."[24] Never had French royal claims to Caesar's heritage been so beautifully and overtly presented.

Numerous additional editions of Caesar's *Commentaries* that included the *Civil Wars* were also printed in the era of Francis I, including a new translation by Estienne Beauvoys in 1531. Published under royal privilege, this version included two color maps and numerous illustrations of bridges and war machines from antiquity. It was reprinted again in 1539 and dedicated to the Admiral of France, Philippes Chabot, who was also the governor general of the king for the duchy of Burgundy. The translator believed that among its many virtues, the writings and example of Caesar were capable of providing military inspiration for the French nobility, who apparently needed some extra help.[25] Another edition of this translation was printed in 1545 again in Paris.

Unfortunately for Francis I and the French nobility dreaming of empire, the future envisioned in the many editions of the *Commentaries* ran into trouble shortly after the first victories in Milan. Again, the problems came from Italy and from the other major pretender to Caesar's title, Charles V. The French conquest of Milan in 1515 was short lived, as Francis I was defeated by Charles V first in 1521 and then again in three more campaigns between 1522 and 1525. The French king suffered the added indignity of being captured and imprisoned in Spain after his final loss at Pavia in 1525. Still undeterred, Francis I sent troops into Italy again in 1527 once he was free. They were again defeated by the armies of Charles V. Also lost during that campaign was the allegiance of Genoa and its fleet under the Doria admirals. Thereafter they would be an important part of Spanish naval forces. Italy, in short, was an unmitigated disaster for Francis I.

---

[23] Lecoq, pp. 229–244. The three volumes of the *Commentaires de la guerre gallique* have been dispersed and are now found separately in London, Paris, and Chantilly.

[24] Ibid., pp. 237–238. "l'épée et le caducée."

[25] *Les Commentaires de Jules Cesar*, trans. Estienne Beauvoys after that of Robert Gaguin (Paris: 1539).

Given the financial and military edge that Charles V enjoyed especially after the conquest of Mexico in 1520, it is hard to imagine that it could have gone differently. Yet Italy was an obsession for French monarchs throughout the entire early modern period, and their desire to control and/or occupy Italian territory was unrelenting. Imperial longing and the desire to claim the mantle of the new Caesars explains much of this. Italy had always been the heart and home of the empire, and having at least some Italian territories was a valuable component of the imperial image. So, too, the possession of the title of Holy Roman Emperor, and that had also been the subject of a fierce bidding war between Charles V and Francis I. But again, the superior treasury and borrowing power of the former won the day as Charles V spent almost 1 million gold florins for the crown.

Francis I also attempted to follow the lead of the Spanish in the quest for both New World territories and new routes to the Far East. The French monarchy never accepted the Treaty of Tordesillas and the monopoly on American settlement that it gave to the Spanish and Portuguese. French voyages to the New World by Le Paulmier de Gonneville to Brazil in 1503 and another to New Foundland in 1506 were of little lasting significance, but they did set a precedent for future French explorations.[26]

Francis I understood the growing importance of the Atlantic world and initiated work on the new port of Le Havre as soon as he assumed power. He also supported, directly or indirectly, Atlantic explorations such as the voyage of Giovanni da Verrazzano to present-day New York in 1524. More significantly, Jacques Cartier made three voyages to North America between 1534 and 1543, discovering in the later voyage the St. Lawrence River.[27] Finally, Jean-François de la Roque de Roberval began the settlement of Canada in 1541. No small accomplishments, these voyages nonetheless pale in comparison with the Spanish conquests of Mexico and Peru occurring in the same years. Francis I was also hoping for treasure, or at least a quick route to the trading riches of Asia. Instead he received news of fish and fur.[28]

Defeated in Italy and severely limited in the New World, Francis I still had France as a place to make his mark as a Renaissance imperial prince. With French commercial life flourishing in his age and the Concordat of 1516 ensuring that more ecclesiastical income stayed in France, the king had a healthy income. A good amount was lost on wars, but he also spent

[26] Frederick Quinn, *The French Overseas Empire* (London: Praeger, 2002), pp. 12–17.
[27] Ibid., pp. 18–29.
[28] Georges Duby, *Storia della Francia*, trans. Francesco Saba Sardi (Milano: Bompiani, 1998), pp. 485–493.

lavishly on art and architecture, a more winning proposition for his reputation and legacy.

It was as a patron of arts and letters that Francis I competed more successfully with Charles V as he, too, built or renovated royal residences that he filled with the literature of ancient Rome and Greece and with paintings and sculptures that followed the ancient style. Stymied in his attempts to maintain a foothold in Italy, he was successful in buying Italian art and attracting Italian artists and architects to his court. Leonardo da Vinci was the most famous among them, but many other Italians were put to work in the building or rebuilding of royal residences, most especially at Fontainebleau and at the Louvre Palace in Paris. They successfully helped the French king develop his image as a new Caesar surrounded with imperial iconography and splendor.

Already in 1518 to 1519, medals were cast commemorating Marignano that depicted Francis I in the dress of a Roman emperor on one side and a battle scene modeled on those of ancient Rome on the reverse.[29] Similarly, the subjects of Francis I demonstrated that they were learning from and following the lead of the Italian courts in their use of the artistic forms from antiquity. In 1517, for example, the city of Rouen erected an ephemeral equestrian monument to celebrate the entry of the king. With strong echoes of a similar entry and ephemeral construction created for the entry of Leo X into Florence in 1515, it was the first example of this part of the ancient Roman artistic repertoire being used to celebrate the French monarchy.[30] But it was far from the last.

Although medals or ephemeral constructions served in a limited way to bolster the image of the imperial monarchy under Francis I, it was in his building projects at Fontainebleau and the Louvre Palace in Paris that the king made a more permanent and dramatic statement. Work began in earnest at Fontainebleau in 1528, and the major construction and substantial decoration was done by the time of the king's death in 1547. Viewed from the perspective of a competition with Charles V, who had started his palace in Granada in the same period, Francis won at least this battle because he was able to actually live in and enjoy his new chateau.

With Fontainebleau, Francis I initiated a major period of palace construction and decoration with the aim of bringing the grandeur of the Italian Renaissance to France and to himself. In the words of Giorgio Vasari, he wanted to make a new Rome at Fontainebleau.[31] To that end, he recruited

[29] Lecoq, pp. 218–219.
[30] Ibid., pp. 224–228.
[31] Quoted in Eugène Plon, *Leone Leoni*, p. 49.

the artists Rosso Fiorentino, Benvenuto Cellini, Giovanni Francesco Rustici, and Francesco Primaticcio to decorate his favorite residence. Built using some of the old walls and foundations of the medieval building, Fontainebleau from the exterior does not follow a classical plan, and there was no intention to recreate an imperial palace like that of Granada. Rather, it is the interior paintings of the building, as well as the collection of sculptures, that animate Fontainebleau with a classical spirit.[32]

It is in the large gallery of Francis I, most especially, that the frescoes of Rosso Fiorentino, framed with elaborate stucco decoration, created an environment of ancient luxury. The subject material for the majority of the thirteen frescoes is taken from ancient mythology: *The Battle of the Centaurs, Venus Frustrated, The Education of Achilles, The Death of Adonis,* and so forth. Although the cycle has no obvious narrative unity or structure and has often posed an interpretive problem or puzzle for scholars, the most convincing interpretation to date is the one that is most consistent with the broader political program of Francis I described thus far. Proposed by André Chastel shortly after the restoration of the gallery in the late 1960s, this reading of the cycle views the frescoes as united not by any historical narrative, but rather by a political program. The frescoes, in short, are allegories of the political principles of the French monarchy.[33]

More specifically, it is the "imperial theme" that unites and explains the images from the triumphal *Elephant* to the fresco titled *The Unity of the State.* The latter image features a Roman emperor crowned with a laurel wreath, holding an imperial symbol of unity and rule, the pomegranate.[34] He is giving a speech to a group of attentive listeners that form a semicircle around him. This is Caesar speaking to the ancient Gauls, but the face of the emperor is a portrait of Francis I. This merging of the king and the ancient Caesar is completely consistent with the literary and iconographic program of Demoulin's edition of Caesar's *Commentaries* and with the continuing political ambitions of the monarch.[35]

So, too, the sculptural program for Fontainebleau entrusted first to the Italian sculptor and painter Francesco Primaticcio. He was sent to Rome in 1540 to get molds of a dozen major ancient sculptures, mainly from the

[32] Henri Zerner, *L'Art De La Renaissance en France* (Paris: Flammarion, 1996), p. 63. The architectural plan of Fontainebleau is described as utilitarian by this author, while the program for the interior decoration takes the place of any strong architectural idea.

[33] Sylvie Béguin, Oreste Binenbaum, André Chastel, W. McAllister Johnson, Sylvia Pressouyre, and Henri Zerner, *La Galerie François Ier au Chateau de Fontainebleau* (Paris: Flammarion, 1972), pp. 147–149.

[34] Cox-Rearick, pp. 13–14.

[35] Chastel, p. 148.

Belvedere Courtyard at the Vatican. These were then used to cast bronze copies at the new foundry in Fontainebleau on Primaticcio's return. Thus, some of the most famous ancient statues from the Vatican collection, including the *Apollo Belvedere*, *Laocoön*, *Venus*, *Hercules Commodus*, *Sleeping Ariadne*, and *Mercury*, took their place in the Galerie François or the gardens of Fontainebleau to give the king's residence splendor and gravitas *all'antica*.[36] In addition, a greater plaster copy of the ancient Marcus Aurelius from the Capitoline Hill was made.[37]

To these were added many new sculptures, including the creations of the other major Italian sculptor working at Fontainebleau, Benvenuto Cellini. The Florentine goldsmith and sculptor stayed in France for five years from 1540 to 1545, during which time he produced, among other works, the *Nymph of Fontainebleau*. The graceful bronze relief sculpture of a reclining nymph with her armed draped around the head of a stag was one of the finest pieces made in the period. It joined dozens of other antique and contemporary sculptures that had been acquired abroad by the king's agents, including, possibly, Michelangelo's *Hercules*.[38]

In addition to Cellini, Francis I had given another major sculptural commission to the Florentine sculptor Giovanni Francesco Rustici. Highly regarded in his home city, where he won the competition to cast the large bronze statue of St. John the Baptist for the Cathedral Baptistery, Rustici was enlisted to cast a bronze equestrian statue of the French king that was to be twice the size of nature. Prefiguring the monument by Giambologna of Henry IV by many decades, the monument would have been an excellent companion and bronze culmination of the many other painted and literary images that depicted Francis I as a new Caesar. But as an apt metaphor of the political agenda of Francis I, it was not finished by the time of his death in 1547. According to Vasari, only the horse had been cast in Paris.[39]

Still, like so many of the political and artistic designs of the ruler many consider France's first Renaissance monarch, Rustici's statue established a precedent: Catherine de' Medici, the wife of the next monarch, Henry II,

[36] Bruce Boucher, "Leone Leoni and Primaticcio's Moulds of Antique Sculpture," in *The Burlington Magazine*, Vol. 123, No. 934, 1981, pp. 23–26. Also E. Plon, *Leone Leoni*, pp. 48–49.

[37] Cox-Rearick, pp. 325–335.

[38] Ibid., pp. 302–307.

[39] Ibid., p. 286, and E. Plon, p. 55. Most art historians assume that Rustici's inspiration for the equestrian monument came from his master Leonardo da Vinci, who had drawn sketches of such a monument for the Sforza in Milan.

also tried to get a bronze equestrian statue made for her husband that was left unfinished. But as Giambologna's work proved, the project was finally accomplished by yet another Medici queen a generation later. Once revived and embraced, this ancient imperial sign of sovereignty exercised an irresistible draw on the French monarchy. The project first promoted by Francis I thus enjoyed success in the long term.

This was also true in the realm of architecture. Again, Francis I can be credited with being the first monarch to promote the Vitruvian revival in France, initially through his patronage of Sebastiano Serlio (1475–1553), who resided in his court from 1541, when he was appointed court architect, to the king's death in 1547. Serlio dedicated the first three books of his major work, *D'Architettura*, to the king with an ode that associated him with the general revival of classical architecture. "In this age the beautiful and useful art of Architecture returns to that height that it had in that happy age of the Romans and Greeks," Serlio wrote. He credited Francis I with the French stage of the revival because he "had ordered the building of many beautiful and magnificent buildings throughout his realm."[40]

In the case of Fontainebleau, Serlio's contributions were modest. He designed a separate house on the grounds in the classical style for Cardinal Ippolito d'Este and also drew up plans for a classical loggia and domed bathing pavilion that were never built.[41] The fact that he arrived when the reconstruction was well underway, combined with the death of the king only six years after he assumed his role as royal architect, partially explain this limited impact.

More important and influential than his buildings, however, was Serlio's book. The most expansive and well-illustrated architectural treatise up to that time, it became a popular guide for craftsmen, who increasingly were called on to use the classical orders for royal construction projects. It was translated into French in 1545. Together with Guillaume Philander's *Annotationes*, a French commentary on Vitruvius published in that same year, and Jean Martin's first French translation of Vitruvius' *On Architecture* from 1547,

[40] Sebastiano Serlio, *D'Architettura, Il Terzo Libro* (Venice: Giovanni Battista and Marchio Sessa, 1559), p. III. The relevant passage of the dedication reads:

E perche in questa età la bella, et util'arte de l'Architettura ritorna a quella altezza, che ella era a quel felice secolo de i Romani, e de i Greci trovatori de le buone arti: et essendo vostra Maestà non solo dotata di tante altre scientie per theorica, e per pratica; ma tanto intendente, et amatore de l'Architettura, quanto ne fan fede tante bellissime, e stupende fabriche da quella ordinate in piu parti del suo gran regno; havendo ciposto ogni mia diligentia, ho voluto collocare questo mio volume sotto i larghissimi rami de la intelligentia di V. Maestà.

[41] Cox-Rearick, pp. 41–42.

4.1. Pierre Lescot, Cour Carre, Louvre, Paris, France. (Photograph: Erich Lessing/Art Resource, NY.)

Serlio's work laid the textual foundation for the Vitruvian revival in France. He is thus credited with being the first architect who gave the French "access to classical architecture and to its principles."[42]

The best example of this revival being applied to palace architecture occurred not in Fontainebleau but in Paris at the Louvre Palace. It was in the renovation and reconstruction of the old medieval fortress of the French kings that the Vitruvian aesthetics of the imperial Renaissance found their strongest and first French expression. Serlio's plan for the city palace of Francis I, inspired especially by Palazzo Te in Mantua, was included in his sixth book on palace architecture. Although never realized, it became a central point of reference for the future designs that were executed over the next century.[43]

Francis I initiated the transformation when he first commissioned Pierre Lescot (Figure 4.1) to draw up plans for a new palace on the grounds of the Louvre. Not built until after Francis I's death, it nonetheless constituted his

[42] Zerner, p. 98. "Les François ont salué en lui un grand initiateur, celui qui leur avait donné accès à l'architecture classique et à ses principes."

[43] Roberto Gargiani, *Idea e costruzione del Louvre* (Bologna: Alinea, 1998), pp. 12–13. This study points out that "Il disegno di Serlio costituirà il riferimento ideale per gil sviluppi del Louvre."

most lasting contribution to the early Vitruvian revival in France when it was finished in 1556. Moreover, it initiated the transformation of the Louvre Palace into one of the foremost classicizing palaces of Renaissance Europe and added further luster to Francis I's reputation as a leading patron of the classical revival.[44]

The façade of the new wing of the palace became the focus of the court-yard, as it evoked the image of an ancient theater. The *Cour Carrée* utilized the Corinthian order and was elaborately decorated with sculptures by Jean Goujon. A relatively small part of what grew to be the most monumental of all French royal palaces, the new wing by Lescot set the classicizing prec-edent that dominated all future additions and renovations.[45]

The Imperial Political Science of Jean Bodin

When Francis I died in 1547, the artistic inheritance that he left to his son Henry II (1519–1559) considerably increased the political grandeur of the monarchy, at least in its material expressions. The richly developed iconog-raphy so lavishly presented at Fontainebleau presented the king as the sec-ond Caesar. But the undeniable reality was that as far as real empire was concerned, Francis I was all crown and no conquests. He had imitated the ancient emperors relatively well as a patron of arts and letters. But after Marignano, he failed badly in the critical realms of winning tangible mili-tary victories and real territorial gains. The sprawling territories of Charles V that also included Peru by 1547 set the gold standard for real empire and put in high relief the shortcomings of Francis I and France as contenders for modern empire.

Henry II tried to change this by challenging his father's old nemesis, Charles V, once he assumed power. In central Europe, he joined with the German Protestant princes in their wars against the emperor in the late 1540s and early 1550s. Together they were successful at blocking Charles V in his attempt to pass on the title of emperor to Philip II. They also scored some important victories against his armies that led to the settlement of Augsburg in 1555 that ensured religious autonomy for the German princes. For his role in the fight, Henry II earned the name Protector of the Empire from the Protestant princes.[46]

---

[44] Zerner, pp. 158–170. Also see André Chastel, "French Renaissance Art in a European Context," in *Sixteenth Century Studies*, Vol. 12, No. 4 (Winter, 1981), pp. 77–103.
[45] Gargiani, pp. 13–14.
[46] T. Brady, pp. 227–228.

In Italy, the French king was not so fortunate. He sent modest aid in the early 1550s to the Republic of Sienna, then at war with Cosimo I de Medici, who was backed by the armies of Charles V. That ended in defeat for Sienna in 1554. Henry II followed with a bolder attempt to challenge Philip II's dominance in Italy in 1557 when he sent armies to aid Paul IV in the Caraffa war. That, too, ended in failure, as did the simultaneous battle at St. Quentin that marked the further ascent of the Spanish. When Henry II died from a wound received in a joust held to celebrate the peace reached with Spain at Cateau-Cambrésis in 1559, it put a tragic end to a dozen years dominated by costly military adventures. Politically and financially weakened, France had to wait for another day and another monarch.

More accurately, virtually all French aspirations toward increased political power, not to mention empire, had to wait for many more years, as the kingdom fell into four decades of sporadic religious civil war and conflict with Spain. In an age when the health, longevity, and political skill of the monarch weighed heavily on the fortunes of European states, France had bad luck with both in the latter half of the sixteenth century. After the early death of Henry II at age forty, his son Francis II (1544–1560) survived for only one year. Charles IX followed but died at only twenty-four (1550–1574), and Henry III (1551–1589), politically weak and misguided, was assassinated before he reached his fortieth birthday.

The wife of Henry II, Catherine de Medici, provided some political leadership and continuity throughout much of this time. She had lived at court under Francis I and clearly understood not only the workings of government but also the importance of the arts in the promotion of the monarchy. During her husband's reign, she had often acted as regent during his frequent military campaigns and also commissioned yet another equestrian monument to honor him that never reached France.

Beginning in 1560, she wielded considerable power, first acting in the name of her son, the ten-year-old king Charles IX. Sometimes as the head of the government and the person who controlled the king's seal and at others as the primary councilor to the king, she was the most influential political figure in the court from 1560 until her death.[47] Even if youth or lack of natural ability limited what her sons could hope to achieve, she aided them in the pursuit of policies that furthered the image and theoretical power of the monarchy.

Under Henry III, for example, there was a strong push to consolidate the power of the king through the promulgation of law codes favorable to royal

---

[47] Katherine Crawford, "Catherine de Médicis and the Performance of Political Motherhood," *The Sixteenth Century Journal*, Vol. 31, No. 3 (Autumn 2000), pp. 643–673.

interests. The ordinance of Blois of 1579 and the Code of Henry III of 1587 revised French ordinances to follow the model and form of Roman law. In theory if not always in fact, these codes substantially reformed laws in a wide range of areas including commerce, noble privileges, government offices, and the economy. They also established an important precedent for future kings and ministers seeking to consolidate royal power.[48]

This revival of Roman law at the service of increased monarchical power was furthered by the publication of the most important piece of French humanist scholarship of the late sixteenth century, *The Six Books of the Republic* by Jean Bodin (1529–1596).[49] First published in French in 1576 and then in a revised Latin version in 1586, it was a milestone in Renaissance political writing and imperial humanism. It was also one of the most successful French political works of the sixteenth and seventeenth centuries judging by its publication record: the French version went to press fourteen times in Paris, Lyon, and Geneva; the Latin version was printed nine times in France, Germany, Geneva, and Strasburg; and translations were printed in Italian (1588), Spanish (1590), German (1592), and English (1606).[50]

Although the educational background that produced such an important work is vague, it is clear that after a few years as a Carmelite monk in his teens, Bodin had pursued the study of law and was teaching that subject at the College of Tolosa by 1559. In 1570, he attained his first royal appointment as a procurator of the king in Normandy, and he also served as a Latin translator for the court in that period. He was favored by Henry III, who enjoyed listening to his learned discourse, and royal support of *The Six Books of the Republic* was strong to the extent that a critic of the text was arrested in 1579.[51]

The work was originally dedicated to one of the king's primary councilors, and Bodin stressed in his opening comments that his writings were meant to help the monarchy maintain its power and rule its subjects.[52] At the same time, an imperial nostalgia colored the dedication, in which Bodin recalled the day when the German empire, the kingdoms of Hungary, Italy, Spain, and all of Gaul up to the Rhine were under "Our Rule."[53] In his earlier work on historical method, *Methodus ad facilem historiarum cognitionem*, he

[48] Georges Duby, *Storia della Francia*, Vol. 1, p. 514.
[49] Jean Bodin, *I Sei Libro dello Stato*, ed. Margherita Isnardi Parente (Turin: Unione Tipografico-Editrice Torinese, 1964), Volumes 1–3.
[50] Ibid., Vol. 1, pp. 109–110.
[51] Ibid., Vol. 1, p. 105.
[52] Ibid., p. 133.
[53] Ibid., p. 134.

had emphasized that it was useful to "compare the empires of our ancestors with our own."[54] In the *Six Books*, he aimed to apply those lessons with an eye toward revival. If the loss of its earlier empire under Charlemagne was not bad enough, Bodin mourned the fact that his France was subject to the predatory acts of internal and external enemies. He subsequently wrote the text hoping that all true Frenchmen would want to see France return to its ancient condition when it flourished in both arms and laws.

This was a Herculean task given the kingdom's plunge into civil religious war that Bodin was a living witness to, and the tools he chose for confronting it were history and law. A great fan of Tacitus and his approach to history, Bodin praised the ancient historian's style as "wonderfully keen and full of prudence," and he relied heavily on the *Annals* both as a model and as a source.[55] At the same time, his extensive knowledge and integration of Roman law in the text distinguished his lengthy study from other purely historical works. At its methodological heart, the *Six Books of the Republic* wove together the author's expansive knowledge of both history and law to break substantial new disciplinary ground. Bodin recognized this when he described the work using his newly coined term "political science."

For all of its novelty, *The Six Books of the Republic* was heavily indebted to humanist historiography stretching back to Petrarch. Like his predecessors, Bodin drew extensively on the examples and writings of ancient Rome. Although his text embraced a wide range of historical examples from antiquity up to his own day, a privileged place was given to the Roman Empire and to the example of its emperors. In this sense, the *Six Books of the Republic* carried on the tradition and work of imperial humanists and represented a strong continuation of rather than any substantial break with that long intellectual movement.

This is apparent in the prominence of the sources that are now familiar as the foundational texts of imperial humanism, most especially Caesar's *Commentaries*, Suetonius, Plutarch, and Tacitus. More broadly, Bodin makes constant and repeated references to the examples of the Roman Empire and emperors to illustrate, justify, and elaborate on the various political and/ or legal points that he wishes to make. Moreover, like many other authors who drew on the texts and history of ancient Rome, the political lessons Bodin drew from imperial Rome were largely those that supported and

---

[54] K. Schellhaus, pp. 110–111.

[55] Quoted from Jacob Soll, "Empirical History and the Transformation of Political Criticism in France from Bodin to Bayle," in *Journal of the History of Ideas*, Vol. 64, No. 2 (April 2003), pp. 297–316, 300.

encouraged a vision of wide-ranging monarchical power and an expansive imperial agenda.

This is largely because Bodin believed, as did so many of his contemporaries, that "The Romans had the greatest empire that ever was."[56] They subsequently became the main point of comparison and source of wisdom for the revival of French power in numerous concrete ways. Bodin, for example, was a great advocate of increased military strength and war. As his introduction stated, he hoped to see French arms flourish again, and he promoted a large standing army.

Bodin pointed approvingly to the example of Francis I, who had maintained "seven legions of six thousand foot soldiers," in 1534. Unfortunately, his successors had failed to continue this practice, and Bodin turned to the example of the emperor Augustus to further bolster his position. Augustus, who "surpassed all who came before or after him in wisdom and happiness," was a central model for Bodin.[57] Specifically, it was the happy emperor's strategic military wisdom that merited imitation. He had maintained forty legions and two navies, thereby "keeping the empire safe from foreign and civil wars." Bodin specifically suggested that four legions of 6,000 men be maintained on France's borders.[58]

Military strength was viewed as leading not only to the successful defense of the empire from outside enemies but also to the suppression of civil strife and war. This was the burning issue of the day for France, and Bodin famously promoted a political philosophy backing strong monarchy as the most effective remedy to the problem. It was during the reign of Augustus that Bodin saw this development first reaching maturity, and he again cited that emperor as his primary role model. Many ancient scholars before the Romans had praised monarchy as the highest form of government, but it was in the age of Augustus that it stuck in Bodin's account. Romans then decided that monarchy was the safest form of government for the largest empire in the world. Although the Romans could not live for ten years without a civil war in the time of the Republic, according to Bodin, Augustus maintained the empire in peace for almost fifty years thanks to a strong monarchy.[59]

---

[56] Quoted from the English version, *The Six Bookes of a Commonweale*, trans. Richard Knolles (London: G. Bishop, 1606), ed. Kenneth Douglas McRae (Cambridge, MA: Harvard University Press, 1962). P. 620.

[57] Ibid., p. 263.

[58] Ibid., p. 611.

[59] Ibid., p. 719. "It was resolved in the time of Augustus that a monarchy was the most safe form of government and that the Romans could not live for 10 years without a civil war in times of republic. But Augustus maintained them in peace for almost 50 years."

Although Augustus received credit for stabilizing and developing monarchical government, and it was the empire under him that constituted the broad imperial ideal, Bodin pointed far more often in his text to the example of Caesar as embodying the qualities of the individual prince. "There was never a more gracious, magnificent, noble, courageous, or courteous prince than Caesar" in the eyes of Bodin.[60] He was the "best captaine of his age" not to mention the "most ambitious man that ever was."[61]

For the greatest early French advocate of absolute monarchical power, these were all admirable qualities. Although he criticized Caesar for not consulting the Senate enough and not taking care of his personal safety once in power by maintaining a personal guard, there is no question that Bodin yearned for a king who embodied the political qualities and strength of Caesar. Speaking of the power given to Caesar by both the Senate and people, he could not contain his enthusiasm for that critical moment in the development of the rule of one:

> [S]o great a power was joined with the hardiest heart that then lived, and the most valiant that ever was, and descended of so noble an house, as that in an oration unto the people he doubted not to say, that by the fathers side he was descended from the gods, and by the mothers side from the kings.[62]

Bodin made strong distinctions between the legal power that Roman emperors held and that of the kings of France. Although the former had been granted their power by the Senate and people who held final sovereignty, the kings of France were ultimately granted their power and sovereignty from God alone. Assassination of a French monarch was subsequently never acceptable, whereas in the ancient Roman model, it was if the ruler had unjustly usurped the sovereignty of the people. The French kings thus had more theoretical power, but as all of the references to the ancient Caesars demonstrated, Bodin knew well that the real power exercised by the ancient Caesars was far greater than that of his own monarchs.

Viewed in this historical contest, Bodin's absolutism must be seen as growing directly out of the tradition of the imperial humanists. He took his political theory one step further by making the king, and royal power, responsible only to God, but the concrete historical model for royal power came first from ancient Rome. In this sense, absolutist theory simply built on

---

[60] Ibid., p. 419.
[61] Ibid., p. 610, "best captaine of his age," and p. 421, Caesar as "the most ambitious man that ever was."
[62] Ibid., p. 419.

the humanist editions, commentaries, and histories that provided the many examples from the Roman Empire. Bodin's exalted view of monarchical power, because it added an extensive treatment of Roman law to the picture, pushed the revival a step further. With the divine grant of sovereignty that Bodin claimed for his monarchs joined to the Roman model, the result was a super-charged theory of the rule of one.

Henry IV and Caesar

For all of their scholarly gravitas and rhetorical sophistication, Bodin's writings and the parallel attempts to strengthen royal authority through the use of law and arms fell far short of being fully acted on in the reign of Henry III. The favorite son of Catherine de Medici never managed to adequately build up his military strength and proved unable to protect even himself. Moreover, his failure to produce an heir created a succession crisis that began even before his assassination in 1589, and it led to yet another major period of civil war. For nine years France entered into a bloody series of conflicts between the Protestant faction, led by Henry of Navarre from the Bourbon dynasty, and the Catholic League, led by the Duke of Guise and strongly supported by Philip II of Spain.

This last phase in the French Wars of Religion was an unlikely location for the emergence of a major new chapter in the imperial Renaissance in France, but that is exactly what it was. The protracted war finally gave the new king, Henry IV, something that all of his sixteenth-century predecessors lacked: a series of epic battles marked by many struggles, more victories than losses, and a final triumph.

Here was a military record that actually echoed that of Caesar, at least in its length and location. It also brought the king a measure of fame and built up his military reputation to an extent enjoyed by none of his Renaissance predecessors. A new wave of literary and iconographic production to celebrate Henry IV as the new Caesar in word and deed subsequently followed.

Standing out among the literature of the imperial Renaissance as the most lengthy, overt, and detailed comparison of Julius Caesar and a contemporary monarch to date was *Les Paralleles de Cesar et de Henry IIII* by Anthoine de Bandole published in 1609. Like Jean Bodin, Bandole was a doctor of law who also had a deep interest in the history of ancient Rome. Politically active as a lawyer at court representing the Parliament of Provence, he wrote his history as a contemporary political guide.[63]

---

[63] Bandole. The author's profession is identified in the royal privilege, which is unpaginated.

The book was dedicated to the king's son, the soon-to-be Louis XIII. As a long hybrid text of almost 1,000 pages, it includes a heavily annotated French edition of the *Commentaries* that is 770 pages long.[64] To these are added brief lives of Henry and Caesar and a 128-page-long essay comparing the two men.

Addressing the Dauphin in the preface, Bandole claimed that "the King, your Father, put into practice the theory of Caesar, and repeated his actions in the conquest of Gaul." For that reason, the writer was dedicating his account of both of their deeds to the young prince with the hope that he would succeed them as the "legitimate son" and heir of their virtue and courage.[65]

For Bandole, the Gallic wars of Caesar were the perfect comparison for the wars that Henry IV had to fight to win France. Like Caesar, whose major nemesis constantly put him to the test, Henry had his own Pompey, Philip II, who aimed to make his own son the king of France. Rather than one opponent, both Caesar and Henry had to fight against multiple foes allied against them, and they both were forced to leave the tranquility of their homes, friends, and families just to guarantee their own lives.

Through all of his trials, Henry IV was victorious because he followed the example of Caesar. At one point when he was counseled by advisors to withdraw from France in the face of his enemies' strong persecutions, he refused because "Caesar would not permit it."[66] After all, Caesar also had to fight for nine years to conquer the Gauls. In battle, Henry thus imitated the perseverance, valor, courage, and strategic wisdom of Caesar above all others. He inspired his men like Caesar and showed clemency in victory like his ancient role model.

To an unprecedented extent, the familiar heroic image of Caesar that had been disseminated throughout Europe by 1600 in many different texts and artistic mediums was now fully transposed onto Henry IV. In victory, the French king increased the authority of the Senate, something Caesar was also credited with in an imaginative reading of the historical record. Just as Caesar had built up Rome after his victory, so too did Henry leave Paris as a city without equal. Both had great architects beautify their cities with monumental buildings, Caesar with a theater and Henry with the

---

[64] Bandole. The annotations for the text were written by Blaise de Vigenere Bourbonois.

[65] Ibid. From the unpaginated dedication. The text reads in part: "le Roy vostre Pere ayant reduit en pratique la theorique de Cesar, et represente' ses actions `a la conqueste des Gaules, il faloit par devoir dedier les faicts de ces deux `a vostre Grandeur, `a la valeur desquels vous devez succeder comme fils legitime de leur vertu et courage."

[66] Ibid., p. 43.

Place Royal. In memory of his greatness, Caesar had triumphal statues made, and Henry IV had numerous equestrian statues of himself erected in public places throughout his kingdom.[67]

Unfortunately for Henry IV but unbeknownst to Bandole when he wrote the text, the French king also followed Caesar in his last act of being assassinated in 1610. But in death, as in life, he continued to enjoy the image of the new Caesar, particularly in his wife's native Florence, where elaborate funeral celebrations were held to mark his reign. Commissioning twenty-six large drawings of the life of Henry IV that were hung in the church for the event, Cosimo II had his artists produce works that followed in the tradition of the arts of triumph.[68]

Frequently depicted mounted on his horse surveying the scene of a victorious battle, the French king was immortalized in the funeral hangings striking a pose similar to that which the workshop of Giambologna used for his statue on the Pont Neuf. The bronze statue had a permanence and power of display that mirrored the historical fame and place that Henry IV won in Renaissance France. Further, it was appropriate that it overlooked the Louvre Palace, the object of his most important architectural patronage.

Besides the new wing of the Louvre initiated by Francis I and executed by Pierre Lescot in the age of Henry II, the royal grounds near the old fortress were also the sight of the new Tuileries Palace initiated by Catherine de Medici beginning in 1564. Set far apart from the old castle and new wing of Lescot, it was only in the reign of Henry IV that a monumental new gallery was built facing the Seine that united the two royal residences.[69]

Following the classical orders and the grand design initiated by Serlio's plan for the Louvre, the Great Gallery of Henry IV comprised another major phase in the construction of the enormous palace complex that increasingly moved to equal or surpass that of El Escorial in its size. Begun in 1595, very shortly after the king's coronation and entry into Paris, the Great Gallery was designed by Jacques Androuet de Cerceau and Louis Métezeau.

---

[67] Ibid., pp. 115–116. "Cesar et Henry ont este' grands architectes pour embellir de beaux edifices leurs villes. L'un fit bastir dans Rome un theatre somptueux pour la plaisir public: Et l'autre la Place Royalle dans Paris." And, "Pour memoire des vaillances de Cesar on luy dressa des Statues triomphantes: Pour memoire des armes d'Henry, ... en une infinite' de lieux publics on a dresses a statue sur un cheval triomphant." P. 116.

[68] Eve Borssok, "Art and Politics in the Medici Court IV: Funeral Décor for Henry IV of France," in *Mitteilungen des Kunsthistorischen Institutes in Florenz*, 14. Bd., H. 2 (Dec., 1969), pp. 201–234. The author notes that "the spirit of triumph and worldly fame were allowed to dominate the esequie of 1610." P. 231.

[69] Gargiani, p. 17.

Completed by 1609, it added further prestige to the king's image as someone who brought his projects to a successful completion.[70]

Louis XIII, Richelieu, and the *Belliqueuse Nation*

Unlike the Great Gallery project, Henry IV left unfinished his plans to reassert French military power in Europe. In a familiar scene that once again slowed French ambitions at home and abroad, the throne was left to the nine-year-old dauphin, Louis XIII (1601–1643), whose mother, Marie de Medici, assumed the role of regent and Queen Mother. Reaching his maturity in 1617, Henry IV came of age just as the uneasy peace in Europe was beginning to unwind. Beginning in Germany in 1618, the Thirty Years War between the Holy Roman Emperor and Protestant Princes of Germany eventually drew both Spain and France into the conflict on opposing sides. The ostensible cause of the war was initially religion, as the Holy Roman Emperor sought to retake lands from rebellious Protestant Princes in Bohemia.

For France and Spain, however, the long series of wars became a struggle not just over the future of European supremacy but also of global empire. France under Richelieu and Louis XIII was driven by a far greater agenda than just stopping Habsburg expansion in central Europe. Rather, it sought to break Spanish hegemony and replace it with a new French hegemony.

This was a task that required, above all else, the new flourishing of arms. Henry IV had begun this revival in terms of scoring some important victories and strengthening military confidence. But it was Louis XIII and Richelieu who reorganized the administration and financing of the military to create the de facto standing army urged by Bodin in *The Six Books of the Republic*. Their efforts led to nothing less than the rise of France as the dominant military power of the seventeenth century, the central development that paved the way for rise of the French Empire.

Warfare more than any other single factor transformed French society and government in the period between 1589 and 1789.[71] The financial and logistical demands of sustained conflict led to an increase in both the real and theoretical power that the monarchy claimed throughout its kingdom. This was nothing new, however, as the heavily taxed citizens of Castile understood dating back to the reign of Charles V. As in many other realms of imperial

---

[70] Ibid., pp. 15–16.

[71] The most important work on this theme is Roland Mousnier, *Les institutions de la France sous la monarchie absolue, 1598–1715*, 2 Vols. (Paris: Presses universitaires de France, 1974–1980).

pursuit, Louis XIII and Richelieu were largely imitating their Spanish opponents as they sought to build up a military machine that could compete.

To this end, they increased the size of the army from an estimated maximum strength of 50,000 to 75,000 troops in the late sixteenth and early seventeenth centuries to an estimated 125,000 to 150,000 soldiers after 1635.[72] Again, this increase in size was simply an attempt to catch up to Spanish imperial forces that had reached that number in the previous century. Similarly, naval forces were expanded as two permanent fleets were built up for the Mediterranean and Atlantic theatres.

To pay for this larger army and navy, the monarchy turned to increased taxes of various kinds. French monarchs had been levying special war taxes throughout the period, but the number and amount of different taxes, as well as revenue from the sale of offices and borrowing against alienated lands, increased significantly under Richelieu by all estimates. In short, the financial instruments for the funding of war became more numerous and sophisticated in the reign of Louis XIII, which allowed for larger military forces fighting longer wars.[73]

Although increased military spending created a burden that contributed to serious unrest and eventual revolt in the 1640s and beyond, the accomplishment of Richelieu and Louis XIII in extracting the necessary revenues to defeat the Spanish Empire is undeniable. The accomplishment is all the more striking when one considers that New World treasure continued to flow into Spanish coffers to fund their war effort in this period, albeit at a slower rate. This was a financial advantage the French did not have but made up for through more effective administration to increase internal revenues.

The Perfect Captain and the Bellicose Nation

In addition to stronger administration and financing of war, there also emerged in seventeenth-century France a more pervasive martial spirit that cannot be quantified with troop rosters or account ledgers. Although larger armies and the money to pay them were essential to the war effort, the monarchy also required ideology to justify wars of unprecedented cost and

[72] David Parrott, *Richelieu's Army: War, Government, and Society in France, 1624–1642* (Port Chester: Cambridge University Press, 2001), p. 9. This study provides a wealth of details on the development of French military power and spending in the seventeenth century. The author notes that accurate numbers are difficult to come by given problems with documentation. Nonetheless, he estimates that the size of the military between 1500 and 1700 multiplied by ten from an estimated 30,000 to 300,000.

[73] Ibid., pp. 225–232.

duration. They also needed texts and narratives to inspire their commanders and to bolster morale.

Here, again, the example and writings of Caesar and of ancient Rome continued to play a central part, most especially in the abridged *Commentaries* of Caesar by Henri de Rohan (1579–1638). Rohan, a Protestant duke from Brittany, was a celebrated military figure who began his career early, fighting against the Spanish at the siege of Amiens in 1597. He was a colonel by 1605 and between 1633 and 1636 led the French troops in a series of battles for control of the strategic Valtellina region in northern Italy. It was shortly before his death from wounds received in battle in 1638 that he wrote his major books.[74]

Titled *The Perfect Captain*, Rohan's most popular text went to press in numerous editions throughout the seventeenth century. It used only short selections of the *Commentaries* as the starting point for expansive reflections on effective military command and rule. Repeating a judgment that had become dominant by the middle of the seventeenth century, Rohan described Caesar as the greatest captain that the world had ever had. He was prudent in his actions and strategies, diligent in their execution, and always showed great fortitude in the face of difficulties. Continuing the comparative motif of Bandole, the author dedicated the book to Louis XIII, proclaiming, "You are the monarch of the Bellicose Nation ... You are like him."[75] Written in 1636 just after war had been declared on Spain, the text encouraged the king to persevere in war following the example of Caesar in order to reap the greatest glory.

Roughly the first third, or ninety pages, of Rohan's text is dedicated to short passages from Caesar's *Commentaries* that are followed by his own *remarques*, or annotations. Partially a reflection on the martial qualities of Caesar and partially a historical commentary on leaders who successfully followed his example, the *remarques* stressed many of the same qualities established previously in the Caesar literature: clemency, the ability to inspire men against the odds, the ability to win battles, and the strength to persevere and follow through on victories.[76]

---

[74] François Bluche, *Dictionnaire du Grand Siècle*, ed. François Bluche (Paris: Fayard, 1990), pp. 1350–1351. Between 1620 and 1629, de Rohan fought for the Huguenot cause in the series of Protestant revolts against the policies of Marie de Medici. This led to his exile in Italy, where he was a mercenary captain for Venice before returning to fight for Louis XIII after the exile of his mother and ascent of Richelieu.

[75] Henri de Rohan, *Le parfait Capitaine* (Paris, 1667). "Vous estes, Sire, le Monarche de la Belliqueuse Nation ... Vous estes commes lui, tellement nourri dans les fatigues de la guerre." From second page of unpaginated preface.

[76] Ibid., p. 76.

Caesar's strategic superiority was emphasized as well. Rohan noted that his hero's armies were always smaller than those of his foes, but Caesar nonetheless dominated in battle because he knew how to take advantage of the speed of smaller forces and the element of surprise this provided.[77] He also knew well that the attacking army was at a distinct advantage, and he followed a strategy of being the first to attack more often than not, as the wars in Egypt revealed.[78]

Besides the specific example of Caesar, Rohan focused his attention on the example of the ancient Romans at war because he found there "the true foundation of all military art."[79] In fact, almost two thirds of his text was concerned with analyzing the military discipline of the Romans and their strategies in war. Although he recognized that gunpowder and canon had significantly altered the nature of warfare in his own time, he maintained that the example of ancient Rome under Caesar continued to offer fundamental insights about strategy, leadership, and the organization of armies.

In an age that was infamous for a frequent lack of military discipline, Rohan was particularly interested in the good order that the Romans were generally able to maintain in their military. He subsequently looked at everything from how soldiers were trained to how they were paid. He emphasized the obedience that was cultivated in the Roman soldiers and the strict discipline that was maintained. He also took note of the penalties and punishment imposed for failure or lack of discipline as well as the prizes given out for success on the battlefield.[80]

Rohan's *The Perfect Captain* was frequently published together with his other major work, *The Interest of Princes* (1634). Well received at court, even if written by a Protestant nobleman who had rebelled earlier in the reign of Louis XIII, that text stressed that advancing the interests of the state had to be the central focus of any foreign policy. In short, it advocated the primacy of reason of state over any moral or theological considerations.

The pairing of Rohan's reflections on ancient Roman war with his contemporary political commentary underlines the inseparable nature of the two. Ancient Rome and the Caesars, in short, provided the central historical foundation and precedent for a political morality that was not tied to Christianity or any other controlling theological system. What made Rome great and justified its actions were its victories and the size of the empire

---

[77] Ibid., p. 88.
[78] Ibid., p. 82.
[79] Ibid. Third page unpaginated preface.
[80] Ibid., pp. 152–159.

it amassed – nothing more and nothing less. What made these victories possible, of course, was dominant military power.

Although Richelieu and his king, like all other monarchs and ministers in Europe, consistently cast themselves as the defenders of Christianity and instruments of God's will, their actions both at home and abroad spoke of an autonomous political morality and quest for increased power.[81] This became increasingly evident with Louis XIII and Richelieu after France declared war on Spain in 1635, entering the war on the side of the Protestant coalition allied against the Habsburgs. Prior to that point, they had aided the Protestants financially but avoided an outright alliance, in part to avoid the inevitable charges that they were aiding the heretics.

The Habsburg victory in 1634 at Nördlingen over Gustavus Adolphus and the German Protestants, however, led Louis XIII to drop any pretense of neutrality and enter the war on the side of the Protestant coalition. The French monarchy had a long history of putting state interests above religious considerations, most infamously by entering into alliances with the Ottomans, as Francis I did in the early sixteenth century. In the case of Richelieu and Louis XIII, the declaration of war on Catholic Spain and the Austrian Habsburgs simply continued this tradition and highlighted that reason of state trumped religious orthodoxy once again. The religious rhetoric that Richelieu cultivated to justify his policies, like that of so many Renaissance statesmen, was little more than an elaborate Machiavellian cloak.

Further evidence of this was the fact that Richelieu mounted an aggressive effort to bolster rebellions against the Spanish crown in Portugal and Catalonia. This made the real goal of French policy clear: the fundamental weakening and breakup of the Spanish Empire. The results of the broad military strategy of the French prime minister and his king are well known: Spain suffered a series of major military defeats at the hands of the French, culminating with the French victory at Rocroi in 1643. At the same time, backed by French aid, Catalonia revolted, forcing Philip IV to spend money and men on that effort. Most devastating was the loss of Portugal and its imperial possessions after a successful revolt placed a new king on the throne in Lisbon.

After 1645, the Spanish Empire under Philip IV continued to be the major global empire, albeit much diminished, with all of its American and Italian possessions intact. But in Europe, France had established itself as the rising

---

[81] John H. Elliott, *Richelieu and Olivares* (Cambridge: Cambridge University Press, 1984), p. 121. Richelieu frequently justified his policies, claiming that France only sought the good of Christendom and a balance of power among Europe's princes.

military power, and the British had also strengthened their navy and army in the context of the Thirty Years War. The Dutch Republic, moreover, had capitalized on the European wars to expand its merchant empire and trading strength in Asia and the Americas. By 1648, when the Treaty of Westphalia was signed, bringing an official end to three decades of war, Europe and its empires had a new political order that included rising imperial competition globally.

In the case of France, it was in the age of Richelieu and Louis XIII that colonization in the Americas got its first major push and that a centralized mercantilist imperial project first took root. Rising military power in Europe was paralleled by rising imperial power abroad, and the most powerful links between the two were Richelieu's administration and a stronger navy. More specifically, Richelieu tripled the naval budget shortly after assuming his office in 1624. He also oversaw the compilation of the Code Michaud that more carefully defined the relationship between the state and merchants. State monopolies were established, and formerly independent merchant centers like La Rochelle were brought under the crown's control.[82]

Richelieu favored colonial expansion, sponsoring new settlements such as the tobacco colony on the island of St. Christophe and new trading ventures like the Compagnie des Isles de l'Amerique that subsequently initiated the settlements of Guadeloupe and Martinique. Other French colonies on the Caribbean islands of Saint Croix, Saint Martin, and Grenada followed with the aim of farming tobacco using imported African slaves.[83]

For all of the earlier French criticism of the harsh nature of Spanish colonization in the Americas, their own tactics were similarly cruel. The native peoples of the islands were killed or driven off, and a slave economy was established, first to produce tobacco and then sugar. By the end of the reign of Louis XIII in 1643 and the death of Richelieu in 1642, more than 3,000 French settlers lived on these islands together with some 1,200 African slaves. This was more than ten times the population of New France, where the largest town, Quebec, counted just more than 300 people.[84]

Although these were relatively small numbers of both settlements and settlers, particularly in comparison with the Spanish New World colonies, they nonetheless comprised a substantial foothold in the Atlantic World and set a precedent for further colonial exploits. Perhaps more importantly, they gave the French monarchy something that it had been dreaming about for

[82] Kenneth Banks, *Chasing Empire Across the Sea: Communications and the State in the French Atlantic, 1713–63* (Montreal: McGill-Queen's University Press, 2002), p. 16.

[83] Ibid., p. 18.

[84] Ibid.

more than a century, namely the beginnings of a real empire to match its imperial image.

The French Empire in the Age of Louis XIV

"To your glory, at the age of Alexander,
you have the prudence and behavior of Caesar."

> N. Perrot, Sieur d'Albancourt, to Louis XIV, in his dedication
> of a new edition of *Les Commentaire de Cesar* (Paris, 1665)

A marble bust of Louis XIV (1638–1715) from around 1644, now preserved in the Louvre, depicts the young king as a noble ancient Roman child wearing the laurel crown. Attributed to Jacques Sarrazin, who had spent his formative years in Rome, the sculpture speaks strongly to the self-image that the six-year-old monarch inherited from the beginning of his life.[85]

The imperial image of monarchy that had been cultivated in France for more than 150 years reached a new peak in the age of Louis XIV. Encouraged in this by his major councilors, Cardinal Mazarin and after him Jean-Baptiste Colbert, Louis XIV embraced and expanded on the theme and agenda like no other monarch before him.[86] It was the unifying factor that explains much of his reign.

In all of the major realms of imperial pursuit that have been charted over the previous chapters – lavish patronage of art, architecture, and letters with a strong emphasis on the imperial motif; enormous expenditures on virtually perpetual warfare; the increase of internal power through more royal control over all areas of administration; and the pursuit of new conquests and territory in Europe and abroad – the age of Louis XIV stands out for its extravagant ambition, success, and excess. The imperial image was joined with a substantial French empire for the first time since Charlemagne, and the Renaissance of Empire in France was thus largely realized in his reign.

That this would be the case was not inevitable or readily apparent in the king's youth. On the contrary, the financial and social strains of the Thirty

---

[85] *The Sun King: Louis XIV and the New World*, ed. Robert R. McDonald (New Orleans: Louisiana Museum Foundation, 1984), p. 185. Jacques Sarrazin returned to Paris after many years in Rome and, together with Vouet, was one of the major protagonists of a new wave of classicism. The same pose used for the sculpture was used on early coins from 1644 to 1645.

[86] Pierre Goubert briefly noted the imperial dream held by ministers like Colbert when he wrote, "They saw a kind of Augustan Rome transposed into the seventeenth century with all the Indies for Empire and all kings turned into good Catholics, gathered respectfully about Louis' throne." In Pierre Goubert, *Louis XIV and Twenty Million Frenchmen*, trans. Anne Carter (New York: Vintage Books, 1970), p. 97.

Years War and especially the last decade after the declaration of war on Spain had left France, like much of Europe, exhausted and unsettled. The wars and rebellions that followed cost the Spanish monarch a substantial part of his empire and the English king his head. Louis XIV, for his part, lost his youth as the rebellion known as the Fronde (1648–1653) forced him to flee Paris at age ten to protect his young life.

Reaching his official majority in 1651, the king was consecrated as king in 1654. During these years, Louis XIV was present at a number of military campaigns against the Spanish, and his formative years were thus marked more by the school of war than by any formal education in humanist letters. Louis XIV's Latin was not advanced, even if he presumably translated the first book of Caesar's *Gallic Wars*, a work that was published by the royal press in 1651.[87] But his taste for war and the glory and fame that it promised was equal to that of the ancient emperors.

Cardinal Mazarin, his first minister, was largely responsible for the early military success of the monarchy in the troubled decade between 1648 and 1659. Besides putting down the rebellious factions that led the Fronde uprising, he guided the military strategy that led to a number of important victories against the Spanish Empire. The Treaty of the Pyrenees between France and Spain (1659), most especially, signaled a French victory in the wars that had dragged on for almost twenty-five years. France acquired some territories in the settlement, and Louis XIV acquired a Spanish bride (and enormous dowry) in the person of the daughter of Philip IV of Spain, Marie-Thérèse d'Autriche.

After Mazarin's death in 1661, however, the twenty-three-year-old monarch chose not to appoint another favorite, or prime minister. Although he made use of a small number of councilors to help him govern throughout his reign, his decisions in the realm of war were largely his own over the next fifty-four years. This inclination toward the rule of one has made the name Louis XIV almost synonymous with that distinctive seventeenth-century theory of kingship known as absolute monarchy. But historians have long recognized that it was his great-grandfather, Philip II of Spain, more than any other early modern monarch, who provided the major model for the personal and secretive style of governance that also characterized Louis XIV. Like Philip II, Louis XIV also worked long hours dictating orders through

---

[87] The publication is titled *La Guerre des Suisses traduite du I. Livre des Commentaires de Jule Cesar par Louis XIV* (Paris: Imprimerie Royale, 1651). The text is eighteen pages long, with three illustrations of battle formations. Published when Louis XIV was thirteen and had just come into his majority, it has the distinct feel of a work produced by a learned courtier but published under the king's name.

his secretaries in order to control the widest range of political decisions possible.[88] Even more than his Spanish ancestor and any French monarch before him, Louis XIV showed how deeply indebted French absolute monarchy was to the idea of reviving and surpassing ancient Roman imperial glory and power.

This was an idea that was also reinforced by the subjects of the king, who themselves had been steeped in the images of ancient empire for more than a century. Literate culture in seventeenth-century France was well versed in classical literature, and the central playwrights, poets, and historians of Louis's court embraced the classical world for models and subject material for their work in large numbers. Classicism, simply another term for the late Renaissance of ancient Roman literature, art, and architecture, was the dominant order of the day in the court of the Sun King.

This also translated into the realm of ritual, and the French became increasingly capable imitators and innovators of the ancient triumph in this period. In 1660, for example, the city of Paris tapped into the language and images of classical triumph for the entry of Louis XIV and his new bride into Paris.[89] The festivities represented a high point in the genre for Paris, as they utilized a full range of ephemeral constructions to celebrate the event.

A large book commemorating the triumph made the overt comparison with the Romans in its opening pages, where the anonymous author noted that it was the ancient Romans who knew best how to honor their illustrious men with different kinds of monuments.[90] "They honored the virtue of some with marble and bronze statues," and they celebrated "the grandeur of others with the columns and pyramids that they raised in their public places." Finally, "triumphal arches were dedicated to their conquerors upon which they carved their memorable deeds for the sake of posterity."[91]

Paris now followed the example of ancient Rome in the triumph they staged for their conqueror, Louis XIV. Many of the various triumphal monuments were brought together and even a few new additions were invented for the celebration. Initially, the king was welcomed outside of Paris at Fauxbourg near the abbey of Saint Anthoine, where a large triumphal

---

[88] Goubert, p. 62.

[89] L'Entrée Triomphante de Leurs Maiestez Louis XIV, Roy de France et de Navarre, et Marie Thérèse D'Austriche Son Espouse (Paris, 1662).

[90] Ibid., p. 1, "Les anciens Romains soigneux plus que tous les autres peoples de marquer l'estime qu'ils faissoient de leurs Hommes Illustres se sont seruy de diverses sortes de monuments, dont on voit encore les vestiges tres considerables après tant de siecles."

[91] Ibid. "Ils honoroient la vertu des uns par les Statues de marbre, et de bronze qu'ils leurs consacroient, ils marquoient la grandeur des autres par les Colomnes et les Pyramides qu'ils elevoient dans les places publiques, ils dressoient des Arcs de triomphes à leurs Conquerans, sur lesquels leurs plus considerables actions estoient taillées et confiées à la posterité."

arch with six large columns following the Doric order had been erected. Loud echoes of Serlio's treatise are found in the description that notes the grandeur of the Doric order and its ability to project the image of power. Latin inscriptions on the arch praised the great king who had subdued the universe.

Once in Paris itself, the king's procession was met with another triumphal arch at the bridge of Notre Dame and yet another in the Marché Neuf. The latter was adorned with numerous relief sculptures at the ground level that employed a variety of imperial images that the author of the text described in some detail. Two relief sculptures on the corners of the monument, for example, represented two aspects of Fortune: the good fortune of the king's safe return from his voyage and the good fortune of having the stability and permanence that came with his presence. The author explained the arch using the somewhat strained ancient parallel of temples:

> [A]ncient Rome often dedicated temples in favor of its emperors, and it did so to give thanks for the happy success of their voyages, or to salute their arrival, in the belief that the good of the state was inseparably joined to the person of the prince; Paris was right to follow this example.[92]

Other related images on the arch, like that personifying the Pax Augustus, underlined that this was particularly appropriate for Louis XIV because he, like the best of the ancient Roman emperors, left the world happy and at peace. In sum, all of the images and inscriptions on the arch were the tribute of the magistrate and people of Paris (described as S.P.Q.P. on the arch) to celebrate the king who had pacified the universe and restored the Gauls to their former glory.

What a difference twelve years had made for Louis XIV and Paris. The young boy forced to flee Paris in 1648 was now welcomed back as literally the conquering hero and new Augustus. It was an image he liked. Two years later in a famous pageant named the *Carousel of Paris*, the king played the part of a Roman emperor and was dressed appropriately. Paired with the triumphal entry, this highly classicized royal drama signaled unequivocally that the theme of imperial revival would loom large throughout the reign of Louis XIV just as it had for most of the previous two centuries.[93]

---

[92] Ibid., p. 23. "L'ancienne Rome luy a souvent dédié des Temples en faveur de ses Empereurs, et soit qu'elle le fit pour a remercier de l'heureux success de leurs voyages, ou pour la saluer à son arrivée, dans la croyance que le bonheur de l'Etat estoit inseperablement attaché à la personne du Prince; Paris a eu raison de suivre cét exemple."

[93] Daniel Rabreau, "Monumental Art, or the Politics of Enchantment," *The Sun King*, pp. 127–130.

In the case of the Sun King, however, the theme was united with that century's most powerful military, substantial empire building in North America, and one of the early modern period's most dramatic dynastic victories that fundamentally reshaped the history of European empires for the next century. Louis XIV, in short, finally succeeded in bringing to completion a large part of the imperial project that his ancestors had been laying the literary, iconographic, and theoretical foundations for ever since Charles VIII invaded Italy. Ironically, the place he was least successful in realizing the dreams of his predecessors was Italy.

At the heart of Louis XIV's success was the continued expansion of the army and navy that Richelieu and Louis XIII had begun. Together with Colbert, to whom he delegated the implementation of many of his military policies and who became head of the navy in 1669, the king roughly doubled the size of the navy and more than doubled the size of the army. The navy grew to number almost 400 ships,[94] and the total numbers of men at arms reached 450,000 on land and 100,000 at sea by the 1680s, a record for the early modern period.[95] Spending roughly two thirds of the entire state budget, or almost 65 million livres, on defense at the end of the century, the warrior king also doubled the amount of his war expenditures compared to the amount spent early in his reign.[96] This was possible, in part because his overall income had almost doubled from an estimated 60 million livres in the 1660s to 100 million by the late 1680s.[97]

Louis XIV built his military to be used, and he sent his forces into battle proactively and often. The king kept France at war for the majority of his reign: between 1661 when Mazarin died and Louis XIV took full control of his government and the time of the king's death in 1715, France was at war for roughly thirty out of fifty-four years. The new age of Augustan-like peace announced by inscriptions and images on the arches of the triumph of 1660 was not destined to last long. The king of the bellicose nation indicated early on that he was prepared to use force to defend his reputation and pursue the expansion of his territory and influence.

---

[94] K. Banks, p. 23. This study gives the number of "nearly 380 vessels" that were either "purchased, constructed or captured" during the reign of Louis XIV.

[95] Vaughn Glasgow, Pierre Lemoine, and Judy Miller, "War of the League of Augsburg, and Peace of Ryswick," in *The Sun King*, p. 319. These numbers are taken from the period of the War of the League of Augsburg, 1688 to 1697.

[96] K. Banks, p. 24. The defense spending numbers are after Jean Meyer.

[97] Goubert, p. 107. The king's total income of 60 million livres in 1667 was four times that of the other European monarchies.

In Rome, for example, Louis XIV attempted to assert French dominance over the papacy and to displace Spain as the dominant foreign patron of the Church and city. As in virtually all areas of imperial pursuit, Louis XIV and his ministers saw Spain as both the power to vanquish and imitate in Rome. They understood well the success of the Spanish project in the city over the previous century, and they wanted to step into the same role as principle protector of the city, papacy, and Church at large. It was a project that was all about reputation because at one and the same time, it allowed Louis XIV to claim the mantle of the ancient Caesars and reassert his role as heir of Charlemagne.

To this end, the Sun King cast himself, not the Spaniards or German Habsburgs, as the main defender of Christendom. Using his ships to bombard North African pirate strongholds and his troops to aid the Holy Roman Emperor against the Ottomans in Hungary, Louis XIV and his ministers aggressively moved to seize the role claimed by the Spanish kings for most of the previous two centuries. As a part of the strategy, they also tried to seize center stage in Rome itself.

An early symbolic indication of this was the equestrian monument of the Sun King that Cardinal Mazarin wanted to plant in the middle of Rome on the new staircase between the Piazza di Spagna and the church of Trinità di Monte. Pope Alexander VII rejected French patronage of the project when he heard about the statue designed by his own court artist, Bernini. The pope clearly understood that such a monument carried an implied claim to sovereignty, and he, not Louis XIV, was the sovereign of Rome.[98]

The pope also rejected French claims to diplomatic immunity for the neighborhood around their new embassy, Palazzo Farnese, yet another sign of Louis XIV's new presumptions in foreign affairs. When the pope's Corsican guard fired on French soldiers guarding the palace after being provoked, it led to a serious diplomatic crisis, the removal of the French ambassador, and threats of military action from both the French parliament and the king.[99]

This was not idle saber rattling. Louis XIV was itching to fight and impose his will on the papacy, and his ecclesiastical councilors at court had to work hard to constrain his response to Rome. In one of the most interesting twists on the Caesar literature that was produced to both praise and guide the king,

[98] Dandelet, *Spanish Rome*, p. 208.
[99] Ibid.

Jacques de Bosc, a court councilor and preacher, wrote *Panégyrique du Roy sur le Suiet de la Paix de Rome: ou la Magnanimité de Louis XIV est Comparée à celle de Jules Cesar*. Published in 1664 and dedicated to the king when tensions with Rome were at a height, the forty-four-page treatise focuses on the clemency of Caesar and the many examples of his legendary ability to pardon and forgive his enemies.[100] At the same time, the text praises Louis XIV for the victory that he has achieved over himself in opting for peace instead of war with Rome.[101]

De Bosc's work was a stark contrast to the earlier French Caesar literature, most noticeably that of Bandole and Rohan, that emphasized the emulation of Caesar as warrior. Instead, the *Panégyrique* celebrated Caesar as peacemaker. It is a notable late example of the many apologies for Caesar that dominated the imperial Renaissance in its exoneration of him for any responsibility for the Civil War. Instead, Caesar is portrayed as rescuing Rome from the chaos brought on by the corrupt senators and restoring peace: "the major work of that emperor was to give peace to his country."[102] Moreover, Caesar is depicted as a ruler who had mastered himself – who had established "l'empire sur soy-mesme" – as reveled in the pardon granted to his enemies after the Civil War.

These were the characteristics that brought true glory, and the treatise opens with an image of Caesar and the king facing one another as they gaze up at two images of ancient and contemporary Rome. Both hold imperial scepters and Louis XIV is about to receive the laurel crown that already rests on Caesar's head. The caption beneath them titled *On the Peace of Rome* reads in part, "Here, the one and the other Caesar give you Peace."[103]

Although Louis XIV may have overcome his interior urge toward full-scale war in the case of Rome, it was one of the few instances in his reign when he successfully exercised *imperium* over that part of himself. Interiorized imperial self-control was not his goal. Caesar as warrior was his true model, and his dominant urge was toward war in the name of French Empire building both in Europe and abroad.

---

[100] Jacques de Bosc, *Panégyrique du Roy sur le Suiet de la Paix de Rome: ou la Magnanimité de Louis XIV est Comparée à celle de Jules Cesar* (Paris: Edme Martin, 1664).

[101] Ibid., a ii. In a note to the reader, the author describes the central theme of his work as follows: "Mon but est de louer le Roy de plusieurs beaux effets de la Magnanimité, mais particulierment de l'empire qu'il a sur luy-mesme ... Cette fermeté, cette clemence, cette force d'esprit sans pareille, et sur tous cette victoire sur soy-mesme, est le principal sujet que je me propose."

[102] Ibid., p. a ii. "Le Chef-d'oeuvre de cét Empereur a esté de donner la Paix à sa Patrie."

[103] Ibid., unpaginated facing page 1. The caption is titled "Sur la Paix de Rome," and the first line reads, "L'un et l'autre Cesar te donne ici la Paix."

In 1667, using as an excuse the failure of Spain to pay the half-million ducat dowry promised in his marriage contract, the king declared war on Spain. French troops marched on the Spanish Netherlands in May of that year and took a number of towns in the south as supposed compensation. The War of Devolution was over quickly, and France added the conquered territory to her own with the treaty signed in May of 1668.[104]

Louis returned home the conquering hero, but the victory also came with a cost. Most noticeably, the United Provinces grew alarmed at the growing French threat and allied itself with England and Sweden. This triple alliance was an early sign of things to come as the ambitions of France both within Europe and in the New World increasingly led to coalitions forming against the French.

This opposition left the French king undeterred. The taste of Spanish territories gained in 1668 only whet Louis XIV's appetite. In 1672 he declared war on the United Provinces, a more costly and lengthy endeavor that lasted seven years. Both the king and Colbert had entered the war with hopes for a conquest that would leave both the territories and commercial riches of the United Provinces under French rule. It was one of their most naked acts of war for the sake of financial gain and territorial expansion, even if religion was used as a principal pretext: Louis XIV donned the old Machiavellian cloak of religion to pose as a good Catholic monarch who went to war against the Protestants in the name of restoring the Low Countries to the Roman fold.[105]

It was an audacious plan that began well with Louis's famous crossing of the Rhine and quick victories over William of Orange and the surrender of Utrecht in 1672. Irresistible material for classicizing playwrights like the royal historian Pierre Corneille and the magistrates of Paris alike, the victories were cast as triumphs that surpassed even those of Caesar in the *Gallic Wars*.

The city of Paris declared a triumph for Louis XIV, whom it now gave the new title of "the Great." It was, in their words, to be a "mark of gratitude it owed to the glorious labors of this hero who bore the honor of His Crown and of the French name far beyond his illustrious predecessor, Julius Caesar, to whose memory ancient Rome had consecrated triumphal works."[106] Pierre Corneille elaborated on this theme of competition with

---

[104] P. Goubert, pp. 107–112.
[105] Ibid., pp. 128–144.
[106] Robert Wyman Hartle, "Louis XIV and the Mirror of Antiquity," in *The Sun King*, p. 115. I adjusted the very literal translation given in this text for the sake of clarity.

the successes of ancient Rome in a long epic poem celebrating the victory of 1672. Dedicated to the king and capturing the imperial hubris of the age better than many long treatises, the poem boldly declared:

> We have nothing more to do with these Batavians
> Whose huge bodies contain the hearts of slaves,
> No, it is not them against whom we must prove ourselves,
> It is Rome and the Caesars that we are going to defy.[107]

The Imperial Arts and Louis XIV

"Your Majesty knows that aside from striking military actions nothing better marks the grandeur and spirit of Princes than buildings."

Colbert to Louis XIV[108]

The military victories of the first twenty years of the Sun King's reign made an undeniable impression on all of Europe and substantial parts of the New World as well. They established him as the most powerful prince of the age. Following the lead of his ancestors and competitors, Louis XIV was determined to perpetuate this image not just by force of arms and treaties but through the mediums of art and architecture as well. Combined with the largest income that any prince of early modern Europe had ever enjoyed, the giant ego of the king led to an unprecedented boom in palace building, painting, and sculpture to "mark the grandeur and spirit" of his monarchy. To put this building spree in economic perspective, it has been estimated that Louis XIV spent as much on his palaces as he did on his navy, or roughly 10 percent of his annual budget.[109]

Far from being a distinct realm only dedicated to private or domestic pleasure, the palaces of Louis XIV were also political stages that played a central role in the king's control of his subjects. As famously described by Norbert Elias, it was in this period that the French nobility were moved to court en masse to be near the king and under his close supervision. With this

---

[107] Pierre Corneille, *Oeuvres de Pierre Corneille*, ed. M. Ch. Marty-Laveaux (Paris: L. Hachette, 1862), p. 268. The stanza reads:

> Nous n'avons plus, dit-il, affaire à ces Bataves
> De qui les corps massifs n'ont que des coeurs d'esclaves;
> Non, ce n'est plus contre eux qu'il nous faut éprouver,
> C'est Rome et les Césars que nous allons braver.

[108] Daniel Rabreau, "Monumental Art, or the Politics of Enchantment," in *The Sun King*, p. 130.

[109] K. Banks, p. 24. The figures are after Jean Meyer.

captive audience, palace art and architecture became all the more important as tools for indoctrinating the nobility with the proper understanding of Louis XIV's exalted self-image. In virtually all of his residences, the imperial motif loomed large as a part of this project.

No style of architecture served this purpose better than the colossal orders of Vitruvius, promoted in the age of Louis XIV through one of the king's primary architects for the continuation of work on the Louvre, Claude Perrault (1613–1688). The author of a new French translation of Vitruvius's *Ten Books of Architecture* (Paris, 1673), Perrault made explicit parallels between his own age and that of the emperor Augustus. In the dedication of that book to Louis XIV, he wrote, "Here for the second time the *Architecture* of Vitruvius has the honor of being dedicated to the greatest prince of the world. Its illustrious author presented it the other time to the emperor Augustus."[110]

Although the heights reached by the Roman emperor rendered it difficult to aspire to anything comparable, Perrault claimed that the conquests and extraordinary virtues of his king once again called for the most superb and beautiful monuments to commemorate them. Moreover, he was confident that just as the science of architecture promoted by Vitruvius served well to reflect the grandeur of Augustus, so too would it add luster to the accomplishments of Louis XIV.[111] In a sonnet that followed this dedication, the poet Charpentier continued the Augustan theme as he celebrated the fact that "under a new Augustus a new Vitruvius" was born.[112]

Perrault saw strong parallels between the historical development of architecture in ancient Rome and in early modern France. Both were "bellicose nations" that were first inclined toward war and the art of ruling other people. But eventually the ancient Romans had embraced the other arts in imitation of the Greeks, just as France, beginning with Francis I, had embraced the arts imported from Italy. Serlio in particular is mentioned by Perrault as one of the greatest architects of his time who taught the French much through his own treatise on architecture.[113]

With this deep sense of his Vitruvian pedigree and indebtedness to Serlio, Perrault joined a team of architects that was appointed by Colbert and

---

[110] Vitruvius, *Les Dix Livres D'Architecture de Vitruve*, ed. Claude Perrault (Paris: Jean Baptiste Coignard, 1673), First page of unpaginated dedication. The text reads: "Voicy la seconde fois que l'Architecture de Vitruve a l'honneur d'estre dediée au plus grand Prince de la Terre."

[111] Ibid., third page of unpaginated dedication. "On peut s'asseurer aussi que cette Science n'aura point à regretter les grandeurs d'Auguste, puisqu'elle trouvera dans celles de V.M. tout ce qui peut donner du luster à ses ouvrages."

[112] Ibid. "Ce Livre te seconde en un dessein si beau, Et fait voir que le Ciel devoit à la Nature, Sous un nouvel Auguste un Vitruve nouveau."

[113] Ibid., p. a.

4.2. Claude Perrault, Colonnade, Louvre, Paris, France. (Photograph: Erich Lessing/Art Resource, NY.)

the king to continue work on the Louvre (Figure 4.2). The Council of Architects included Charles Le Brun (1619–1690), Louis Le Vau (1612–1670), and François d'Orbay (1634–1697).[114] Perrault is widely considered to be the principal force behind their major work, the façade of the Louvre on the exterior of the Square Court that faces Saint-Germain L'Auxerrois. It was built starting in 1667 and has been described as "*the* monument of architectural classicism" in France.[115]

Consistent with the aim of imperial architecture, the building projected strength, grandeur, and solemnity with its long colonnades of paired columns. Unfortunately for the architects in charge of the project, it languished after Louis XIV turned his full attention and passion to Versailles in the 1670s, but it was eventually finished and remains one of the strongest testimonies to the Vitruvian revival in the France of the Sun King.

[114] *The Sun King*, p. 235.
[115] Daniel Rabreau, "Monumental Art, or the Politics of Enchantment," in *The Sun King*, p. 133.

Louis XIV's commitment to finishing the Louvre Palace had strong parallels with that of Philip II in finishing Charles V's palace in Granada. It was an act of filial duty and important for the image of the monarchy, but neither king ever had his heart in the project. In the case of Louis XIV, that passion was left for Versailles, his answer to El Escorial.

Although a detailed analysis of the building or iconography of Versailles is far beyond the scope of this work, it is possible to highlight some of the major expressions of the imperial theme that unites Versailles with other palaces, including the Louvre. First among these is the monumental scale of the building and grounds. Versailles alone is estimated to have cost 82 million livres between 1661 and 1715, or as much as was spent on the French navy in eight years.[116] Although critics saw in the building a grotesque lack of taste, not to mention restraint, no one could deny the impact of a palace complex of such monumental dimensions: the enormous Great Gallery alone stretched out over 73 meters.[117]

Following the classical design attributed largely to Louis Le Vau, the principal architect for the new complex from 1666 until his death in 1670, Versailles was inspired by the same broad Vitruvian project that animated Claude Perrault and Le Vau at the Louvre. Although the final project departed from a strict interpretation of classical orders, the exterior, at least, speaks much more strongly of a restrained classicism than it does of a lavish Italian baroque design.[118]

More direct expressions of the imperial theme included busts of Roman emperors that were included in designs for the exterior of the Hall of Mirrors. On the interior, niches were designed to hold the king's finest ancient Roman statuary, including the busts of four emperors. Similarly, a large copy of an ancient statue of the emperor Commodus posing as Hercules, sculpted by Nicolas Coustou, who had been trained at the French academy on Rome, stood in the famous gardens of the palace.[119]

All of these references to the ancient Roman Empire served to establish the historical context and frame within which the triumphs of Louis XIV, the main topic of the palace decoration, were to be viewed. Although many other layers of mythological meaning and allegory were represented in the palace and garden decoration, it was the references to ancient Rome and the monumental architecture itself that most clearly evoked the imperial

[116] Jean-François Solnon, "Versailles," in *Dictionnaire du Grand Siècle*, ed. François Bluche (Paris: Fayard, 1990), p. 1581.
[117] Ibid.
[118] *The Sun King*, p. 242.
[119] Ibid., pp. 251–254.

political genealogy claimed by the king and his artists. Versailles, in short, presented Louis XIV as the true heir of the ancient empire.

This corresponded with the contemporary agenda of the Great Gallery cycle of paintings created by Charles Le Brun, the king's primary artist for Versailles. Historical narrative paintings that celebrated the king's victories in the 1660s and 1670s, the nine major *tableaux* that lined the Great Gallery, took as one of their dominant themes the French defeat of the Habsburgs and especially of the Spanish Empire.

The eighth painting that depicted the king's conquest of Gent in 1668, for example, was described by a contemporary as showing how the victory undermined the entire political strategy of the House of Austria. In one corner of the painting, Spain was depicted as a lion that stood over a fallen woman representing the subjugated provinces of Flanders. Another allegorical figure was of an armed woman with images of a leopard and "the famous book of Machiavelli" at her feet. These represented "the cruelty and dangerous maxims of Spanish politics."[120] Included in this scene were soldiers near a chateau in ruins, and nearby were two columns representing the device of Charles V with the famous *Plus Ultra* carved on them. They were shown tilting and about to fall.[121] At the same time, a triumphal carriage in another corner of the painting pulled along cities that had been liberated by Louis XIV.

The French Empire in North America

Even as the European triumphs of the king dominated the large paintings of Versailles, there was also a smaller painting in the gallery that celebrated the "revival of navigation" that was counted as another of Louis XIV's accomplishments. The image showed the prince on his throne with a trident in his hand. A merchant mariner walked in front of him, and behind the throne was a pile of goods. Together they represented the abundance and wealth that came from his establishment of the West India Company (1664) that was established to give the crown a monopoly over trade in the French Atlantic.[122]

The smaller scale of the painting was an accurate metaphor for the place that direct New World expansion occupied in the political strategy and

---

[120] *Explication des Tableaux de la Galerie de Versailles* (Versailles: François Muguet, 1687), p. 42. "Elle a á ses pieds un Léopard, et le fameux livre de Machiavel, symbols de la cruauté et des dangereuses maxims de la politique Espagnole."

[121] Ibid., p. 43.

[122] Ibid., p. 63.

budget of Louis XIV. Still, even smaller projects in his reign made previous efforts pale by comparison. In the two decades between 1664 and 1684, the king, and after 1669 Colbert, imposed a new level of order on the French Atlantic colonies. All trading companies and colonies were brought under direct royal control, as was the Church and its missionary activity. The king controlled the appointment of governors and other administrators and supported efforts to impose uniform taxes and laws. Behind all of these efforts was the construction of a navy large enough to include a regular convoy of ships, both merchant and military, for the Atlantic project.[123]

At the heart of French colonial policy in this period was income. Wealth from rising global trade translated directly into military power, a lesson the Dutch were demonstrating all too well. Colbert, on whom fell the task of raising money for the interminable wars of his master, understood this and moved to establish two new companies under royal control to supply African slaves to the French Caribbean sugar plantations. The sugar and slave trade was increasingly the big money maker in the late seventeenth century, and it became a major factor in imperial contest and war in the Atlantic world.[124]

At the same time, French efforts to take more territory in North America also grew under Louis XIV and Colbert, who sponsored the Atlantic voyage of Alexander de Prouville, Sieur De Tracy, with six ships and 1,200 men in 1664. Sailing first to the French Caribbean islands and then to Canada, this military operation imposed royal governors on already established colonies and then strengthened the French presence in the St. Lawrence valley largely by crushing Iroquois resistance. This successful mission was followed by numerous Mississippi River expeditions, including that of Louis Jolliet in 1673.[125]

More significantly, Robert Cavelier de La Salle pushed further south down the Mississippi river in 1678 and claimed much of the river valley down to the Gulf of Mexico for his king. By 1685, increasing numbers of Frenchmen were making their way to North America to trade furs in North American outposts throughout the Great Lakes region or seek their fortunes in the new lands of Louisiana. The quarter century between 1664 and 1689 subsequently witnessed the most significant period of French American conquest and colonization to date. It represented another important step in the quest for real empire and the accompanying increase in glory and reputation that drove Louis XIV.[126]

[123] K. Banks, *French Atlantic*, pp. 22–23.
[124] Ibid., p. 24.
[125] *Sun King*, pp. 313–315.
[126] K. Banks, p. 25.

The French colonies in the Americas would continue to develop in the last twenty-five years of Louis's reign as sugar production increased along with the slave trade in the Caribbean. New settlements in North America continued to the extent that by the early eighteenth century, thousands of French settlers occupied towns from the Gulf of Mexico to Quebec.

In terms of serious wealth, however, the income that France derived from the New World in the late seventeenth century was small in comparison with the wealth that Spain still brought in from both the silver mines and the lucrative monopoly on the slave trade to the Spanish colonies as well as other Spanish American trade. For all of France's military strength and success against the Spanish in the latter half of the seventeenth century, the Spanish Empire continued to stay afloat in part because of its New World income. Moreover, the sheer size of the Spanish Empire, with its many large cities and large population of settlers, put it in a different imperial league where territories and colonies were concerned.

This is a fact that is often overlooked or understated by historians of this period who see only decline and decay in Spain. Louis XIV did not make this mistake. He saw clearly that the Spanish monarchy still ruled over a vast empire that produced serious agricultural, mineral, and commercial wealth. But the Spanish monarchy and its administration were clearly ill. In fact, the Spanish monarchy was on the verge of biological failure since the last Habsburg king, Carlos II, son of Philip IV, was unable to produce an heir.

This created an enormous problem of succession in Europe because both Louis XIV and the Austrian Habsburg prince Charles III had legitimate dynastic claims to the throne. For Louis XIV, it was an enormous opportunity. If he could not hope to conquer an empire the size of Spain's in the New World, the crisis of the Spanish succession offered him the chance to claim the Spanish Empire itself, if not directly for himself, then for his grandson.

Imperial Transitions

In 1699, yet another monumental equestrian sculpture (Figure 4.3) appeared in Paris, this time of Louis XIV in the Place de Louis Le Grande. A large book describing the casting of the bronze statue proudly noted that it was the first equestrian statue cast in one piece since antiquity, when the statue of Marcus Aurelius was done in a similar fashion.[127]

---

[127] Germain Boffrand, *Description de ce qui a été pratiqué pour fonder en bronze d'un seul jet la figure Equestre de Louis XIV* (Paris: Guillaume Cavelier, 1743), p. 1.

FIGURE EQUESTRE DE LOUIS XIV.
que la Ville de Paris a elevée dans la Place de Louis le Grand en 1699
Avec Privilège du Roy

4.3. Germaine Boffand, Equestrian Monument of Louis XIV, 1743. (*Description de ce qui a été pratiqué por fonder en bronze d'un seul jet la figure equestre de Louis XIV*) (Paris: Guillaume Cavelier, 1743). Vatican Library, Cicognara.IX3485.

It was certainly the largest and most accomplished statue of Louis XIV done in that style in the period, but it was far from the only one. In fact, the king had ordered many equestrian monuments of himself to be cast and sent out to various corners of his empire, including the city of Quebec.[128] A particularly striking example of the way in which the Sun King embraced and expanded on the iconographic inheritance of the imperial Renaissance, the Paris statue was also a powerful reminder to his subjects of his many military victories.

So too was the book that the Jesuit priest J. E. Du Londel dedicated to the king in 1694. Titled *Les Fastes de Louis Le Grand*, it was a political chronology of the king's life including the major battles, treaties, and above all else, victories from his birth in 1638 to 1694. In the words of the author, it was an exact recounting of "the events that most distinguished the king's reign," using as much brevity as possible. Du Londel emphasized that this type of history was not suitable for most other kings because their reigns were too short or lacking enough notable deeds, whereas those of Louis filled forty-seven pages. In fact, there was only one comparable historical parallel: "Rome alone, and then Rome in its beautiful centuries, has left us a model, which as accomplished as it is, will never surpass that which your majesty has done."[129]

In a political twist on the Quarrel of the Ancients and the Moderns, increasing numbers of French writers depicted Louis XIV as surpassing even the greatness of ancient Rome in his conquests and general military success. Surrounded by such men and living in the midst of the vast artistic and architectural splendor that he had spent a fortune on over fifty years, the king's imperial ambitions grew only stronger. Very much like Philip II, who in the last decade of his reign harbored the dream of placing his grandson on the French throne and also of conquering England, Louis XIV was reaching for his own version of universal monarchy.

This was an opinion elaborated on at length by one of his critics in a treatise titled *The Parallels of Philip II and of Louis XIV* published in Cologne in 1709. The author took the pen name of Mr. I. I. Q., and he was no fan of either monarch. The subtitle that opened the pro–English polemic was "On the Overthrow of Universal Monarchy," a task that fell to the English

---

[128] S. A. Callisen, "The Equestrian Statue of Louis XIV in Dijon and Related Monuments," *The Art Bulletin*, Vol. 3, No. 2 (Jun. 1941), pp. 131–140.

[129] J. E. Du Londel, *Les Fastes de Louis Le Grand* (Paris: Imprimerie Royale, 1694), a–ai. "Rome seul, e encore Rome dans ses beaux siecles, nous en laissé un modelle, qui tout achevé qu'il est, n'effacera jamais ce qu'a fait Votre Majesté."

Queen Anne. Just as Spain under Philip II was "the example of an empire in a perfect decadence," that was finally stopped thanks to the work of Queen Elizabeth, so, too, the desire of Louis XIV to dominate Europe and conquer the world was an "unjust and tyrannical" ambition that had to be opposed.[130]

The text was written in the middle of the War of the Spanish Succession (1702–1713). Yet another long war that consumed all of Europe, it was above all else about the future of European empires. More specifically, it was about which European power would emerge as the dominant empire of its day with the potential claim to rule over the world's largest empire.

When it became clear in the last decade of the seventeenth century that Carlos II, the king of Spain, would die childless, all of Europe began debating and strategizing about the future. The two main claimants to the Spanish throne by virtue of dynastic claims were Louis XIV and the Holy Roman Emperor, Leopold. Both were the sons of Spanish infantas, and both had married daughters of the Spanish king, Philip IV.

It was supposedly left to the deranged Carlos II to choose his successor, and the final version of his will named the grandson of Louis XIV as the rightful heir of his vast empire. The only condition was that the future Philip V renounce any claim to the French throne, a move meant to keep the two great powers separate. Welcomed by Louis XIV, who accepted the terms of the will, the decision was not accepted by Leopold. It also disturbed the Dutch and English, who feared that the wealth and trade of the Indies was the real aim of Louis XIV. The French nonetheless moved quickly to install Philip V in Madrid with a carefully chosen group of ministers that answered to Louis XIV, and in 1701 the French king confirmed his opponent's fears by confirming his grandson's right to inherit the French throne should the other two Bourbons who stood in front of him for that spot die.[131]

This declaration, together with the facts that Spanish policy was being directed by Louis XIV and his ministers in Madrid, and French merchants and ships were trading freely in the Indies and Spain, made it clear to all of Europe that a de facto merging of the Spanish Empire and French Empire was underway. For a short time, at least, the grandiose dreams of the old French Caesar were close to being realized, a development that caused concern and anxiety throughout Europe and her colonies.

---

[130] Mr. I. I. Q., *Le Parellele de Philippe II et de Louis XIV* (Cologne: Jaques Le Sincere, 1709), pp. 34, 16.
[131] Goubert, pp. 231–238.

The War of the Spanish Succession and the End of
Louis XIV's Imperial Project

Louis XIV aimed to impose the remedy of Empire on Europe and the world with his dynastic conquest of the Spanish Empire. But it was not a cure that the other European powers wanted to take. By 1702, an alliance of England, the Dutch, and the Holy Roman Empire had formed against France and another long decade of war followed. Although the two main competitors at the beginning of the contest were France and the Empire, by 1702 the British and Dutch had entered the war on the side of the emperor, in large part to contest French domination of Atlantic trade.

The fact that the War of the Spanish Succession was, at its heart, a war over the riches that came from imperial trade was first revealed by the major event that drew the British and Dutch into the battle: the granting of the *asiento*, or monopoly on the African slave trade in Spanish America, to a French company in September of 1701. The formal alliance against France was signed very shortly after this decision, and the slave trade remained a central aspect of the war all the way through the final negotiations that brought it to an end.[132] Louis XIV himself acknowledged in a letter of 1709 that "the trade of the Indies" was the real "object" of the war.[133]

That said, much of the war was fought in Europe, as virtually the entire continent and England witnessed battles infamous for the large numbers of lives lost. Although the first years of the war were marked by a mix of victories and losses for France and Spain, by 1709 the tide had turned on Louis XIV, whose armies were repeatedly beaten by a coalition of Germans, Dutch, and Savoyards and whose weak navy was increasingly defeated by the superior Dutch and English naval forces. With his finances drained, Louis sought peace on terms that eventually left his kingdom in tact but his empire and imperial dreams in tatters. The old monarch who wanted so badly to be an emperor, and who came close to the goal, was reduced at the end of his life to the same humbling circumstances that marked the last years of Philip II. It was all he could do to leave his kingdom at peace in the hopes that his young heir, Louis XV, would have time to assume his role.

As for the Spanish Empire of his grandson, Philip V, it retained its New World colonies but lost the Italian territories that it had held for almost two centuries. It also lost the monopoly on New World trade for many decades

---

[132] Goubert, pp. 236–238.

[133] Dale Miquelon, "Envisioning the French Empire: Utrecht, 1711–13," in *French Historical Studies*, Vol. 24, No. 4 (Fall 2001), p. 653. (653–677.)

to come and had to grant the English the coveted *asiento* for the African slave trade. Clearly, Great Britain was the biggest winner of the wars, as it assumed the mantle of the new dominant imperial power in Europe. Britain had been a relative latecomer to the imperial Renaissance, but by the end of the wars of 1702 to 1713, she was beating the other powers at the great game they had started.

5

BRITAIN AS LATE RENAISSANCE EMPIRE

Not Caesar's deeds, nor all his honours won
In these West-parts; nor, when the war was done,
The name of *Pompey* for an Enemy;
Cato to boot; *Rome*, and her liberty;
All yielding to his fortune: nor, the while,
To have ingrav'd these Acts with his own stile;
And that so strong, and deep, as might be thought
He wrote with the same spirit that he fought;
Not that his Work liv'd, in the hands of foes,
Un argu'd then; and (yet) hath fame from those:
Not all these, *Edmonds*, or what else put to,
Can so speak Caesar, as thy Labours do.
For, where his person liv'd scarce one just age,
And that 'midst envy and Parts; then, fell by rage;
His deeds too dying, save in Books: (whose good
How few have read! how fewer understood!)
Thy learned hand, and true Promethean Art,
As by a new creation, part by part,
In every Counsel, Stratagem, Design,
Action, or Engine, worth a Note of thine,
T'all future time not only doth restore
His life, but makes that he can die no more.

> Ben Johnson, "To my friend master Clement Edmonds,
> Epigramme," in Clement Edmonds, *Observations
> Upon Caesar's Commentaries* (London, 1609)

Of the major European monarchies that eventually ruled new global empires in the early modern period, the British monarchy stands out for the slow, halting, and crooked path that eventually led to its own distinctive Imperial Renaissance in the late sixteenth, seventeenth, and eighteenth centuries. The "first empire," commonly viewed as spanning the two centuries between the claiming of Newfoundland in 1583 and the loss of the American colonies to 1783, lagged behind the Spanish by more than a century in terms of real colonization in North America. Compared to their continental rivals, the British monarchs in the sixteenth and seventeenth centuries had fewer resources, greater political and religious internal divisions, and less military power, all of which stood in the way of imperial aspirations.[1]

Serious cultural distinctions also played a role in this contrast, most noticeably weaker direct ties to the ancient Roman Empire and the corresponding literary and artistic development of the Italian Renaissance. Although England did enjoy a flowering of humanist learning in the late fifteenth and early sixteenth centuries, it was far removed from the imperial humanism of Petrarch and the many that followed him on the continent. Rather, the early Renaissance in England was first and foremost an intellectual movement that initially grew out of contacts between England and Florence such as those between John Colet and Marsilio Ficino. As in Spain, Erasmus was an important figure for the advancement of humanism in England but not for the form that inspired the revival of the Roman Empire.[2]

Influential both in university life and at court, the humanists of the early English Renaissance during the reign of Henry VIII (1509–1547) nonetheless established an important foundation for a revival of Latin letters. Like their counterparts on the continent, English humanists aspired to Ciceronian Latinity and knowledge of Greek and Hebrew. Students and scholars at Oxford and Cambridge benefited from the new learning and a proliferation of classical texts thanks to the printing press and the introduction of the new humanist curriculum, most noticeably at Cambridge and St. Paul's School. Initially, at least, the age of Henry VIII promised a revival like that of his peers, Francis I or Charles V.[3]

Increased interest in and knowledge of Roman history was predictably central to this movement, and a few contemporary works like *Richard III* by Thomas More successfully modeled themselves after Roman historians. In a related vein, the publication of new editions of ancient works by Livy,

[1] For a recent treatment of the British Empire that generally follows this chronology, see *The Oxford History of the British Empire*, Vol. 1, *The Origins of Empire*, ed. Nicholas Canny (Oxford: Oxford University Press, 1998–1999).

[2] For a succinct treatment of early English humanism, see Paul Dean, "Tudor Humanism and the Roman Past: A Background to Shakespeare," in *Renaissance Quarterly*, Vol. 41, No. 1 (Spring 1988), pp. 84–111.

[3] For additional details on the revival, see Maria Dowling, *Humanism in the Age of Henry VIII* (London: Croom Helm, 1986).

Caesar, Suetonius, and Plutarch appeared and became a part of the education of the ruling class. This included the Tudor monarchs Henry VIII, Edward VI, and Elizabeth I, who all reportedly read a wide range of Roman historians and philosophers.[4]

Unlike the fifteenth-century Italians or the sixteenth-century Spaniards and French, however, this early English Renaissance fell short of producing a substantial Imperial Renaissance on the level of learning, the arts, or political life. Few early English humanists urged their monarchs to imitate the *pagan* emperors or actively encouraged the reading of ancient imperial history specifically for political guidance. There was no strong political tradition that urged imitation of the ancient Roman model, either Republican or Imperial.

This was also true in the realms of artistic and architectural production, where England also had more limited contact with Italy than Spain, France, and Germany. It noticeably lacked any substantial number of native artists and architects who embraced the revival of ancient Roman aesthetics in painting, sculpture, or architecture. The Gothic aesthetic, in short, continued to dominate the artistic and architectural tastes of the British monarchy and ruling class for most of the sixteenth century.

Cultural and intellectual distance from developments in Italy was only increased when Henry VIII married Anne Boleyn and divorced Catherine of Aragon in 1533. With this act, he not only openly broke with Rome but also with the Holy Roman Emperor, Charles V, the nephew of Catherine and cousin of her daughter Mary. For the remaining years of his reign, the English king was consumed with internal religious strife, political upheaval, warfare both in Britain and on the continent, and endless marital drama with his many wives. Although Henry VIII spent large sums on his building projects, most noticeably Whitehall Palace in London, he fell far short of being part of a classical revival. The English king paled in comparison with his contemporaries, Charles V and Francis I, as a Renaissance patron, and he had no serious imperial agenda in those areas, unlike his counterparts.

On the other hand, Henry VIII and his ministers, out of necessity, did make one of the first major steps toward claiming a distinctive English imperial identity. Seeking to counter the status and real power of the king's new enemies, Charles V and the papacy, they claimed that England, too, was an empire. More specifically, the idea of England as an empire ruled over by a Christian emperor was first expressed briefly in the English Reformation context in the Restraint of Appeals of 1533, in which England is first

---

[4] P. Dean, p. 98, note 54.

described as an empire.[5] The apparent innovation of Thomas Cromwell as he searched for a suitable historical justification for the political presumptions of his master, Henry VIII, this text, together with the Act of Supremacy of 1534, claimed for the English monarchy a supremacy over the church that echoed the rights of Byzantine emperors without ever mentioning that historical model explicitly.[6]

This was an important moment in the early development of English imperial political ideology, but its more extensive elaboration appeared during the reign of Henry VIII's successor, Edward VI (1537–1553).[7] By the time the young prince assumed power in 1547, his ministers were already cultivating imperial iconography for his monarchy, most noticeably the use of the imperial crown for his coat of arms that was used in images printed repeatedly on bibles and religious treatises.[8]

Beyond images, however, the most expansive and elaborate source of imperial theory came not from an English churchman or humanist. Rather, it was the work of Martin Bucer, the dejected leader of the Reformation in Strasbourg, who left that city for England in April of 1549.

Bucer and Edward VI as the New Constantine

After more than twenty-five years of service as a teacher, theologian, and preacher, Bucer had been suspended from his duties by the city Senate

---

[5] *Documents Illustrative of the English Church*, ed. Henry Gee and William John Hardy (London: Macmillan), 1896, p. 187: The relevant text reads: "Where by divers sundry old authentic histories and chronicles, it is manifestly declared and expressed, that this realm of England is an empire, and so hath been accepted in the world, governed by one supreme head and king, having the dignity and royal estate of the imperial crown of the same, unto whom a body politic, compact of all sorts and degrees of people, divided in terms, and by names of spirituality and temporality, be bounden and ought to bear, next to God, a natural and humble obedience."

[6] G. R. Elton, "The Reformation in England," pp. 234–235, in *The New Cambridge Modern History, volume II, The Reformation*, ed. G. R. Elton (Cambridge: Cambridge University Press), 1975.

[7] On the proliferation of imperial images during Edward's reign, see especially Stephen Alford, *Kingship and Politics in the Reign of Edward VI* (West Nyack, NY: Cambridge University Press, 2002), p. 53. "Edward was an emperor: Printers used every opportunity to emphasize the power of imperial kingship in their editions of sermons, homilies, injunctions, and bibles."

[8] On the image of the imperial crown, see Dale Hoak, "The Iconography of the Crown Imperial," in *Tudor Political Culture*, ed. Dale Hoak (Cambridge: Cambridge University Press, 1993), pp. 54–103. Also see David Armitage, *The Ideological Origins of the British Empire* (Port Chester, NY: Cambridge University Press, 2000), p. 34. He notes that already in 1517, Cuthbert Tunstall had told Henry VIII that "the Crown of England is an Empire of hitselff," although such a propositions had yet to be attached to any law.

because he refused to accept their decision to abide by the conditions of the peace interim imposed by the Holy Roman emperor Charles V on the city in 1547. The interim restored various privileges and properties to the Catholics of Strasbourg, including the right to celebrate the mass. Bucer refused to compromise with a power that he considered to be siding with the Antichrist in Rome.[9]

Indirectly driven into exile by an emperor whose religious decisions he found anything but holy, Bucer spent the last two years of his life writing a book that served, in part, to create a Protestant version of the Holy Roman Emperor. Highly respected by the king's ecclesiastical councilors, Bucer was appointed as the influential Regius Professor of Divinity at Cambridge during these years.[10] A client of the young king Edward VI, his text, like Mexia's history dedicated to Philip II only a few years earlier, was written as a primer for a young monarch.

Dedicated to his royal patron, *De Regno Christi* was first published in 1551, the year of Bucer's death. It was a lengthy reflection on the proper relationship between the kingdom of God and the earthly kingdoms of men and the necessary laws for creating a Christian society. Particularly concerned with the right relationship between kings and the Church, it constituted one of the most extensive works of political theology that came out of the first generation of Protestant reformers.[11]

Understood in the context of Bucer's exile and bitter experience with Charles V, together with the still embryonic state of a distinctly Protestant English political theology, *De Regno Christi* represented a bold claim to still largely unchartered territory in the English Reformation. A clear challenge to the prevailing Catholic understanding of the relationship between secular and ecclesiastical power, it was also a departure from his earlier work and that of continental Calvinism more generally that had focused

---

[9] Thomas A. Brady, *Protestant Politics: Jacob Sturm (1489–1553) and the German Reformation* (Atlantic Highlands, NJ: Humanities Press), 1995, p. 333 and pp. 345–346.

[10] The most recent bibliography of Bucer scholarship published in 2005 lists no fewer than 3,314 entries for the period between 1523 and 2004. *Martin Bucer-Bibliographie*, ed. Holger Pils, Stephan Ruderer, and Petra Schaffrodt (Gütersloh: Gütersloher Verlagshaus, 2005). Among these many titles, a small fraction touch on Bucer's time in England, including most recently Basil Hall, "Martin Bucer in England," in *Martin Bucer*, ed. David F. Wright (Cambridge: Cambridge University Press, 1994), pp. 144–160; and David F. Wright, "Martin Bucer and England – and Scotland," in *Martin Bucer and Sixteenth Century Europe*, ed. Christian Kriegger and Marc Leinhard (Leiden: Brill, 1993), Vol. 2, pp. 523–533. None of these texts provide an analysis of *De Regno Christi* and its political implications or context.

[11] *Melanchton and Bucer*, ed. Wilhelm Pauck (London: SCM Press LTD, 1969), pp. 157–158.

on the right of Protestant republics to rebel against Catholic monarchs and the emperor.[12]

It is the role of Bucer as a champion of Protestant republicanism that has been emphasized in much of the historical literature.[13] But the later political model fashioned by Bucer in the English context, the Protestant imperial model, was the longer-lasting and more influential of the two in the early modern period.

Writing for an established, if threatened, Protestant monarchy in 1551, Bucer stressed in his last work the power, rights, and duties of Christian monarchy. He turned first to biblical and early Patristic precedents, but the primary model that he held up for imitation in England came from the late Roman Empire. It was the Byzantine church of Constantine and Justinian that provided the historical precedent that allowed for a dominant monarchical role vis-à-vis the Church. State supremacy over the Church, Bucer argued, was clearly the reality in the time of Constantine, who became the primary role model proposed for the young king Edward VI.

This was an ecclesiastical history that fit well with English secular histories from the same period that emphasized the unity of the British Isles under the Roman Empire and particularly under Constantine, who was himself born in England. But Bucer's history was far more extensive, and he was the first of the English theologians to develop a more comprehensive analysis of the relationship between monarch and Church specifically supported by the Byzantine example. In so doing, he also wrote the first detailed historical justification for royal supremacy over the Church. His ideas, moreover, remained a lasting foundation of imperial Protestant political theology in early modern England that produced strong, if often unacknowledged, imitators in the decades that followed. This was particularly true during the reign of Elizabeth I and James I.

These later monarchs and their theologians developed a form of Protestant caesaro-papism that drew explicit parallels with the examples of Constantine, Theodosius, and Justinian. As part of the wider debate that later

---

[12] The most recent text that is concerned specifically with Bucer's political theology is Andreas Gäumann, *Reich Christi und Obrigkeit* (Bern: Peter Lang, 2001), pp. 133 and 225. This text focuses primarily on Bucer's work and political experience before he reaches England, and it does briefly note Bucer's use of the Constantinian example for establishing the nature of Christian monarchy. It falls short, however, of providing an analysis of the shifts in Bucer's political theology in the English context, and of charting the elaboration of the Byzantine model that I will be looking at in the pages that follow.

[13] Quentin Skinner, *The Foundations of Modern Political Thought*, Vol. II, pp. 207, 228. Skinner notes Hans Baron's 1939 article in *Church History* on "Protestant Republicanism" that in turn notes the role that Bucer played in its formulation.

included the Venetian interdict controversy and the writings of Paolo Sarpi, the English theologians wrote many of their treatises drawing on Bucer's ideas as they sought to counter the central scholastic defenders of papal supremacy. Cesare Baronio, Robert Bellarmine, and Francisco Suarez wrote for their own Constantine, usually the Spanish kings, as noted in Chapter 3. Later, Bossuet also made the parallel between the early Christian emperors and Louis XIV.

Bucer's text drew on early church historians, and especially Eusebius, to develop a view of the early Church that saw the reign of Constantine as the first historical moment when God decided to grant the Christian Church a monarch of its own and a time of true grace and peace. After reflecting on the broad tradition of monarchy in ancient history, he reaches the following central conclusion about the divine plan:

> The lord promised the people such kings through the prophets, on condition that they fully accept the Kingdom of his son. But in order to show the secret and celestial power of his Son's Kingdom, from the first revelation of his Kingdom to the Gentiles until Saint Constantine, he gave no kings to his people.[14]

This is the pivotal move in Bucer's historical analysis that shapes his text and leads him to repeatedly return to Constantine's example as he progresses through the fifteen major areas of reform that he chooses to comment on for young King Edward. What is striking about the passage is the description of Constantine as a saint, a status recognized by the Eastern Orthodox Church but not by the Roman Catholic Church in Bucer's time. Clearly, Bucer singles out the Constantinian example as the golden age of Christian monarchy and empire and in so doing pushes the Church of England and the English monarchy along an imperial path.

By developing a political theology that justified the king's superiority over the Church using the example of the first Christian emperors of ancient Rome, Bucer provided later English monarchs and theologians with the intellectual framework for an increasingly imperial political mentality and royal self-conception. The Reformation in England thus merged with the Imperial Renaissance to further the theoretical foundations for early modern imperial ambition in the West.[15]

[14] Ibid., p. 190–191.
[15] For a more detailed analysis of Bucer's text and especially the historical examples he uses to bolster his political theology, see my article: "Creating a Protestant Constantine: Martin Bucer's *De Regno Christi* and the Foundations of English Imperial Political Theology," in

Elizabeth I: From Constantine to Caesar

Although Bucer's death in 1551 and the king's death shortly thereafter in 1553 meant that *De Regno Christi* had little chance to be acted on by its first intended student, the Constantinian model and image that it promoted clearly lived on. It was in the reign of Queen Elizabeth I (1556–1603) that her theologians and historians began to more fully incorporate the imperial image and language with the English monarchy. On the level of political theology and polemic, it was John Jewel, student of Peter Martyr Vermigli at Oxford and eventual bishop of Salisbury, who picked up where Bucer had left off.

Jewel's major late work, *An Apology of the Church of England*, first published in 1564, also promoted the Byzantine political theology and historical examples elaborated on by Bucer.[16] The text would have certainly been known to Jewel and his teacher, Peter Martyr, a fellow exile from the continent who had much contact with Bucer.

Jewel's work has frequently been cited as the primary work that formed the imperial political theology for the English Reformation under the young queen Elizabeth.[17] And the text did present one of the most eloquent and detailed defenses of royal supremacy to that date. Bucer's earlier and more elaborate formulation of the imperial theme, however, has not been understood or acknowledged in the contemporary literature. But the dependence of Jewel on Bucer's main ideas is very clear.

This is obvious in the treatment of the theme of the authority of the ancient Christian emperors to call and preside over Church councils. Just as Bucer had pointed to Constantine's role at Nicea as a critical precedent and example of imperial authority over the bishops and entire Church, so too did Jewel make this precedent the focus of his justification of royal supremacy. More specifically, Jewel wrote, "The Christian Emperors in old time appointed the councils of the bishops. Constantine called the Council of Nicaea. Theodosius the First called the council at Constantinople. Theodosius the Second, the council of Ephesus. Marcian, the council at Chalcedon."[18]

Politics and Reformations: Communities, Politics, Nations and Empires, ed. C. Ocker, M. Printy, P. Starenko, and P. Wallace (Leiden: Brill, 2007), pp. 539–550.

[16] John Jewel, *An Apology of the Church of England*, ed. J. E. Booty (Ithaca, NY: Cornell University Press), 1963.

[17] See especially Frances A. Yates, *Astraea*, pp. 39–42. Yates does not mention Bucer in her work on Elizabeth, and it is not apparent that she knew his work.

[18] John Jewel, *Apology*, p. 116.

Bucer had emphasized the royal role in attending to Church order and governance, and Jewel followed him, adding for further emphasis that "Continually, for the space of five hundred years, the Emperor alone appointed the ecclesiastical assemblies and called the councils of the bishops together."[19]

Although this view was not historically accurate because it neglected the councils called by early medieval kings like the Visigoths in Spain beginning in the late sixth century, it did serve the polemical purposes of both Bucer and Jewel, who sought to elevate the Byzantine model. And again, for Jewel it was the example of Constantine, above all others, who justified the English monarchs' own claims to royal authority over the church: "Greater authority than Constantinus the emperor had and used our princes require none."[20] Moreover, the fact that Constantine had been born in England only added to his popularity as a model and precedent for the English monarchs.

The authority that Jewel exercised as the bishop of Salisbury and one of the most loyal ecclesiastical servants of Queen Elizabeth ensured that his Constantinian view of royal authority would enjoy a level of influence probably never imagined by Bucer. By 1563, John Foxe, too, had jumped on this bandwagon and was fashioning Elizabeth as the English Constantine who had brought an end to the sixteenth-century age of martyrdom.[21] Playing Eusebius to Elizabeth's Constantine, Foxe included an image of Elizabeth framed by the C that began a section on Constantine in his famous *Book of Martyrs*.[22]

The use of imperial imagery grew as Elizabeth's reign progressed, and by the later sixteenth century, it had begun to appear in other genres of literature that more closely resembled the continental model from earlier in the century. Much of the ecclesiastical history early in her realm, with its Constantinian focus, had the practical purpose of undermining the competing theory of papal supremacy over the Church that was then being defended at the last sessions of the Council of Trent. But as military conflict with Spain grew in the 1580s, humanist cultural production dedicated to

---

[19] Ibid., p. 117.

[20] Quoted in Yates, p. 42. The view that English political theology is modeled after the example of Constantine and the early Christian emperors was first argued by Yates, who writes after this quote from Jewel: "We thus find that the official apologist for the Church of England bases the right of the crown to be head of both church and state on the position of the early Christian emperors in the early church." The only thing lacking in this analysis is the fact that the first architect of such a view was Bucer and not Jewel, something never recognized by Yates.

[21] Ibid.

[22] Ibid., p. 43.

Elizabeth finally discovered the power of Julius Caesar and ancient Rome as a point of reference for the queen and her military that had successfully waged war against Philip II and the Spanish Empire.

This was the case, for instance, when Elizabeth staged a Roman triumph in London after the defeat of the Spanish armada in 1588. The queen paraded through the streets in a triumphal carriage, or "chariot throne," proving that she, too, could play the role of Caesar, gender differences notwithstanding.[23]

Nothing that compared with the triumphs of Charles V from fifty years earlier, the Elizabethan triumph nonetheless signaled that England was also up to imitating the ancient Caesars. The political uses and revival of the pagan Caesars came later to England in part because the historical connection between the English monarchy and the Roman emperors and empire was never as thick as it was between the major monarchs on the continent. Both ancient and humanist histories that focused on the pagan Caesars subsequently did not enjoy the same prominence as instructional texts that were considered useful to the other imperial monarchs in the age of Elizabeth.

But as England imposed its control over Wales, Ireland, and Scotland in varying measure over the course of the sixteenth century and then began to challenge the Spanish Empire in the Atlantic, interest in the example of the ancient empire and her Caesars grew. Increased military power, wars of conquest, the accompanying increased militarization of society, and the example of England's competitors on the continent made this development almost inevitable.[24]

That did not mean that Caesar or the ancient Roman Empire suddenly became a major role model, but they did become increasingly popular, as reflected in the growing numbers of new translations, editions, and contemporary literary production based on Roman ancient themes. As with the other monarchies, the big political questions raised by empire both for the individual ruler and for the state led humanists to look to ancient Rome as a fertile location for reflecting on the serious problems of governance in their own day.[25]

---

[23] Lisa Hopkins, *Cultural Uses of the Caesars on the English Renaissance Stage* (Abingdon: Ashgate, 2008), p. 1.

[24] For the relationship between sixteenth-century English conquest in Ireland and later American conquests, see John Patrick Montaño, *The Roots of English Colonialism in Ireland* (Cambridge: Cambridge University Press, 2011).

[25] For the application of Roman texts to the early American context, see Andrew Fitzmaurice, *Humanism and America* (Cambridge: Cambridge University Press, 2003). This work emphasizes the Ciceronian tendencies of members of the Virginia Company and their supporters and argues that they were not out to conquer or claim empire but rather to bring civilization to the barbarian natives much as the Romans had brought civility to the ancient

No English author reflected this development more than William Shakespeare (1564–1616), and no play from the period better reflected the interpretive tensions and ambiguities with which Elizabethan England approached the Roman Empire than his *Julius Caesar*. Shakespeare was no imperial humanist or champion of Caesar. But he also presented Brutus and the other assassins of Caesar in a less than heroic light. The play falls far short of celebrating the Republic or condemning the Empire. In the end, Shakespeare produced what one contemporary scholar has called a "supremely ambivalent drama" that leaves the ancient question of whether the assassination of Caesar was justified unanswered.[26]

This ambivalence forces the reader or viewer of the play to wrestle not just with the meaning of Caesar's rise to power and eventual murder but also with the legitimacy of empire itself. The tyrannicide debate that marked the revival of Caesar from the fourteenth century onward is certainly not resolved here, and neither is the question of which form of government is superior. The only thing that seems beyond question is that the life and death of Caesar was a tragedy, not a triumph, for both him and his foes.

All of Shakespeare's Roman plays are tragedies, a very basic fact that points to the author's deep unease with the looming, dark memories of the ancient world's dominant power. *Anthony and Cleopatra*, *Coriolanus*, and *Titus Andronicus* all carry warnings about the often grim consequences of the quest for power. Betrayal, revenge, bloodlust, violence, pride, and treachery of various and assorted kinds are the ingredients of Roman history from this perspective. If there is any core lesson, either implied or overt, it seems to be that ancient Rome was a dangerous and dark chapter of human history and any repetition of it is best avoided. Empire is to be feared, not loved.

Shakespeare's Roman plays are central examples of Renaissance drama, as they revive and reflect on ancient Roman historical memory. But they are not a call for a rebirth or imitation of that history. It is impossible to read them as encouragement for empire builders or aspiring emperors. They thus differ quite radically from the humanist histories that offered the Roman past as a guide and model to political glory.[27]

Britons. He acknowledges the popularity of Tacitus but proposes that the "dominant understanding of Tacitus was one of nostalgia for a lost civic virtue. In this sense, Tacitism was an extension of Ciceronian humanism." P. 160.

[26] Robert S. Miola, "Julius Caesar and the Tyrannicide Debate," in *Renaissance Quarterly*, Vol. 38, No. 2 (Summer 1985), pp. 271–289. Quote from p. 273.

[27] Probing the many different interpretations that can be read into Shakespeare's Caesar is far beyond the bounds of this work, as is any further reading of the expansive uses of ancient Roman history found in the historical plays. For uses of the Roman past in Shakespeare, see

In the English context, they differ most obviously with a contemporary of Shakespeare, whose translation and publication of the first five books of Caesar's *Commentaries* coincided with the first performance of *Julius Caesar* in 1600. Clement Edmonds's *Observations Upon the Five First Books of Caesars Commentaries* was initially dedicated to Sir Francis Vere, the chief commander of the English forces that had fought the Spanish in the United Provinces. Edmonds noted in the dedication that "this worke of Caesar hath alwaies beene held in your particular recommendation, as the Breviarie of soldiers."[28]

English translations of some parts of Caesar's *Commentaries* had appeared as early as 1530, first with John Tiptoft's *Julius Cesars Commentaryes*. The poor quality of the book, together with its lack of dedication and supporting materials, were indicative of the relatively low level of interest the work then generated for a broader reading public. The same held true of other English editions of 1565 and 1590. There were also no Latin editions dedicated to the monarchs to rival those of the French humanists and kings.

This was not the case with Edmond's work, the first edition of which went to press again in 1604. More importantly, and pointing to a dramatic political change with the coming to power of James I in 1603, Edmonds published a much-expanded version of his text in 1609 that coincided with and contributed to the dawning of the first major phase of the Imperial Renaissance in Britain.

James I and the "Imperial Crown of Great Britain"

The second and expanded edition of Edmonds's work was dedicated to the ill-fated prince Henry, son of King James I (1603–1625). Like the work of Guevara, Mexia, or de Bandole (published in the same year), Edmonds's second edition of the *Commentaries* was also a primer for the presumed heir of a kingdom with growing imperial presumptions. Deepening associations between the monarchy and the ancient Caesars was illustrated by a portrait of Prince Henry on the front page of the text. It was framed in an oval that rested atop a classical arch with two Caesars in front of the supporting columns. In the dedication, the author urged the young prince and son of James I to take Caesar's life and work as a "chief pattern and Master-piece

---

J. Leeds Barrol, "Shakespeare and Roman History," *Modern Language Review*, Vol. 53 (1958), 327–43.

[28] Clement Edmonds, *Observations Upon Caesar's Commentaries* (London: Peter Short, 1600). I consulted the 1600, 1604, 1609, and 1655 editions found in the British Library.

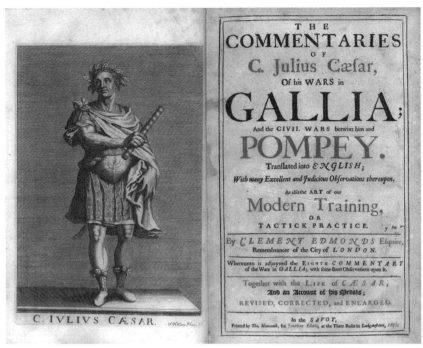

THE
COMMENTARIES
OF
C. Julius Cæfar,
Of his WARS in
GALLIA;
And the CIVIL WARS betwixt him and
POMPEY.
Tranſlated into ENGLISH;
With many Excellent and Judicious Obſervations thereupon.
As alſo the ART of our
Modern Training,
OR
TACTICK PRACTICE.
By CLEMENT EDMONDS Eſquire,
Remembrancer of the City of LONDON.
Whereunto is adjoyned the EIGHTH COMMENTARY
of the Wars in GALLIA; with ſome ſhort Obſervations upon it.
Together with the LIFE of CÆSAR,
And an Account of his Medals;
REVISED, CORRECTED, and ENLARGED.
In the SAVOY,
Printed by Tho. Newcomb, for Jacobus Edwin, at the Three Roſes in Ludgate-ſtreet, 1677.

C. IVLIVS CÆSAR.

5.1. Clement Edmonds, *Observations Upon Caesar's Commentaries*, 1677 edition.

of the art of war."[29] He was especially "emboldened" to make this recommendation because of the king's endorsement. Caesar's work, he noted, "in the deep judgment of his most excellent Majesty, is preferred above all other profane histories; and so commended, by his sacred Authority."[30] This more lavish edition included the *Commentaries on the Civil Wars*, a short biography of Caesar, a section on ancient Roman coins, and the two poems by Ben Johnson praising the work, the first of which opened this chapter.

From its relatively modest beginnings, Edmonds's work had grown over the course of a decade to become the most expansive English example of a high Renaissance humanist celebration of Caesar. It was of a piece with the long line of biographies, vernacular editors, and commentators on Caesar that began in Italy 250 years earlier. But in this case it was a harbinger of Britain's imperial future in the seventeenth and eighteenth centuries (Figure 5.1).

[29] Ibid., p a3r. Quote taken from 1655 edition.
[30] Ibid.

Three different, and always larger, editions of Edmonds's text went to press six times between 1600 and 1695, a tangible literary example of the growing interest in the imperial theme in seventeenth-century Britain. Eventually, the longest editions of 1655 and 1695 included numismatic sections, some of the commentaries of Henri de Rohan, a short life of Caesar, numerous maps depicting battles, and a geographical index with maps. Ben Johnson was right in praising Edmonds for ensuring that the memory and words of Caesar would "die no more" in Britain thanks to his work.

This rebirth of interest in Caesar as an admirable role model was but one manifestation of the fact that James I and his court increasingly saw themselves as the center of a new Britannic Empire. The succession of James VI of Scotland to the English throne as James I in 1603 united the Scottish and English crowns and made the king ruler over the island that Caesar himself had first named Britain in 55 BC. Although there were numerous medieval and early modern literary and political precedents for James I to draw on in constructing his idea of a British Empire, it was contemporary competition and models that played the central role in this development.[31]

By the time James I and VI came to power, increasing contact with Spain and France made it almost inevitable that the British monarchs would move to develop their own imperial image and agenda more fully. This meant drawing on the full range of examples offered by the increasingly familiar corpus of classical literature from the age of empire. It also meant the first full flourishing of imperial Renaissance letters and arts in Britain, including the first stage of a Vitruvian revival. On the concrete level of acquiring New World colonies, it was also in the reign of James I that Britain first moved aggressively to compete for a real empire in the Atlantic world.

The Imperial Renaissance came late to Britain, but it did come, perhaps against the odds, in the seventeenth century. The lure of Caesar's fame, the wealth and glory that came from real empire, and the architectural grandeur of the Vitruvian revival had created a momentum of their own that was able to withstand and eventually overcome even the great convulsions of civil war, religious revolution, and intrigues over royal succession. The lure of wealth from North American colonies and global trade also loomed large in pushing Britain to reach for a true global empire. At the same time, more contact with Italy also encouraged the development of classical aesthetics,

---

[31] For the early uses of the terms "Greater Britain," "Britain," and "King of Britain," see Andrew D. Nicholls, *The Jacobean Union* (London: Greenwood Press, 1999), pp. 4–5. On James I's self-perception as founder of a Britannic Empire, see Allan I. Macinnes, *Union and Empire* (Cambridge: Cambridge University Press, 2007), pp. 54–55.

particularly with the most important English Renaissance architect to date, Inigo Jones.

An early indicator that James I and VI was raising his imperial profile appeared in the polemic that surrounded yet another round of debate over Church and State relations. More specifically, papal authority was once again at the center of the controversy that gave rise to the third generation of Constantinian political theology in Britain. The Venetian Interdict controversy at the beginning of the seventeenth century drew in numerous antagonists from distant shores, including the new king of England and Scotland. But this king surpassed his predecessors in authoring numerous works that bore the distinctive Constantinian claim. And his theologians were steeped in the precedents that the new monarch was claiming as his own.

The historical foundations and rhetoric had also expanded to include the pagan emperors. This was clear in the collected works of King James edited by the Bishop of Winton and Dean of the Royal Chapel. More specifically, in the introduction to *The Workes of the Most High and Mightie Prince, James by the Grace of God, King of Great Britaine, France, and Ireland Defender of the Faith*, the bishop first drew parallels between earlier imperial authors and his monarch. He pointed out that King James, in leaving writings to his sons, was following the example of emperors: "Basilius, Constantinus, Manuell, and Charles the fifth – left instructions for their sons."[32] He also made further parallels with imperial authors, noting that "Amongst the Romans, which of their Emperours did not advance his fame by Letters. Julius Caesar, besides many other things, writ his Commentaries after the example of Cyrus."[33] The author goes even further with his imperial model to claim that the example of Caesar was a good precedent "for our Augustus to follow." And among Christian emperors, "That one example of Constantine amongst the Christian emperors shall suffice."[34]

The *Defence of Constantine* by the theologian Richard Crakanthorp, published in 1621 just a few years before the death of James I, constituted the most explicit and strident example of the Constantinian polemic from the Anglican perspective. A more accurate title might have been *The Defence of Constantine and James I*, because the author dedicated his book to the king,

---

[32] *The Workes of the Most High and Mightie Prince, James by the Grace of God, King of Great Britaine, France, and Ireland Defender of the Faith*, ed. and with introduction by James Bishop of Winton, Dean of the Royal Chapel (London: Robert Barker and John Bill, 1616). The dedication is found in folios a 1–4, followed by introduction folios b 1–4, c 1–4, d 1–4, and e 1–3. Then regular pagination begins but by folio.

[33] Ibid., p. c2r.

[34] Ibid., p. c3r.

whom he described as "the Great Constantine of these later Ages." He elaborated on the theme, stating that, almost like mirror images of one another, both men were "the Inheritors and Possessors of the Imperiall Crowne of great Brittaine" who had been endowed with the now familiar imperial virtues of "prudence, justice, clemency, and magnanimity."[35] Both, moreover, were fully endowed with temporal authority over the Church, the major point of the book that the author argues against the papal interpretation of Constantine for the next 283 pages.

James I, the English Augustus and Constantine, clearly saw himself as a champion and torch bearer of the imperial rights of monarchs against the claims of the papacy to an extent that would have made Martin Bucer proud. In his treatise *A Premonition to all Most Mightie Monarchs, Kings, Free Princes, and States of Christendome,* James called on all European princes to refuse to submit to the arguments for papal supremacy. Pressing a historical analysis that echoed *De Regno Christi,* he argued that

> [A]ll Christian Emperours were for a long time so farre from acknowledging the Pope's Superioritie over them, as by the contrary the popes acknowledged themselves for their Vassals, reverencing and obeying the Emperours as their Lords, for proofe whereof, I remit you to my Apologie.[36]

Repeating many of the same historical arguments as those made by Jewel and Bucer before him, King James proved to be the good student that Bucer had hoped Edward VI might be. He was the most intellectually inclined king that Britain had in the period, and he embraced a large range of ancient texts in true humanist fashion to bolster the arguments and messages of his writings. In the famous primer for his son, *Basilikon Doron,* he drew on Plato, Aristotle, Cicero, and Xenophon, all of whom provided various lessons for imperial kingship.[37] As a book by the king himself, it spoke strongly to the exalted nature of the British monarchy he advocated as he sought to connect his rule with that of the great classical and biblical rulers of antiquity. These aspirations also went far beyond literary claims. Once he had assumed the crown of England as well as that of Scotland, the king developed a much more expansive imperial agenda. As a builder and patron of the arts, for example, he sought to imitate no less an emperor than Augustus.

---

[35] Richard Crakanthorp, *The Defence of Constantine* (London: Bernard Alsop, 1621), p. A2v.

[36] Pp. 287–338. Quote from p. 297.

[37] John Cramsie, "The Philosophy of Imperial Kingship and the Interpretation of James VI and I," in *James VI and I,* ed. Ralph Houlbrooke (Hampshire: Ashgate Publishing, 2006), pp. 49–53.

Inigo Jones and the Vitruvian Revival in Britain

In 1615, the king issued a famous proclamation that constituted a royal building code for London. Besides banning further construction except on old foundations, James also ordered that all new buildings be made of brick, not wood. His goal was to make London the greatest city in the world, and his role model was Augustus:

> As it was said of the first emperor of Rome [Augustus] that he found the city of Rome of brick and left it of marble, so we, whom God have honored to be the first King of Great Britain, might be able to say in some proportion that we found our city and suburbs of London of sticks, and left them of brick, being a material far more durable, safe from fire and beautiful and magnificent.[38]

A mixture of pretension and modesty, this early architectural agenda lacked any specifics about the preferred style of architecture. But the fire of 1619 that destroyed one of the central ceremonial rooms of the monarchy, the Banqueting House at Whitehall Palace, gave James I the chance to reveal his tastes. In true Augustan fashion, the king chose Inigo Jones (1573–1652), the first British Renaissance architect to embrace the Vitruvian revival, to design the new Banqueting House (Figure 5.2).[39]

The Banqueting Hall commission, together with the earlier commission from 1616 that Jones had won to design the Queen's House at Greenwich, marked the true beginning of the Imperial Renaissance in architecture in Great Britain. Jones had traveled to Italy for an extended stay in 1613 to 1614, when he had the chance to visit Milan, Mantua, Padua, Venice, Vicenza, Florence, and Rome. He subsequently had firsthand knowledge of both ancient buildings and the many Renaissance palaces and churches designed by Bramante, Michelangelo, Giulio Romano, Giuliano da San Gallo, and Palladio, among others. He also purchased numerous drawings by Palladio that he brought back to England, which he added to knowledge acquired from Palladio's highly influential text, *The Four Books of Architecture*, itself an ode to Vitruvius.[40]

Fresh from this immersion in the Italian tradition, Jones returned to London, where he was named Surveyor of the King's Works. With the support

---

[38] Michael Leapman, *Inigo* (London: Review, 2003), p. 184.

[39] Among the best recent works on Inigo Jones and the Vitruvian tradition are John Harris and Gordon Higgott, *Inigo Jones, Complete Architectural Drawings* (London: Philip Wilson, 1989); Christy Anderson, *Inigo Jones and the Classical Tradition* (Cambridge: Cambridge University Press, 2007); and Annarosa Cerutti Fusco, *Inigo Jones, Vitruvius Britannicus* (Rimini: Magioli, 1985).

[40] John Harris and Gordon Higgott, *Inigo Jones, Complete Architectural Drawings*, p. 16.

5.2. Inigo Jones, The Banqueting House, Whitehall, 1619–1622. (Vanni Archive/Art Resource, NY.)

of both king and queen, he went to work on the design and construction of the buildings that, when completed, changed the architectural landscape and future of Britain dramatically. The "British Vitruvius," as he was called by his contemporary John Webb, imported the language of classical architecture into Britain and ensured that classicism would be a dominant style of British royal buildings from that point forward.[41]

[41] Christy Anderson, *Inigo Jones and the Classical Tradition*, pp. 5–7.

The classicism of Jones has been described as a masculine, literate style based on the reason of proportion.[42] It was all of that, but it also carried strong political meaning because it represented a radical departure from the local English style that was still overwhelmingly Gothic and, by implied contrast, feminine, illiterate, and lacking reason. The importation of neo–Roman palaces signaled that James I was embracing the architecture and architect favored by ancient emperors and contemporary imperial monarchs alike. It was a move that did little to calm the anxieties of English parliamentarians who feared the political implications of the building that clearly paralleled the increasingly absolutist claims and behavior of their king.

Although the Banquet House at Whitehall had been used as a theater prior to the fire of 1619 and was initially rebuilt with that same use in mind, by 1621 Peter Paul Rubens had been asked to paint the ceiling of the new building. This meant that it could no longer be used as a theater because the burning of torches for evening lighting would ruin the painting. Both monarch and architect had other intentions for the building in mind. Used as both theater and hall of state in the later 1620s, after Rubens delivered the paintings in 1638, it was used solely as the major hall of state and throne room where the king received his important visitors, including foreign ambassadors.[43]

As the king's "most public statement of his court's cultural achievements and political aspirations," the Banqueting Hall was meant to compete with the other great halls of state and throne rooms in Spain, France, and Italy.[44] All of these were characterized by the classical grandeur of the Vitruvian orders, and so too was the Banqueting House both within and without. As with the other imperial monarchs, the king's authority was closely linked with classical architecture.[45]

On the exterior of the building, the façade is articulated by the Roman orders with two stories of four Doric columns framing the three central bays. These are flanked by two additional bays on either side, all of which rest on a heavily rusticated ground floor. In total, fourteen windows grace the façade, allowing a good deal of natural light into the interior.[46]

---

[42] Ibid., p. 6.

[43] J. Harris, pp. 108–109.

[44] C. Anderson, p. 166.

[45] Ibid., p. 176. The author illustrates this point with the 1620 painting of the king by Paul van Somer titled *James I in Front of the Banqueting House, Whitehall* that prominently features the building directly behind the king dressed in his most elaborate royal apparel.

[46] Ibid., pp. 168–169.

Although the exterior of the room makes a powerful statement about the new Roman moment that was dawning in Britain, it was in the interior that Jones created a classical space that served as the monarch's primary "stage for the display of royal might and glory."[47] The events that were held there included high diplomatic ceremonies such as the signing of treaties with foreign ambassadors, the reception of the Houses of Parliament, and the granting of new titles.[48] In short, it was the location of the most important political ceremonies.

Some scholars have seen the interior decoration of the Banqueting House as Jones's greatest achievement because he applied the language of Roman antiquity gleaned from Palladio in an original way for the ornamentation.[49] Two rows of Ionic columns run the length of the hall, and tapestries based on cartoons of Raphael were commissioned to hang in the first-story windows. By 1638, the ceiling paintings of Rubens celebrating the reign of James I completed the opulent décor. For good reason, the great Roman hall has frequently been described as one of the two most important buildings to be erected in seventeenth-century Britain.

Colonies for the Imperial Crown

The example of the Spaniards excited other European princes to establish colonies in America, which is now inhabited from north to south by Europeans, who have almost extirpated the natives, and formed a kind of collateral power to the European states. The New World has enriched the Old; which has improved the New. Armies have been sent from Europe to fight in America; just as the Roman legions were sent to Asia to determine the fate of nations.

The History of the British Dominions in North America
(London: Printed for W. Strahan and T. Becket
and Co. in the *Strand*, 1773)

As important as the Banqueting Hall was for the image of the British monarchy, James I was confronted with the same challenge as that faced by the French monarchs at the beginning of the seventeenth century and by his predecessor Elizabeth I. For all of his imperial pretenses in arts and letters, he lacked an empire that competed in a meaningful way with that of

---

[47] Per Palme, *Triumph of Peace: A Study of the Whitehall Banqueting House* (London: Thames and Hudson, 1957), p. 120.

[48] Ibid.

[49] J. Harris, p. 17.

Spain. Although the more local conquest of Ireland went forward as part of the consolidation of the British Isles under one crown and also served as a colonial laboratory for the British, it produced neither the wealth nor the prestige of the global territories of the Spanish monarchs.[50]

James I subsequently moved to establish the first major British colonies in North America. The close connection between the rise of the new imperial identity of Great Britain and the colonial impulse was underlined by the name given to the first colony, New Britain. A new code of laws created for Virginia Britannia in 1612 pointed to hopes that the settlement would stick rather than to the reality of an already viable colony.[51] But it underlined that the monarch's feigned ignorance of this colonization in the face of challenges by the Spanish ambassador was a ruse. The British king wanted a piece of the Americas and was actively moving to make his claim along with the French.

James I clearly hoped that Jamestown would succeed, even if it was the initiatives of English settlers and investors that ultimately guaranteed its survival. The search for wealth, more than reputation, drove the investors who were instrumental in early colonization. Specifically, it was the formation of plantation companies that marked the first stage of British colonization: they were formed for Virginia in 1606 and 1624, Newfoundland in 1610, Bermuda in 1611, and New England in 1620.[52] Natural resources like fish, fur, and tobacco were the first objects of commercialization, but there were always hopes for the discovery of gold or silver as well.

By the end of the reign of James I in 1625, roughly 10,000 settlers from Britain were living in British colonies in North America. It was a relatively modest beginning, but it established a precedent for James's successor Charles I. A dutiful son who carried through the completion of the Banqueting Hall with paintings that celebrated his father's accomplishments, the new king also pushed colonization of the Americas. Dramatically, in the first fifteen years of his rule, emigration to the New World increased to more than 80,000. Although many died from disease, violence, or the rigors of the voyage, by 1640 the population had reached 53,700. The global British Empire had truly begun.[53]

---

[50] D. Armitage, p. 49. The English were already attempting to establish plantations in Northern Ireland in the age of Elizabeth. Armitage notes that between 1572 and 1575, Thomas Smith tried three times to establish a colony in Ireland.

[51] A. Macinnes, pp. 138–139.

[52] Ibid., p. 142.

[53] A. Games, *Migration and the Origins of the English Atlantic World* (Cambridge, MA: Harvard University Press, 1999), p. 4.

As these numbers show, Charles I inherited a strong sense of imperial mission and identity that he meant to build on. In the area of colonization, it was during his reign that the monarchy expanded a policy of forced emigration on a scale that dwarfed any similar moves on the part of Spain and France.[54] This was motivated in large part by both the internal pressures on London, which had grown to be the largest city in Europe at 300,000, and the need of the plantation companies for cheap labor.

But it also paralleled a policy that was counted among those that contributed significantly to ancient Rome's greatness. More specifically, Jean Bodin had praised the Romans for establishing colonies that both "freed their cities from beggars, mutinies and idle persons" and "fortified their territories with their own people who then intermarried with the natives." By this means, the Romans "filled the world with their colonies, with an immortal glory of their justice wisdom and power."[55] Caesar, more specifically, was credited by Bodin with sending 170,000 Romans who were on public assistance to the colonies, thus taking pressure off both the treasury and urban fabric of the ancient world's largest city.[56]

Bodin had been translated into English in 1605 by Richard Knolles and dedicated to Sir Peter Manwood. It was printed in London in 1606 and subsequently gained a wider audience. Whether or not James I or Charles I personally read Bodin is not clear, but it is certain that his text was well known in England by the ruling class. On the level of practice, moreover, the parallels between British colonial policies and those of the Romans praised by Bodin are obvious. Among all of the early modern European states, none sent more people to the colonies or were more successful at replacing the native populations with their own. By accident or design, the British were the most successful at imitating the Roman colonization strategy over the long term.

This success meant disaster for the Native American population on par with that suffered by the native peoples of Latin America. A combination of smallpox, hepatitis, other diseases, and warfare with the British decimated the Indian population of the Northeast, estimated at roughly 347,000 people before colonization in 1600. A century later, it is estimated that the number had dropped to roughly 150,000.[57]

---

[54] Godfrey Davies, *The Early Stuarts, 1603–1660* (Oxford: Clarendon Press, 1959), p. 321. This study notes that "there were not a few who had little choice in their emigration."

[55] Jean Bodin, *The Six Bookes of a Commonweale*, p. 656.

[56] Ibid., p. 421.

[57] Douglas Ubelaker, "North American Indian Population Size," in *Disease and Demography in the Americas*, ed. John W. Verano and Douglas Ubelaker (Washington, DC: Smithsonian Institution Press, 1992), p. 173.

The fact that the settlers spanned a range of Protestant Christian positions meant that there was no single religious ideology behind the conquest. The monarchs certainly sponsored no great debate among scholastic theologians as Charles V had done. It is impossible to say that a particular form of Renaissance intellectual discourse played a significant role in English colonization in the same way that it did in Spain.

Scholastic reasoning forced the Spanish conquerors to acknowledge the humanity and some rights of Native Americans, even while using Aristotle to justify their social and economic subordination and exploitation as natural slaves. Renaissance scholasticism thus both supported and placed limits on Spanish imperial domination.

The English debate on the issue was fragmented and ultimately produced no such limits. At the same time, the monarchy in the age of James I and Charles I exercised weak control over colonial policy toward the Indians. Some colonists tried to evangelize the Indians not killed by disease during the first two generations of colonization. But after the war with the Algonquians in 1675 – King Philip's War – the British attitude hardened and most Indians were pushed out of New England, onto reservations, or into servitude.[58] In the Mohawk Valley, to give one example, the Indian population estimated at roughly 8,000 in 1634 was reduced to an estimated 440 by 1698.[59] The British Renaissance of Empire came at a great cost for them.

Unbeknownst to Charles I, it would also come at a great cost to him. The exalted perception of imperial monarchy embraced by the king drove him to acquire not just colonies in North America but also more of the material possessions that marked the courts of his continental peers. As a young man, the prince had traveled to Madrid in 1623 to woo the Spanish princess and sister of Philip IV. Although he failed in that purpose, his six-month stay served the pedagogical purpose of introducing the prince to one of the most lavish courts of Europe, including its extensive art collection. The English royal collection could boast many fine tapestries and paintings such as those by Hans Holbein, but it did not compare with the continental collections, especially where Roman antiquities or Italian Renaissance painting and sculpture were concerned. Elizabeth I, in particular, had been Spartan as a collector compared with the major sixteenth-century kings.

---

[58] Colin G. Calloway, "Surviving the Dark Ages," in *After King Philip's War*, ed. Colin G. Calloway (Hanover, NH: University Press of New England, 1997), p. 4.

[59] Dean R. Snow, "Disease and Population Decline in the Northeast," in *Disease and Demography in the Americas*, p. 181.

Charles I set out to correct this perceived deficiency both by commissioning new works of art and also by moving aggressively to buy art. During his Spanish sojourn, he had taken the occasion to purchase numerous pieces, including two paintings by Titian and a number of ancient statues, including busts of Marcus Aurelius and Apollo.[60] Later, he also ordered copies of three antique busts that he had seen at the palace at Aranjuez of Caesar, Marcus Aurelius, and Hannibal.[61]

These were minor purchases compared to his major effort of 1628, when he acquired a large number of paintings and sculptures from one of the great collections of an early center of the Imperial Renaissance in Italy, namely that of the Gonzaga family of Mantua. A combination of financial distress and weak leadership forced the Gonzaga to sell many prized pieces of the vast collection built up by Isabella d'Este, Duke Federigo II, and numerous other Gonzaga princes over a period of three centuries. The tragedy for Mantua was a triumph for Charles I, as he acquired a substantial part of one of the great Renaissance collections in a single large purchase. At least 157 statues were documented in the inventories of sale together with dozens of paintings, some by Titian and Raphael.[62]

Most important among the paintings was the *Triumph of Caesar* cycle by Mantegna. Central icons of the Imperial Renaissance, Mantegna's panels transferred to the British king's palace represented an artistic *translatio imperii*. Potent symbols of the ascent of Great Britain to imperial status, they became some of the most valued possessions of the British monarchs.

Initially, they also stood as powerful symbols of the imperial tastes of Charles I. Although the price that the king paid for the Mantua collection was modest by the standards of the day, his growing number of critics in the late 1620s and 1630s viewed royal spending on art as extravagant. This criticism was amplified by the fact that all of these purchases came at the same time that the monarchy was increasing taxes and spending for war.

Although both James I and Charles I were successful cultivators of the imperial arts and also played an important role in the expansion of the British Empire, especially in the New World, neither of these accomplishments was profitable. They brought increased reputation, but that did not pay the bills. Unlike the Spanish conquests that resulted in a dramatic

---

[60] Jonathan Brown, "Artistic Relations Between Spain and England, 1604–1655," in *The Sale of the Century*, ed. Jonathan Brown and John Elliott (New Haven, CT: Yale University Press, 2002), pp. 46–49.

[61] Ibid., p. 58.

[62] A. H. Scott-Elliot, "The Statues from Mantua in the Collection of King Charles I," in *The Burlington Magazine*, Vol. 101, No. 675 (June 1959), pp. 218–227.

increase in the revenues of the Spanish monarchs and many others, no such bonanza initially resulted from Virginia tobacco plantations or New England fisheries.

At the same time, both James I and Charles I failed in another crucial area of imperial pursuit: waging war. James I famously fashioned himself a peacemaker, and his main victory was his succession to the throne of England without much struggle. During the twenty-two years that followed, however, he rarely got involved in military confrontations, and it was only at the end of his life that he had decided to go to war against Spain. Charles I faithfully followed his father's plans, and four years of war between 1625 and 1629 followed his succession to the throne, but with no noticeable gain on the part of Great Britain. On the contrary, the protracted conflict left the British treasury strained to the limit and revenue from trade in decline.

The failed military and economic policies of Charles I eventually led to a full-scale depression that reached its depths by 1640, when angry parliamentarians and merchants revolted against the failed leadership of the king. Although there were numerous causes behind the Civil War that followed, viewed from the perspective of the Imperial Renaissance, a central problem was that the monarchs had assumed the costume and stage of the Caesars without ever playing their most important role: winning serious battles and bringing home treasure. The most successful imperial monarchs – Charles V, Philip II, Henry IV, and Louis XIV – could all back up their imperial pretensions with a winning record on the battle field. This was decidedly not the case with the Stuarts.

Art and architecture could only go so far as tools of monarchical power, and no event or setting drove home this lesson more powerfully than the execution of Charles I in 1649 on a scaffold attached to the Banqueting House. The same building that was meant to bolster the authority of James I through its classical Roman associations was used instead as the stage for the beheading of his son. It was a tragedy worthy of Shakespeare that shocked Europe and starkly underlined the limits of the Imperial Renaissance in Great Britain.

As an additional blow against the king's reputation and prestige of the monarchy expressed through art, Cromwell and the Puritan parliament that he led moved to sell a large part of the royal collection that Charles I and his predecessors had acquired. Lasting until 1653, the sale stripped from the royal collection an estimated 1,570 paintings together with many other objects.[63] Among those that were not lost, however, was the *Triumph of Caesar* by

---

[63] J. Brown, *Sale of the Century*, p. 59.

Mantegna, whose artistic and symbolic value even Cromwell apparently understood.

In a literary move that paralleled the usurpation of a major stage of imperial monarchy, a number of humanists working in Britain contributed to the revolt against Charles I using Tacitus as a weapon. Guicciardini had long ago written that the ancient Roman historian could be used to both teach tyrants how to maintain power and to show their opponents how to overthrow them. But in the case of the Spain and France, imperial humanists had claimed Tacitus as a source of instruction in the art of ruling. In the case of Charles I, however, historians enlisted Tacitus to illustrate first the nature of tyranny and then to show how the Stuart king fit that definition. Isaac Dorislaus, a Dutch lawyer and historian, was the major protagonist in this development. Appointed to the first chair in history at Cambridge in 1627 to lecture on Tacitus, he only managed to give a few lectures before being silenced by the royalist party, who rightly saw in his lectures a critique of the king.[64]

Later, Dorislaus became a principal advisor to the prosecution in the trial as he helped them define the nature of the tyranny of Charles I using Tacitus as a major source. An initial winner in the struggle given the result of the trial, Dorislaus was himself murdered by British royalists in Holland when he traveled there shortly after the execution of the king in 1649.[65]

The overt use of Tacitus to undermine imperial monarchy was a central example of a distinctive development in British humanist discourse. It contributed to a decidedly different political trajectory for seventeenth-century Britain that eventually led to a more limited constitutional monarchy. This option was already advocated in the work of John Eliot, the *Monarchie of Man*, written while the author and fan of Tacitus was in prison in 1626 for criticizing the monarchy.[66]

As for the option of a more pure republican form of government advocated by many of Cromwell's followers, Great Britain was clearly not quite ready to embrace it in the 1650s. Even in the midst of the first major republican moment in early modern English and British history, many of Cromwell's supporters fashioned him an emperor, and there were widespread rumors

---

[64] Ronald Mellor, "Tacitus, Academic Politics, and Regicide in the Reign of Charles I: The Tragedy of Dr. Isaac Dorislaus," in *International Journal of the Classical Tradition*, Vol. 11, No. 2 (Fall 2004), pp. 153–193. The author points out that serious interest in Tacitus first emerged in Britain in the reign of James I among opponents of absolutism like John Eliot. P. 175. For details on the lectures of 1627 see especially pp. 177–180.

[65] Ibid., p. 183.

[66] Ibid., p. 175.

that the parliament meant to declare him the emperor of Great Britain. For all practical purposes, he was an imperial monarch without the title.[67]

The restoration of Charles II to the throne in 1660 after the short Puritan republican experiment under the Protectorate of Oliver Cromwell revealed that Great Britain was not quite ready for a republican reading of Tacitus. On the contrary, it inspired serious opposition from champions of absolutism like Thomas Hobbes, who specifically found in the reading of ancient Greek and Latin authors a common source of rebellion and even regicide.

Without specifically citing Tacitus, Hobbes wrote in the *Leviathan* (1651):

> And as to rebellion in particular against monarchy; one of the most frequent causes of it, is the reading of books of policy, and histories of the ancient Greeks and Romans ... From the reading, I say, of such books, men have undertaken to kill their kings, because the Greek and Latin writers in their books, and discourses of policy, make it lawful, and laudable, for any man so to do; provided, before he do it, he call him a tyrant.[68]

Hobbes subsequently urged careful guidance for the young men reading the books, an obvious call for loyalist university professors who knew how to control their classics.

Charles II and the Ancients

The continuing lure of imperial monarchy and the art, architecture, and letters that supported and accompanied it was still strong in Great Britain in 1660. Cromwell had given the empire more military victories than it had enjoyed since the time of Elizabeth, and he successfully strengthened the colonies. But the language of empire built up over the previous 150 years in all of its artistic, architectural, and literary manifestations was tightly bound up with the monarchy. A Puritan commoner, regardless of his military abilities, would not suffice to lead a new Rome.

Charles II was received back in Great Britain by promoters of arts and letters, not to mention imperial splendor, with a sigh of relief. The parliament voted the king a generous annual allowance of more than 1 million

---

[67] David Armitage, "The Cromwellian Protectorate and the Languages of Empire," *The Historical Journal*, Vol. 35, No. 3 (Sept. 1992), pp. 531–555. The author notes the imperial language and associations attached to Cromwell, and he also describes his reign as an imperial monarchy. P. 532. This article is noteworthy as an early call for more attention to be given to the "imperialism of the English republic" and for its admonition that "the intellectual history of Britain must attend to the languages of empire as keenly as to the words of republicanism which have effectively drowned them out." P. 533.

[68] Thomas Hobbes, *Leviathan* (Oxford: Oxford University Press, 1996), pp. 216–217.

pounds, even if money was still in short supply. Picking up where Charles I had left off, the court quickly resumed with the same late-seventeenth-century enthusiasm for a continued classical revival that characterized the continental courts.[69]

The king had spent a part of his exile in France and subsequently had first-hand knowledge of the growing splendors of Paris. When he finally returned home in 1660, he was anxious both to make up for lost time and to keep up with his competitors as they built ever-more-extravagant imperial courts. Over the twenty-five years that he ruled, a combination of talented men, fire, and adequate political savvy helped him preside over a culminating chapter in the Imperial Renaissance of the First British Empire.

An unexpected result of the Civil War that contributed to this development was an increase in educated Englishmen who had first-hand experience of Italy. Many royalists slipped away to the continent during the dangerous years of Puritan rule and took advantage of their exile to see the antiquities of Rome that they previously knew only from books. John Evelyn followed the example of Thomas Howard, Earl of Arundel and famous collector of ancient sculpture, who introduced the younger Evelyn to the ancient sights of Rome in the 1640s. As he wrote to a friend back home, "Each day you call to mind the ages past and their Heroick actions, and never put foot to ground but in the footsteps of Caesar."[70]

When Evelyn returned from his Italian and French sojourn, he had a convert's zeal for the classical revival in art and architecture, and he became one of its major advocates in the London of Charles II and Christopher Wren. A champion and close friend of Wren, he also had personal connections to court and access to the king that he used to promote artists like the Dutch woodcarver and aspiring sculptor Grinling Gibbons. A regular and celebrated artist in the pay of the king, Gibbons's sculpture in stone and metal fell far short of the great Renaissance works of the Italian masters. But he did succeed in casting a gilded copper statue of Charles II in 1676 in the pose of an ancient emperor for Whitehall Palace. It was moved after the king's death to one of his lasting contributions to London, the classically inspired Royal Hospital Chelsea, where it still stands.[71]

The imperial image of Charles II by Gibbon was a strong symbol of the revived imperial aspirations of the grandson of James I. Like his grandfather, he was yet another monarch regularly referred to as a new Augustus by humanists

[69] George Clark, *The Later Stuarts, 1660–1714* (Oxford: Clarendon Press, 1955), p. 7.

[70] Joseph M. Levine, *Between the Ancient and the Moderns* (New Haven, CT: Yale University Press, 1999), pp. 6–7.

[71] Ibid., pp. 20–21.

like Evelyn. They yearned for a revival, a classical Renaissance that equaled those of Italy, Spain, and France. It was not to be in the realms of sculpture or painting, where British artists generally fell short of their continental peers. Imperial humanist production also lagged behind that of the continent.

But in the realm of architecture, the age of Charles II witnessed the greatest Vitruvian revival yet in Great Britain. Unlike the building boom that was occurring at the same time in France under the Sun King, the dramatic transformation of London in the latter half of the seventeenth century was not primarily the product of extravagant royal spending. Charles II did have big plans for Whitehall Palace and some of his other residences, but his budget fell short of his ambitions. He did not want to repeat the mistake of his father in projecting unreasonable extravagance, and those projects subsequently remained unfinished at his death in 1685.

But dozens of other major building projects went ahead funded by the parliament, the Church, and the people of London, who were determined to rebuild London after the great fire of 1666. By some contemporary accounts, the disaster destroyed more than 13,000 houses and eighty-seven churches, or an estimated seven eighths of the city.[72] In addition, dozens of churches and public buildings were destroyed, including St. Paul's, the symbolic center of the Anglican Church.

The devastation unexpectedly gave Charles II the chance to fulfill the ambition of his grandfather, who had dreamt of following Augustus, after a fashion, by transforming a city of wood into a city of brick. The king and city government moved quickly to appoint a Commission to submit a design for the rebuilding of London. Among the three men chosen by Charles II was Christopher Wren (1632–1723), the designer and architect who most closely followed Inigo Jones as the next "English Vitruvius," as he was eventually called by his peers.[73]

Wren was perhaps Britain's most accomplished Renaissance man, with strong interests and accomplishments in astronomy, a topic he first taught at university, as well as various other fields of the sciences. At the same time, he had been immersed in classical literature as a child and had good Latin. His admiration of ancient Rome was well known by friends. More specifically, a fellow member of the Royal Society, Thomas Prat, noted that he and Wren had agreed that of all ages in human history, "Rome in the reign of Augustus, was to be preferr'd before all others."[74]

---

[72] Margaret Whinney, *Wren* (New York: Thames and Hudson, 1971), pp. 37, 45.

[73] J. Levine, p. 178. This was a name given to him after one of his first buildings, the Sheldonian Theatre at Oxford, was built.

[74] Ibid., p. 177.

With such views, it was no surprise that Wren proposed a plan for the rebuilding of London that, although not exactly modeled after that of classical Rome, followed the closest contemporary approximation, namely Renaissance Rome. Wren had never made it to Rome, but he had many drawings and had traveled to Paris shortly prior to the great fire, where he hoped to meet Bernini, apparently in search of drawings from the Roman master. The design he submitted subsequently had strong echoes of the urban design that emerged in Rome in the age of Sixtus V, with its broad streets connecting major piazzas.[75]

Although this plan was rejected in part because of the difficulty of clearing old foundations, Wren succeeded in leaving a classical stamp on the reconstruction efforts, especially after he was named the chief surveyor of the King's Works in 1669. He held that office for the next fifty years, during which time work progressed quickly on the reconstruction of the city to the extent that by 1677, foreign observers estimated that a majority of the houses had been rebuilt. As a testimony to the accomplishment, a triumphal column was built by Wren in that year that constituted yet another architectural genre of the Imperial Renaissance in the England of Charles II.[76]

Modeled after ancient columns like that of Trajan in Rome, the column commemorating the fire was placed at the spot where the blaze had started near the old London Bridge. Latin inscriptions that were then quite rare in London were inscribed on three sides of the pedestal. They made "intimate, often verbatim connections to the admired and minutely studied history of ancient Rome." More specifically, they strongly echoed Tacitus and his history of the great fire that destroyed ancient Rome.[77]

In a reversal of the negative uses of Tacitus that had characterized the Republican forces in the Civil War, Wren and his collaborators used Tacitus to make positive associations between Charles II and the good emperors such as Augustus who had built up Rome. To emphasize the point, a relief sculpture graced one side of the pedestal that depicted Charles II dressed as a Roman emperor and patron of architecture. The king had played an admirable role during the fire, and the column emphasized the rebuilding of the city as his personal triumph.[78]

---

[75] M. Whinney, pp. 38–39.

[76] John E. Moore, "The Monument, or Christopher Wren's Roman Accent," *The Art Bulletin*, Vol. 80, No. 3 (Sept. 1998), pp. 498–533. The author provides a rich analysis of the meaning of the column and more particularly its intentional associations with Tacitus and the great fire of ancient Rome that he recorded.

[77] Ibid., p. 498.

[78] Ibid., pp. 504–505.

An important symbolic part of Wren's work, the monument has been understandably overshadowed by the extraordinary number of other buildings that Wren built in the decades after the fire. Drawing extensively on Vitruvius as he was translated and transmitted through his Renaissance disciples – Serlio, Palladio, Bernini, and Claude Perrault, among others – Wren applied a discipline and rigor reminiscent of Michelangelo in designing a remarkable number of classical buildings over a period of more than fifty years.

Besides being responsible for the design and supervision of fifty-two churches that were rebuilt over the quarter century following the fire, he also designed the library for Trinity College at Cambridge, Chelsea Hospital, and, late in his career, Hampton Court Palace. All of these buildings incorporated Vitruvian principles to one extent or another. Collectively they ensured that the classical style became the dominant architectural tradition of London. No building reinforces this fact more than the most famous among all of Wren's works, New St. Paul's Cathedral, rebuilt between 1675 and 1710. It is an essential part of the genealogy of the Imperial Renaissance in architecture.

By 1675, New St. Peter's Basilica in Rome was largely finished. The great dome of Michelangelo had finally been finished in 1590, the façade was in place by 1620, the great bronze baldachin of Bernini covered the main altar by 1650, and the colossal colonnade of Bernini encircled the piazza in front of the church, providing a monumental liturgical space for the throngs of pilgrims. It was a building that Wren's friend John Evelyn had described as "the most stupendous and incomparable basilicam, far surpassing anything in the World."[79]

That, of course, was a subjective judgment, but it was undeniable that St. Peter's was one of the great accomplishments of Renaissance architecture and testimony to the joined economic and cultural power of Catholic Empire. For Wren and his patrons, the crown and Church of England, it was the new benchmark of imperial churches, and they set out to equal or surpass it.

Built over a period of 35 years compared to the 150 years it took to complete St. Peter's, St. Paul's was a potent sign of a Protestant Empire rising in the North of Europe. The great dome that looked out over the Thames could not claim the originality of the one that cast a shadow towards the Tiber, but that did not matter to its admirers, who fashioned Wren as Virgil while Michelangelo played Homer (Figure 5.3).

[79] J. Levine, p. 7.

5.3. Sir Christopher Wren, Exterior of St. Paul's Cathedral, London, Great Britain. (Photograph: James Morris/Art Resource, NY.)

Paid for largely by a coal tax, not crusade indulgences, St. Paul's drew on a variety of sources for different features of the building. Wren had a full range of Renaissance architectural books at his disposal, and he used them. But for the parts of the building described as "the summit of Wren's achievement," namely the west towers and the dome, he drew directly from Bramante and Michelangelo.[80] Built on those early Renaissance foundations, it became the crowning achievement of the late Renaissance in England.

Not accidentally, it was in precisely those years that Great Britain made its first major steps toward becoming the preeminent empire in the Atlantic World and a rising global empire. Charles II claimed credit for the growth of British power in the New World as his soldiers claimed New Amsterdam for Britain and renamed it New York in honor of his brother James, Duke of York. The defeat of the Indian rebellion in 1675 cleared the way for further settlement of New England, and William Penn furthered English interests with the settlement of Pennsylvania beginning in 1682. In the East, the marriage of Charles II to the Portuguese princess, Catherine of Braganza, brought Bombay to Great Britain as part of the dowry.

Slowly but surely, Great Britain was developing the Atlantic World's most powerful navy, in part because of the growing colonies and merchant fleets but also to advance its interests closer to home. As briefly outlined in Chapter 4, it was the Spanish War of Succession that led to the definitive arrival of Great Britain as Europe's dominant naval power and rising global empire as well.

But by 1688, the nature of the British imperial government had also changed dramatically because of the Glorious Revolution of 1688 that left William and Mary on the throne, but with much-reduced power. The age of imperial monarchy was giving way to a new political hybrid that gave more power to Parliament. Great Britain, in short, was moving definitively away from a Roman imperial model that valued the rule of one, however qualified that was throughout the preceding centuries, to a Republican Empire that maintained imperial monarchs for their value as unifying figures and arbiters between political factions.

This was a new day that did not mean the end of empire by any means, but it did mean the close of the chapter of the Imperial Renaissance that advocated the rule of one. The British Caesars now served together with a powerful senate, even if they kept many of the trappings of imperial rule. This would prove to be an effective imperial hybrid that combined the strengths of two systems previously thought to be at odds with one another.

[80] M. Whinney, p. 113.

The great accomplishment of the British Empire in the two centuries that followed, and a major key to its success, was the fact that it reconciled the Republican and Imperial Renaissances, drawing on the strengths of each.

Henri de Rohan had observed many decades earlier that the strength of absolute imperial monarchs was that they were better at conquering territories and winning empire because they could move quickly in wars of conquest, unencumbered by the need to get the approval of the senate. But the Republican government was deemed better at holding empire because it was not susceptible to the weaknesses that came from dynastic rule: the uneven quality of monarchs and frequent battles over succession.

This was not exactly the case with the British Empire, but the success of the parliament in guiding Great Britain through the tumultuous years of the War of the Spanish Succession did prove the latter point. Regardless of the problems of succession and generally weak monarchical rule between the reigns of William and Mary, Anne and George I, Great Britain pursued a successful military strategy that not only gained territories for the Empire but also enriched its merchants. This would not hold true, however, in the case with the war against the American colonies. It was subsequently a bitter blow to merchants and monarchs alike when the American Revolution brought about the effective end of the First Empire in 1783.

CONCLUSION

In 1724, the premiere of George Frideric Handel's new opera, *Julius Caesar*, was performed at the King's Theatre in London under the patronage of King George I. Met with much praise, the performance presented Caesar in a heroic light as he successfully defeated Ptolemy and took control of Egypt.[1] Many additional productions followed as Caesar remained popular.[2] Opera was well suited for advancing his fame and for celebrating the history of the Roman Empire, and it was a telling sign that the premiere was performed in the capital of Europe's rising empire, Great Britain. Gone was the ambiguous characterization of Shakespeare's Caesar from a century earlier. In his operatic incarnation, Handel's Caesar was the conquering hero of Clement Edmonds.

In addition to the opera stage, the urban stages of Europe's cosmopolitan centers celebrated empire for the growing populations of London, Paris, Madrid, Lisbon, and Rome. Palaces and temples inspired by Vitruvian principles, large plazas with classicized equestrian monuments of their most illustrious monarchs, and broad streets punctuated with columns and fountains were the fruits of the triumphs of their armies and the treasure that they extracted from their new colonies. They were the most visible signs of the Imperial Renaissance and the tangible fulfillment of the dreams of reviving ancient Rome. These cities left no doubt that Europe had been immutably transformed by the cultural and political movement set in motion by Italian humanists and princes almost four centuries earlier.

This was true above all else for the ruling class. The noble families prided themselves on the opulent palace culture that they had created in imitation

---

[1] Anthony Hicks, "George Frideric Handel," in *The New Grove Dictionary of Opera*, ed. Stanley Sadie (New York: Macmillan Press, 1992), Vol. 2, pp. 614–636.

[2] Ibid., Paul Corneilson, "Julius Caesar," pp. 929–930.

of their monarchs. They filled the enormous galleries of their classicized palaces with paintings and sculpture, collected jewels, books, and other precious objects, and strolled in gardens manicured to imitate the ancient villas of the emperors. Their libraries were filled with the texts of the imperial humanists and the new editions of Caesar, Tacitus, and Seutonius. Not surprisingly, many of them took it for granted that they were born to rule much as the ancient Romans had assumed the same thing.

And rule they did. The global expansion of European empires had far surpassed the imaginations of the early Renaissance humanists as well as the size and grandeur of ancient Rome. The Spanish Empire, even in its diminished eighteenth-century configuration, remained the world's largest empire in terms of territory. The Bourbon kings of Spain still commanded large navies and substantial armies that kept their Latin American and Pacific territories tied to Madrid. Centuries of Spanish rule had succeeded in transforming these conquered lands much as four centuries of Roman rule had transformed ancient Gaul, Britain, Iberia, Italy, and Germany. In the realms of language, law, religion, culture, military organization, governance, economy, and urbanization, Spanish rule radically and irreversibly altered the societies of the conquered peoples as it created new hybrid colonial cultures.

The same held true for Brazil where the Portuguese monarchs continued to hold sway. They had successfully promoted an imperial project that had many of the same characteristics of the Spanish with the additional ignoble distinction of being the most dependent on African slaves. The lucrative slave trade was present in many of the American colonies, of course, and it was this economic prize that inspired imperial competition even more than the quest for gold or silver mines.

Following the Spanish and Portuguese monarchs in the quest for political glory and treasure, the British and French had successfully imposed their government, cultural forms, economic systems, religions, and laws on various Native American nations in North America and the Caribbean by the eighteenth century. The imperial imprint of the British would never match that of the Spanish in the Americas, and British rule would be much shorter than that of the Spanish kings. But the rebellious children of the British monarchs, the American colonies, managed to carry on their work of cultural conquest and domination even if it was under a democratic government.

Similarly, the French imperial project in the Americas was more limited in its impact and success at imposing French culture and rule and in extracting treasure for the metropolitan center. But the French monarchs, too, claimed much glory from the conquests that they did preside over. Quebec may have only had a few hundred inhabitants in the age of Louis XIV, but it merited an equestrian statue of the monarch nonetheless. What it lacked in material wealth it gave to the monarch in terms of reputation: with the other American territories, it gave him claim to the fame of ruling over an empire.

This remained a central conceit of the French monarchs throughout much of the eighteenth century. In 1745, Voltaire wrote the libretto for an operetta performed at Versailles for Louis XV. Set to music composed by Rameau, it was titled the *Temple de la gloire*, and it featured the emperor Trajan in a flattering light with obvious references to the French king. If the point needed any clarification, the pandering courtier offered it when he reportedly inquired of the king after the performance: "Is Trajan content?"[3] The vignette and Voltaire himself embodied the continuity and change that marked the imperial revival in the age of the Enlightenment. While a young Voltaire knew how to imitate an old and time-honored script that the French court had been using for centuries, it was also true that as he matured he turned "against Trajan." Increasingly his writings offered a sharp critique of despotism, if not absolute monarchy, that would eventually help stoke the fires of revolution.

Indeed, a growing chorus of criticism and complaint against the old regimes of Europe was emerging not only in Europe but in their colonies as well. Language that echoed early Renaissance criticisms of empires and tyranny found strong new voices in the philosophers of the Enlightenment who paved the way for revolutions that not only called for more liberty and equality but also for the heads of the Caesars of their day.

It was an older Voltaire, the rebellious courtier, who served as perhaps the best harbinger of the bloody days to come. One of his last plays, published posthumously in 1781, was titled *The Death of Caesar*, and it gave full voice to the republican critique of tyranny and the sins of Caesar.[4] Even more than Shakespeare, to whom he was heavily indebted, Voltaire showed little sympathy for the founder of the Roman Empire. Rather, he gave pride of place to the dictator's assassins who asked only for liberty.

Read as a prophetic critic of the monarchs of his own day and their empires, and as an advocate for the revival of republican liberty, Voltaire was rightly claimed as a hero of the French Revolution. The French Caesar of his later years, Louis XVI, met a fate similar to that of the first Caesar, even if the instrument of his death was the guillotine of the state instead of the swords of a group of assassins. Together with the American Revolution that

3 Peter Gay, *Voltaire's Politics* (New York: Vintage Books, 1965), p. 116.
4 Ibid., pp. 117–143.

had witnessed the first successful colonial rebellion from an early modern empire, the French Revolution made it appear that the Imperial Renaissance was at a definitive end by 1800.

But just as the death of Julius Caesar did not necessarily mean the end of the Roman Empire, neither did the execution of Louis XVI mean the death of imperial ambition in France or the rest of Europe. The ideas and temptation of empire died hard. New powers like the Russia of Peter and Catherine the Great, yet additional competitors in the great game of empire building, were proof of this. Even more so was the last great pretender to the empire of the Caesars, Napoleon.

Epilogue

Petrarch and Napoleon

If Francesco Petrarca had returned to his beloved Italy in 1812, he would have found one of his greatest wishes fulfilled: the Italian peninsula was united under one emperor for the first time since antiquity. Perhaps beginning his visit in Milan, then the capital of the Kingdom of Italy, the poet would have marveled at the large new triumphal arch being built at the north end of the city to honor the emperor. Throughout the city, signs of imperial revival, such as the busts of the twelve Caesars that decorated the sixteenth-century façade of the nearby Erba Odescalchi palace or the new heroic nude sculpture of the current emperor sculpted by Canova now in the Brera museum, testified to the rebirth of ancient Roman imperial aesthetics and ideals.

Evidence of the most current wave of the revival stretched from one end of the Po River Valley to the other: in Bologna, the Neo-classical Villa Aldini, built by the emperor's minister of the same name, was rising on a prominent hill overlooking the city. A short distance away in Ferrara, a column originally built for a statue of the d'Este ruler of the city was now topped with a statue of the new emperor instead. Even proudly independent Venice had fallen to the new Caesar, Napoleon, who also claimed a palace in that city overlooking St. Mark's square.

Undoubtedly anxious to visit Rome, Petrarch would have found a former papal palace on the Quirinal Hill being renovated for the new emperor. But that project paled in comparison with the revival of colossal imperial architecture built by Michelangelo on the Capitoline Hill, at New St. Peter's, or at Palazzo Farnese. Almost certainly this earlier rebirth of Rome would have made the greatest impression on the poet who could no longer lament that

"Rome was." The city had undoubtedly been reborn even if it was known as the second city of the Empire in the age of Napoleon.

To see the first city and the emperor responsible for unifying Italy, Petrarch needed to travel to Paris. It was there that yet another great urban concentration of Vitruvian-inspired palaces and temples, large triumphal arches under construction, and numerous equestrian monuments including those of Henry IV and Louis XIV awaited him. Perhaps Napoleon would have given the poet a tour of his art collection including the hundreds of paintings and ancient sculptures taken from Italy and especially the Vatican. Or perhaps the emperor would have offered Petrarch a contemporary history lesson complete with an explanation of his conquests including those of Italy, Egypt, Spain, and France itself. The paradox of a revolutionary republic mutating into a global empire and of a former military leader of that republic seizing the imperial crown may have appeared to need some explanation. But on that count, at least, Petrarch needed no instruction. The original Renaissance student and biographer of Julius Caesar had seen it all before.

SELECT BIBLIOGRAPHY

PRIMARY SOURCES

Alamos De Barrientos, Baltasar, *Tacito Español*. Madrid: Luis Sanchez, 1614.

Alberti, Leon Battista. *De Equo Animante*. Trans. Antonio Videtta. Ed. Antonio Videtta. Napoli: Ce.S.M.E.T., 1991.

Momo O Del Principe. Trans. and ed. Giuseppe Martini. Bologna: Niccola Zanichelli, 1942.

Bandole, Anthoine de. *Les Paralleles De Cesar et De Henry IIII*. Paris: Jean Richer, 1609.

Baronio, Cesare. *Annales Ecclesiastici*. Vol. 3. Antwerp: Plantiniana, 1593.

Barros, Joao de. *Dell'asia*. Trans. Alfonso Ulloa. Venice, 1561.

Biondo, Flavio. *Roma Trionfante*. Trans. Lucio Fauno. Venice: Michele Tramezzino, 1544.

Bodin, Jean. *I Sei Libri dello Stato*. Ed. Margherita Isnardi Parente. Vols. 1–3. Turin: Unione Tipografico-Editrice Torinese, 1964.

The Six Bookes of a Commonweale. Trans. Richard Knolles. London: G. Bishop, 1606. Ed. Kenneth DouglasMcRae. Cambridge, MA: Harvard University Press, 1962.

Boffrand, Germain. *Description de ce qui a été pratiqué pour fonderen bronze d'un seul jet la figure Equestre de Louis XIV*. Paris: Guillaume Cavelier, 1743.

Bosc, Jacques de. *Panégyrique du Roy sur le Suiet de la Paix de Rome: ou la Magnanimité de Louis XIV est Comparée à celle de Jules Cesar*. Paris: Edme Martin, 1664.

Botero, Giovanni. *Della Ragion Di Stato*. Venice: Gioliti, 1589.

Caesar, Caius Julius. *The Gallic War*. Trans. H.J. Edwards. Cambridge, MA: Harvard University Press, 1986.

The Civil Wars. Trans. A. G. Peskett. Cambridge, MA: Harvard University Press, 1996.

Les Commentaires de Julius Cesar. Trans. Robert Gaguin. Paris: Anthoine Verad, 1488.

Chacón, Alfonso. *Historia Ceu Verissima a Columniis Multorum Vindicata*. Rome: F. Zanetti, 1576.

Corneille, Pierre. *Oeuvres de Pierre Corneille*. Ed. M.Ch. Marty-Laveaux. Paris: L. Hachette, 1862.

Crakanthorp, Richard. *The Defence of Constantine*. London: Bernard Alsop, 1621.

Du Londel, J. E. *Les Fastes de Louis Le Grand*. Paris: ImprimerieRoyale, 1694.

Edmonds, Clement. *Observations Upon Caesar's Commentaries*, London: Peter Short, 1600.

Explication des Tableaux de la Galerie de Versailles. Versailles: François Muguet, 1687.

Franchi Conestaggio, Gerolamo de. *Dell'unione Del Regno Di Portogallo Alla Corona Di Castiglia*. Genoa: Giralomo Bartoli: 1585.

Giovio, Paolo. *Commentario De Le Cose De' Turchi, Di Paolo Giovio, Vescovo Di Nocera, a Carlo Quinto Imperadore Augusto*. Rome: Antonio Blado d'Asola, 1532.

    La Seconda Parte Dell'istorie Del Suo Tempo Di Monsignore Paolo Giovio. Trans. Lodovico Domenichi. Venice: Bonelli, 1560.

    Storia. Trans. Lodovico Domenichi. Vol. 2. Venice: Giovan Maria Bonelli, 1560.

Gomara, Francesco Lopez de. *Historia Dell Nuove Indie*. Trans. Agostino di Cravalie. Venice: Francesco Lorenzini da Turino, 1560.

Guevara, Antonio de. *Libro Di Marco Aurelio Con L'horologio De Prencipi*. Venezia: Pietro Ricciardi, 1606.

    Marco Aurelio Con El Relox De Principes. Seville: Cromberger, 1534.

Guicciardini, Francesco. *The History of Italy*. Trans. Sidney Alexander. Princeton: Princeton University Press, 1984.

    Discorsi Politici: Opere Inedite Di Francesco Guicciardini. Ed. Piero and Luigi Guicciardini. Florence: Barbara, Bianchi, e comp., 1857.

Guicciardini, Lodovico. *Descrittione Di Tutti Paesi Bassi, Altrimenti Detti Germania Inferiore*. Anversa: Guglielmo Silvio, 1567.

Herrera y Tordesillas, Antonio. *Historia General de los Hechos de los Castellanos en las Islas y Tierra Firme del Mar Oceano*. Madrid: Juan Flamenco, 1601.

    La Chronica de los Turcos, 1565.

James I. *The Workes of the Most High and Mightie Prince, James by the Grace of God, King of Great Britaine, France, and Ireland Defender of the Faith*. Ed. James Bishop of Winton, Dean of the Royal Chapel. London: Robert Barker and John Bill, 1616.

Jewel, John. *An Apology of the Church of England*. Ed. J.E. Booty. Ithaca: Cornell University Press, 1963.

L'Entrée Triomphante de Leurs Maiestez Louis XIV, Roy de France et de Navarre, et Marie Thérèse D'Austriche Son Espouse. Paris, 1662.

Lettenhove, Kervyn de. *Commentaires De Charles Quint*. Paris: Firmin-Didot, 1862.

Llaguno y Amirola, Eugenio, and Juan Augustín Ceán Bermúdez. *Noticias De Los Arquitectos Y Arquitectura De España Desde Su Restauración*. Madrid, 1798.

Machiavelli, Niccolò. *The Art of War*. Trans. Christopher Lynch. Chicago: University of Chicago, 2003.

    The Prince. Trans. Luigi Ricci. Ed. E.R.P. Vincent. New York: Random House, 1950.

    The Discourses, The Legations, and The Prince. Trans. Allan Gilbert. Vol. 1. Durham, NC: Duke University Press, 1965.

Mariana, Juan de. *Historia General De España*. Madrid: Andres Garcia de la Iglesia, 1669.

Mexia, Pedro. *Historia Del Emperador Carlos V*. Trans. Francesco Cazzamini-Mussi. Ed. Juan de Mata Carriazo. Madrid: Espasa-Calpe, 1945.

    Historia Imperial Y Cesarea. Seville: Dominico de Robertis, 1547.

    La Selva Di Varia Lettione. Trans. Mambrino da Fabriano. Venice: Michele Tramezzino, 1549.

Mexia, Pedro, and Giralomo Bardi Fiorentino. *Le Vite Di Tutti Gl'imperadori Da Giulio Cesare Insino a Massimiliano*. Trans. Lodovico Dolce. Venice: Olivier Alberti, 1597.

Morales, Ambrosio. *Coronica General De Espana by Florian De Ocampo*. Ed. B. Cano. Vol. 1. Madrid: Quiroga, 1791.

Napoleon III. *La Guerre des Gaules par Napoleon III, Histoire de Jules Cesar.* Paris: Editions Errance, 2001.

Petrarca, Francesco. *De Gestis Cesaris.* Ed. Giuliana Crevatin. Pisa: Scuola Normale, 2003.

De Viris Illustribus. Ed. Guido Martellotti. Florence: Sansoni, 1964.

Gli Uomini Illustri Vita Di Giulio Cesare. Ed. Ugo Dotti. Torino: Einaudi, 2007.

Plutarque. *Les Vies Des Hommes Illustres Grecs Et Romains.* Trans. Jaques Amyot. Gent: Jacob Stoer, 1642.

Rohan, Henri de. *Le parfait Capitaine.* Paris, 1667.

Salutati, Coluccio. *De Tyranno.* Trans. Francesco Ercole. Ed. Francesco Ercole. Bologna: Nicola Zanichelli, 1942.

Sepúlveda, Juan Ginés de. *Obras Completas I and II: Historia De Carlos V.* Trans. E. Rodríguez Peregrina. Salamanca: Europa Artes Gráficas, 1995–1996.

Obras Completas III: Democrates Segundo. Trans. A. Coroleu Lletget. Vol. III. Salamanca: Europa Atres Gráficas, 1997.

Serlio, Sebastiano. *D'Architettura, Il Terzo Libro.* Venice: Giovanni Battista and Marchio Sessa, 1559.

Suetonius. *The Twelve Caesars.* Trans. Robert Graves. Baltimore: Penguin Books, 1962.

Tacitus. *Complete Works of Tacitus.* Trans. John Church and William Jackson Brodribb. Ed. Moses Hadas. New York: Random House, 1942.

Veronese, Guarino. "Letter 670." *Epistolario Di Guarino Veronese.* Ed. Remegio Sabbadini. Vol. 2. Venice: C. Ferrari, 1919. 221–254.

Vitruvius. *Ten Books of Architecture.* Trans. Ingrid Rowland. Cambridge: Cambridge University Press, 1999.

Les Dix Livres D'Architecture de Vitruve, ed. Claude Perrault. Paris: Jean Baptiste Coignard, 1673.

SECONDARY SOURCES

Ackerman, James S. *The Architecture of Michelangelo.* London: A. Zwemmer, 1966.

Agosti, Barbara. *Paolo Giovi.* Florence: Olshcki, 2008.

Alford, Stephen. *Kingship and Politics in the Reign of Edward VI.* New York: Cambridge University Press, 2002.

Anderson, Christy. *Inigo Jones and the Classical Tradition.* Cambridge: Cambridge University Press, 2007.

Armitage, David. "The Cromwellian Protectorate and the Languages of Empire," *The Historical Journal,* Vol. 35, No. 3, Sept. 1992, 531–555.

The Ideological Origins of the British Empire. PortChester: Cambridge University Press, 2000.

ed. *Theories of Empire, 1450–1800.* Aldershot: Ashgate, 1998.

Alvar Ezquerra, Alfredo. *El Duque De Lerma.* Madrid: La Esfera de los Libros, 2010.

Álvarez, Manuel Fernández. *Felipe Ii Y Su Tiempo.* Madrid: Editorial Espasa Calpe, 1998.

Anatra, Bruno, ed. *Carlo V. Fonti.* Vol. 1. Florence: La Nuovo Italia, 1974.

Avery, Charles. *Giambologna: The Complete Sculpture.* London: Phaidon Press, 1993.

Banks, Kenneth. *Chasing Empire Across the Sea: Communications and the State in the French Atlantic, 1713–63*. Montreal: McGill-Queen's University Press, 2002.

Barkan, Leonard. *Unearthing the Past: Archeology and Aesthetics in the Making of Renaissance Culture*. New Haven: Yale University Press, 1999.

Baron, Hans. *The Crisis of the Early Italian Renaissance*. Princeton: Princeton University Press, 1966.

Barrol, J. Leeds. "Shakespeare and Roman History," *Modern Language Review*, Vol. 53, 1958, pp. 327–343.

Baxandall, Michael. "A Dialogue on Art from the Court of Leonello D'este: Angelo Decembrio's De Politia Litteraria Pars LXVIII," *Journal of the Warburg and Courtauld Institutes*, Vol. 26, No. 3/4, 1963, pp. 304–326.

Bazzotti, Ugo, ed. *Palazzo Te Mantua*. Milan: Skira, 2007.

Beard, Mary. *The Roman Triumph*. Cambridge, MA: Harvard University Press, 2007.

Béguin, Sylvie, Oreste Binenbaum, André Chastel, W. McAllister Johnson, Sylvia Pressouyre, and Henri Zerner. *La Galerie François Ier au Chateau de Fontainebleau*. Paris: Flammarion, 1972.

Belluzzi, Amadeo, and Walter Capezzali. *Il Palazzo Dei Lucidi Inganni: Palazzo Te a Mantova*. Florence: Ourubus, 1976.

Belluzzi, Amedeo, and Kurt W. Forster. "Giulio Romano, Architect at the Court of the Gonzagas." *Giulio Romano Architect*. Cambridge: Cambridge University Press, 1998. 90–128.

"Palazzo Te." *Giulio Romano Architect*. Cambridge: Cambridge University Press, 1998. 165–177.

Bentini, Jadranka, ed. *Gli Este a Ferrara: Un Corte Nel Rinascimento*. Milan: Silvano Editore, 2004.

Bertozzi, Marco, ed. *Alla Corte Degli Estensi*. Ferrara: Università degli Studi, 1992.

Boucher, Bruce. "Leone Leoni and Primaticcio's Moulds of Antique Sculpture," *The Burlington Magazine*, Vol. 123, No. 934, 1981, 23–26.

Brady, Thomas A. *German Histories in the Age of the Reformations, 1400–1650*. Cambridge: Cambridge University Press, 2009.

Brandi, Karl. *The Emperor Charles V*. London: J. Cape, 1960.

Braudel, Fernand. *The Mediterranean and the Mediterranean World in the Age of Philip II*. Trans. Sian Reynolds. New York: Harper Collins, 1973.

Brothers, Cammy. "The Renaissance Reception of the Alhambra: The Letters of Andrea Navagero and the Palace of Charles V," *Muqarnas*, Vol. 11, 1994, 79–102.

Brown, Clifford M. "'Fruste et Strache nel Fabbricare', Isabella D'este's Apartments in the Corte Vecchia of the Ducal Palace in Mantua," *La Corte Di Mantova Nell'età Di Andrea Mantegna*, 1997, 295–336.

Per Dare Qualche Splendore a La Gloriosa Città Di Mantua: Documents for the Antiquarian Collection of Isabella D'este. Rome: Bulzoni, 2002.

Brown, Jonathan. "Artistic Relations Between Spain and England, 1604–1655." *The Sale of the Century*, ed. Jonathan Brown and John Elliott. New Haven: Yale University Press, 2002, 41–68.

Brown, Virginia. *The Textual Transmission of Caesar's Civil War*. Mnemosyne. Vol. Special Supplement Volume. Leiden: Brill, 1972.

Burke, Peter. "A Survey of the Popularity of Ancient Historians," *History and Theory*, Vol. 5, No. 2, 1966, 135–152.

The European Renaissance. Oxford: Blackwell, 1998.

Burns, Howard. "'Quelle Cose Antique Et Moderne Belle De Roma'. Giulio Romano, the Theatre and the Antique." *Giulio Romano Architect*. Cambridge: Cambridge University Press, 1998, 129–142.

Cadenas y Vicent, Vicente de. *Carlos I De Castilla, Señor De Las Indias*. Madrid: Hidalguia, 1988.

Diario Del Emperador Carlos V. Madrid: Hidalguia, 1992.

Doble Coronacion De Carlos V en Bologna. Madrid: Hidalguia, 1985.

Calloway, Colin G. "Surviving the Dark Ages," *After King Philip's War*. Hanover: University Press of New England, 1997, 1–28.

Castelli, Patrizia, ed. *L'ideale Classico a Ferrara E in Italia Nel Rinascimento*. Florence: Leo S. Olschke, 1998.

Cebrià, Ernest Belenguer, ed. *Felipe II y El Mediterráneo*. 4 Vols. Madrid: Closas-Orcoyen, S.L., 1999.

Cerutti Fusco, Annarosa. *Inigo Jones, Vitruvius Britannicus*. Rimini: Magioli, 1985.

Chastel, André. "French Renaissance Art in a European Context," *Sixteenth Century Studies*, Vol. 12, No. 4, Winter 1981, 77–103.

Checa Cremades, Fernando. *Carlos V, La Imagen Del Poder En El Rinacimiento*. Madrid: El Viso, 1999.

Clark, George. *The Later Stuarts, 1660–1714*. Oxford: Clarendon Press, 1955.

Cochrane, Erich. *Florence in the Forgotten Centuries: 1527–1800*. Chicago: Chicago University Press, 1973.

Cole, Jeffrey A. "An Abolitionism Born of Frustration: The Conde de Lemos and the Potosí Mita, 1667–73," *Hispanic American Historical Review*, Vol. 63, No. 2, 1983, 307–333.

Cordara, Michele, ed. *Mantegna's Camera Degli Sposi*. New York: Abbeville, 1993.

Cox-Rearick, Janet. *The Collection of Francis I: Royal Treasures*. Antwerp: Fonds Mercator Paribas, 1995.

Cramsie, John. "The Philosophy of Imperial Kingship and the Interpretation of James VI and I," *James VI and I*, ed. Ralph Houlbrooke. Hampshire: Ashgate Publishing, 2006, 43–60.

Crawford, Katherine. "Catherine de Médicis and the Performance of Political Motherhood," *The Sixteenth Century Journal*, Vol. 31, No. 3, Autumn, 2000, 643–673.

D'Amico, John. *Renaissance Humanism in Papal Rome*. Baltimore: Johns Hopkins University Press, 1983.

Dandelet, Thomas. "Financing New St. Peter's, 1506–1700." *Sankt Peter's Von Rom*. Eds. Georg Satzinger and Sebastian Schutze. Munich: Hirmer, 2008, 41–48.

Spanish Rome. New Haven: Yale University Press, 2001.

Dandelet, Thomas and John Marino, eds. *Spain in Italy: Politics, Religion and Society, 1500–1700*. Leiden: Brill, 2007.

Davies, Godfrey. *The Early Stuarts, 1603–1660*. Oxford: Clarendon Press, 1959.

Davis, Robert C. *Christian Slaves and Muslim Masters*. New York: Palgrave, 2003.

Dean, Paul. "Tudor Humanism and the Roman Past: A Background to Shakespeare," *Renaissance Quarterly*, Vol. 41, No. 1, Spring, 1988, 84–111.

Diamond, Jared. *Guns, Germs, and Steel*. New York: W.W. Norton, 1997.

Disney, A.R. *A History of Portugal and the Portuguese Empire*. Vol. 2. Cambridge: Cambridge University Press, 2009.

Dowling, Maria. *Humanism in the Age of Henry VIII*. London: Croom Helm, 1986.

Duby, George. *Storia della Francia*, Trans. Francesco Saba Sardi, Milano: Bompiani, 1998.

Elliot, John. *Empires of the Atlantic World*. New Haven: Yale University Press, 2006.

    Imperial Spain, 1469–1716. London: Penguin, 1988.

    Richelieu and Olivares. Cambridge: Cambridge University Press, 1984.

Ferguson, Niall. *Empire*. New York: Basic Books, 2004.

Fernández Alvarez, Manuel. *Carlos V*. Madrid: Publicaciones Españolas, 1974.

Fernández-Santamaria, José. "Baltasar Alamos De Barrientos' Ciencia De Contigentes: A SpanishView of Statecraft as Science During the Baroque." *Bibliotheque d'Humanisme et Renaissance*, Vol. 41, No. 2, 1979, 293–304.

Feros, Antonio. *Kingship and Favorotism in the Spain of Philip III, 1598–1621*. Cambridge: Cambridge University Press, 2000.

Fitzmaurice, Andrew. *Humanism and America*. Cambridge: Cambridge University Press, 2003.

Forster, Kurt. "Metaphors of Rule. Political Ideology and History in the Portraits of Cosimo I De' Medici," *Mitteilungen des Kunsthistorischen Institutes in Florenz*, Vol. 15, No. 1, 1971, 65–104.

Frommel, Christoph Luitpold. *Architettura e Commitenza da Alberti a Bramante*. Castello: Leo S. Olschi, 2006.

Games, A. *Migration and the Origins of the English Atlantic World*. Cambridge, MA: Harvard University Press, 1999.

Gargiani, Robert. *Idea e costruzione del Louvre*. Bologna: Alinea, 1998.

Gäumann, Andreas. *Reich Christi und Obrigkeit*. Bern: Peter Lang, 2001.

Gaztimbide, Jose Goñi. *Historia De La Bula De Cruzada En España*. Vitoria, Editorial del Seminario, 1958.

Gibellini, Cecilia. *L'immagine Di Lepanto*. Venice: Marsilio, 2008.

Goldman, William S. "Spain and the Founding of Jamestown." *The William and Mary Quarterly*, Vol. 68, No. 3, 2011, 427–450.

Goubert, Pierre. *Louis XIV and Twenty Million Frenchmen*. Trans. Anne Carter. New York: Vintage Books, 1970.

Grafton, Anthony. *Forgers and Critics*. Princeton: PrincetonUniversity Press, 1990.

    "Historia and Istoria: Alberti's Terminology in Context," *I Tatti Studies: Essays in the Renaissance*, Vol. 8, 1999, 37–68.

    Leon Battista Alberti. Cambridge, MA: Harvard University Press, 2000.

Grandi, Paola Tosetti. *I Trionfi Di Cesare Di Andrea Mantegna*. Mantua: Sometti, 2008.

Hale, John. *The Civilization of Europe in the Renaissance*. New York: Atheneum, 1994.

Hall, Basil. "Martin Bucer in England." *Martin Bucer*, ed. David F. Wright. Cambridge: Cambridge University Press, 1994, 144–160.

Hanke, Lewis. *All Mankind Is One*. Dekalb: Northern Illinois University Press, 1974.

Harris, John and Gordon Higgott. *Inigo Jones, Complete Architectural Drawings*. London: Philip Wilson, 1989.

Hartt, Frederick. *Giulio Romano*. New Haven: Yale University Press, 1958.

Hayden, J. Michael. "Continuity in the France of Henry IV and Louis XIII: French Foreign Policy, 1598–1615," in *The Journal of Modern History*, Vol. 45, No. 1 (Mar., 1973), pp. 1–23.

Headley, John M. *The Emperor and His Chancellor*. New York: Cambridge University Press, 1983.

Hoak, Dale. "The Iconography of the Crown Imperial." *Tudor Political Culture*, ed. Dale Hoak. Cambridge: Cambridge University Press, 1993.54–103.

Hopkins, Lisa. *Cultural Uses of the Caesars on the English Renaissance Stage*. Abingdon: Ashgate, 2008.

James, Harold. *The Roman Predicament*. Princeton: Princeton University Press, 2008.

Johnson, Eugene J. S. *Andrea in Mantua*. University Park and London: The Pennsylvania State University Press, 1975.

Kallendorf, Craig. "The Historical Petrarch," *The American Historical Review*, Vol. 101, No. 1, 1996, 130–141.

Kamen, Henry. *Empire*. New York: Perennial, 2004.

Kaufman, Thomas DaCosta. *Variations on the Imperial Theme: Studies in Ceremonial, Art, and Collecting in the Age of Maximilian II and Rudolf II*. New York: Garland Publishing, 1978.

Kohl, Benjamin G. "Petrarch's Prefaces to De Viris Illustribus," *History and Theory*, Vol. 13, No. 2, 1974, 132–144.

Krinsky, Carole Herselle. "Seventy-Eight Vitruvius Manuscripts," *Journal of the Warburg and Courthauld Institutes*, Vol. 30, 1967, 36–70.

Kristellar, Paul. *Andrea Mantegna*. London: Longman Green and Co., 1901.

Kristellar, Paul Oskar. "Studies in Renaissance Humanism in the Last Twenty Years," *Studies in the Renaissance*, Vol. 9, 1962, 7–30.

Kroeber, C.B. "The Mobilization of Philip Ii's Revenues in Peru, 1590–1596," *The Economic History Review, New Series*, Vol. 10, No. 3, 1958, 439–449.

Kubler, George. *La Obra Del Escorial*. Madrid: Allianza, 1983.

Lavin, Irving. "On Illusion and Allusion in Italian Sixteenth-Century Portrait Busts," *Proceedings of the American Philosophical Society*, Vol. 119, No. 5, 1975, 353–362.

Lecoq, Anne-Marie. *François I imaginaire*. Paris: Macula, 1987.

Levine, Joseph M. *Between the Ancient and the Moderns*. New Haven: Yale University Press, 1999.

"Giambattista Vico and the Quarrel between the Ancients and the Moderns," *Journal of the History of Ideas*, Vol. 52, No. 1, Jan.–Mar. 1991, 55–79.

Lightbown, Ronald. *Mantegna*. Berkeley: University of California Press, 1986.

Lotti, L., and R. Villari, eds. *Filippo II e Il Mediterraneo*. Rome: Laterza, 2003.

Lowe, K.J.P., ed. *Cultural Links between Portugal and Italy in the Renaissance*. Oxford: Oxford University Press, 2000.

Lupher, David A. *Romans in the New World*. Ann Arbor: University of Michigan Press, 2009.

Lynch, John. *Spain under the Habsburgs*. Vol. 1. Oxford: Blackwell, 1981.

MacCormack, Sabine. *On the Wings of Time*. Princeton: Princeton University Press, 2007.

Macinnes, Allan I. *Union and Empire*. Cambridge: Cambridge University Press, 2007.

Malacarne, Giancarlo. "Il Sogno Del Potere Da Gianfrancesco a Francesco II (1432–1519)." *I Gonzaga Di Mantova*, Vol. 2, 6 vols. Modena: Il Bulino, 2010.

"I Gonzaga Duchi Da Federico II a Guglielmo (1519–1587)." *I Gonzaga Di Mantova*, Vol. 3, 6 vols. Modena: Il Bulino, 2010.

Maltby, William. *The Reign of Charles V*. New York: Palgrave, 2002.

Maravall, J.A. "La Corriénte Doctrinal Del Tacitismo Politico En España," *Cuadernos Hispanoamericanos*, Vol. 240, 1969, 645–667.

Martindale, Andrew. *The Triumphs of Caesar by Andrea Mantegna*. London: Harvey Miller, 1979.

Matteini, Anna Maria Testaverde. "La Decorazione Festivi E L'itinerario Di 'Rifondazione' Della Città Negli Ingressi Trionfali a Firenze Tra XV E XVI Secolo," *Mitteilungen des Kunsthistorischen Institutes in Florenz*, Vol. 2, No. 3, 1988, 323–352.

Mazzocco, Angelo. "Petrarch: Founder of Renaissance Humanism?" *Interpretations of Renaissance Humanism*. Ed. Angelo Mazzocco. Boston: Brill Academic Publishers, 2006. 215–242.

McAlister, Lyle N. *Spain and Portugal in the New World, 1492–1700*. Minneapolis: University of Minnesota Press, 1984.

McDonald, Robert, ed. *The Sun King: Louis XIV and the New World*. New Orleans: Louisiana Museum Foundation, 1984.

McEwen, Indra Kagis. *Vitruvius*. Cambridge, MA: MIT Press, 2003.

Mellor, Ronald. "Tacitus, Academic Politics, and Regicide in the Reign of Charles I: The Tragedy of Dr. Isaac Dorislaus," *International Journal of the Classical Tradition*, Vol. 11, No. 2, Fall 2004, 153–193.

Meserve, Margaret. *Empires of Islam in Renaissance Historical Thought*. Cambridge, MA: Harvard University Press, 2008.

Miola, Robert S. "Julius Caesar and the Tyrannicide Debate," *Renaissance Quarterly*, Vol. 38, No. 2, Summer 1985, 271–289.

Miquelon, Dale. "Envisioning the French Empire: Utrecht, 1711–13," *French Historical Studies*, Vol. 24, No. 4, Fall 2001, 653–677.

Mitchell, Bonner. *The Majesty of the State*. Florence: Olshcki, 1986.

Molinié-Bertrand, Annie. *Au Siècle D'or L'espagne Et Ses Homes: La Population De Royaume De Castille Au Xvie Siècle*. Paris: Econimica, 1985.

Momigliano, Arnaldo. "The First Political Commentary on Tacitus," *The Journal of Roman Studies*, Vol. 37, Nos. 1–2, 1947, 91–101.

Montaño, John Patrick. *The Roots of English Colonialism in Ireland*, Cambridge: Cambridge University Press, 2011.

Moore, John E. "The Monument, or Christopher Wren's Roman Accent," *The Art Bulletin*, Vol. 80, No. 3, Sep. 1998, 498–533.

Morford, Mark. "Tacitean Prudentia and the Doctrines of Justus Lipsius." *Tacitus and the Tacitean Tradition*. Eds. T.J. Luce and A.J. Woodman. Princeton: Princeton University Press, 1993. 129–151.

Mousnier, Roland. *Les institutions de la France sous la monarchie absolue, 1598–1789*, 2 vols. Paris: Presses universitaires de France, 1974–1980.

Muir, Edward. "The Italian Renaissance in America," *The American Historical Review*, Vol. 100, No. 4, 1995, 1095–1118.

Müntz, M. Eugène. *La Renaissance en Italie et en France a L'Époque de Charles VIII*. Paris: Firmin-Didot, 1885.

Nader, Helen. *The Mendoza Family in the Spanish Renaissance*. New Brunswick: Rutgers University Press, 1979.

Nederman, Cary N. "Humanism and Empire: Aeneas Sylvius Piccolomini, Cicero, and the Imperial Ideal," *The Historical Journal*, Vol. 36, No. 3, 1993, 499–515.

Negri, Antonio, and Michael Hardt. *Empire*. Cambridge, MA: Harvard University Press, 2000.

Nicolini, Fausto. *La Giovinezza di Giambattista Vico*. Bari: Laterza, 1932.

O'Brien, Emily. "Arms and Letters: Julius Caesar, the Commentaries of Pope Pius II, and the Politicization of Papal Imagery," *Renaissance Quarterly*, Vol. 62, No. 4, 2009, 1057–1097.

Osorio, Alejandro. "La Entrada Del Virrey Y El Ejercicio De Poder En La Lima Del Siglo XVII," *Historia Mexicana*, Vol. 55, No. 3, 2006, 767–831.

Pade, Marianne. "Guarino and Caesar at the Court of the Este." *The Court of Ferrara and Its Patronage, 1441–1598*. Eds. Marianne Pade, Lene Waage Peteersen, and Daniela Quarta. Ferrara: Edizione Panini, 1990, 71–91.

Pagden, Anthony. *La Caduta Dell'Uomo Naturale*. Trans. Igor Lagati. Torino: Einaudi, 1989.

Lords of All the World. New Haven and London: Yale University Press, 1995.

Pallotta, Augustus. "Reappraising Croce's Influence on Hispanic Studies in Italy: The Case of Guevara and Mexia," *Modern Language Studies*, Vol. 22, No. 3, 1992, 44–52.

Palme, Per. *Triumph of Peace: A Study of the Whitehall Banqueting House*. London: Thames and Hudson, 1957.

Panofsky, Erwin. *The Life and Art of Albrecht Durer*. Princeton Princeton University Press, 2005.

Parker, Geoffrey. *Philip II*. Chicago: Open Court, 1995.

The Grand Strategy of Philip II. New Haven: Yale University Press, 1998.

Parrott, David. *Richelieu's Army: War, Government, and Society in France, 1624–1642*. Port Chester: Cambridge University Press, 2001.

Partner, Peter. *Renaissance Rome, 1500–1559*. Berkeley: University of California Press, 1976.

The Papal State under Martin V. London: British School at Rome, 1958.

Pauck, William, ed. *Melanchton and Bucer*. London: SCM Press LTD, 1969.

Pérez, Joseph. *L'espagne De Philippe II*. Paris: Fayard, 1999.

Pernis, Maria Grazia. "Fifteenth-Century Patrons and the Scipio-Caesar Controversy," *Text*, Vol. 6, 1994, 181–195.

Pettegree, Andrew. *The Book in the Renaissance*. New Haven: Yale University Press, 2011.

Pincelli, Maria Agata. "La Roma Triumphans E La Nascita Dell'antiquaria: Biondo Flavio E Andrea Mantegna." *Mantegna E Roma*. Eds. Teresa Calvano, Claudia Cieri Via and Leandro Ventura. Rome: Bulzoni, 2010. 79–98.

Plon, Eugène. *Leone Leoni Et Pompeo Leoni*. Paris: E. Plon, 1887.

Pomper, Philip, ed. "The History and Theory of Empire," *History and Theory*, Vol. 44, 2005, 1–27.

Prem, Hanns J. "Spanish Colonization and Indian Property in Central Mexico, 1521–1620," *Annals of the Association of American Geographers*, Vol. 82, No. 3, 1992, 444–459.

Rabreau, Daniel. "Monumental Art, or the Politics of Enchantment." *The Sun King*. Ed. Robert R. McDonald. New Orleans: Louisiana Museum Foundation, 1984, 126–135.

Rausa, Federico. "'Li Disegni Delle Statue Et Busti Sono Rotolate Drento Le Stampe'. L'arredo Di Sculture Antiche Delle Residenze Dei Gonzaga Nei Disegni Seicenteschi Della Royal Library a Windson Castle." *Gonzaga: La Celeste Galeria*. Ed. Raffaella Morselli. Milan: Skira, 2002. 67–91.

Redondo, Augustin. *Antonio De Guevara et l'espagne de son temps*. Geneva: Droz, 1976.

Reyes y mecenas: los Reyes Católicos, Maximiliano I y los inicios de la casa De Austria en España. Museo de Santa Cruz, Toledo: Ministerio de Cultura, España, 1992. 233–251.

Richardson, John. *The Language of Empire*. Cambridge: Cambridge University Press, 2008.

Rinaldi, Rinaldo. "Princes and Culture in the Fifteenth-Century Italian Po Valley Courts." *Princes and Princely Culture 1450–1650*. Eds. Martin Grosman, Alasdair MacDonald, and Arjo Vanderjagt. Vol. 2. Leiden: Brill, 2005. 23–42.

Rodríguez-Salgado, M.J. "Terracotta and Iron: Mantua Politics (ca. 1450–ca. 1550)." *La Corte Di Mantova Nell'età Di Andrea Mantegna*. Eds. Cesare Mozzarelli, Robert Oresko and Leandro Ventura. Rome: Bulzoni, 1997. 15–59.

Rosenberg, C.M. *The Este Monuments and Urban Development in Renaissance Ferrara*. Cambridge: Cambridge University Press, 1997.

Rosenthal, David. "The Genealogy of Empires: Ritual Politics and State Building in Early Modern Florence." *I Tatti Studies: Essays in the Renaissance*, Vol. 8. Florence: Leo S. Olschki, 1999, 197–234.

Rosenthal, Earl. "Non Plus Ultra, and the Columnar Device of Emperor Charles V," *Journal of the Warburg and Courthald Institutes*, Vol. 34, 1971, 204–228.

The Palace of Charles V in Granada. Princeton: Princeton University Press, 1985.

Rosier, Bart. "The Victories of Charles V: A Series of Prints by Maarten Van Heemskerck, 1555–56," *Simiolus: Netherlands Quarterly for the History of Art*, Vol. 20, No. 1, 1990–1991, 24–38.

Rowland, Ingrid D. *The Culture of the High Renaissance*. Cambridge: Cambridge University Press, 2000.

Sabbadini, Remigio. *La Scuola Di Guarino Guarini Veronese*. Catania: Francesco Galati, 1896.

Said, Edward. *Culture and Imperialism*. New York: Vintage Books, 1993.

Saignes, Thierry. "Notes on the Regional Contribution to the Mita in Potosí in the Early Seventeenth Century," *Bulletin of Latin American Research*, Vol. 4, No. 1, 1985, 65–76.

Sandys, John Edwyn. *A History of Classical Scholarship*. New York: Hafner, 1967.

Scheller, Robert W. "French Royal Symbolism in the Age of Louis XIII," *Simiolus: Netherlands Quarterly for the History of Art*, Vol. 13, No. 2, 1983, 75–141.

"Imperial Themes in Art and Literature of the Early French Renaissance: The Period of Charles VIII," *Simiolus: Netherlands Quarterly for the History of Art*, Vol. 12, No. 1, 1981–1982, 5–69.

"Louis XII and Italy 1499–1508," *Simiolus: Netherlands Quarterly for the History of Art*, Vol. 15, No. 1, 1985, 26–29.

Schellhase, Kenneth C. *Tacitus in Renaissance Political Thought*. Chicago: University of Chicago Press, 1976.

Scott-Elliot, A. H. "The Statues from Mantua in the Collection of King Charles I," *The Burlington Magazine*, Vol. 101, No. 675, June, 1959, 218–227.

Sherman, Michael. "Pomp and Circumstances: Pageantry, Politics, and Propaganda in France during the Reign of Louis XII, 1498–1515," *The Sixteenth Century Journal*, Vol. 9, No. 4, Winter, 1978, 13–32.

Skinner, Quentin. *The Foundations of Modern Political Thought*. 2 vols. Cambridge: Cambridge University Press, 1978.

Soll, Jacob. "Empirical History and the Tansformation of Political Criticism in France from Bodin to Bayle," *Journal of the History of Ideas*, Vol. 64, No. 2, Apr. 2003, 297–316.

Soly, Hugo, ed. *Charles V, 1500–1558*. Antwerp: Mercatorfonds, 1999.

Starn, Randolph, and Loren Partridge. *Arts of Power*. Berkeley: University of California Press, 1992.

Stinger, Charles. *The Renaissance in Rome*. Bloomington: Indiana University Press, 1998.

Strong, Donald. *Roman Art*. Harmondsworth: Penguin Books, 1982.

Suppa, Silvio Suppa, ed. *Tacito e Tacitismo in Italia da Machiavelli a Vico*. Naples: Archivio della Ragion di Stato, 2003.

Tandeter, Enrique. "Forced and Free Labor in Late Colonial Potosí," *Past and Present*, Vol. 93, 1981, 98–136.

Tanner, Marie. *Jerusalem on the Hill: Rome and the Vision of St. Peter's in the Renaissance*. London: Harvey Miller Publishers, 2010.

The Last Descendant of Aeneas. New Haven: Yale University Press, 1993.

TePaske, John J. *A New World of Gold and Silver*. Ed. Kendall W. Brown. Leiden: Brill, 2010.

Toffanello, Marcello. *Le Arti a Ferrara Nel Quattrocento, Gli Artisit E La Corte*. Ferrara: Edisai, 2010.

Tracy, James. *Charles V, Impresario of War*. Cambridge: Cambridge University Press, 2002.

Trevisani, Filippo, ed. *Andrea Mantegna e I Gonzaga*. Verona: Mondadori Electa, 2006.

Tuohy, Thomas. *Herculean Ferrara*. Cambridge: Cambridge University Press, 1996.

Ubelaker, Douglas. "North American Indian Population Size." *Disease and Demography in the Americas*, ed. John W. Verano and Douglas Ubelaker. Washington, DC: Smithsonian Institution Press, 1992.

Veronese, Guarino. *Epistolario Di Guarino Veronese*. Ed. Remegio Sabbadini. Vol. 3. Venice: C. Ferrari, 1919.

Vidoni, Mariarosa Scaramuzza. *Retorica E Narrazione Nella "Historia Imperial" Di Pedro Mexía*. Rome: Bulzoni, 1989.

Visceglia, Maria, ed. *L'Italia di Carlo V*. Rome: Viella, 2003.

Vosters, Simon A. *Antonio De Guevara Y Europa*. Salamanca: Ediciones Universidad Salamanca, 2009.

Whinney, Margaret. *Wren*. New York: Thames and Hudson, 1971.

Wilkins, Ernest Hatch. *The Life of Petrarch*. Chicago: University of Chicago Press, 1956.

Williams, Patrick. *Philip II*. New York: Palgrave, 2001.

"Philip III and the Restoration of Spanish Government, 1598–1603," *The English Historical Review*, Vol. 88, No. 349, 1973, 751–769.

Wright, David F. "Martin Bucer and England – and Scotland." *Martin Bucer and Sixteenth Century Europe*, eds. Christian Kriegger and Marc Leinhard. Vol. 2. Leiden: Brill, 1993, 523–533.

Yates, Frances A. *Astrae*. London: Routledge and Kegan Paul, 1975.

"Petrarch's Conception of the 'Dark Ages'." *Medieval and Renaissance Studies*. Ed. E.F. Rice, Jr. Ithaca: Cornell University Press, 1959. 106–29.

Zerner, Catherine Wilkinson. *Juan De Herrera*. New Haven: Yale University Press, 1993.

Zerner, Henri. *L'Art De La Renaissance en France*. Paris: Flammarion, 1996.

Zimmermann, T. C. Price. *Paolo Giovio: The Historian and the Crisis of Sixteenth-Century Italy*. Princeton: Princeton University Press, 1995.

INDEX